THE FILMS OF DOUGLAS SIRK

Douglas Sirk, January 1987. Bertrand LAFORET / Getty Images.

THE FILMS OF
Douglas Sirk

EXQUISITE IRONIES AND MAGNIFICENT OBSESSIONS

TOM RYAN

UNIVERSITY PRESS OF MISSISSIPPI • JACKSON

The University Press of Mississippi is the scholarly publishing agency of
the Mississippi Institutions of Higher Learning: Alcorn State University,
Delta State University, Jackson State University, Mississippi State University,
Mississippi University for Women, Mississippi Valley State University,
University of Mississippi, and University of Southern Mississippi.

www.upress.state.ms.us

Designed by Peter D. Halverson

The University Press of Mississippi is a member of
the Association of University Presses.

Four chapters of this book are extensive overhauls of commentary that first appeared in *Senses of Cinema* between 2004 and 2015, and in Bruce Babington and Charles Barr, eds., *The Call of the Heart: John M. Stahl and Hollywood Melodrama* (2018).

Copyright © 2019 by University Press of Mississippi
All rights reserved

First printing 2019
∞

Library of Congress Cataloging-in-Publication Data

Names: Ryan, Tom (Film writer), author.
Title: The films of Douglas Sirk : exquisite ironies and magnificent obsessions /
Tom Ryan.
Description: Jackson : University Press of Mississippi, [2019] | Includes bibliographical references and index. |
Identifiers: LCCN 2018051026 (print) | LCCN 2018054109 (ebook) | ISBN 9781496822383 (epub single) | ISBN 9781496822369 (epub institutional) | ISBN 9781496822390 (pdf single) | ISBN 9781496822406 (pdf institutional) | ISBN (cloth : alk. paper) | ISBN 9781496822376 (pbk. : alk. paper)
Subjects: LCSH: Sirk, Douglas, 1897–1987—Criticism and interpretation. | Motion picture producers and directors—United States—20th century. | Motion picture producers and directors—Germany—20th century. | LCGFT: Informational works.
Classification: LCC PN1998.3.S57 (ebook) | LCC PN1998.3.S57 R93 2019 (print) |
DDC 791.4302/33092—dc23
LC record available at https://lccn.loc.gov/2018051026

British Library Cataloging-in-Publication Data available

FOR DEBI & IN MEMORY OF HILDE

CONTENTS

ACKNOWLEDGMENTS IX
INTRODUCTION 3
CHAPTER ONE. Detlef Sierck in Europe 17
CHAPTER TWO. American Beginnings: The European Legacy 58
CHAPTER THREE. In the Shadows: Sirk and the Noir Inclination 82
CHAPTER FOUR. The Uncomfortable Comedies. 98
CHAPTER FIVE. Sirk and God: "The Pure Ambiguity of Experience" 113
CHAPTER SIX. Pastoral Yearnings: Sirk and the Musical 129
CHAPTER SEVEN. Hollywood, Rock Hudson, and the Idea of the Hero. . . . 143
CHAPTER EIGHT. Sirk, the Family Melodrama, and the Production Code . . 158
CHAPTER NINE. Sirk and John M. Stahl: Adaptations and Remakes. 193
CHAPTER TEN. Out of the Past 231
CHAPTER ELEVEN. Into the Future: Sirk's Legacy 251
FILMOGRAPHY 257
NOTES 266
BIBLIOGRAPHY 291
INDEX 298

ACKNOWLEDGMENTS

With grateful thanks for their invaluable assistance and encouragement to the late Robin Wood, John Anderson, Virginia Soukup, Jean-Loup and Eithne Bourget, Jon Halliday, Adrian Martin, David Stratton, Robert E. Smith, John Belton, the late Roger McNiven, Michael Stern, Bill Paul, Scott Meek, Michael Walker, Charles Barr, Rolando Caputo, Evi Nelson, Isabelle Mangeot-Hewison, the late Kaye Coghlan, and Cerise Howard. Also to technical advisor extraordinaire Barry White; Ned Comstock at the Doheny Library's Department of Special Collections at the University of Southern California; Catherine Gillam, chief librarian at the Australian Film Institute Research Library at the Royal Melbourne Institute of Technology in Melbourne, and her assistant, Alex Gionfriddo; Roslyn Pachoca at the Library of Congress in Washington; the National Film Archive in London; and Ben Pollock at Madman Pictures in Australia. And especially to my ever-supportive daughter, Madeleine, and to my wonderful wife and soul-mate, Debi Enker, for her undying patience, editorial advice, and love.

THE FILMS OF DOUGLAS SIRK

Introduction

*"Your characters have to remain innocent of
what your picture is after."*
—DOUGLAS SIRK, 1971[1]

DOUGLAS SIRK WAS ONE OF THE TWENTIETH-CENTURY CINEMA'S GREAT ironists. And perhaps the most distinctive characteristic of the films he made in Europe and America is the rigor with which they create a gulf between how his characters see themselves and our view of them.

They're forever grappling with the same problems that have always afflicted men and women and parents and children, to do with love, death, and social circumstance. In some cases, they do so in a world of melodrama; in others, they're immersed in the trappings of genre films, such as crime thrillers, musicals, war dramas, and Westerns. Whatever the contexts, though, Sirk adds another layer to their dramatic shape and to his characters' struggles within them.

All around, but beyond the reach of their vision, are forces which define the parameters of their lives. These are evident at the most basic level, in the way that the plots almost always hinge on problems for which the only solution becomes a convenient plot-bound miracle, a *deus ex machina*. As Sirk told journalist Wolfgang Limmer in 1973, "These happy endings all express the weak and sly promise that the world is not rotten and out of joint but meaningful and ultimately in excellent condition. One could follow these thoughts endlessly through Dante, Moliere, Calderon, and even in the grandiose, celestial, operetta-like ending of the second part of *Faust*."[2]

There's also an air of fatalism in the way that social customs and the material world acquire lives of their own in Sirk's stories, stifling the characters' sense of what's possible and limiting their options. From *Das*

"It's remarkable how often carousels, merry-go-rounds, and other rotating objects turn up as background detail in Sirk's films." Rock Hudson in *The Tarnished Angels*.

Madchen vom Moorhof/The Girl from the Marsh Croft (1935) and *Boefje* (1939) through *Summer Storm* (1944) and *Has Anybody Seen My Gal* (1951)—which begins with a caption reading "This is a story about money. Remember it?"—to *The Tarnished Angels* (1957) and *Imitation of Life* (1959), characters' choices seem to be determined by a combination of ideological decree and financial capacity.

Most compellingly of all, forces of repression are signaled through Sirk's imagery. In his work, *mise-en-scène* is as crucial to meaning as narrative form. Outlining the material and psychological parameters of his characters' lives and delineating the limits of their liberty, Sirk's often baroque visual style points to the ways in which human aspiration is largely determined by the tenor of its surroundings.

Homes that are supposed to be havens start to look like prisons as the décor comes to dominate the compositions. The characters' reflections are all around them, and it often seems as if they're entrapped in what is tantamount to a hall of mirrors, a realm made up of reflections of reflections. They're also frequently framed through the bars of staircases or in low-angle shots that make it seem as if ceilings are pressing down on them. Objects that are supposed to be items of support actually seem to be taking over their lives. Their traumas become the logical extensions of the workings of the world around them.[3]

And, at least until the "happy endings" arrive, there seems to be no way out for them, for they're also regularly locked inside cyclical narratives which suggest a legacy being passed from one generation to the next. It's remarkable how often carousels, merry-go-rounds, and other rotating objects turn up as background details in Sirk's films.

Melodrama was the most potent weapon in Sirk's arsenal. Critic and playwright Eric Bentley's simple definition of its modus operandi best defines the source of its emotional power. "Melodramatic vision is paranoid: we are being persecuted, and we hold that all things, living and dead, are combining to persecute us . . . Popular Victorian melodrama made extensive use of bad weather and dangerous landscape."[4] In the women's film in general, and Sirk's work in particular, the natural world of Victorian melodrama is replaced by social circumstance: family breakdowns, the loss of a husband or wife, an individual's alienation from his or her world, the consequences of the divisions wrought by class.

In *All That Heaven Allows* (1955), a New England widow (Jane Wyman) falls in love with her gardener (Rock Hudson), a younger man, much to the chagrin of the local community and her grown-up children (William Reynolds and Gloria Talbott). They have other plans for her: a TV set; a safe, respectable suitor of her age and social standing (Conrad Nagel); a comfortable, orderly life. In Sirk's hands (as in its source), this troubled romance unfolds as an indictment of the social mores that make it troubled, mores that not only exist outside the central figures, embodied in how they're treated by others, but that also seep through their own behavior and are ever-present in the ways in which they think about themselves.

In such a context, when the curtains finally close on them, characters who'd seemed to have overcome their problems emerge in a very different light. Endings that might otherwise be deemed to be happy become far less reassuring. Unsettling ironies cast a shadow across any sense of achievement, not so much invalidating it as offering other ways of viewing it. The miracle that brings *The First Legion* (1950) to a close might persuade Father Arnoux (Charles Boyer) and Dr. Morell (Lyle Bettger) of the existence of God and the power of faith, but Sirk ensures that we also understand both the event and their reaction to it as an indication of the final incomprehensibility of the world, what John Belton refers to as "the pure ambiguity of experience,"[5] and of their limited understandings of their place in it.

The resolutions to *Magnificent Obsession* (1954) and *Battle Hymn* (1957) work in much the same way. While acknowledging the changes that have taken place in the lives of their protagonists (played in both films by Rock Hudson) and their heroic efforts on behalf of others, the films also call into question the nature of their spiritual conversions, suggesting the two men's limited grasp of the personal needs that have been driving them. Sirk's observations to Jon Halliday in relation to *Imitation of Life* are especially pertinent to the view of the world that emerges through his work: "There is a wonderful expression: seeing through a glass darkly.

Everything, even life, is inevitably removed from you. You can't reach, or touch, the real. You just see reflections."[6]

. . .

Sirk is now entrenched as an esteemed Hollywood *auteur*. But perhaps the most astonishing facet of his career is that it took until he left the US for Switzerland at the end of the 1950s (and at the age of sixty-three) for any serious critical attention to be paid to his work. The April 1959 issue of *Cahiers du cinema* is probably where it began, with Jean-Luc Godard's enthusiastic review of *A Time To Love and A Time To Die* (1958), Sirk's anguished 1957 adaptation of the Erich Maria Remarque novel of the same name.

However, it was *Cahiers'* April 1967 issue that really set the ball rolling: it included an extended interview conducted by Serge Daney and Jean-Louis Noames;[7] a thoughtful (and influential) appreciation written by Jean-Louis Comolli, entitled "L'aveugle et le miroir ou l'impossible cinema de Douglas Sirk" ("The Blind Man and the Mirror or The Impossible Cinema of Douglas Sirk"); and a "biofilmographie" compiled by Patrick Brion and Dominique Rabourdin. And, in 1972, Jean-Loup Bourget's insightful writings about Sirk for *Cahiers'* rival, *Positif*, indicated that the director was no passing fad.

Published in 1968, *The American Cinema*, Andrew Sarris's pioneering book on American directors, placed Sirk on "The Far Side of Paradise," drawing attention to his distinctive visual style, somewhat guardedly observing that "the essence of Sirkian cinema is the direct confrontation of all material, however fanciful and improbable," and predicting that "time, if nothing else, will vindicate Douglas Sirk as it already has Josef von Sternberg."[8]

But it wasn't until the publication of Jon Halliday's seminal, book-length interview in 1971 that Sirk became known in the English-speaking world as something more than the director of glossy melodramas and other genre films at Universal. The Sirk that emerges from the interview is a cultured intellectual, a filmmaker who arrived in Hollywood with a very clear vision, leaving behind him an established career in German theatre and film.[9]

At around the same time, largely as a result of director Rainer Werner Fassbinder's enthusiasm, which appeared in his tribute to Sirk in *Fernsehen und Film* in February 1971, German critics began to take notice of Sirk's work. In 1972, a retrospective in Munich paid tribute to the director, followed by Heinz-Gerd Rasner and Reinard Wulf's extended interview with him in *Filmkritik*, in November 1973, and Wolfgang Limmer's soon afterwards in Munich's widely read *Suddeutsche Zeitung*. The country of his birth was now paying attention too.

In England during the 1970s, several probing articles by writers such as Paul Willemen and Fred Camper published in the British theoretical journal, *Screen* (Summer 1971), further enhanced Sirk's prestige. They were followed by the programming of a twenty-film retrospective at the 1972 Edinburgh Film Festival, at which Sirk was a guest. The event solidified his reputation and led to the publication of a book of essays, edited by Halliday and Laura Mulvey. It offered new material as well as a selection of articles originally published elsewhere, including Thomas Elsaesser's translation of Fassbinder's tribute and an essay by a young American filmmaker-in-waiting named Tim Hunter on *Summer Storm*.

A downside of much of the writing about Sirk during the 1970s and '80s was the almost reflexive condescension towards the sources for his films, the insistence that he was somehow borrowing from the trash heap and transforming what he found there into masterworks. For example, James Harvey writes in the late 1970s that "an intelligent director confronting the world of Fannie Hurst or of Lloyd C. Douglas confronts not only banality but a more virulent kind of falsity: the self-deceptions and consoling lies about life and human character that the tearjerking mode exists to supply us with."[10] This view is also prevalent throughout Halliday's book, and Sirk himself, at least as quoted—I never encountered this kind of tone from him during my interviews with him—appears to have concurred.[11]

One gets the sense from the lack of any detail about these sources that what was being espoused here was a borrowed truth rather than the result of any firsthand encounter with the novels or plays being so summarily dismissed. In the Halliday interview, Sirk frequently observes that he didn't read the books or stories from which his films were adapted or watch the original versions of the films he was remaking. In several cases, these sources were entirely overlooked. It wasn't until I began researching this book that I became aware that *Slightly French* (1949) is a remake of *Let's Fall in Love* (1933), which was based on a story by Herbert Fields, and that *There's Always Tomorrow* (1956) is a remake of a 1934 film of the same name (sometimes known as *Too Late for Love*), which was based on a story by Ursula Parrott.

Where possible I have tracked down these sources as part of my efforts to identify the creative strategies Sirk brought to the material, to try to make sense of exactly how he was bending them to his style. And enough

Published 1952, G. P. Putnam's Sons, New York.

have proved to be sufficiently worthy of attention in their own right—rather than simply being seen as starting-points for Sirk's projects—to make it clear that one should remain skeptical about any glib put-downs.

For example, Edna Lee's novel, *All That Heaven Allows*, might have been available during the early 1950s and at the time of the release of Sirk's film, and viewers might well have been compelled to set the two alongside each other in their assessments. But by the time Sirk had been "discovered," Lee's work no longer had any traction, and no commentaries I've come across about the film offer any more than a passing note.

Even more obscure is Gene Markey's 1951 novel, *The Great Companions*, which served as the source for Sirk's 1953 musical, *Take Me to Town*, and, as far as I can tell, was only ever published in the *Ladies' Home Journal*. Nowhere does any commentary reflect on what Markey's work might have contributed to Sirk's, or how choices made by the filmmakers might have been inspired by it.

In 1974, the University of Connecticut Film Society programmed an ambitious tribute to Sirk,[12] offering a complete retrospective of the director's American films and inviting him to attend. However, on the way to the airport for the flight to New York, and the eagerly anticipated return to the US, Sirk suffered a hemorrhage that seriously impaired the vision in his left eye, an ailment that was to trouble him for the remainder of his life. "If I couldn't read, I couldn't live," he said shortly afterwards.[13] But it wasn't long before he lost most of the sight of his other eye.[14]

However, by this time, his reputation was firmly established, even if he felt uncomfortable with some of the terms in which his work was being discussed. In particular, he was uneasy about the way he'd been cast as an unequivocal critic of all things American, as in Halliday's account of his work as a commentary on "the barren ideology" of '50s America.[15]

Much of the subsequent writing on Sirk's films took up Halliday's approach, casting the director as something akin to a latterday Bertolt Brecht, identifying his methods of "distanciation" as a way of casting a critical eye over the workings of classical storytelling and the failures of the American bourgeoisie. While acknowledging Brecht's influence and expressing his admiration for him (he'd directed a production of *The Threepenny Opera* in Germany), Sirk was uncomfortable with the way his work was being regarded in the same light.

For example, the robot figure in *There's Always Tomorrow* can be viewed as a metaphor for the way Fred MacMurray's protagonist is living his life, but it reveals nothing of the torment he suffers during the course of the film. Here and elsewhere, Sirk's films offer critiques of their characters' ideologies, but also extend to them an understanding and an empathy that acknowledges their humanity. While the director was delighted to find that the social commentary embedded in his work was being recognized, he was dismayed by the way it was often reduced to its didactic elements.

"When I went to the United States," he recalled in 1975, "I was making films about American society, and it is true that I never felt at home there, except perhaps when my wife and I lived on a farm in the San Fernando Valley. But I always wanted my characters to be more than cyphers for the failings of their world. And I never had to look too hard to find a part of myself in them."

It was a view upon which he elaborated in an interview with Peter Lehman in 1980. "You have to think with the heart," he said. "There's a thinking of the heart, too. At the same time as you can be an intellectual; you can be very sophisticated. I think the great artists, especially in literature, have always thought with the heart."[16]

Among those who contributed to the wave of critical interest in Sirk at this time were a number of critics well-equipped to situate his work in the context of so-called "women's pictures" and to explore its sexual politics. Foremost among them were Elsaesser, whose seminal essay on the family melodrama laid solid foundations for what was to follow.[17] Two other prominent and influential contributors to this discussion during the 1970s were Molly Haskell[18] and Laura Mulvey.[19]

Without wanting to promote a straightforward cause-effect reasoning here, I suspect that it's not entirely by coincidence that much of the commentary about Sirk and the 1950s melodramas occurred during the '70s, just as the resurgent feminist movement of the time was becoming a potent social force. As revealed in the interviews he was giving, Sirk was clearly a man with social and sexual politics on his mind, and the films for which he initially became famous were dealing with what history had long defined as the woman's domain, the home.

Much of the commentary, like that on display in the invaluable 1991 collection edited by Lucy Fischer for *Imitation of Life: Douglas Sirk, Director*,[20] focuses on the ways in which Sirk's films probe the circumstances of women in American society. Barbara Klinger's *Melodrama & Meaning: History, Culture and the Films of Douglas Sirk*,[21] published in 1994, also provides an insightful context for the exploration of Sirk's standing as an auteur. Not all of the critical work was waving the Sirk flag; some of the writers disagreed with the prevailing view for a variety of reasons. But the sustained critique and its focal points made significant contributions to Sirk commentary, whatever conclusions the various critics reached.

As a result, however, Sirk's critical reputation currently rests heavily on four of the melodramas he made during the 1950s: *All That Heaven Allows*, *Written on the Wind* (1956), *The Tarnished Angels*, and *Imitation of Life*. And some recognition has been given to three other films from this period, including *All I Desire* (1953),[22] *There's Always Tomorrow*[23] and *A Time To Love and A Time to Die* (1958).[24] Of the work he did before going to America, only *Schlussakkord/Final Chord* (1936),[25] *Zu neuen Ufern/To Distant Shores*,[26] and *La Habanera* (both 1937)[27] have received substantial critical scrutiny.

These films all deserve the attention paid to them and their configurations play an important part in the commentary that follows. However, the preoccupation with them and the social and political priorities that came to the fore during the 1970s and '80s meant that other works that were equally deserving of attention were pushed into the background.

In his book, Michael Stern exemplifies the skewed thinking that resulted from this. "*Sleep My Love* has as poor a reputation as *Lured* among Sirk's admirers," he writes, "and, in fact, it shares with its predecessor the mystery/jeopardy plot that seems so out of place in the hands of a director whose concerns are social and psychological."[28]

It's true that some of Sirk's early work in Hollywood suffers to a degree from the limited budgets that were available to him and from the other constraints under which he was operating. But much of it also indicates that, even before the 1950s melodramas, he was a filmmaker with a finely developed sensibility who was fully in control of his medium. In fact, his work in Europe makes him a significant figure in world cinema even before he went to the US. He might not have been free to choose projects in line with his personal interests, but he was an artist who brought those interests with him to whatever material he tackled.

That said, not everyone who has written about Sirk has been positive about his work. In 1991, Paul Coates summarily dismissed the director as an opportunist, accusing him of "reducing the imperative of art to the small matter of retaining a tasteful tone, while explicating his supposed true intentions in interviews dispensed after the fact to eager auteurists."[29] Robert B. Ray's smug put-down in his book *How a Film Theory Got Lost*, of Sirk's "opportunistic" engagement with commentators about his work, is similarly instructive in its condescension: "Aberrant decoding [such as Sirk's] enables individual readers [or groups, cf. feminist scholars] ... to remotivate Hollywood's product for other purposes."[30]

Along the same lines, several hostile articles appeared in a 1999 double issue of the American magazine, *Film Criticism*, that had been devoted to Sirk and that followed a 1997 conference at Dartmouth College in New Hampshire. Therein, he was accused of inadvertently playing into the hands of the Nazis by making films at UFA after Hitler came to power, and any admirers of his work were charged with being guilty of "unreflected fandom" [*sic*][31] and accused of missing the point. "The renaissance of Sirk," wrote Gertrud Koch in an extremely convoluted article, "is informed by a duplicity in the interpretation of his oeuvre. The emphasis on the 'tender,' 'human,' 'non-despising' aspects of his films brushes aside elements which are central to his films—elitism, sadism, and sealed surfaces."[32] Then, in 2005, the *New German Critique* published an essay by Eric Rentschler asserting that "Sirk's undialectical approach to social criticism does not further understanding, but instead compels the viewer to retreat into interiority when the world outside offers no solace."[33]

Much of this commentary, which is described by Linda Schulte-Sasse in her 1998 article in the *Germanic Review*, as "the backlash discourse,"[34] is filled with factual error and snide innuendo, and is certainly not unduly overburdened with critical acumen. Dissenting views about Sirk's work should open up further discussion about it, but the dismissive tone of this commentary runs entirely counter to that. The accusation that Sirk was using the interviews he did with Halliday and others to guide the way his work would be discussed totally misrepresents the openness Sirk would bring to discussions about his art. And it also displays an appalling arrogance in its charge that a generation of film critics and scholars had allowed the wool to be pulled over their eyes.

When critic Fred Camper observed that "no critic has been as perceptive as Sirk himself in articulating some of [his] themes,"[35] he was showing an appropriate respect for the filmmaker's intelligence as a commentator on his own work. And the quotations from Sirk sprinkled throughout this book indicate the richness of the insights he had to offer. However, any critic worth his or her salt will always adhere to D. H. Lawrence's dictum: "Never trust the teller, trust the tale." Nobody can control meaning and it is never fixed. Furthermore, the quality of any reading of any text—Sirk's and anyone else's—depends on the insights and understandings it has to offer. The director's reputation mattered to him, of course, but his readiness to discuss and debate the meanings of his films pointed to his appreciation of Lawrence's position on the subject.

• • •

From the vantage point of 2018, Sirk's work looks very different from the way it did in the 1970s. My extended introduction to it back then came via one-off screenings, on TV (hosted by knowing Australian cinephiles such as Ivan Hutchinson in Melbourne and Bill Collins in Sydney), as part of National Film Theatre schedules (in Melbourne and London), during the teaching of courses at colleges and universities (in Melbourne and the UK), at the National Film Archive in London, and courtesy of enthusiastic and unfailingly generous film collectors (in Melbourne and New York). However, it's a logistically very different matter to examine them from the perspective of the early years of the twenty-first century than from anywhere between 1960—by which time their director had departed Hollywood—and the 1990s.

Scribblings made in the dark and post-screening reflections made on the run used to be all that I or anybody else was able to do by way of note-taking. Unless, of course, one was able to view the films on a Steenbeck editing table. That invaluable but now-antiquated contraption provided an early and very crude model for the closer kinds of viewings available today, via DVD, on television, or online (on YouTube and elsewhere). Armchair viewings now allow remote-controlled opportunities to pause and rewind at will.

Furthermore, it's more than half a century since *Cahiers* first turned the spotlight on Sirk's work and most of his films are far more readily available. So, one of the chief goals of this book is to provide a comprehensive overview of *all* of Sirk's features. Another is to propose a view of them that looks beyond their political critiques and their concern with the social oppression of women to a wider view of the human condition that incorporates those critical issues but looks beyond them.

Following Schulte-Sasse's lead, my commentary also draws upon the notion of a "reflexive space"[36] which Sirk's films (or at least most of them) invite us to occupy as we contemplate their stories and their surfaces. That is, the space in which an audience finds itself when it comes to recognize that "form should not be understood as opposed to content, but as a formal system that constructs and complicates meaning." This thesis is akin to the one proposed by Victoria L. Evans in her analysis of Sirk's use of "apertures, grids, drapes, screens and vortices . . . [to create] a state of sympathetic attention in the observer that combines emotional engagement with more thoughtful deliberations."[37] To a degree, that project is also part of a wider one: to lay claim to Sirk's work as classical in its form, self-aware, and finding room for rupture, but never abandoning the coherence of its characters or the seamlessness of its fictions.

My "interviews" with Sirk were more like conversations. He asked almost as many questions of me as I did of him. Along with his published responses to others over the years, his comments appear here to indicate his thoughts about his work and life. As my disagreements with him indicate, they are not intended in any sense to provide a final word on the subject.

• • •

Sirk was born Hans Detlef Sierck on April 26, 1897, in Hamburg. His parents were Danish, his father a newspaperman. By the time he was fourteen, he had discovered the theatre, in particular Shakespeare's history plays. He'd also begun to frequent the cinema, where the Danish-born silent era star, Asta Nielsen (1881–1972), became a favorite and where he had his first encounters with what he was later to describe as "dramas of swollen emotions."

In 1919, he enrolled to study law at Munich University, before moving to the newly established Hamburg University, where he turned his attention to philosophy and the history of art. Years later, he still remembered lectures given there by Albert Einstein (presumably as a visitor) and Erwin Panofsky (who was chair of the art history department). To finance his studies, he wrote for newspapers and began to work in the theatre.

In 1922, he directed his first production in Hamburg, Hermann Bossdorf's *Bahnmeister Tod/Stationmaster Death*, and began a career which saw him become one of the foremost theatre directors in Weimar Germany.

While continuing that side of his career, which he was finding increasingly stressful in the context of the social changes of the time, he also began work at UFA studios in 1934. He directed three shorts there before making his feature debut in 1935 with *April! April!* (an alternative version was made in Dutch).

Throughout his time in Germany, he maintained an intense interest in painting (which he pursued in his spare time) and in art movements across history. When I first visited him and his wife, former stage actress Hilde Jary, in 1975, it was clear that this interest was eclectic and hadn't waned over the years. A Korean tapestry denoting the seasons was hanging by the entrance doorway, presented to him during the location filming for *Battle Hymn*. On opposite walls of their living room were a modern Japanese painting and one striking work entitled "Negro Ritual," done by Hilde during her time as a student, before she turned her hand to singing and acting. And on their dining room wall was a Constable original.

Sirk would welcome the chance to talk about art and the ways in which it fueled his theatre and film work. "I was bored by expressionism and unhappy about the gradual shift to more realist forms," he said, subsequently identifying two nineteenth-century painters, Honore Daumier (1808–1879) and Eugene Delacroix (1798–1863), as having left "their imprint on the visual style of my melodramas."

After *April! April!*, Sirk made six more films at UFA, before leaving Germany in 1937 to join Hilde, who'd traveled to Rome not long beforehand. Sirk made his escape by pretending to be scouting locations for what he explained to UFA executives was to be his next film, *Wilton's Zoo*. That film was never made, but it became his way out. While there were admirers of his work in high places in the Nazi government—Goebbels foremost among them—he had become increasingly dismayed by what was happening in Germany and what he referred to as "the abyss of Hitlerism."[38] Along with his concern for Hilde, this was a key reason for his hasty departure.

One of the reasons he had remained as long as he did was his hope for a chance to reunite with his son, Claus, from whom he had become estranged after divorcing his first wife, Lydia Brinken. After leaving Germany, he never saw her or Claus again. She died of cancer in 1945; a year earlier, Claus had been killed on the Russian Front, although Sirk didn't learn of this until much later.

Arriving in the US in 1941, he found it hard to get a foothold in the film business. Eventually he made *Hitler's Madman* (1942), which provided him with an opportunity to dramatize some of the horror he'd been able to leave behind. Then came *Summer Storm*, which was based on Chekhov's

The Shooting Party and led to a collaboration and long friendship with George Sanders (1906–1972), whom he described as "really the only actor with whom I had anything in common in Hollywood."

Sirk's star gradually ascended in America, his partnerships with producers Ross Hunter (nine films) and Albert Zugsmith (two) at Universal-International proving especially fruitful.

When Hunter visited Australia during the early 1970s to promote *Lost Horizon* (1973), he remembered Sirk as "a sweet man, but very out of place in Hollywood." For his part, Sirk found Hunter equally congenial company, even if they were on entirely different wavelengths. Zugsmith gave him his freedom, for which he was grateful, and he would speak of "Zug" with affection, although he also confessed to finding the cigar-smoking mogul "awfully crass."

Largely as a result of the workings of the studio system, Sirk was able to gather around him a group of regular collaborators, including Rock Hudson ("a lovely young man who was treated abominably by the studio"), screenwriter George Zuckerman ("the only writer I ever felt an allegiance to"), cinematographer Russell Metty ("a man with a great eye for detail and an appreciation of what I wanted"), and art director Alexander Golitzen. However, he lamented long after his retirement, "I was, and to a large extent still am, too much of a loner."

His affair with Hollywood was very much a love-hate relationship. "At that time, we Europeans called Hollywood a prison, and that it was. But although it appears paradoxical, the system had its advantages. An artist needs walls against which to fight, even if they are prison walls. Total freedom is only for the genius, and even that is open to doubt. Attacking these walls makes a man cunning and inventive. It strengthens the muscles of his talent."[39] But, while he enjoyed the challenge of "bending the material to [his] style" in an environment seemingly designed to cramp his creativity, neither Sirk nor Hilde ever felt comfortable with its excesses. He remembered being shocked when he went to a party at Zugsmith's lavish LA home and found "naked women frolicking in the pool."

Partially because of his ill health, but largely because he'd had enough, he and Hilde left the US in 1959. Until his death in January 1987, they lived in Lugano, in an apartment high on the Ruvigliana hillside looking out over the beautiful lake. It provided them with the peace and the solitude they loved, although they regularly greeted friends from afar. Hilde died in 1989.[40]

Encouraged by Rainer Werner Fassbinder, with whom he became friendly after the then-*enfant terrible* of the German cinema visited him in Lugano, Sirk also did some teaching during the late 1970s at the film school in Munich, where he made three short films with his students. When he died, he was still "studying the classics," as he put it, and being excited by more recent discoveries, especially the work of Gabriel Garcia Marquez and Patrick White.

CHAPTER ONE

Detlef Sierck in Europe

"I didn't expect the Nazis to last. I was wrong about that. First of all, like a lot of people, I didn't ever expect them to get power—and then, when they did get in, I didn't believe they could hold on to it."
—DOUGLAS SIRK, 1970[1]

IN 1934, AFTER TWO UFA (UNIVERSUM FILM-AKTIEN GESELLSCHAFT) executives attended a performance of Sirk's stage production of *Twelfth Night* in Berlin, the director was invited to work for the Berlin-based film company. It had been established in 1917 as a corporation run by a consortium whose business was making films and money. In 1927, it was bought by Alfred Hugenberg, an extreme right-wing financier with close ties to the Nazi Party. In 1933, Hitler came to power and appointed Joseph Goebbels as minister of propaganda; his goal was to assume control of the media in all forms, and that included UFA. Public book burnings began soon afterwards, although the types of films coming out of UFA remained relatively constant.

There are several reasons for this, including the fact that the company was not only an established part of the business landscape but was also prosperous. As Marc Silberman puts it, "except for the exclusion of 'undesirables' [notably Jews and Leftists], there was a remarkable continuity in the personnel on the management level of the film industry before and after January 1933 . . . In other words, the main social function of National Socialism in the film industry was to sustain the capitalist industrial structure to the advantage of big business and at the expense of small and midsized operations."[2]

While Sirk, whose work in the theatre had made him a well-known figure of the left, became one of numerous "undesirables" to find or maintain a place at UFA, others departed the scene, many in fear for their lives. Although little detailed biographical information is available about this period of Sirk's career, it appears that he managed to do things his own way not only because his films were successful but because, despite the oppressive circumstances, he found himself working with like-minded individuals.

In fact, even after UFA had been nationalized in 1937, bringing it formally under the control of the government's propaganda ministry, Goebbels regarded it as a problem. As historian Klaus Kreimeier points out, despite official policy, not only was it "still employing unreliable types capable of equivocation," but "the contingent of National Socialist Party adherents (working there) was small, and even in their presence criticism was repeatedly voiced."[3]

In his interview with Jon Halliday, Sirk confirmed this, recalling that, during his time at UFA, "the workers and technicians were mainly anti-Nazi, much more so than the intellectuals."[4] He also went on to explain that, just as he later found ways to deal with Hollywood on his own terms, he also managed to negotiate his way past prohibitions at UFA: "You could still get away with extraordinary things under the Nazis. It took time for everything to seize up, and at UFA there was still a certain amount of room to manoeuvre."[5]

Part of the reason for this was that Goebbels was concerned that the films being made at UFA should, for the most part at least, adhere to the principles of popular entertainment rather than pitching hard-line propaganda. The problem created by his attempt to, in the words of historian Eric Rentschler, "aestheticize the political in order to anaesthetize the public"[6] was that he was inadvertently giving filmmakers license to inflect "the political" in ways that he hadn't anticipated. In other words, to tell stories their own way. The critical question for those exploring Sirk's work, and for this chapter, is the kind of use the director made of the prevailing circumstances at UFA during his short time there.

Between 1935 and 1937, he made seven feature films under the company banner, five about female characters colliding with hostile circumstances. Three travel across oceans—in *Schlussakord* (1936) and *Zu neuen Ufern* and *La Habanera* (both 1937)—but they and their soul-sisters are all on metaphorical journeys. In *Das Madchen vom Moorhof* (1935), Helga (Hansi Knoteck) is an unwed mother confronted by social prejudice and hypocrisy. But, although she is the title character, the protagonist is the man who, eventually, stands by her. The tone is lighter in *Das Hofkonzert* (1936), an operetta, but Christine (Martha Eggerth), a singer, is equally subject to a fraught situation in which she's cast as an unwelcome outsider.

While this might seem to confirm the notion that the character focus of the films that Sirk made in Germany was sustained into his career in Hollywood, it doesn't. In fact, although he's long been best known for his films about women, only nine of the twenty-nine films he made after leaving Europe have females as their central characters. But even if the connections between the two phases of his career lie elsewhere, in these films it's the woman's plight that drives the plot.

Although all five are distinguished by compelling performances from their female leads, Sirk's two collaborations with Zarah Leander—in *Zu neuen Ufern* and *La Habanera*—are what stand out. Despite her reputation as being generally troublesome,[7] and Goebbels's famous dislike for her—he is reputed to have described her as an "enemy of Germany"—the Swedish-born actress became a star in Nazi Germany. Only after she returned to Sweden in 1943 did the press turn on her.

In an interview with Eckhardt Schmidt,[8] Sirk recounted visiting her backstage in Vienna in 1936 while she was performing in the musical, *Axel an der Himmelstur*. During the casting for *Zu neuen Ufern*, he'd been sent there by UFA production boss, Ernst Hugo Correll, and was immediately taken by what he describes as "the whole strange Nordic landscape of her face": "It was as if she was covered by a blanket of ice," he continues. "Rarely was there any movement in her face, but she had wonderful eyes and exuded a great calm." He knew almost at once that she was right for the role of the tormented chanteuse in *Zu neuen Ufern*, although, after three days of screen tests, UFA executives became troubled by her "strange blend of femininity and masculinity." "Everything about her was in a minor key," Sirk says, "even her voice."

As in much of the rest of the world at the time, the prevailing wisdom in Nazi Germany was that a woman's place was in the home looking after her children. In his commentary on *La Habanera*, Bruce Babington identifies "National Socialism's perverse ability to colonise themes and language not in themselves Nazi."[9] So, like the German cinema's wider roster of female stars, Leander represented a problem for the authorities. As critic Antje Ascheid observes, "The very presence and immense popularity of a star like Leander exemplify the ideological inconsistencies that existed in everyday life under Nazi rule."[10] Further evidence that, despite the strict measures that Goebbels put into place, the film business was a very difficult one to control.

For Sirk, Leander was perfect casting, and he constantly draws on the tensions between her public persona as a woman very much in control of her life and the traumas encountered by the characters she played for him. Her exterior might have signified a magisterial stillness, but violent storms raged within. And, in both *Zu neuen Ufern* and *La Habanera*, despite the ostensible "happy endings," those tensions remain unresolved.

Sirk made two other features for UFA, both directly linked to his time in the theatre. The first was the Moliere-inspired *April! April!*; the second, the Ibsen adaptation, *Stutzen der Gesellschaft*. Both deal loosely with the workings of class and capitalism, never far away throughout Sirk's career. His stylistic range is further illustrated by the neorealist *Boefje*, which he made in Holland after leaving Germany and shortly before his departure from Europe for the US.

APRIL! APRIL! (1935)

> "If he does not assert a system of virtues, he identifies the reverse of them, pretentiousness, insincerity, hypocrisy; finds amusement in the contrasts between what men are and what they think themselves, what they endeavour to do and what is in their nature to be: he reveals things which deform men, separate them from their fellows, and magnify their differences."
>
> —JOHN WOOD ON MOLIERE, 1953[11]

A deliciously funny screwball farce, Sirk's feature debut is very much in the mode of *Le Bourgeois Gentilhomme/The Would-Be Gentleman*. And theatre producer John Wood's above observations about the seventeenth-century playwright are equally applicable to *April! April!* In fact, they also encapsulate a general view of the world akin to Sirk's, even though much of the director's work was in the realm of melodrama rather than comedy.

The film's title sets the tone for what is to follow. "April! April!" is the exclamation you'll hear in Germany after someone has made you the butt of an April Fools' Day hoax. In most countries, citizens could expect to find themselves free of pranksters by midday, since custom has it that the joke rebounds on the joker after then. However, in Sirk's film, written by H. W. Litschke and Rudo Ritter (best known for the opera, *Penthesilea*), the games go on long after the appropriate hour has passed and the ricocheting chaos can even continue into the following day.

The central character is Julius Lampe (Erhard Siedel), an endearing buffoon with upwardly mobile aspirations who, nominally at least, is in

The family maid (Hilde Schneider) delivers the letter to befuddled noodle-maker Julius Lampe (Erhard Siedel) that sets the plot of *April! April!* in motion.

charge of Lampe's Nudelfabrik, a noodle-making factory. I'm not entirely sure why, but "noodle," or "nudel," is an automatically funny word, the humor only enhanced when it's spoken in German. Lampe's wife, Mathilde (Lina Carstens), appears to be the one who really cares about climbing the social ladder—like Harriet Blaisdell (Lynn Bari) in Sirk's later *Has Anybody Seen My Gal*—although her husband seems willing enough to push aside his discomfort with the required airs and graces and go along for the ride. He used to be a humble baker, she a cook, and they have now, somehow, managed to hit the jackpot.

We first find him sleeping his way through a Sunday-morning recital by his daughter, Mirna (Charlott Daudert), and her goofy beau, Reinhold Leisegang (Werner Finck). The finely attired guests, anticipating the snooty attendees at the country club party in *All That Heaven Allows*, politely applaud their performance, while turning down their noses at the family's ambitious affectations. One of them, Finke (Paul Westermeier), sardonically asides, "Thank God, I'm not musical."

While all this is happening, the family maid (Hilde Schneider) is scurrying across the room towards the slumbering man of the house, carrying the letter that is to set the loopy plot in motion. It is from Prince von

Hosten-Bohlau (Albrecht Schoenhals), containing an order for noodles, and it leads a very excited Mathilde to see opportunity knocking, call the recital to a halt, announce the family's very close relationship to local royalty, and regard poor Leisegang as no longer a suitable marriage prospect for Mirna.

For Finke and his friend (Herbert Weissbach), the Lampes' pomposity is "intolerable," so, given that it's April 1, they conspire to put them in their place. Pretending to be the prince, Finke phones Julius and announces an imminent visit. The guests are dispensed with, the newspapers are contacted, the Lampes' mansion is prepared, and bedlam ensues.

It should have been avoided when Leisegang discovers the prank that is being played and tells Julius . . . actually, he has to persuade him because Julius is not especially quick on the uptake. But instead of immediately calling the preparations for the visit to a halt, Julius decides that they need someone to play the part of the illustrious visitor. Given the public humiliation if the prince doesn't appear, he sees no alternative. The force of social expectations is just too great.

Thus, Mueller (Hubert von Meyerinck), a traveling salesman who just happens to be passing through, is cast in the role. Meanwhile, after the prince reads about his forthcoming visit in the newspaper, he assumes that his secretary (Annemarie Korff) has forgotten to tell him and decides to make his own way to the Lampes'. And then . . . never mind: I'm sure you get the general idea.

What follows is a crescendo of mistaken identities, verbal misunderstandings, and false rumors, with characters forever pretending to be somebody they're not or to have done something they didn't. The interlocking misjudgements and deceptions are as hilarious as they are seemingly endless. And driving them all are the ways in which the characters' sense of their place in the world is determined by an insidious social hierarchy.

While the film's ending might seem to restore a semblance of order, the mindsets of most of those involved suggest that their place in that order is far from fixed. With a very raised eyebrow at the proposed outcomes—Mirna settles for Leisegang because all other options seem exhausted; her parents go back to business as usual—Sirk is simply placing the mayhem in pause mode and suggesting that it's very likely to continue indefinitely.

At the same time, however, the possibility of rising above such divisions and confusions is embodied in the romantic relationship that develops between the prince and Julius's secretary, Friedl Bild (Carola Hohn). A godsend for her employer—she is smart and down-to-earth, and knows how to write letters to princes—she's also the film's Cinderella. When she and her prince fall in love, she's unaware that he's actually a prince—in the film's ongoing network of intrigues, she believes he's the traveling-salesman impostor rather than the real thing—and he's happy to go along with her mistake. That they're made for each other is clear from the start in the actors' easygoing, naturalistic performances, in sharp contrast to the bombast on display elsewhere.

Despite the Lampes' pomposity, Sirk depicts them as dolts rather than devils. Julius, in fact, is the heart and soul of the film. If *April! April!* were a Hollywood screwball comedy, he might be played by Edward Everett Horton or, perhaps, Eugene Pallette. But Siedel is a joy to watch, fluttering to and fro as his character tries to do the right thing, as he sees it, but forever missing the point. In appearance, his Julius could easily be one of George Grosz's allegorical caricatures of the bourgeoisie.[12] But whereas Grosz's art was driven by his anger at the plight of Germany between the World Wars, Sirk's approach in *April! April!* is much gentler, even affectionate, the equivalent of a wry smile rather than a savage snarl.

During his time in the theatre, Sirk had directed Moliere,[13] and his pursuit of the cinematic potential in Moliere's experimental fusions of music, dance, and drama—in particular in *Le Bourgeois Gentilhomme*—is clear in the approach he took to *April! April!* The musical rhythms underpinning the play are evident in some of Moliere's stage directions: for example, "Four tailor boys dance up to Mr. Jourdain [Moliere's equivalent to the befuddled Julius]. Two take off the breeches in which he did his exercises; the others remove his jacket, after which they dress him in his new suit. Mr. Jourdain struts round to be admired in time with the music."[14]

At times, Sirk's smooth staging of the action and his direction of the actors—a few of whom he'd previously worked with in the theatre, including Siedel—evoke the impression of a dance. A couple of smartly edited montage sequences of servants going about their business are effectively the equivalent of dance numbers in a musical. And Siedel's rushings-around are akin to quicksteps. His physical grace is remarkable.

Along similar lines, in her commentary on the film, Katie Trumpener likens the film's upstairs-downstairs aspects to "a contrapuntal household symphony."[15] However, for her, its chief influence stems from the ways in which Rene Clair's early sound films (such as *Sous les toits de Paris*, *Le Million*, and *A nous la liberte*) "offer poetic, and ultimately political, meditations on the nature of everyday (and working-class) experience."[16]

To this point, Trumpener aside, there has been a scarcity of substantial critical commentary about *April! April!*—perhaps because no print with

English subtitles has been available.[17] In a 2016 article, Valerie Weinstein dealt with it at length but without insight; her dogged, doctrinaire discussion of what she sees as the film's inadvertent racism and anti-Semitism is as muddle-headed in its commentary as it is condescending.

Her subject is the depiction of the "white Jew" in German cinema of the 1930s. Explaining that the label was "a common insult in the Third Reich used to criticize non-Jews perceived as corrupted by and behaving like 'Jews,'"[18] she proposes that, for parts of German audiences at the time, the Lampes would have been so labeled. "The film gives spectators little reason to assume the Lampes are Jewish," she adds, "although in Nazi Germany there well could have been spectators who understood them as such."[19]

For what it tells us about the way in which films can be viewed at different times in history by viewers with a wide variety of dispositions, this is of interest. But it has little of value to offer about the workings of *April! April!* or about the perspectives it offers on its characters and the values they embody.

Equally misguided is Weinstein's put-down of Sirk as a "fledging director" and her charge that *April! April!* was "not a project controlled by an artistically independent, mature director with a recognizable stylistic signature and social agenda."[20] In fact, Sirk was coming to film with a significant body of work in the German theatre of the 1920s and early '30s on his curriculum vitae (not that he needed one). He'd sought refuge at UFA after the Nazis closed down his production of Georg Kaiser and Kurt Weill's play *Der Silbersee Ein Wintermarchen/The Silver Lake, A Winter's Tale* at the Altes Theatre in Leipzig and vetoed his appointment as head of the Berliner Staatstheater. He recalled being told by the theatre's administrative head, "My dear friend, you must realize it's out of the question for you to take over the theatre since, I'm sorry to say, you have a Jewish wife."[21]

Following a trio of shorts he made for the studio—one of which was adapted (by Rudo Ritter, again, and I. A. L. Muller) from Moliere's *La Malade Imaginaire* (1934)—*April! April!* was his first feature. But, far from pointing to its director as an anonymous novice, it is very sophisticated, extremely assured, stylistically adventurous, and entirely irresistible.

THE GIRL FROM THE MARSH CROFT/DAS MADCHEN VOM MOORHOF (1935)

"This was not a project of my choosing, but it gave me an opportunity to keep working, which is what I do best."
—DOUGLAS SIRK, 1981

Sirk's second feature—released less than a week after *April! April!*—is an adaptation of Swedish Nobel Prize-winning novelist Selma Lagerlof's novella of the same name (originally included in her 1908 collection entitled *En saga om en saga och andra sagor*).[22] Lagerlof's well-received book had been previously adapted by fellow Swede Victor Sjostrom in 1917 and by Turkish director Muhsin Ertugrul in 1934. Subsequent renderings have come from Finland (1940), Sweden again (1947), Denmark (1952), and West Germany (1958).

Written by Philipp Lothar Mayring,[23] Sirk's version is the first of his films about women struggling to survive in worlds which pay scant attention to their needs. It's a point of reference in several of the interviews he did during the time of his "rediscovery,"[24] although it's only discussed in passing, perhaps because of his vague recollection of it. I never spoke to him about it in any detail, mainly because I hadn't seen it at the time. But in what he does have to say, Sirk shows no awareness of Sjostrom's version, telling Halliday that the screenplay "deviated quite a bit from the original"—he doesn't elaborate in what ways—and expressing regret that the Swedish setting of the novel had been replaced by a North German one. "People in Scandinavia are different from the Germans," he said. "The peasantry there are more highly educated than anywhere else in Europe." What's implied here also remains unclear.

Sirk's observations are especially perplexing given that both his and Sjostrom's films turn out to be what are generally referred to as "faithful adaptations"—that is, each adheres fairly closely to the details of Lagerlof's plot, if not their precise narrative order.

Helga is the novelist's title character, "a poor farmer's daughter,"[25] whose moral goodness comes to serve as a shining example to all who encounter her. She withdraws her claim for financial assistance from the well-off landowner who has fathered her child after he shows that he's willing to lie on oath if necessary to avoid humiliation. Believing that "there is nothing so terrible as perjury,"[26] she can't bear the idea that the child's father should so damn himself in the eyes of God. Her actions win the respect of all in the courtroom, the judge observing their transformation in the "light in their faces, as though they had seen something very beautiful, which had made them happy all the way into their souls."[27]

Gudmund is a local farmer's son, betrothed to Hildur, the daughter of a wealthy village elder. When the young man's mother, an invalid, takes pity on the impoverished Helga and offers her work in their home as a maid, Hildur's snobbish objections stem in part from an undeclared sexual jealousy. As a result, Gudmund starts to see his fiance in a different light, as "petty and heartless."[28] His recognition of "the wealth and good social position which awaited him" as Hildur's husband still takes precedence over his doubts about her. But what had once appeared clear no longer does, for "Helga had become for him the standard by which he measured people."[29]

In addition to being divided by class, their community is a God-fearing one and Gudmund strives to follow the dictates of his conscience. After a drunken evening with friends in a local tavern, he believes that he's responsible for the death of a man in a brawl there. Although he can't remember what happened, he regards his clasp-knife's broken blade as clear evidence that he is the killer and considers that he is bound to confess to the crime.

Unaware until later that Helga had borrowed the knife from him to shave firewood and was responsible for its condition, he is horrified by what he thinks he must have done. To spare his bride-to-be and her family public embarrassment, he calls off the wedding and resigns himself to a different kind of future from the one he'd been planning.

After Helga discovers that Gudmund has mistakenly implicated himself, she goes to Hildur to explain, urging her to forgive him and take him back. Amazed at Helga's selflessness—"I can't comprehend that you should come to me today with the desire to help me"[30]—Hildur achieves a dignity that had previously seemed beyond her, goes to Gudmund, and opens the door on new possibilities for his relationship with Helga.

In the novel, Sagerlof frequently backtracks in her narration, placing us at a particular point in the story and then looking back to reveal how the characters have arrived there. On the other hand, the trajectory of both films is relentlessly forward-moving—that is, with one exception. A flashback near the end of the Sjostrom film expands on the earlier scene in which Helga (Greta Almroth) borrows Gudmund's knife. Sirk deems it unnecessary to revisit the original incident.

Lagerlof's backtracking formally insists that the past shapes the present. This not only bears upon the specific interactions between the characters but also on the social expectations that have led them to act in the way that they do. At the same time, her plotting insists that the choices they make aren't solely determined by their social and personal histories. Sjostrom and Sirk's methods are different, but these elements still remain crucial to the stories they tell.

In all three versions of *The Girl from the Marsh Croft*, the characters finally and poignantly adhere to a shared sense of decency and to moral principles that allow them to rise above the forces limiting their options. That the road serves as a recurring setting for the meetings between the three main characters underlines the notion that theirs are lives in transit, however potent the social factors seeming to constrain them.

The opening scenes of Sjostrom's exquisitely gentle film (released in the US as *The Woman He Chose*) methodically establish the key characters' places in the social hierarchy. The first shot introduces the humble marsh-side cottage where Helga lives with her parents (Thekla Borg and William Larsson), before cutting to the interior where she tends to her baby and they look on, concerned. The next scene introduces the more comfortably furnished farmhouse which Gudmund (Lars Hansson) shares with his parents (Concordia and Hjalmer Selander, themselves a married couple). Then, finally, the film presents the more luxurious home where Hildur (Karin Molander) resides with her parents (Georg Blomstedt and Jenny Tschernichin-Larsson, the wife of fellow cast member William Larsson).

In contrast to Sjostrom's measured opening, Sirk's film begins, like the novel, *in media res*. While Sagerlof immediately inserts us in the courtroom where Helga is pleading her case, Sirk situates us in a crowded town square where a "servant sale" is in progress. The courtroom scene occurs immediately afterwards. Apparently in line with the transfer of the setting from Sweden to Germany, Sirk's adaptation also turns Gudmund into Karsten and Hildur into Gertrud while leaving Helga's name unchanged.

As it opens, Karsten (Kurt Fischer-Fehling) is moving through the crowd minding his own business when the camera picks out a disapproving old crone who is in the midst of gossiping about Helga (Hansi Knoteck). She prattles on about how the young woman used to work at the Marshland Farm until she was compelled to leave to avoid a scandal. That turn of events is later repeated when Helga is forced to leave her new place of employment, this time because of the jealous Gertrud's misplaced concern about her working for Karsten's parents (Jeanette Bethge and Friedrich Kaybler).

Sirk allows the social world to emerge as the characters pass through it, even at this early stage in his film career showing a firm grasp of the

Sirk and superstition: Helga (Hansi Knoteck) sprinkles the ashes in *Girl from the Marsh Croft*.

workings of *mise-en-scene*.[31] It's likely that his extensive work in the theatre helped to make the shift of medium such a seamless one. His theatrical productions are said to have been supported by an adventurous style in which the stage functioned as far more than a mere background setting for the characters, and lighting served the needs of tone rather than simply operating in a naturalistic mode.[32]

His version of *The Girl from the Marsh Croft* sets Helga's moral strength against the flawed humanity of its other characters. At the same time, with the capable assistance of Willie Winterstein (who was also cinematographer on *April! April!* and Sirk's UFA shorts), it discovers a lyrical beauty in the harsh rural surroundings. The marshland is muddy, but it's also home to meadowlands where flowers grow; the wind blows through the cornfields; and workers there are regularly framed heroically against the sky as if in reference to Dziga Vertov's films from the previous decade.

Nevertheless, while Sirk joins Sagerlof and Sjostrom in their celebrations of the ways in which humanity can rise above its failings, his adaptation remains skeptical about their views on the rules according to which the world turns. Given her God-fearing beliefs, Helga's refusal to allow her child's father to damage his soul is nobly altruistic, making her thoroughly deserving of the respect she earns from everyone in the courtroom. But Sirk qualifies this by placing it in the same context as the superstitions which have pervaded the way the locals think about their lives.

Sjostrom offers no such reservation, while Lagerlof only hints at it when Helga tells Gudmund the old wives' tale about a remedy for homesickness: "I remembered having once heard someone say that if one took the ashes from the hearth in one's own home and strewed them on the fire, one would be rid of homesickness."[33] Sirk, on the other hand, deliberately sets out to stress the strangeness of such customs: his Helga explains her collection and sprinkling of ashes well after the fact, leaving viewers in an extended state of uncertainty about what she's doing.

Furthermore, he adds to this a variety of other superstitions to which the townspeople adhere. When news arrives about the death of the man in the tavern brawl, a local layabout (Erich Dunskus) says he already knew it was "a cursed night": "Full moon!" he exclaims. "Turns everyone into wild animals. They say a cow gave birth to a five-legged calf." Sirk has also previously given us a reflection shot of one of the brawlers hurling a bottled ship into a mirror in the tavern, its fracturing conventionally announcing the impending arrival of bad luck.[34]

This skeptical view of the peculiar beliefs that preoccupy humanity points to a key difference between Sirk's telling of this tale and its predecessors'. But it doesn't alter the perspective his film provides on its characters. And what all three versions of the story offer is a firm grasp of the layers of complexity that underlie human behavior: Gudmund/Karsten torn between his recognition of his fiance's mistreatment of Helga and his wish not to cut himself off from the social advantages that a marriage to her would provide; Hildur's initially ruthless treatment of Helga eventually replaced by an empathy for her. In this way, taking their lead from the novel, both films refuse to damn any characters for their failings and assert a moving belief in humanity's potential to transcend its limitations.

PILLARS OF SOCIETY/STUTZEN DER GESELLSCHAFT (1935)

> "Today, it is the artist's responsibility to expose the evils of capitalism."
> —DOUGLAS SIRK, 1981

The opening credits announce that *Pillars of Society* has been "freely drawn from Henrik Ibsen," and, indeed, Sirk's film has made a number of key alterations to the Norwegian writer's 1877 play (aka *The Pillars of the Community*).[35] Several characters have been neatly excised in the

Pompous potentate Bernick (Heinrich George) with his wife (Maria Krahn), one in a long line of deeply flawed matriarchs in Sirk's films.

interests of economy, the ending has been changed in significant and revealing ways, and the vantage point from which the action is viewed has shifted.

Nevertheless, the two works also have much in common. In remarkably prescient ways, both are concerned with questions of social class and with how the pursuit of power can corrupt, and each tells more or less the same story: about a ruthless shipping magnate in a coastal town who uses his position as the burgh's consul to further his own ends (a consul is an approximate equivalent to a mayor). His life is an ongoing series of negotiations—with his extended family, his social circle, his employees, and other members of the local community—to ensure the success of his business ventures and strengthen his social standing.[36] But there are secrets buried in his past that are destined to bring him undone.

In the absence of anything more than general accounts of Sirk's work in the German theatre during the 1920s and '30s, one can only imagine what his 1923 staging of Ibsen's play might have been like, and what liberties he might have taken with it.[37] Clearly, one of the things that would have drawn him to it in the first place—given his left-leaning political views and the inclinations evident in many of his American films—is its critique of the workings of capitalism. More than a decade later, his approach in his screen adaptation—officially co-written by Karl Peter Gillmann and Georg C. Klaren—is much sterner in its appraisal of the characters than Ibsen had been. Sirk's characters remain more or less the way they are when we first meet them, whereas Ibsen depicts them as capable of change.

The film's Bernick, played by Heinrich George,[38] is a pompous potentate, charismatic but shallow. After the unveiling of a bust that has been sculpted in his honor, he's introduced delivering a platitude-packed speech about his commitment to the community. Setting the statue alongside the pontificating Bernick, Sirk underlines the artifice of both.

Soon afterwards, Bernick blows smoke in the face of a journalist (Hansjoachim Buttner) who has dared to question his credentials, warning him to keep his mouth shut in the future, "otherwise I would have to ask your editor to find more progressive writers." This archetypal exchange has lost none of its relevance in the eighty-plus years since the film was made.

The contempt with which Bernick treats his wife (Maria Krahn) suggests that his bullying behavior in public extends to his private life. And we subsequently learn that his wealth and reputation have been acquired by displacing charges that should have been directed at him—an extramarital affair and the embezzlement of funds from the family business—on to his brother-in-law, Johan Tonnessen (Albrecht Schoenhals), who had left Norway for America twenty years earlier.

However, the eager-to-please strain that flavors his exchanges with his niece, Dina (Suse Graf)—later to be revealed as his daughter—and his gentle attentiveness to his young son, Olaf (Horst Teetzmann), go some way towards softening the hard edges of Sirk's general portrayal of the character, as does his eventual attempt to make reparations to Johan for the damage he had done to his brother-in-law's reputation.

Ibsen is, finally, more generous to Bernick, whom he has coming clean to everyone about most of his improprieties, and receiving their forgiveness. Even the wife whom he has cruelly deceived expresses her relief at his confession. "Do you know, Karsten," she tells him, "you have just shown me the happiest prospect I have seen for many a year?"[39] Sirk allows her no such silver lining, contemptuously condemning her as an embodiment of mindless class condescension. Denied any redeeming qualities, she occupies a prominent place in the long line of deeply flawed matriarchs in his films.

In the play, Bernick's admissions of guilt also allow him to declare himself cleansed. "Now I feel as if I had come to my senses after being poisoned," he says in the final scene.[40] Nevertheless, Ibsen ensures that we see him differently. As translator Una Ellis-Fermor perceptively points out in her introduction to the play, his public declarations are never to be trusted. "Bernick's habit of explaining his own motives," she writes, "of explaining what kind of a man he is, is at once a subtle piece of self-deception and the result of a lifelong habit of arguing with his subdued but not yet silenced conscience."[41]

And what he omits when he's testifying about his sins is the truth about the immediately preceding events. By permitting an unfit vessel to embark on a journey which he knew was likely to lead to the demise of all aboard, he had knowingly sent Johan and Dina to their deaths, his malicious negligence also putting Olaf at risk. They all survive, but only through good fortune.

So Ibsen's play arrives at a very qualified happy ending. While an onlooker explains that "the spirit of truth and the spirit of freedom, they are the pillars of the community" in the final line, Bernick's and his community's future still remain works in progress.

However, there's no such light at the end of the tunnel that Sirk has built for him. To a degree, the consul does repent his sins, but only after he realizes that he's inadvertently put his son's life at risk. And when he dies of an apparent heart attack at the water's edge, the raging storm all around is like an embodiment of the universe's anger at him. With his dying breath, he passes his authority on to Johan, but by this point it has become evident that it's a poisoned chalice. Furthermore, it seems like a perfunctory gesture at a point where he recognizes that all is lost rather than the product of any sincere regret.

The largely one-dimensional thrust of Sirk's adaptation is sustained in his depiction of many of the secondary characters. Johan is an unequivocally positive figure, as is Dina (there's some ambiguity about who her father is in the play, but not in the film). Aune (Karl Dannemann), a shipbuilder and one of Bernick's chief opponents, represents the interests of the men in his employ and stands firm on their behalf. The film simply casts him as a warrior for workers' rights. However, again pointing to Ibsen's readiness to complicate rather than simplify the issues, the play makes him a much more ambiguous and interesting figure, a man so committed to his cause that, like Bernick, he's prepared to risk lives in order to achieve his ends.

The play was written during the early years of the industrial age, and the tensions of the time were writ large in it. Sirk's film, however, was made in very different political circumstances, two years after Hitler came to power. An angry melodrama about evils perpetrated by people in power, it offers no direct commentary about the Reich or its Fuhrer. But such a critique is implicit throughout and is much less measured than Ibsen's account of the changing times and the ways of a tyrant. It's a striking example of the "room to manoeuvre" that was inadvertently allowed at UFA.

The liberties Sirk takes with the play also extend to the way he has structured the drama. The least effective of the changes he makes is the often frantic crosscutting that prevents scenes from unfolding at their own pace and too forcefully insists on the connections between them. What appears to be an attempt to do on screen what would be impossible on stage builds a degree of melodramatic urgency but also seems like dramatic overkill.

More successful are the contrasts that Sirk creates between the spaces the characters occupy, lending the locations an immediacy that's absent from the play. For example, whereas all of the play takes place in "the garden room at the Bernicks' house," the film moves back and forth between the bawdy, everyday world of the town café, where ship-workers and fisherman gather to carouse, and the tea-party proprieties that rule in Bernick's home. One of the positive aspects of this "opening out" of the play is that it enables Sirk to depict the messy lives of the town's citizens which Ibsen's methods leave as an abstraction.

More crucially, whereas Ibsen immediately immerses us in Bernick's circumstances and the kind of social life that passes through his home, Sirk begins in America with Johan, who has been pursuing the life of a rancher there. Urbini (Walther Sussenguth), a circus-director friend, is planning a trip to Europe with his troupe and invites Johan to join them. Once he hears that Norway will be on the itinerary, the initially reluctant but homesick Johan agrees to go.

Right from the beginning, then, he is placed at the center of the action. His vantage point on it becomes primary and a sharp contrast is created between the openness of the West and the closed world over which Bernick presides.

A cut via matched close-ups of the Norwegian flag takes us from America to Norway, where Bernick is then introduced. But rather than being the focal point for all that ensues—as he is in the play—he is forced to share the spotlight with Johan. The ripples that accompany his brother-in-law's appearance soon afterwards thus carry a different kind of dramatic weight. In the film, it's as if, by being placed alongside Johan, we're observing what takes place through the eyes of an outsider.

The structure here echoes the one Sirk later took with *All I Desire*, where Naomi Murdoch (Barbara Stanwyck) returns home to the small town where she'd lived with her husband and children years before. The structure ensures that we see what she finds when she arrives there through her eyes, rather than those of her family. In this context, when Dina tells Johan that she has been "suffocating" in the town where she's grown up and longs to "travel the world," as he has, she serves as the equivalent of Naomi's daughter (Lori Nelson), who yearns to follow in her mother's footsteps.[42]

In the play, Johan and Dina are important characters, but because of the ways in which they impact upon Bernick's life rather than in their own right. They vanish early in the final act when they leave together for America, with the rest of the play unfolding in their absence. Their fate is discussed, but their further presence is deemed unnecessary. Given the direction that the film has taken, and the dramatic expectations it has created, such a decision would be unthinkable.

Both Ibsen's approach and the variations Sirk plays on it make dramatic sense, each going its own way for its own reasons. Ibsen's inward-looking drama ends with an exchange in which characters reflect on what has gone before and bring a moral perspective to it. Sirk's, in contrast, ends with what Eric Bentley describes in his account of the workings of melodrama as "an elevated rhetoric (in which) ordinary conversation would be incongruous and anti-climactic":[43] that is, a storm and a death, a visually spectacular explosion of action in which nature seems to have the final say.

SCHLUSSAKKORD/FINAL CHORD (1936)

> "Any discussion of cinematic melodrama inevitably returns to Douglas Sirk and what is seen as his distinctive filmic style and aesthetic vision."
> —JOHN MERCER & MARTIN SHINGLER, 2005[44]

An all-stops-out melodrama in which music is likened to a "subliminal force" driving individuals' actions, *Schlussakkord*—like *The Girl from the Marsh Croft*—pivots on the plight of a mother and her child. However, whereas, in the earlier film, Helga is effectively a supporting player in Gudmund's story, Hanna (Mária v. Tasnádi, wife of the film's producer, Bruno Duday) is the protagonist here. The film sets us alongside her as she travels home from New York to Berlin to reclaim the child whom she has left behind, and it's her situation that determines the emotional trajectory of the ensuing drama.

Written by Sirk and Karl Heuser, *Schlussakkord* begins amid the jazz-club gaiety of New Year's Eve celebrations in a snowbound New York City. But then the body of Hanna's embezzler husband is found in Central Park. After she collapses in distress on learning that he has committed suicide, the camera sweeps across the ocean to Berlin, to introduce her abandoned son, Peter (Peter Bosse), and the other characters who are to play significant roles in what follows: music-loving orphanage director Professor Obereit (Theodor Loos); his famous conductor friend, Erich Garvenberg (Willy Birgel); Garvenberg's socialite wife, Charlotte (Lil Dagover); and her unscrupulous lover, Carl-Otto (Albert Lippert), an oily astrologer.

With consummate skill, Sirk economically winds their stories together: The Garvenberg-conducted performance of Beethoven's Ninth Symphony at the Berlin Philharmonie; the empty chair in the front row, because Charlotte is attending an astrology function at Carl-Otto's and has lost track of the time; the radio in the ailing Hanna's New York apartment on which she and her carers listen to a live broadcast of the Beethoven concert; her restoration from the depths of despair by the adagio and by the words of Friedrich Schiller's "Ode to Joy" poem, with which Beethoven brings the symphony to a close ("And the cherub stands before God"); Garvenberg's estrangement from Charlotte and the decision to adopt a child, Peter, in an attempt to save their marriage.[45]

What follows is as inevitable as it is engrossing. As if drawn by the music, Hanna returns home and sets out to find Peter; Professor Obereit proposes that she become the boy's nanny to help out Garvenberg and Charlotte, but makes her promise not to reveal who she is; the tormented Charlotte and her sinister housemaid, Freese (Maria Koppenhofer), become increasingly unsettled by the ease of the relationship Hanna shares with Peter. Events build to a climax which results in her being accused of poisoning Charlotte and put on trial for her murder.

Criticism has been directed against the film for the way in which it has gone about "staging the drama of femininity through the open confrontation of two female stereotypes."[46] That is between the so-called good woman, Hanna, the biological mother, and the sexual woman, Charlotte, the unfaithful wife—except that it's far from being so simple.

For one commentator, the opposition is a product of the film's "malignant gaze," a way of seeing that the writer links to Nazi film production and its patriarchal preoccupations. Thus, family will be restored and "in the end, the authoritarian gesture of the conductor and his controlling and directing gaze will triumph."[47] According to this line of thinking, Garvenberg becomes, implicitly, a Hitler surrogate in control of what takes place. For another critic, Sirk's perceived endorsement of Garvenberg exemplifies the way in which, generally, his films constitute "a cinema that is characterized by an authoritarian and evil gaze—with Sirk the sadist being a direct descendant of Sierck, der Sadist."[48]

While the motives for the animus underlying this kind of commentary are best left to others to explore, its critical failings are worth noting for they point to what most of the "backlash critics" have in common: a failure to address the details of the films except in the most selective, limited, and limiting ways.

By way of contrast, in her fine book, *Douglas Sirk, Aesthetic Modernism and the Culture of Modernity*, Victoria L. Evans makes a very different kind of sense of *Schlussakkord* in her examination of the ways in which the film's visual design subtly, and subversively, offers a critique of Nazi Germany. She argues that, in the film's Berlin, "the splendour of the surroundings can't disguise the fact that Germany is a deeply divided society, whose fissures can't be papered over by an application of ornament."[49]

The most telling flaw shared by these revisionist critics is their inability to deal with the ways in which Sirk's use of irony inflects and complicates the meanings of his work. Or, in some cases, even to recognize his use of it. In fact, it's only through a close attention to detail and an appreciation of Sirk's dramatic strategies that the worlds he creates and his humanist impulses are best understood. *Schlussakkord* rewards such an approach, extending a sympathy to all of the film's characters, aside from Carl-Otto and his cohorts, whose ruthlessness can be seen as representative of the Third Reich.[50]

The film is, in fact, a compendium of narrative strategies, plot situations, character types, and motifs that recur throughout the director's career. Far from a straightforward contrast between good and bad, the reflections on mothering raised here recur in *Imitation of Life*. The estranged mother who returns home to stake her claim is also the central character in *All I Desire*. The charismatic conductor with the troubled wife turns up again in *Interlude*. The masks worn by the partygoers who burst into Hanna's apartment at the start and that adorn the walls of Carl-Otto's home prefigure those worn by the Mardi Gras merrymakers in *The Tarnished Angels*. One of the guests at Carl Otto's, Frau Czerwonska (Hella Graf), has much in common with the country club gossip (Jacqueline deWit) in *All That Heaven Allows*. Peter riding the four-seater merry-go-round in his bedroom is a precursor to young Jack Shuman (Chris Olsen) on the aeroplane carousel in *The Tarnished Angels*. The courtroom climax in which the protagonist is accused of murder turns up again in *Written on the Wind*. And Carl-Otto's hedonistic gathering anticipates the one with the piano-playing Nazi in *A Time To Love and A Time to Die*.

More substantially, Sirk places us at a distance from the characters in *Schlussakkord* in the way they seem to be forever putting on a show, either professionally or as part of their everyday lives. As Schulte-Sasse points out, the film is structured around a series of performances, "consisting of different types of musical and non-musical shows (a symphony, a ballet, a puppet show, an opera, a courtroom scene and an oratorio)."[51] The settings for these are mostly public spaces, although even in private ones the characters assume a theatrical air: Carl-Otto pompously presents himself as an "experimental astrologer" to the guests who gather at the soiree in his home; Peter puts on an elaborate puppet show for Garvenberg and Hanna in his bedroom.

But, whatever the location, the audiences at all of these events are performing too, playing their roles without question.[52] They dress and act in line with strictly defined social codes and what they do, consciously or unconsciously, makes up what Adrian Martin astutely refers to as "a social *mise-en-scene*."[53] Those attending the performance of Beethoven's Ninth near the start of *Schlussakord* wear dinner suits and gowns, take their seats in an orderly fashion, and silently listen to the music. Those who create disturbances or arrive late—Charlotte does both—are frowned upon for breaking the rules.

When Peter puts on his puppet show the setting is an informal one, but his audience of two knows that the same rules apply, more or less. The show is "Snow White and the Six Dwarfs"—"The seventh is broken," he disarmingly explains—and Garvenberg and Hanna's responses see them self-consciously adopting the same roles as those adopted by the concert audience (or assumed by those listening to the radio broadcast of it).

Sirk also presents his characters' theatrics away from these highly formalized settings as performances, not just in the terms of the unfolding plot—as when Hanna assumes the role of Peter's nanny and conceals her true motives—but also in the wider context he creates for them. Swirling around the characters is a host of references to fairy tales and time-honored archetypes: *Snow White* with its wicked stepmother; the opera that Hanna attends with its "drop of hemlock, sweet and deadly," which features a murder by poisoning; the Madonna and child statue above the stage on which Garvenberg is conducting the Oratorio from Handel's *Judas*

At rear of image, the reunited mother and child (Mária v. Tasnádi and Peter Bosse) sharing the frame with the Madonna statue in *Schlussakord*'s closing shot.

Maccabaeus. And they all infiltrate the situations in which the characters find themselves.

The resultant effect is not only the sense that the characters in *Schlussakkord* are playing out a familiar ritual, but that, with *The Nutcracker*'s "Dance of the Sugar Plum Fairy" heard over the opening credits, the film is presenting itself as a distorting mirror of its various fictional references.

The links are ongoing. When Charlotte visits Carl-Otto to call an end to their affair, he pays her no heed, literally sweeping her off her feet before Sirk cuts directly to a shot of a male ballet dancer doing the same with his on-stage partner in "The Dance of the Sugar Plum Fairy." Like Snow White's wicked stepmother looking in the mirror and asking who is the fairest of them all, Charlotte regularly surveys her own reflection to reassure herself that her glamor has not faded ("Erich once told me that I am the most beautiful woman in the world"). Professor Obereit performs the function of a fairy godfather in the way he guides Hanna into the lives of Peter and Garvenberg and sets the stage for a happy ending. And, after the camera has swept high above the action in the film's final scene, it finally comes to rest on the reunited mother and child, sharing the frame with and becoming a mirror reflection of the Madonna and child statue standing alongside them.

At the same time as Sirk engages us with his story, then, he is working to remind us of its artifice, of the ways in which it is like *other* stories. His artistry lies in the way he's able to balance these two aspects without ever losing sight of either.

Simultaneously drawing us in and keeping us at a distance, *Schlussakkord* also provides us with bravura filmmaking at its best: the delirious momentum created by Robert Baberske's fluid camera moves; Milo Harbich's editing and Sirk's consummate staging of the action; the forceful flow of the music (the film won the Best Musical Film award at the Venice Film Festival in 1936); the flamboyant and highly evocative visual design by Erich Kettelhut, who was art director for Fritz Lang on the first *Dr. Mabuse* film (1922) and *Metropolis* (1926).

But the pyrotechnics aren't simply an end in themselves. At the same time as their affect is wholly immersive—it's impossible not to be swept along—the excess of style strategically draws attention to itself, and thus, again, to the film's artifice. In other words, not only are all of the film's characters involved in performances of one kind or another, so too is the film. This is what is meant when Sirk is described as an ironist: he invites us to care about his characters as if they're real people, but he also spends much of his time finding ways to remind us that they're not.

Schlussakkord self-consciously inserts itself into a roundabout of stories that have been told and retold, the recycling locking its characters on to preexisting paths even as they try to overcome the obstacles strewn in their way. This sense of circularity is also reinforced visually by a host of circular motifs: in the privacy of his bedroom, Peter shares his four-seater merry-go-round with his Teddy bear; elsewhere in the house, a turntable with twirling figurines on top plays a record; *The Nutcracker* features pirouetting dancers; and so on.

In addition to the sense of life forever duplicating itself with variations that is a function of the film's ongoing references to other stories, numerous sequences become repetitions of earlier ones. There are two suicides: Hanna's husband in New York at the start; Charlotte's at the end. Hanna is bedridden at the start; Charlotte near the end. In paired sequences, Garvenberg introduces Peter to potential mothers: firstly to Charlotte, the boy's stepmother; then to Hanna, who is to be his nanny (although, ironically of course, she is his biological mother). There are two party scenes: one at Carl-Otto's; the other at the home Charlotte shares with Garvenberg (a possible third, the New Year's Eve revelry in New York, is largely kept off-screen). The film begins and closes with a concert performance.

Schlussakord was Sirk's fourth feature. It is also his first masterpiece.

DAS HOFKONZERT/THE PALACE CONCERT (1936)

> "It was suitably stylised and, in a way, close to the Offenbach of *The Grand Duchess of Gerolstein*. There was a little satire, a little music, a little drama, a little sentiment."
> —DOUGLAS SIRK, 1963[54]

Sirk dismissed it as "a piece of Viennese pastry,"[55] something light and fluffy that he could work on after the melodramatic intensity of *Schlussakord*. And the description fits. Featuring a hodgepodge of songs written by Edmund Nick and Ferenc Vecsey, among others, *Das Hofkonzert* is an enjoyably playful operetta set in the mid-nineteenth century in the sunny principality of Immendingen, which, according to its ruling prince (Otto Tressler), "covers only a few kilometers but reaches to the stars." But the endearing humor, charm, and style that Sirk brings to the film lend it a special distinction and even make it a worthy companion piece to Ernst Lubitsch's estimable contemporaneous contributions to the genre, such as *One Hour with You* (1932) and *The Merry Widow* (1934).

At the time *Das Hofkonzert* was made, the film operetta was well-established as a UFA staple. Under the inspired guidance of production boss Erich Pommer, the studio took advantage of the coming of sound[56] and led other parts of the filmmaking world—most notably, Britain, France, and the US—to appreciate that there was an audience eager for such fare. Even after Pommer fled Germany in 1933, UFA persisted with it. As historian Klaus Kreimeier observes, "Goebbels knew well that 'unpolitical' entertainment helped to stabilize the 'national body politic,' to neutralize unfocused discontent, and to reconcile people to their fate as obedient consumers."[57]

Regardless of the ways in which that notion might have filtered its way into the UFA management's decision-making, Sirk was given a relatively free hand with *Das Hofkonzert*. Shot between late August and mid-November in 1936 at Veitshochheim Castle near Wurzburg and at the UFA studios, the film was rushed into release before the end of the year.

The success of *Schlussakord* had assured the director of a decent budget, and it shows: in the casting, the costumes, the sets, and the graceful visual choreography,[58] which includes some clever special effects. It also gave him the chance to make the material his own. With Kurt Heinecke and Franz Wallner-Baste, he adapted the screenplay from Paul Verhoeven and Toni Impekoven's play, *The Little Palace Concert*.[59]

The setting is a fairy tale kingdom: a palace by a lake, verdant gardens, a nearby fairground (with a carousel), cobbled village streets and picturesque cottages, fountains, a peaceful countryside stretched out all around, all of it guarded by a multitude of handsomely costumed soldiers. Statues of frolicking cherubs and nymphs abound, watching over Immendingen from the opening credits onwards, with a Cupid thrown in for good measure at the end. This is a blessed realm, an earthly paradise, although somehow a stone demon has found its way into the mix of decorative ornaments.

The thesis about the spaces created by operettas for subversive elements is yet to be written, probably with good reason. Nevertheless, Sirk still manages to gently poke fun at the genre, drenching the film in an overflow of kitsch, but also engaging affectionately with its excesses and the possibilities it offers for creative play. As is customary in this particular subspecies of the musical genre, everyday places come alive with music and song, the settings seamlessly transforming themselves into stages on which the characters perform, often singing, occasionally dancing, and always putting on shows for each other's benefit. Given that this is a recurring theme in Sirk's work, he was clearly at home here.

The plot is straightforward. Christine Holm (Martha Eggerth), a young woman graced by golden locks and a fine trill, arrives by coach from Munich looking for the father she's never met. The amiable prince, known to his obsequious minions as "your highness," is worried that his annual concert might not take place because the court soprano, tempestuous Tamara (Iwa Wanja), has come down with a sore throat.

Actually, her ailment is a little more complicated than that. She tells her physician (Hans Holder) that her condition is a symptom of her love life, explaining that "when my heart hurts me, my throat hurts me too"—which he diagnoses slightly differently, telling the prince that her affliction is "a frontal kinetic tenderness attached to a chloritic neoplexia, which could lead to a maniafonitis." Like *April! April!*, this is a film with a very screwball sensibility, leading one to wonder about the kinds of films Sirk might have made had he gone to America a decade earlier than he did.

As revealed in her numerous songs in the film—standing at the window of her hotel room, seated on a swing, passing through the village square, splashing around in a bathtub with a cake of soap and a sponge as her props, and, finally, performing at the palace concert—Caroline is no prima donna. This stands in sharp contrast to the diva she is destined to replace. And all of her numbers more or less amount to the same thing: "It's wonderful to be in love." Walter van Arnegg (Johannes Heesters),

Christine (Martha Eggerth) turns taking a bath into a musical number in *Das Hofkonzert*.

the allegedly dashing lieutenant who becomes her suitor, lends his tenor voice to several duets with her, their harmonies meant to indicate that they were made for each other.

The prince shares Caroline's world view, even if his mood throughout the film remains melancholy, at least until he discovers that the vivacious visitor to the palace is the daughter he never knew he had. "Music and love are the only things that make life worth living," he tells no one in particular as he becomes aware in the film's opening scene that not only does he have no one to love but his treasured concert might not go ahead.

Like *Schlussakord*, but without the melodrama, *Das Hofkonzert* is emotionally anchored in a woman's efforts to restore the sense of family that has been missing from her life. And it's also grounded in the same sense of human existence as an ongoing series of repetitions with variations. Caroline and her lieutenant's romance is mirrored by the one shared by palace maid Babette (Ingeborg von Kusserow) and her soldier boyfriend (Kurt Meisel, later to play the sadistic concentration camp commandant in *A Time To Love and A Time To Die*). Christine arrives in Immendingen twice, first as an anonymous visitor and then, under the stage name of Bellini, as the singer whom the prince has invited to replace the ailing Tamara.

And the past lingers on in the film's present, creating an impression of history repeating itself. Christine's mother was a famous opera singer who had sung at the same court concert more than twenty years earlier. The lyrics of the song that has been performed there every year since—"Denkst Du nie daran, was kommen mag" ("Never Do You Think About What May Come")—are borrowed from a love letter which was sent to her by the prince. But it had actually been written by a Cyrano-like poet (Alfred Abel) who, as we see, is still offering the same service to prospective lovers. Brief flashbacks of the performance by Christine's mother (who is also played by Eggerth) twice interrupt the present: first taking us back to it via a painting which the poet shows to Christine, and again when the prince is reminded of it by her performance. And the filming of Christine's song to the court duplicates the compositions used in those flashbacks.

While it hardly ranks as a major work, *Das Hofkonzert* deserves more attention than it has so far received. It is to Sirk's German melodramas what the director's musicals are to his American ones.

ZU NEUEN UFERN/*TO NEW SHORES* (1937)

> "You've come too late, Albert. I'm on another shore now."
> —GLORIA VANE (ZARAH LEANDER) TO ALBERT FINSBURY (WILLY BIRGEL) IN
> *ZU NEUEN UFERN*

Earlier commentaries about *Zu neuen Ufern* have largely ignored the fact that, whatever else the film is, it is a romantic melodrama. Based on a 1936 novel by Lovis Hans Lorenz and adapted to the screen by Sirk and Kurt Heuser, who'd previously collaborated on *Schlussakord*, it tells the story of a love affair gone wrong in a world where the patriarchy rules and social division is rampant.[60] Opening in London in 1846 with a couple of vignettes establishing the social circumstances of the time, the film pivots on the choices which glamorous torch singer Gloria Vane (Leander) makes about her life. And things do not go well.

First, her self-admiring lover, aristocrat Sir Albert Finsbury (Birgel)— "the most elegant man in London," according to his layabout friend, Bobby "Pudding" Wells (Robert Dorsay)—accepts an officer's commission to the penal colony of Australia. Although he vows that their relationship is not over, she knows better and is heartbroken. Then, after he forges a check in Pudding's name to discharge debts before his departure, she takes the rap for him and also ends up in the distant colony, having being transported there to serve a seven-year sentence in the women's prison in Parramatta (which is misspelled throughout the film).

The clothes she wears trace the course of her adversity. The first time we see her, she's dressed in an alluring stage costume at London's Adelphi Theatre, where she's singing her raunchy siren song "Yes, Sir." Elsewhere in the city (perhaps it's Hyde Park Corner?), Bible-thumpers have been pontificating about her: "Not only does she sing the most impudent songs," a speaker (Hansjoachim Buttner) declares, "but she also wears almost nothing." The description grabs the attention of at least two puritan types who, immediately afterwards, join the audience at the Adelphi.

A short time later, Gloria attends Pudding's farewell party for Sir Albert, more relaxed in fashionable evening wear, but still putting on a show for the other guests. A low-cut dress with a velvet jacket and a lace-trimmed hood serve as her costume for the second song in the film, the lovelorn ballad "Ich steh' im Regen (I'm Standing in the Rain)."[61] For her appearance in court, Gloria dons a more demure but still elegant outfit with a stylish, broad-brimmed hat. Then, once she's arrived in Australia, she's clad in a grimly anonymous prison uniform bearing the number 218.

One of the British Empire's strategies for developing its sunburnt colony was to ensure that there were wives for free settlers, and Gloria's only chance of an early release is for one of them to agree to marry her. She smuggles a letter out of the prison to Albert, who is stationed in nearby Sydney, telling him, "You are my only hope." He's dismayed when he learns that she's in prison, although he can't find out what she's done to deserve such a fate. Trying to help, he speaks on her behalf to the prison wardress (Lina Lossen) and the colony's governor (Edward Jurgensen). But he isn't prepared to put his social standing in the colony at risk by acting as selflessly for her as she had for him, and he avoids any contact with her. While still a man about town—he's embroiled in an affair with Fanny (Hilde von Stolz), the wife of the local doctor (Erich Ziegel)—he's also highly regarded, about to be appointed personal adjutant to the governor, and to become engaged to the governor's daughter (Carola Hohn).

A further option for Gloria appears in the form of Henry Hoyer (Viktor Staal), the doctor's cousin and a wealthy local farmer. A socially upstanding citizen, Henry offers her a chance for a new start—a new shore—promising her stability, a home, and a future as a wife and mother. Desperate, she accepts his proposal, but only in order to find her way back to her beloved. At the same time as she learns of Sir Albert's coming wedding, he finds out that she'd taken responsibility for the crime he had committed and goes to her. Too late. She has lost faith in him. And after his (off-screen) suicide, she returns to Henry.

Some of the writing about *Zu neuen Ufern* offers useful insights into its workings. In discussing its fusion of music and drama, Thomas Nadar perceptively pays tribute to the ways in which, in it and *La Habenera*, Sirk "attempts to create a new form of film melodrama closely following the principles of Brecht and Weill."[62] Marc Silberman considers it in terms that might be equally applicable to the melodramas that Sirk made in Hollywood during the 1950s. Noting that it "conforms closely to the hundreds of escapist films produced during the Third Reich in which a happy end, prompted by social authority, can redeem even the most complicated and morally questionable situations,"[63] he then constructively reflects on some of the ways in which *Zu neuen Ufern*'s ending becomes problematic.

Other commentaries seem to be discussing an entirely different film. Jan-Christopher Horak, for example, seems completely misguided in an article about UFA when he asserts that "Leander, in particular, became wildly popular in such films as *Zu neuen Ufern* (which) addressed women's desire, all the while subtly inserting fascist attitudes in order to prepare women for war."[64] No argument is presented here, or in his other writing about Sirk, to establish any basis for such a view. And much of the disapproving commentary along these lines has been content to draw on the broad sweep of the film's story rather than examining the way it has been told.

Lutz Koepnick's approach is also curiously misguided. "The film first construes what amounts to a repulsive image of female sexuality only to resort to ritual acts of cleansing," he writes. "Sirk privileges a gaze that moves from aversion to purification, and in so doing, he arrests the female body as a deformed, disciplined fetish."[65] The idea that *Zu neuen Ufern* is somehow endorsing the puritanical hysteria given voice during the film's second scene is, frankly, absurd. And while a street balladeer outside the courtroom where Gloria is on trial does refer to Parramatta as a "purgatory," the notion that she is somehow purified by her Australian experience is entirely at odds with the film's details and its careful structuring of sympathies.

And it's here, in the way viewers are invited to respond to the characters and their circumstances, and via the distinctive route that it navigates across the conventions of the romantic melodrama, that one is best able to make sense of the film.

If this were one of Sirk's American films, Leander's protagonist might have been played by Jane Wyman (even if she didn't sing like Leander) or maybe even Lauren Bacall. All too aware of the obstacles that have been strewn across her path simply because she's a woman, Gloria maintains her dignity despite the betrayals that have consigned her to a godforsaken place in the middle of nowhere.⁶⁶ But her controlled demeanor is a performance, a way of keeping her pain at bay.

This is superbly illustrated in the four-shot scene where she and Albert bid farewell to each other after Pudding's party. Their exchange is commonplace in the genre: two lovers separating but promising each other that it's only temporary, that they'll be back together soon. After an establishing shot of their horse-drawn carriage being driven down a dark, rainy London street, Sirk cuts to a brief exterior angle on the couple seated inside. She is to the left of the frame, looking straight ahead; he is on the right, watching her as he tries to reassure her of his loyalty; from our vantage point, a window frame separates them. On the soundtrack is the orchestral version of the sad song she'd sung at the party.

A further cut places us inside the carriage as he continues, she looking at him for the first time in the scene as he says, "This is the beginning of something new . . . Really . . . In a year, I'll come and get you, I swear." "Really?" she asks. They both want to believe the roles that they're playing, but they gradually become aware that they're acting out a scene that has been played many times before, saying what they're supposed to say, telling the lies that lovers tell each other when they can't bear to face the truth.

"Will you always stand by me?" he asks, still looking at her. "Always, Albert. I love you," she replies, looking away into the middle distance. "And will you wait for me?" he continues. "Always, Albert," she repeats, looking further away from him, off to her right. Then a dissolve finds her watching his ship sail away into the foggy distance, the plaintive score speaking of her pain as the image fades to black.

From that point, the film traces their trajectory back towards each other. She has remained loyal to him; despite the lies, she'd kept her promise. But he has betrayed her. Once again, he arrives on the scene while she's on stage, this time at the Sydney Casino, singing the same sad song about standing in the rain, and being heckled by a crowd eager for something livelier. Earlier at the Adelphi, he'd leapt on to the stage when the two puritans from the earlier sequence had interrupted her "Yes, Sir!" number, gallantly coming to her defense, happy to share her spotlight, declaring his authorship of the song. This time, he believes he has too much to lose and he does nothing—and loses everything.

Gloria Vane (Leander) and Albert (Willy Birgel) exchanging the lies that lovers tell each other when they can't bear to face the truth in *Zu neuen Ufern*.

Yet for all his flaws, Sir Albert remains a sympathetic figure, reminiscent of the troubled misfits that Robert Stack later played for Sirk. A man forever poised between one state and another—in the opening scene, he describes himself as "a dubious aristocrat"—he never seems at ease and remains constantly on the move. A prisoner of his character and his class, he's caught between his ambition and his ego and his love for Gloria.

Forever in pursuit of the admiration of those around him, he's eventually shattered when he is brought face to face with the part he has played in what has happened to Gloria and learns of her disillusionment with him. In a scene reminiscent of George Sanders hurling a violin at his reflection in *Summer Storm* and Robert Stack tossing a drink at his in *Written on the Wind*, Sir Albert is confronted by his failures, his self-loathing made palpable in the image where he stands at a rain-streaked window, with darkness all around and the echo of Gloria's song on the soundtrack. Paradoxically, by arriving at this point, he achieves a kind of redemption. Like the Rock Hudson character in *Magnificent Obsession*, he comes to understand the disaster that has resulted from his inability to take responsibility for his actions, and to repent the wrongs he has done.

His death creates a potent absence in the film, which has been driven by Gloria's passion for him. Henry is handsome, sympathetic and well-meaning, even if not quite as appealing as Rock Hudson's Nature Boy in *All That Heaven Allows*. But he is an unlikely replacement for Albert in her life, and her decision to accept his renewed proposal speaks more about the limited options available to her than anything else. She has already tried to return to the Parramatta prison but been denied re-entry; a different kind of prison, perhaps one with more warmth, but a prison nonetheless, now awaits. Sirk always argued that happy endings were tricks being played on audiences, providing emergency exits for those "who must not know that they can be failures, in their professions, in love, in their struggles with themselves."[67] And the ending of *Zu neuen Ufern* is one among many Sirk endings that suggest one thing—which was, apparently, enough to satisfy the demands of UFA's National Socialist management—but mean something else altogether.

LA HABANERA (1937)

> "The wind has sung me a song
> Of happiness too beautiful to describe.
> It knows what causes my heart to long,
> For whom it beats and burns like fire.
> Come, come . . ."
> —"LA HABANERA (THE WIND HAS SUNG ME A SONG)"[68]

Sirk began shooting his final film for UFA in March 1937, only a month or so after production finished on *Zu neuen Ufern*. Just as, years later, Universal tried to capitalize on the success of *Magnificent Obsession* with *All That Heaven Allows*—seeing the combination of Sirk, producer Ross Hunter, and stars Rock Hudson and Jane Wyman as a potential goldmine[69]—UFA was punting on the box-office appeal of a further film featuring Sirk, Leander, and a romantic triangle. The studio also threw one of its most successful screenwriters into the mix, Gerhard Menzel, who, if he wasn't openly a Nazi supporter at the time, subsequently became one.[70]

During the eighty or so years that have passed since the film's release, it has been described in various ways: routinely, as a Zarah Leander vehicle; controversially, as yet another example of the ways in which UFA's entertainment features were a more subtle part of the Third Reich's propaganda machine; and accurately, as further evidence of Sirk's filmmaking talents long before he made the 1950s melodramas for which he has long been best known.

However, if one simply outlines the film's plot, it's not difficult to see how a racist film *could* have been made from the material. Two Swedish women, Astree Sternhjelm (Zarah Leander) and her wealthy aunt Ana (Julia Serda), arrive in Puerto Rico for a holiday. Despite Ana's xenophobia—"The savages and the vermin here are really too much for me"—Astree is won over by its exotic charm and by a local nobleman, Don Pedro de Avila (Ferdinand Marian).

Ten years later, Astree and Don Pedro have a young son, Juan (Michael Schluz-Dornburg), although their marriage appears to be on the rocks and a custody battle looms.[71] Astree now sees Puerto Rico differently—"It's not paradise, it's hell"—and the island is stricken by a fever for which there appears to be no cure. She yearns to return to her homeland, and to take her son with her. And, in the film's closing sequence, she does, accompanied by a Swedish doctor, Sven Nagel (Karl Martell). He has been sent to Puerto Rico by her aunt, whose charitable foundation has funded his trip to study the fever and to make contact with Astree.

For some commentators, this is enough. The lesson Astree learns about the foreign place that initially appeared so attractive to her is seen to be an endorsement of the National Socialist agenda. Paul Coates, for example, posits that "the absolute dualism characteristic of melodrama pervades *La Habanera*."[72] He goes on to cite what he sees as the film's black-and-white opposition of Aryan durability and Latin Otherness as irrefutable evidence of this and to charge that the film's final scene makes it "clear that no self-respecting Nordic would find (Puerto Rico) alluring any longer."[73] His clichéd notion of melodrama is simply misguided, but his blindness to the subtleties and complexities of *La Habanera* seems almost willful.

Along the same lines, but less simplistically, Eric Rentschler argues that the choices which Astree makes "separate her from the authentic sources of security and stability" and links her travels and travails with other "Nazi fables about travelers [who] come undone in the topographies of alien cultures."[74] And Gertrud Koch follows more or less the same route, conceding that Sirk "was obviously not a Nazi and held no sympathies for them" but insisting that his "Nazi features [*sic*] are a good example to show how personal attitude can be eclipsed by a studio system."[75]

However, the exact reverse is true here, as it is also when applied to Sirk's entire career. While one can postulate about the politics that guided

Menzel's writing of the screenplay, the film based on it remains very much "a work by Douglas Sirk." In his comments about the final scene of *La Habanera*, which was rereleased in London in 1981, British critic Geoff Brown astutely and concisely identifies the gap that can emerge between a writer and director sharing credits on the same production. "For Menzel, presumably, Ms. Leander was escaping from tropical delusions to pure Aryan bliss," he writes. "But for Sirk, she was sailing away from her melodramatic past with the most ambiguous feelings, undoubtedly shared by her director."[76]

As with any narrative text, on the page, on the stage, or on a screen, point of view is paramount in *La Habanera*. Rather than inviting us to see Astree's Puerto Rican adventures through her eyes, Sirk places us alongside her. The difference is crucial: at the same time as Sirk allows us to share the initial excitement of her discoveries and her later disillusionment with it, he steers us towards a critical distance from her, guiding us into a "reflexive space" where we come to see her differently.

Near the start, Astree is clearly attracted by the earthiness and the musicality of the people on the island, and by the sense of abandon that seems prevalent there. Born of high society—as indicated in the brief sequence in Sweden where her aunt hosts a group of guests in her home—Astree sees Puerto Rico as an opportunity to make a permanent escape from a world of pretense, the oh-so-civilized rituals of good manners and party conversation, and a future as "a stockbroker's wife in Stockholm." However, her aunt warns her to beware this alien place and the aristocratic Don Pedro, describing Puerto Rico as "stifling," the locals as "barbarians," and him as "a Creole from the Middle Ages."

Our sympathies at this point are entirely with Astree. Her aunt is a stuffy old woman who clearly doesn't appreciate the romance that Puerto Rico has to offer, her experience of the place confirming what she's read in her *Baedeker* (to which she makes approving reference). This is the German travel guide that began publication in 1827 and has continued to the present day in one form or another. During the 1930s, it was vetted by the Nazis to ensure that it adhered to the party line about the world.

Near the end, disillusioned by her marriage and a life where she feels "cut off from everything," Astree tries to explain what it's really like to the doctor who has become her aunt's emissary. Echoing her aunt's disapproving words ten years earlier, she warns him of the dangers he faces there—"You don't know the island, you don't know Don Pedro"—and asks him to take her and Juan back to the safety of Sweden.

Our sympathies at this point might again be with her, but, by having her sentiments about Puerto Rico echo those of her aunt, Sirk complicates the issue in ways that simply can't be resolved. Living with Don Pedro hasn't been easy, she has no friends and the only person she seems close to is little Juan, to whom she talks incessantly about the joys of life in the country she'd previously described as "that cold and dreary place."[77]

To further unsettle matters, just as Sirk declined the option of reducing *Zu neuen Ufern*'s tortured Albert (Willy Birgel) to an unqualified villain, he also makes Don Pedro a divided character, ruthless and duplicitous but deeply troubled. Both men die as a direct consequence of their actions. Albert commits suicide, and Don Pedro effectively does the same. For business reasons, he orders the destruction of the antidote that the visiting doctor and his Hitler-moustached assistant (Boris Alekin) have discovered, only to be himself stricken by the fever. Just as the fate that befalls Bernick (Heinrich George) in *Pillars of Society* is an inadvertent consequence of his abuses of power, so too is what happens to Don Pedro here.

Furthermore, like farmer Henry Hoyer (Viktor Staal), who provides a final haven for Leander's character in *Zu neuen Ufern*, the Swedish doctor here becomes Astree's last resort. Although her aunt's introductory description of him as "the Don Juan of Swedish doctors" calls his reliability into question, his determination to find an antidote and his long-held affection for Astree are evident. But her interest in him seems opportunistic rather than heartfelt. And when she leaves with him on the boat, her declaration that she has no regrets about her departure is contradicted by her lingering backward look as the film ends. As Linda Schulte-Sasse eloquently puts it, "Sirk never fails to complicate the constellation and thus to destabilize audience identification."[78]

However, Sirk's masterstroke, and the key to Astree's inner life, is the film's use of music. It, and the wonderfully melodic "La Habanera" in particular, is what initially so attracts her about Puerto Rico and so exasperates her aunt: "It's all I've heard on this island for the past two weeks," she fumes. Astree is not just being coy when, having decided not to sail home with her aunt, she tells Don Pedro that her last-minute decision "was more because of 'The Habanera' than you." Indeed, just before she abandons ship, the editing makes it seem as if she's been intoxicated by the gypsy troupe's dockside rendition of the song. They're singing it again as she leaves at the end, and it's clear that it continues to haunt her.

However, her disillusionment with Puerto Rico is given expression in the songs she performs for Juan. In them, her yearning is for Sweden,

The declaration by Astree Sternhjelm (Zarah Leander) that she has no regrets about her departure from Puerto Rico is contradicted by her lingering backward look as *La Habanera* ends.

snow has become "frozen angel tears," and the life she left behind there is alluring rather than "pretentious." Desire draws her on, always towards something that is absent. Just as the river comes to represent a lost paradise for the characters in *Written on the Wind*, Astree's melancholy songs about Sweden (featuring lyrics written by Sirk) speak of a yearning, but also point to a fantasy that will always lie beyond reach.

Her decision to return to "the homeland" at the end might, if taken out of context, suggest a condemnation of what Puerto Rico represents. However, what it indicates in context is how the island's reality is in the eye of the beholder and how, in Schulte-Sasse's words, "the structure of desire demands . . . a perpetual process of trading in."[79] In other words, Astree—like the rest of us—is doomed to a life of restlessness, a quest without an end. The homeland is no haven. As Bruce Babington observes in his excellent commentary, "[I]n *La Habanera*, details play against the restorative narrative drive."[80]

Rentschler dismisses those who read the film along such lines as foolishly believing that its "subversive" undercurrents had "somehow 'slipped by' the censors or that party functionaries were so dim that irony and tongue-in-cheek escaped them."[81] It apparently never crosses his mind that, just as it came as a surprise to many when Sirk's oeuvre was "rediscovered" long after his retirement, it also might have come as a surprise to German authorities, audiences, and critics during the 1930s to find that there was much more going on in *La Habanera* (and Sirk's other work) than they had believed. Nor does it occur to him that, just as he has misread and undervalued the film, so too might have Goebbels and his henchmen.

BOEFJE (HOLLAND, 1939)

> "I shot the whole picture myself in Holland, but it was edited after I left . . . As far as I can remember, the only interesting thing about it is that the lead part of the boy is played by a girl, Annie van Ees, who had done the part on the stage. But it was a ridiculously small-budget film."
>
> —DOUGLAS SIRK, 1970[82]

After spending time in Paris, where he worked on *Accord Final*,[83] plus several projects that never came to fruition,[84] Sirk moved to Holland, drawn there by the offer to shoot *Boefje*.[85] The title means "rascal" or "ragamuffin" in English. Set in Rotterdam, the film was his final project before leaving Europe for the US and it brought together a number of recent German émigrés alongside its director. The producer was Leo Meyer, who'd fled Germany in the early 1930s and made his home in Holland; the screenplay came from playwrights Carl Zuckmayer, whose work was prohibited in Germany after the Nazis came to power, and Curt Alexander, a regular Max Ophuls collaborator who was murdered in a German concentration camp in 1943; and the cinematographer was Hungarian-born Akos Farkas, who'd worked in Germany before making his escape in 1933.[86]

Sirk and Hilde fled to the US before editing had been completed on *Boefje* and before it was nominated for the Palme d'or in what was to have been the first Cannes Film Festival in September 1939. The festival opening was postponed when Germany invaded Poland on September 1, and then abandoned when war was declared two days later. On May 14, 1940, Rotterdam was bombed by the German Luftwaffe, leaving the city (and the waterside locations used in the film) in ruins. *Boefje* was banned after the occupation, but is now regarded as a classic of Dutch cinema.[87]

The original source for the film is Rotterdam journalist Marie Joseph Brusse's famous children's book of the same name first published in 1903. Brusse also adapted it for the stage in 1923, where his central character, sixteen-year-old street urchin Jan Grovers, was played more than 1,500 times by well-known Dutch actress Annie van Ees. She also took on the role for Sirk—at the age of forty-five—in what was to be her only film performance.[88]

On screen, she makes the boy a force field of irrepressible energy. Her cropped hair and androgynous look make her reminiscent of singer k.d. lang, and she lends Jan a self-assurance and bravado that render the age difference and gender divide irrelevant. Along with this, she makes Jan's theatricality—his fallback position whenever cornered is to make up a story—the key to his inner life, a way of disguising the vulnerability that only comes to the fore a couple of times: when he's behind bars, alone and despairing of his future.

Jan is a delinquent with a decent streak and a dreamer yearning for a better life. Like many of the characters in Sirk's early films, and indeed Sirk himself at the time of the film's production, he looks to America as a land of hope. He can't read or write, but his knavish friend, Pietje (Guus Brox), excitedly introduces him to the comic book world of Chicago gangster Ben Morrison and a make-believe life away from the Rotterdam slums that are their stomping ground. Puffing cigars, the two tough-guy wannabes share a fantasy of a faraway future in which money will be no problem, enabling Jan to bring back presents for his parents (Piet Bron and Enny Heymans-Snijders) and younger sisters, Lientje, Mientje, and Fientje: "For my father, a big box of cigars. For my mother, a hat with feathers. And, for my sisters, a bag filled with candy."

Only the intervention of the local pastor (Albert van Dalsum) saves Jan from disaster. Impressed by the way the boy takes it upon himself to rescue a drowning cat and amused by his cheek, the pastor helps him to evade the law, takes him under his kindly wing, and arranges for him to go to a haven for lost boys run by Christian Brothers in the southern province of Brabant. Soon after his arrival there, Jan runs away, not because he's fleeing anything in particular but simply because that's what he does. His restlessness is an instinct that makes him unpredictable but also appealing. He joins up again with Pietje, becoming a reluctant accomplice as his partner-in-crime steals money from the parson's housekeeper, then uses his share of the proceeds to buy food, cigars, and candy for his family—the same presents that he'd innocently dreamed of bringing back from his American adventures.

The waterfront world of *Boefje* is one afflicted by poverty and riven by class. Jan is mischievous rather than malicious, but he and Pietje roam the streets, playing pranks on the unwary, and opportunistically stealing whatever they can lay their hands on (a bucket of herrings left unattended, a bicycle pump when a shopkeeper isn't looking). Jan's mother is a force to be reckoned with, and she needs to be as she struggles hard to keep her family together with little help.

"All you do is spend the whole day wandering and begging," she tells Jan. "You know how to steal and fight and be rude to me, but helping out . . . !" And she is forced to turn to her unsympathetic milk-seller father (Piet Kohler) for financial help. Meanwhile, across the road, Pietje's mother (Mien Duymaer Van Twist) looks through her window and down her nose at Jan's family and blames Jan for her son's misdemeanors. And, like his friend's mother, the pastor's snooty housekeeper regards him as "scum," offended by his lack of decorum and blind to his virtues.

Pietje's mother and the housekeeper aside, Sirk depicts his characters here with affection, leavening their uncouth ways with a gentle humor. He might refer to *Boefje* as "a ridiculously small-budget film," but it has provided him with an opportunity to depict a society in distress and to present its outsider protagonist as a life force. Just as the warmhearted pastor spends much of his time smiling benignly at Jan's antics and wanting the best for him, so too does the film.

Only when Jan is charged with stealing and winds up in court near the end of the film does Sirk overplay his hand. After the pastor speaks on his behalf, a supercilious psychologist describes the boy as "a prolonged case of degeneration" who has been produced by his environment, thus making him "unaccountable for his actions." What had remained implicit throughout the film abruptly becomes explicit, even if the words are placed in the mouth of a condescending babbler.

In his discussion of the film, Jan-Christopher Horak insightfully proposes an intriguing subtext for *Boefje*, linking it thematically with other German exile films of the time, which he describes as "part of an alternative German film history, a parallel track to developments in the Third Reich." He writes, "The prejudices encountered by (Jan) as a member of the lumpenproleteriat reflect the situation of German Jewish refugees in Europe in the 1930s. Often without passports, residency permits, or working papers, they were literally hounded from country to country like common criminals."

Regardless of how one reads *Boefje*, though, it now seems nothing less than a fore-runner of the neorealist movement that grew up in post–World

The supportive pastor (Albert van Dalsum) and the vagabond Jan (Annie van Ees) in *Boefje*.

War II Italy (around films such as *Rome Open City*, *Shoeshine*, and *Bicycle Thieves*). The film's subject matter seems to have been drawn from working-class lives rather than more glamorous existences. And, even if a number of street scenes were filmed on studio sets,[90] the camerawork and lighting have a documentary feel, creating the impression that it was being made on the run. As in the Italian films, many in the cast were non-professionals.

At the same time, seen from the vantage point of the twenty-first century and in the context of Sirk's completed oeuvre, the film's most striking aspect is that it's perhaps closest in tone to the three Technicolor musicals he made in Hollywood in the thirteen months between October 1951, and November 1952 (*Has Anybody Seen My Gal*, *Meet Me at the Fair*, and *Take Me to Town*). While *Boefje* depicts a world divided between haves and have-nots, its ending is a relatively happy one, largely devoid of ambiguity and allowing Jan some respite from his troubled life and hope for the future. Perhaps the reason for this was Sirk's wish to remain true to the spirit of the film's source; perhaps he didn't have time to refine the work as otherwise he might have wanted; or perhaps (given that the film was edited without his oversight) it has ended up at a different point from the one he had intended?

Whatever the reason(s), though, what emerges from the film is that institutions and individuals that are presented elsewhere in Sirk's work as limited in their perceptions, however well-meaning, are here able to achieve understanding and insight. Far removed from the clerical figures grappling with existential crises in later Sirk films (from *The First Legion* through to *Battle Hymn*), the parson here is a man with his feet planted firmly on the ground, a potent moral force who not only emerges as Jan's guardian angel but guides the film towards an emotionally uplifting ending. And the Brothers at the Brabant home for boys are presented in a similar light.

Events come to a close with a now optimistic Jan returning to the nurturing influence of the Brothers. In a sequence echoing the one that concludes *Schlussakkord*, Brother Nardus plays a grand organ with a chorale surge on the soundtrack accompanied by the camera's crane movement to a Madonna flanked by two trumpeting angels. While the social conditions that had cast their shadow across Jan's life remain unchanged, the home is unambiguously celebrated in a way that the restoration of the family in *Schlussakord* is not.

CHAPTER TWO

American Beginnings
The European Legacy

> "What I brought with me to America, as a gift from UFA, were two things: I had really perfected my technical skills there and I had learned how the star system worked."
> —DOUGLAS SIRK, 1980[1]

> "In some of the first films which I made in Hollywood, I had a freer hand, right from the story through to the distribution . . . With the exception of *The First Legion*, all these films played within a European setting, which indicated that I was avoiding the depiction of American attitudes. Soon after, however, only American themes came to interest me."
> —DOUGLAS SIRK, 1973[2]

FOR SIRK AND HILDE, THE EMIGRATION TO THE US LATE IN 1939 WAS like "starting all over again."[3] They'd left Europe under duress, but he at least had an invitation from Warner Bros. in hand—to remake *Zu neuen Ufern*—and "the phantasmagoria of America" was promising much: "the broad, powerful, epic landscapes"; the chance to share the possibilities of the exciting new world depicted by writers like Hemingway, Fitzgerald, Faulkner, and Thomas Wolfe; and more.[4] Then he arrived in Hollywood, where all that mattered was the box-office and the glitter.

The offer from Warners was withdrawn in 1940. A remake of a film originally produced by a studio now under Nazi control was no longer on the cards. Sirk got some work as a script editor for Columbia and MGM, but his prospects were bleak. "I thought my American movie career was probably over," he told Jon Halliday, "and eventually the Hitler business would be finished and I could go back to pictures in Germany."[5]

On their arrival in the US, the Sirks had chosen to live away from Los Angeles. First, they bought a chicken farm in the San Fernando Valley and then, a year later, an alfalfa plantation in Pomona County, about forty miles from LA, where they stayed for a couple of years. He remembered it as one of the happiest times of his life, a period when he really discovered America, even if he wasn't personally attuned to a life on the land. "Mrs. Sirk is the farmer in the family," he explained to James Harvey in 1978. "I was useless."[6]

However, he retrospectively recognized the value of the time he and Hilde spent away from the business of filmmaking. "What I learned here was not lost in my later series of films: it was an exact knowledge of American small-town society, a continuous, intimate association with the people who lived there, an understanding of their hopes and memories. Something that few who came from Europe at the time managed to acquire."[7]

Around this time, in 1941, a chance meeting with a fellow refugee from Europe, Freddy Fromm, led to Sirk making a short documentary in color—*The Christian Brothers at Mont La Salle*—about a group of wine-making monks in the Napa Valley, north of San Francisco.[8] Creative muscles were being flexed, but, from a position of relative control at UFA, where he was respected as an intellectual force who'd moved from theatre to film with considerable success, Sirk was struggling to find a place for himself. For the most part, the studios weren't interested in what he was offering, or in the European sensibility that he was bringing to his work.

But, soon afterwards, opportunity came calling, once more through the agency of émigrés from Europe, and he got the chance to direct his first Hollywood feature. *Hitler's Madman* and the three films that followed between 1942 and 1946 introduced him to the erratic realities of the Hollywood studio system. The door had opened, even if the budgets were smaller than he was used to. And while current history might remember Sirk for "the Universal years," the energy, intelligence, and artistry he brought to his early work in America make it equally deserving of attention.

Loosely speaking, his first four films there could all properly be ascribed to the crime genre. *Hitler's Madman* is about a mass killing perpetrated by occupying Nazi forces; *Summer Storm* is about the murder of a young woman; *A Scandal in Paris* is about a thief who becomes a detective; and *Lured* is about a serial killer. But, while they draw on the genre's conventions, they're far from formulaic.

George Sanders is the star of all but *Hitler's Madman*. There would have been a further collaboration had Sirk got to make his adaptation of Alexandre Dumas's *Memoirs of a Physician* (aka *Balsamo, the Magician*), in which Sanders had been set to play the famous hypnotist, Cagliostro. And Sirk and Sanders worked together again, unofficially, on *The Strange Woman* (1946).

The British-born actor (1906–1972) brought a distinctive air of urbanity with him when he moved to the US in the mid-'30s. He was quickly in demand, playing Simon Templar in five of the Saint films (1939–41), and he worked with some of the best directors at the time, including Hitchcock, Lang, and Renoir, before teaming up with Sirk. Perhaps it was Sanders's air of theatricality that drew Sirk to him, for he seemed to be the living embodiment of the notion that life is all about putting on a show, metaphorically shaking his head in bewilderment at those around who were taking themselves way too seriously for his liking.

His persona was that of the dapper English gentleman, an upper-class aristocrat who found himself slumming in a world that he knew was beneath him—America, a former colony of the Empire!—barely tolerating his inferiors, but still somehow managing to charm them. Sirk saw him as one of the few people in Hollywood with whom he had anything in common, and Sanders was a regular visitor in the Sirks' home. Such was his contribution to the three films they made together that they're unimaginable without him. A few years later, he won a Best Supporting Actor Oscar for his performance in Joseph L. Mankiewicz's *All About Eve* (1950).

One could be forgiven for seeing the Sirk of this early American period as an émigré filmmaker who was working in the US but whose heart and mind were still based elsewhere. Many of his projects never saw the light of day, but, in the films that eventually launched his American career, there is a clear suggestion that he was drawing on the kind of material he felt safe with. As he pointed out, they're all set away from the US: the anger-fueled *Hitler's Madman* in Czechoslovakia; the classically inclined *Summer Storm*, based on Anton Chekhov's only novel, *The Shooting Party*, in Russia; *Scandal in Paris* (which he regularly told interviewers was his favorite work) in France; and *Lured* (aka *Personal Column*) in London, remaking and relocating Robert Siodmak's French-language, Paris-based *Pièges*. The noir inclinations, discussed in the next chapter, are also here in evidence, most notably in *Lured* and *Summer Storm*.

As Thomas Elsaesser observed in 1972, likening Sirk's "sophisticated irony" to "the dry, unmistakeably cerebral tone of mockery and self-mockery" so evident in the work of Orson Welles,[9] it really wasn't until after the period represented by these four films that Sirk moved towards forms more readily accepted by popular audiences in the US. His art lay in his ability to make this move so seamlessly.

HITLER'S MADMAN (1942)

> "No, comrades. The name of the community has not been obliterated. The name of the community has been immortalized."
> —TOWN OFFICIAL IN HUMPHREY JENNINGS'S *THE SILENT VILLAGE*, 1943

On June 10, 1942, by way of reprisal for the assassination of Reich Protector Reinhard Heydrich, also known as "Heydrich the Hangman," the German occupying forces wiped out the Czechoslovakian village of Lidice, about 20 kilometers from Prague, executing the entire male population over the age of fifteen and deporting all women and children to concentration camps. In the immediate wake of the atrocity, by way of drawing it to the world's attention, three films went into production.[10]

The first was esteemed British filmmaker Humphrey Jennings's striking thirty-four-minute docudrama, *The Silent Village*. Made by the Crown Film Unit, which was attached to the British Government's Ministry of Information, it began shooting in September 1942—barely three months after the event—and ended in December. Set in the Welsh coal-mining village of Cwmgiedd, which was chosen for its similarities to Lidice, and featuring a cast of non-professional locals, the film is a moving fictionalization of what took place in the Czech village.

As Jim Hillier notes, "Jennings' talent was in observing actuality,"[11] and his focus here is on the impact of a Nazi occupation on the lives of ordinary people, the peaceful stillness and everyday routines of the film's opening abruptly shattered by an intruder: a black car with a megaphone. *The Silent Village* was made as both an explicit memorial to the people of Lidice and a warning about what the future could hold if the nation failed to take a stand against a looming threat—a precursor, if you like, to Peter Watkins's *The War Game* (1965). Made all the more powerful by its restraint, it was released in the UK in June 1943 and in the US in October, shortly after US troops landed in Sicily.

Shot in the US, Fritz Lang's *Hangmen Also Die!* (1943) was also clearly planned as part of "the war effort": that is, Hollywood films designed to expose American audiences to the tragedies unfolding in German-occupied Europe, albeit in fictional contexts. Effectively a call-to-arms, the film closes with a chorale singing "No Surrender," filling the screen with a giant "NOT" that is then replaced with "The End." But it deals with the assassination and its aftermath in a very different way from the Jennings film.

According to Lang, he and Bertolt Brecht began work on the project ten days after Heydrich's death,[12] although it wasn't until late October 1942 that it went into production. It was completed in mid-December and went into general release in the US on April 15, 1943. Written by John Wexley, with adaptation and story credits going to Bert Brecht (as the credits read) and Lang,[13] and produced by Arnold Pressburger (*A Scandal in Paris*), it doesn't mention Lidice but is set in Prague just before Heydrich's assassination and then in the days immediately following.

Its tale about the Czech Resistance and the assassin (Brian Donlevy) who has been assigned to kill Heydrich becomes a dramatized debate that asks what might be the best form of resistance to the Nazis. It also deals with the moral quandary facing those whose underground activities lead to further atrocities against the local population by the occupying forces.

As Lang put it, "I wanted to explain to an American audience what it means if a country is overrun by foreign soldiers, by foreign governments, by foreign powers, with absolutely other ideals as political ideals. Therefore, as it plays in Czechoslovakia, I made all the Czechs Americans and all the Germans German."[14]

But whereas *Hangmen Also Die!* is immersed in the idioms of American popular culture—a conventional thriller-plot structure as the assassin tries to avoid detection; Nazi officials as sadistic villains who become almost comic in their absurdities; their henchmen cast in the mold of goons out of a 1930s Warners' gangster movie—*Hitler's Madman* strategically sets them aside.

Early on, it might seem to be simulating the style of a conventional British war movie, introducing its protagonist, Lidice-born and British-trained commando Karel Vavra (Alan Curtis), as he parachutes in to the Czech countryside with sabotage on his mind. Karel's assignment is to form a local resistance to carry out the assassination. But soon after Heydrich's death, he abruptly disappears from the scene, his mission accomplished. The locals are left to the fate that awaits them, with a vengeful Himmler (Howard Freeman) making the decision to wipe out Lidice as a warning to anyone planning to defy the might of the German war-machine: "They won't say Himmler is too weak," he snarls. "Not after the 10th of June." There are no conventional heroes here, and there is no happy ending to this story. When it's over, all the good people are dead or in a concentration camp.

Sirk's account of the Lidice massacre is fueled by an anger that is more evident here than in any of his other films. This is not surprising, given the circumstances and the personal histories of the filmmakers. The anger is chiefly directed at the psychopathic Heydrich (superbly played with steely vindictiveness and totally without nuance by John Carradine) and the other Nazis in the film. But civilians who have collaborated with the occupying forces—like the town mayor (Ludwig Stossel)—are also treated with contempt. And, even after his death, the unmitigated evil that Heydrich represents casts a long shadow across unfolding events.

Hitler's Madman might be a B-movie, but even today, it packs a powerful emotional punch. Few are likely to remain unmoved by it and a key reason for this is the feeling of violation that it's able to create, similar to the one in *The Silent Village*. Like *The Girl from the Marsh Croft*, *Pillars of Community*, and much of Sirk's American work, it's a telling portrait of the life of a small community. This time, however, the danger primarily comes from beyond its boundaries, rather than from within.

The film is framed by two montage sequences, both accompanied by—and effectively illustrating—verses from Edna St. Vincent Millay's poem "The Murder of Lidice," first published on October 17, 1942, in the *Saturday Review of Literature*.[15] The first lyrically celebrates how Lidice was born "in the year of Our Lord, 1623"; the second records and mourns its tragic passing. In between, the villagers grapple with the reality unfolding around them and the hell into which history has cast them.

Initially, they're divided about how best to deal with the intrusion of jackboots into their peaceful existence. For some, it's a matter of maintaining the status quo and trusting in God to see them through; for others, it's about making a stand. After the opening montage, the first scene neatly and quietly encapsulates the issues. With a crucifix looking over them from the kitchen wall (and introduced in close-up), a family gathers around a meal table. At the head is Hanka (Ralph Morgan), who says grace with his head bowed. The prayer over, his son (John Good) adds, "And someday, Our Father, give us Czechs back our freedom . . ."

Hanka disapproves, explaining how it's been down the ages—"We plough, we sow, we have patience to wait for the harvest . . ."—and the discussion is over. But the terms of the debate have been introduced, and it follows along the same lines as the one in *Hangmen Also Die!* Should the townspeople do as they're told, or should they unite against the common enemy?

That they really have no choice against an enemy such as this becomes evident in what follows. The scene in which Heydrich and his thugs invade a lecture theatre at Prague University, mocking the learning taking place there and selecting female students for the pleasure of officers at the front, is deeply unsettling. No less horrifying is the mayhem and

On the edge of chaos. Hanka (Ralph Morgan) restrained by Lidice's parish priest (Al Shean) as Reich Protector Heydrich (John Carradine) looms in *Hitler's Madman*.

murder that ensues when he intrudes into the blessing-the-fields celebration being conducted by Lidice's parish priest (Al Shean). But the closing scenes—in which the villagers gather around the statue of Saint Sebastian in the town square to be told of their fate, and the men are herded to the churchyard to be executed alongside the figure of a guardian angel—are totally shattering.

According to Jan-Christopher Horak's account,[16] Sirk's film began as an idea conceived soon after the massacre by two German émigrés, noted biographer Emil Ludwig and playwright Albrecht Joseph. It also draws on Bart Lytton's 1943 story *Hangman's Village*, with at least four other writers contributing to the screenplay, three officially—Yiddish-language playwright Peretz Hirschbien, Melvin Levy, and Doris Malloy—while Edgar G. Ulmer's additional work went uncredited. Rudolph Joseph, Albrecht's brother, who subsequently worked on *Summer Storm* and *The First Legion*, became associate producer alongside Seymour Nebenzal and invited Sirk to direct his first film in the US.

Although the filmmakers couldn't have known it at the time, the assassination of Heydrich had been planned in London (under the name of Operation Anthropoid) by the Czech government-in-exile with a team of commandos headed by British-trained Czech nationals who had parachuted into their German-occupied homeland in late December 1941. However, intriguingly, the ambush scene in the film bears a marked similarity to one of the early proposals for the mission, eventually abandoned. And Nazi intelligence initially (it turned out, falsely) believed Lidice had given asylum to the assassins.[17]

Hitler's Madman was made under the auspices of the "Poverty Row" studio, PRC, and shot in one week in November 1942.[18] Nooses and their shadows still fill the screen behind the opening credits, but the working-title of *Hitler's Hangman* was changed to avoid confusion after the filmmakers became aware that *Hangmen Also Die!* was also in the works.

The original plan was to distribute *Hitler's Madman* through Republic Pictures. However, it's no surprise to learn that, after a screening arranged by Nebenzal for MGM boss, Louis B. Mayer, it was taken up for distribution by the studio. With extra funding on offer, it was partially reshot by Sirk in May 1943,[19] before being released in the US in July 1943 and in the UK in October. For Sirk, it was an auspicious American debut.

SUMMER STORM (1944)

> "I hired Jimmy Cain for a writer—he was someone I had a very high regard for, particularly *The Postman Always Rings Twice*. [He] was crazy about the treatment and the story, but he Americanized it so much that by the end you'd have thought Chekhov had been writing about Milwaukee."
> —DOUGLAS SIRK, 1970[20]

A project Sirk had begun developing while he was at UFA, *Summer Storm* finds the director determined to ensure that its setting *isn't* mistaken for Milwaukee. Adapted from Anton Chekhov's only novel, *The Shooting Party*,[21] the film begins in 1912 in a township in the Russian countryside where the effects of the 1905 revolution that overthrew the Tsarist government are everywhere in evidence. Soon afterwards, it moves into an extended flashback occurring twelve years earlier.

The first character to appear is a former aristocrat who used to be known as Count Volsky (Edward Everett Horton). Now he's a scruffily dressed man anonymously shuffling along a cobblestone street; in fact, the film opens with a shot of his muddied shoes. Looking for the *Karhoff Times* building, he asks a passer-by for directions. "Excuse me, my good man," he says, before correcting himself. "Uh, uh . . . comrade."

When he enters the newspaper offices, a manuscript tucked under his arm, he's treated with contempt by the clerk behind the desk (Byron Foulger). It's clearly the kind of response he's had to become used to. When the clerk deigns to notice him, he asks to see the editor, whom he says he used to know, only to be told that he has died and been replaced by his daughter, Nadena Kalenin (Anna Lee).

She wants to have nothing to do with the visitor. We learn during the flashback that she's always loathed the count as someone who represents "everything that's wrong with Russia." But after he inveigles his way into her office and she notices his impoverished appearance, her compassion wins out. He mumbles on about his misfortune and how his spectacles were taken away with his estate; she politely explains that she's not interested in the manuscript he's trying to sell.

The loss of his spectacles suggests that he hasn't even read it. As far as he's concerned, all it represents is a way to put some money in his pocket. Only when she realizes who wrote it does she change her mind. The author is Fyodor Michailovitch Petroff (George Sanders), formerly the region's examining magistrate to whom she had been engaged.[22]

With the nuanced exchanges between the characters evoking tensions whose sources are yet to be established, Sirk's attention to detail is meticulous. The sparse décor speaks of a world where luxuries have no place. A photograph of a rifle-wielding soldier on the wall looks down on Volsky's exchange with the clerk. And throughout the subsequent flashback, the cluttered decor is equally oppressive, pressing in on the action in a manner that had become part of Sirk's modus operandi long before he arrived in the US. The characters are regularly forced to share the frame with large statues and other objects, which sometimes even obstruct our view of them.

Obviously, given that it was written in 1883, the novel is set before the revolution had taken place, although the social stresses it depicts correspond to those in the film. However, given the vantage point that time has allowed him on Russian history, Sirk is able to suggest not only that Russia's Tsarist era was a time of brutal class oppression but also that the revolution grew logically out of it. In *Hitler's Madman*, a philosophy lecturer cites Emmanuel Kant's thesis about how pressure always produces counter-pressure. That notion is as applicable here as it was to Sirk's depiction of the Nazi occupation of Czechoslovakia.

It's also worth noting that *Summer Storm* invites comparison with Renoir's *La regle du jeu* (1939), not just because of the shooting party referred to by the title of Chekhov's novel but also in its portrait of a society on the brink of a breakdown. And, as in Renoir's film, the upper classes frequently rub shoulders with those whom the social order deems to be inferior while unspoken tensions simmer away.

Petroff's memoir makes up the entire flashback and most of the film's running time (as well as including several events that occur when he's not present). And, in both novel and film, he's shown to be a very unreliable narrator. In the book, he's the one pitching the manuscript to a male editor, whose suspicions about what he's reading are presented (somewhat redundantly) in the form of footnotes. Chekhov also includes another character, an idealistic doctor, who doesn't appear in the film and whose assessment of Petroff as "something of a psychopath"[23] makes perfect sense. In the film, Petroff certainly omits crucial bits of information, but his untrustworthiness is subtly evident throughout in Sanders' compelling performance.

The events covered in the manuscript reveal Petroff's boredom with his privileged life and his wantonness. They also deal with his strained friendship with Count Volsky and his ill-fated affair with Olga (Linda Darnell), the daughter of the alcoholic woodcutter who lives on Volsky's estate (Sig Ruman). Their relationship begins soon after she has married Volsky's bookkeeper, the unfortunate Urbenin (Hugo Haas), and leads to the demise of his engagement to Nadena. The flashback ends with Olga's murder and the trial in which Urbenin is found guilty of the crime.

Deliberately or otherwise, Olga is cast in the mold of the classic *femme fatale*. Seen in such a light, she belongs to a rank-and-file sisterhood that includes the likes of sad Stella (Darnell again) in *Fallen Angel* (1945), troubled Cora (Lana Turner) in *The Postman Always Rings Twice* (1946), and, indeed, Hedy Lamarr's upwardly mobile Jenny Hager in Edgar G. Ulmer's *The Strange Woman* (1946), to which Sirk made an uncredited contribution. But these defining characteristics primarily stem from the novel where Petroff's manuscript describes her as a cold-blooded manipulator who "appears with all the vain grandeur of a beautiful woman who has plumbed the depths of depravity."[24]

If Olga is a *femme fatale*, Nadena is a "good woman" (that is, a nonsexual one). Whereas the duplicitous Olga flaunts her sexuality, the upright Nadena remains demure. Like Joyce (Marcia Henderson) when boyfriend Russ (Richard Long) kisses her in street outside her home near the start of Sirk's *All I Desire*, Nadena is embarrassed when, early in the film, Petroff embraces her outside a cake shop. "Fejor," she exclaims, "we'll be the talk of the whole village." "It's too late for that now," he replies dismissively, and that's clearly not the kind of thing he worries about anyway.

Olga (Linda Darnell) putting on a show for Petroff (George Sanders) and Count Volsky (Edward Everett Horton) in *Summer Storm*.

Olga is not the only character in the film who regards her life as a stage on which to play out a role, but that trait both defines and destroys her. It's how she's introduced, in the key scene set in the gazebo outside Volsky's home during a summer storm: roused from her slumbers by a thunderclap and the arrival of Petroff and the count, she pretends to still be asleep and then goes through the motions of awakening, this time stretching seductively and feigning surprise at their presence.

And it's how she acts throughout the film, at least until the moving scene on her deathbed where she faces the man who has murdered her but doesn't acknowledge his guilt. She is a walking melodrama, and her theatrical ways wreak havoc with the aristocracy's sense of order. Petroff sees the danger—"Why is it that you degrade everything you touch?" he asks her—but he can't help himself.

Considered in the wider context of Sirk's work, *Summer Storm* can be found lurking in the wings throughout *Written on the Wind*. In their different ways, the two films both depict doomed aristocracies, with their demise all but sealed into place by a flashback structure. Petroff is akin to Kyle Hadley (Robert Stack). Both men are stricken by melancholy and hate what they see when they look in the mirror: Petroff attempts to erase his reflection by tossing a violin into a bar mirror; for Kyle, it's a glass of scotch.

"If only a small part of the past could be retrieved," Petroff says in voice-over as the flashback begins, except that it becomes clear in what follows that the past he's talking about is evidence of his, and Tsarist Russia's, decay. His sentiment is echoed by Kyle's yearning to go back to the river and his childhood, and both films show that the past the two men are trying to summon is not the reality of a happier time but simply an illusion. Furthermore, Olga and Marylee (Dorothy Malone) are sisters beneath the skin, both lost souls estranged from the worlds they inhabit but drawn by its empty promises.

As the flashback ends, Count Volsky returns to the cramped lodgings he's been sharing with Petroff and explains to him what he's done with his manuscript. Horrified by having provided Nadena with what amounts to a confession, Petroff rushes off to her. Having read it and learned that he'd kept her discarded dance card on which he'd written "I love you," she's placed his memoir in an envelope addressed to the public prosecutor, but hasn't mailed it. "I was too weak to give you away," she tells him, passing the envelope—and the decision about whether or not to post it—over to him.

It's his last chance at redemption and the last hope for the innocent Urbenin, who has been languishing in Siberia. Petroff's impulse for good, earlier displayed when he'd tried to speak up during Urbenin's trial but had been silenced, again emerges. But it's finally suppressed when he steals the envelope back from the postman, only to be shot by police as he tries to flee the scene. The envelope and the dance card memento end up in a rubbish bin as the film ends.

Written by Rowland Leigh and Sirk, under the pseudonym Michael O'Hara,[25] with additional dialogue by Robert Thoeren, who fled Germany in 1933, *Summer Storm* is a savage film about the workings of the class system. Immensely rich, it's arguably more polished than its source, and its devastating final sequence leaves behind only an aching sense of waste. As in *Hitler's Madman*, there's no room for a happy ending.

A SCANDAL IN PARIS (1945)

> "Probably the most brilliant dialogue I worked with was the script that Ellis St. Joseph did for *A Scandal in Paris*. In fact, if you talk of art, I consider *A Scandal in Paris* my best film—even above the Chekhov picture . . . But it's a European film really—in a totally European style."
> —DOUGLAS SIRK, 1978[26]

Although he comes from the mean streets of Paris, or thereabouts, there's nothing hard-boiled about Eugene Francois Vidocq. As played by George Sanders, the protagonist and occasional narrator of *A Scandal in Paris* is as smooth as silk, a soul brother to sleuths as various as Arthur J. Raffles, Arsene Lupin, Nick Charles (of *The Thin Man* series), and even the screen versions of James Bond (especially as incarnated by Sean Connery, Roger Moore, and Pierce Brosnan). He's also the consummate gentleman con artist.

The credits announce that the film is based on his memoirs.[27] However, aside from a broad narrative arc that sees Vidocq transform himself from a thief to the prefect of police, there's little plot overlap between them and the film. Vidocq's account, for example, has him "brought into the world on the 23rd of July, 1775, in a house adjoining that in which Robespierre was born, sixteen years before."[28] The film's Vidocq, however, introduces himself in voice-over as one who was born in prison and now finds himself "spending another birthday at home." And it's not until much later in the film that he even acquires the name of Vidocq, when, standing alongside the tombstone of one Baron Vidocq, he asserts a family connection.

In fact, as scholar Kristopher Mecholsky points out, there are greater similarities between *A Scandal in Paris* and *The Memoirs of Casanova* than there are between the film and its officially ascribed source.[29] Vidocq himself appears to endorse such a view: as Sirk's camera pans from him reclining in his cell to a close-up of a copy of *The Adventures of Casanova* at his side, he explains in voice-over that he has been spending his "monastic seclusion devoted to a study of the classics, particularly one from which I acquired my style, not only in literature but in my brilliant career of love and crime."

A carefully worded opening scroll, citing the *Encylopaedia Britannica*, has already called Vidocq's account of his life into question: "He published two volumes of what *purported* to be the true history of his adventurous career" (my emphasis). A couple of later comments by characters likening him to Casanova serve as playful reminders that all may not be as it seems here.

What *A Scandal in Paris* does take from Vidocq's memoir, however, is its tone. In their different ways, both present themselves with a knowing wink: believe us at your peril, they seem to say. The raised-eyebrow wordiness of Vidocq's first-person narration on the page conveys the sense that he's the kind of storyteller who's not going to allow mundane truths to get in the way of the fanciful yarn he's spinning. And so too does the dry, wry tone of Sanders' delivery, providing a clear warning that we shouldn't be taking anything he tells us at face value. As Mecholsky puts it, "The 'reality' of the film the audience views contrasts sharply and humorously with the grandiose language (of the voice-over) that accompanies it."[30]

The film's picaresque plot is launched by Vidocq's escape from jail with his witless "flatmate," Emile (Akim Tamiroff), a cutthroat with a knife ever at the ready. Assisted by Emile's family, an oddball bunch of born criminals,[31] they assume new identities, "stolen uniforms and counterfeit papers" allowing Vidocq—who's not yet known as Vidocq—to become First Lieutenant Rousseau and Emile his orderly, a role that this fellow traveler slips into as if it were the natural order of things. The plan is for them to join Napoleon at Marseilles prior to his departure for Egypt.

However, Vidocq explains that, before they head off, he needs an important accessory, a woman, and so Loretta (Carole Landis), a nightclub singer, enters the picture with a temptress number entitled "Flame Song."[32] In a sequence reminiscent of the one in Josef von Sternberg's *Morocco* (1930), where soldier Gary Cooper catches the eye of songstress Marlene Dietrich, he acquires the required playmate . . . and her garter. The sexual connotations are irresistible and the outrage of her husband-to-be, Richet (Gene Lockhart), the prefect of the Paris police, is perfectly understandable.

Vidocq and Emile's military adventures occur off-screen, and their next encounter, which our narrator explains takes place two years later, after their return to France, has them serving as models for an artist (Fritz Leiber) who is restoring a mural of St. George and the Dragon outside St. George's church in a village not far from Paris. Ever the opportunist, Vidocq steals St. George's horse and they move on to the nearby domain of the Marquise de Pierremont (Alma Kruger) and her family, son Houdon (Alan Napier), the police minister, granddaughter Therese (Signe Hasso), and her ten-year-old sister, Mimi (Jo Anne Marlowe).

One could be easily forgiven for seeing what ensues as, at least in part, an eighteenth-century blueprint for Alfred Hitchcock's *To Catch a Thief*

The restored St. George mural in *A Scandal in Paris*.

(1955). Viewed in this light, Vidocq becomes a costumed precursor to Cary Grant's enigmatic cat burglar, the countess's granddaughter serves as a more demure equivalent for Grace Kelly's heiress, investigator Houdon becomes John Williams's Lloyds Insurance man, and the countess herself provides the model for Jessie Royce Landis's no-nonsense mother. In both cases, jewelry is the prize.

At the same time, *A Scandal in Paris* slowly turns into a thinly disguised heist movie as Vidocq and Emile look beyond the countess's stash to the 22 million francs held in the vaults of the Bank of Paris. Vidocq's two-part plan is ingenious. First, he and Emile steal the countess's jewels, after which he helps the police minister to recover them, displaying skills of detection so impressive that he gets to replace the unfortunate Richet as prefect of police. "I am what you might call a connoisseur of crime," he teasingly tells the minister. Then, in the interests of making the bank burglar-proof, he installs Emile's family there, just waiting for the right moment to empty the vault.

Smartly written by short story writer Ellis St. Joseph, Sirk's playfully ironic film is deliciously funny, its amiable bent prefiguring that of his later trio of smalltown musicals. To Vidocq's explanation to Emile that his family will be given a percentage of the profits, the bonehead barks back, "No percentage, just a cut." (Tamiroff is as amusing as his character is dangerous.) Playing Holmes to the police minister's Watson, Vidocq declares that it's all "elementary, my dear Houdon." To the now-married Loretta's complaint about her life with Richet, he indicates that he's willing to help in whatever way he can, sympathetically explaining, "Sometimes the chains of matrimony are so heavy, they have to be carried by three."

Central to the film is its play with seeming and being, and it creates a world where appearances are constantly deceptive. Even if one is a dapper charmer and the other embodies a totally maladjusted menace, Vidocq and Emile's shared modus operandi is pretense. And they're not alone in this: disguises are everywhere, as people try to hide their motives. Endeavoring to discover the identity of the shadowy figure who's ruining his life, the forlorn Richet dons a ridiculous beard and—perhaps in a throwaway reference to Papageno in Mozart's *The Magic Flute*—stumbles around under the weight of the birdcages on his back. For her part, Loretta's disguise is made up of the gifts that God has given her—and a wardrobe full of hats—which she deploys in order to get what she wants. She and Vidocq have much in common, certainly more than he and the reserved Therese do.

Doublings pervade the film. Mirrors are everywhere, reflecting characters and objects back at themselves; the paintings on the walls around the characters forever seem to be imposing themselves on the spaces they occupy and also serve to underline the status of the action in the foreground as a series of images. One part of a scene seems to emulate another, as in what unfolds when Vidocq and Emile first meet the countess.

The setting is a cemetery. She is trying to persuade her mischievous chimp, Satan, to climb down from a gravestone. Perhaps channeling Cagliostro in *Black Magic* (1949), Sirk's aborted project immediately before making *A Scandal in Paris*, Vidocq comes to the rescue. Swinging his eye-piece chain backwards and forwards, he hynotizes the recalcitrant creature. Meanwhile, looking on, the countess unconsciously mirrors Vidocq's movements with her necklace. As a result, Emile, who has been gazing greedily at the ornament, is in turn mesmerized by it.

"My dear, in all of us, there is a St. George and a dragon," Therese's priest (Pedro de Cordoba) explains. "That is the true meaning of the legend of St. George." The problem is the difficulty of distinguishing between them. Vidocq's face has provided St. George with a suitably virtuous visage and Emile with a villainous one, at least as far as the artist is concerned: as the priest puts it, "He saw, or fancied he saw, the extremes of good and evil." And Therese obviously shares his view of St. George, falling in love

Vidocq (George Sanders) readying to slay the Dragon in *A Scandal in Paris*.

at first sight with the mural's noble knight. But, when he posed for the painting, Vidocq was most definitely not to be trusted.

Ambiguity reigns throughout. On the one hand, it can be said that the film provides a narrative record of both Vidocq's rise in the ranks and the route he takes to redemption. At the start, he is a member of the criminal underclass; at the end, he is an aristocrat. But questions remain unanswered. To what extent is his decision to abandon his life of crime a consequence of his having achieved what he set out to do? And to what extent is it the result of his actually "going moral," as Emile puts it? The same queries could be directed at Emile's family when they settle for steady jobs at the Bank of Paris rather than taking the risk of trying to rob it.

Vidocq declares to Therese that he's going to start afresh with her and that his days of playing around with women like Loretta are over. "In her eyes, I see myself as I am," he tells her. "In your eyes, I see myself as I could be, as I hope to be." It's a good line, but Sanders's delivery of it is a beautiful mix of total conviction and utter insincerity. Likewise, his confessions to the marquise and Houdon about his crimes.

The only time he appears entirely genuine is when he assures the dying Richet that he will grant his final wish. Unaware that Vidocq is the specter who has been haunting his life—not only because of his affair with Loretta but also because he has tricked his way into his job—the dying man begs him to pledge that justice will be done. "Promise me you'll put an end to him," he urges. "I have already put an end to him," Vidocq assures him, aware that he is at least partially responsible for the fate that has befallen Richet. And yet . . .

Vidocq says and does the kinds of things that he should in order to achieve redemption and, for all intents and purposes, he ends up smelling like roses. But he would, wouldn't he? It's his story and he's told it his way, with only the occasional scene-Richet's demise, Vidocq's fight to the death with Emile—suggesting something darker lurking beneath his winningly waggish eloquence. What Sirk leaves us with is a happy enough ending under the circumstances, but one which in which appearances are all and reality becomes a never-ending puzzle. Which sounds about right to me.

LURED (1947)

> "We have read the script for your proposed production, *Personal Column*, and regret to advise that this story is unacceptable under the provisions of the Production Code because of the characterizations of Fleury, a man who has had many sex affairs, and Jules, a man who murders young women because of his sex frustrations. In addition, there is an inference of white slavery and many sex suggestive lines and scenes which could not be approved."
>
> —LETTER FROM JOSEPH BREEN, JUNE 3, 1946, TO PRODUCER HENRY KESLER[33]

Sirk's third film with George Sanders is a hugely enjoyable companion piece to *A Scandal in Paris*. Graced by a bubbly Lucille Ball, a knowing script, and a distinctly European flavor, *Lured* is a remake of Robert Siodmak's *Pièges* (1939), which was written by Jacques Companeez (*Casque d'or*), Ernst Neubach, and Simon Gantillon. The Jewish Siodmak had fled the wrath of Goebbels in 1933, spending six years based in Paris before again escaping the Nazis and heading to the US. *Pièges* (aka *Snares*, aka *Personal Column*) was the last film he made in France.

Although its plot is effectively a variation on the Jack the Ripper story, *Pièges* is less a horror film than a comedy-thriller, even if it visits some dark places en route to its reassuring denouement. A serial killer is terrorizing Paris. Adrienne Charpentier (Marie Dea), a self-assured young taxi dancer,[34] is asked by Police Commissioner Tenier (Andre Brunot) if she'd be willing to help them in their investigation of the disappearance of her taxi-dancer friend (Catherine Farel), the most recent woman to go missing after responding to a personal column advertisement (a precursor to online dating). Essentially, this entails Adrienne becoming the bait to catch the killer and her assignment finds her adopting a variety of identities, eventually leading her into the arms of nightclub owner/singer Robert Fleury (Maurice Chevalier), to whom she becomes engaged. He's arrested for the crimes and ends up on death row. But perhaps the police should be looking more closely at the activities of his business partner/personal assistant, Bremontiere (Pierre Renoir, Jean's older brother) . . .

In *Lured*, whose working title was *Personal Column*, Paris becomes London, the taxi dancer is an American renamed Sandra Carpenter and played by Ball, Fleury becomes the urbane Robert Fleming (Sanders), his partner is Anglicized as the effete Julian Wilde (Sir Cedric Hardwicke), and the investigating policeman is the fatherly Inspector Harley Temple (Charles Coburn), whom Sirk has compared to Maigret.[35] Although the film removes a couple of scenes and lends a very different edge to the ending, its plot otherwise draws extensively on its source.

There has been some debate about whether or not the original story was inspired by or even borrowed from crime writer Cornell Woolrich,[36] but the important element here is that the material was deemed to have much in common with the novelist's noirish beat. That is in line with the visual styles of the two versions, although their tone is much lighter, primarily leavened in the Siodmak film by Maurice Chevalier's mugging and Dea's amiable presence and, in the generally underrated *Lured*, by Sirk's playful approach to the material.

Like *Pièges*, *Lured* opens in darkness with the credits on plaques being illuminated by a torchlight/spotlight moving across a wall. It's foggy London at night. A bus passenger (Florence Wix) is on her way to a date she's made with a man named John via a personal column: a clipping in her hand informs her that he'll be wearing a red carnation. They meet shortly afterwards in a dimly lit cobblestone street, with anonymous passers-by all around. Only she is visible; he's framed behind a building, reduced to a shadow falling across the footpath. As she introduces herself to him, a man carrying a sandwich board moves across the foreground of the image: "'Murder in Soho.' Now Playing. Beltman Theatre," it reads.

The intrusion certainly doesn't break the narrative flow any more than any of the other reminders throughout *Lured* of the calculated artifice of what's unfolding on-screen. But it does underline, once again, the binding theme of so much of Sirk's work: that all the world is indeed a stage and that all of us are merely players, making entrances and exits, playing many parts, sometimes knowingly, sometimes innocent of the parameters of the roles on offer.

The chief difference between *Lured* and *Pièges* can be found in the sustained way in which Sirk draws upon the theatricality implicit in the characters' interactions and in the circumstances that draw them together. Whereas the characters in the Siodmak film follow more or less the same narrative route as the ones in *Lured*, Sirk, working with a screenplay that has been adapted from Companeez's original by Leo Rosten, colors their every step with an air of theatricality.

Everybody in the film is either putting on a show or laying the foundations for one. Sandra is a taxi dancer, a working girl and a showgirl, who becomes an undercover investigator for the Metropolitan Police. In order to do her job, she attends what she calls "auditions," responding to personal column invitations that invite her to assume particular roles. For the eccentric Charles van Druten, "the greatest designer that ever lived" (Boris Karloff hamming it up as he takes over the part played by Erich von Stroheim in the original), Sandra becomes a model wearing his outfits. For Lyle Maxwell (Alan Mowbray), a butler in a household that serves as a front for some shady activities, she becomes a parlor maid and an object of desire. For Fleming, who doesn't know she's working with the police, she becomes the latest in a long line of paramours.

For his part, he's the kind of individual who likes a spotlight. He's turned his life as a sophisticated man-about-town into an art form and he's as adept at drawing a crowd as he is at winning hearts. When Wilde, his business partner, wonders why he favors small entrances for his club, he explains that appearances matter, that "the more crowded the effect the more prosperous the impression."

As a seducer, he follows a well-rehearsed scenario, in line with the bemused observation from a spurned lover (Lynn Baggett) who has been watching him in full performance mode with Sandra. "The old Fleming pattern!" she declares to a friend (Mary Jane French) as Fleming guides his latest catch on to the dance floor. "With a graceful bow, he takes her in his arms and they dance a few steps in beautiful harmonious silence while his busy little brain composes charming little speeches." Cut to Fleming and Sandra dancing, then back to the self-appointed commentator. "He tells her how exciting she is and how fortunate he is and how fond he is of red hair, or black, or purple . . ." The same scene is in *Pièges*, but absent the life-as-theatre context.

As an experienced taxi dancer, however, Sandra is only too familiar with this kind of shtick. "Don't say it, Mr. Fleming. Let me guess. I'm sure it's been said before." And their relationship unfolds like a cat-and-mouse game, with each putting on a show that, despite the constraints imposed by the Production Office, reveals as much about the art of seduction as it does about their characters. When he makes a move she doesn't anticipate (before they've met, he's pretended to be "Fleming's secretary"), she draws on her arsenal of one-liners: "My IQ must've been flying at half-mast," she quips. Theirs is a relationship akin to the ones that were unfolding in the screwball comedies of the era, both characters cast as equals in the battle of the sexes regardless of the places they occupy on the social hierarchy.

Meanwhile, the search for the killer goes on, the police gathered in their offices as they work their way through the evidence. That includes poems which the killer sends to them each time he finds a new victim. Inspector Temple seeks out professional help with the investigation, including forensic experts to identify the typescript and the paper on which the poems have been printed, as well as a professor of literature (Alex Frazer) who identifies Baudelaire as the killer's literary inspiration. That's enough for Temple to conclude that the poet is "one of the most fantastic madmen who ever lived."

This kind of attention to the way the investigators go about their business could, if seen in a particular light, make *Lured* something of a police procedural. However, in the context Sirk has created, the officers become like critics mulling over the details of a production, debating its possible meanings. The evidence points to Fleming as the villain, but Temple comes to believe that he's been set up and Wilde becomes his chief suspect.

His interrogation of Wilde becomes another cat-and-mouse game: Temple doesn't accuse him directly, but instead makes his case by implication. Wilde never openly acknowledges that he knows the game the policeman is playing, but he's clearly well aware of it. "Mr. Wilde, may I have your copy of Baudelaire?" Temple asks. "Baudelaire? But that's a very unusual request . . . I don't think I have a copy here," Wilde fudges. "I am sure you have," insists Temple. "You're right as usual," says Wilde, surrendering to the inevitable and taking *Flowers of Evil* from his bookshelf.

Sirk's direction of the actors and his framings of their conversation, moving between two-shots and close-ups, emphasize the sense of play in the exchange, Coburn assuming the role of predator with authoritative aplomb and Hardwicke's eyes widening behind his spectacles as he almost forgets about the cigarette he's smoking. Yet throughout their exchange, Temple and Wilde maintain polite demeanors alongside their knowing theatricality.

In *Pièges*, the scene is played differently, suggesting that the killer actually wants to be caught. In *Lured*, he's a villain from whose troubled psyche one might extract a deluge of repressed homosexual urges. But Sirk is less interested in the subtleties of Wilde's motivations than in the spectacle of the two men competing for the limelight.

Commentary over the years about *Lured* has seen it as a straightforward genre film, a whodunit with a feisty female lead. But what's lost if the film is reduced to this level are the very qualities that make it so rich—not just the wit and the playfulness that turn the pulp material in on itself, but also Sirk's ability to find in it a mirror for human interactions in general.

In *Sirk on Sirk*, the director tells Jon Halliday that producer Hunt Stromberg gave him "a very free hand, on the cutting and everything."[37] And one should take this information at face value. This was an opportunity for Sirk to move into a realm where he'd never been before: he took a straightforward crime film and made it his own. *Lured* is exactly what he wanted to make and it deserves a far more prominent place in his oeuvre.

Postscript

BLACK MAGIC (GREGORY RATOFF AND, UNCREDITED, ORSON WELLES, 1949)

> "I worked on it for quite a while, and had a complete script ready. I had cast Sanders in the lead as Count Cagliostro, and Akim Tamiroff as his sidekick. Cagliostro was one of those vacillating characters."
> —DOUGLAS SIRK, 1971[38]

Shot at Scalera Studios in Rome in late 1947, *Black Magic* was the fifth Alexandre Dumas adaptation for independent producer Edward Small. It's preceded on his extensive resume by *The Count of Monte Cristo* (1934), *The Man in the Iron Mask* (1939), *The Son of Monte Cristo* (1940), and *The Corsican Brothers* (1941). According to reports in the *Hollywood Reporter*,[39] Irving Pichel was originally slated as director, with a cast headed by Charles Boyer and Akim Tamiroff. Nine months later, in August 1944, Small announced Pichel and Boyer had been replaced by Sirk and Sanders.

About a year later, Sirk began shooting *A Scandal in Paris*, which took him from September to December 1945, to complete; in December 1945, he also did some uncredited work on *The Strange Woman*; after which came *Lured* (October–December 1946) and *Sleep, My Love* (May–August 1947). Given his workload during these years, one can reasonably presume that, by the time he began preparing *A Scandal in Paris*, Sirk was no longer involved with *Black Magic*. The latter film finally went into production in October 1947, with Russian-born, Hollywood-based Gregory Ratoff as director, Orson Welles as his lead actor, and Tamiroff still on board in a supporting role.[40]

Like *A Scandal in Paris*, Ratoff's film is the tale of a charismatic scoundrel told in flashback. Written by Charles Bennett (a regular Hitchcock collaborator from 1937 to 1940), with additional scenes and dialogue by veteran screenwriter Richard Schayer, it begins in Paris in 1848 with a conversation between writer Dumas (Berry Kroeger) and his son (Raymond Burr) concerning a book he's writing about the life of the notorious Italian magician-hypnotist, Cagliostro. "Oh, the eighteenth-century charlatan!" exclaims Dumas *fils*. "Was he?" asks Dumas *pere*. "Devil, mountebank, fool? I'm still wondering."

Cagliostro is thus introduced as an enigmatic figure, like Sirk's Vidocq. However, there's nothing the slightest bit enigmatic about the character we meet in the ensuing flashback, via Dumas's perfunctory narration and Ratoff's ham-fisted melodramatics. The film's Cagliostro, who'd been born Joseph Balsamo, is rescued by gypsies after his parents are hanged on the orders of the villainous Viscount de Montagne (Stephen Bekassy), and initiated into the nomadic life where he grows into "an insolent, devil-may-care vagabond." At which point, Welles assumes the role, replacing the youthful Annielo Mele (who'd starred in Vittorio De Sica's *Shoeshine* three years earlier).

Guided by the noble Dr. Mesmer (Charles Goldner), he goes from being a sideshow magician-hynotist to a man who could, if he chose, use his ability to revolutionize medical science. The doctor points out to him that, since most illnesses start in the mind, "we can conquer man's greatest enemy: himself." But whereas he is an idealist, Cagliostro is an opportunist who prefers comfort to gratitude. And Dr. Mesmer has, inadvertently, set him on a path to achieving his ends.

In what follows, the con artist inveigles his way into the court of Louis XV—the French Revolution is still in the offing—and, along with seeking revenge for the murder of his parents, is willing to do whatever it takes to achieve power and enjoy the favors the court has to offer. But while his life might follow the same upwardly mobile direction as Vidocq's, there's little doubt about what we're supposed to make of this con man.

Welles plays him like a Byronic psychopath, Ratoff's chiaroscuro lighting emphasizing his wide-eyed stare as he goes about his business. A master manipulator, Cogliostro is striving to turn all around him into puppets ruled by his whim. He's a megalomaniac, a dictator in the making . . . perhaps even a filmmaker trying to achieve complete control. And, in his cunning manipulation of events, he's not unlike Sirk's Vidocq whose "solving" of the burglary which he has committed leads to his appointment as the prefect of police.

Welles could ham it up better than most, but it's difficult to believe that he could turn in the overwrought performance he delivers here—especially if, as it has long been believed, he shared directing responsibilities on the film. His mannered excess works much more effectively in the far more adventurous screen adaptation of *Macbeth* (1948), which he was editing at the same time as he was working on *Black Magic*.

One is left to ponder what Sirk's plans might have been for the unmade *Cagliostro*. If, as Kristopher Mecholsky reasonably surmises on the basis of the time frame, "the thematic thrust of his completed *Cagliostro* manuscript carries over into *A Scandal in Paris*,"[41] then it is a matter for considerable regret that he was denied the chance to complete it. Or chose not to.

CHAPTER THREE

In the Shadows
Sirk and the Noir Inclination

> "Film noir is not a genre . . . It is not defined, as are the western and gangster genres, by conventions of setting and conflict, but rather by the more subtle qualities of tone and mood."
> —PAUL SCHRADER, 1972[1]

NOWHERE IN INTERVIEWS DOES SIRK HAVE ANYTHING TO SAY ABOUT film noir. The term that now rolls so easily off the tongue had only gained currency in Europe a few years before the films being discussed here were made,[2] so it's likely that he'd never even encountered it when he made them. Yet it's possible to argue that, in terms of the sensibility that one can identify in Sirk's oeuvre, in "the subtle qualities of tone and mood," he and noir have much in common. Furthermore, several of the character types and themes that turn up in films that are customarily classified as noir—men obsessed with dangerous women; sexual triangles evolving into murder; people trapped by oppressive environments; individuals transgressing and losing themselves in the shadows—also appear in Sirk's work. In that context, films such as *Summer Storm* and *Lured* would fit with the concerns of this chapter, but are discussed elsewhere in another context.

Over the years, two of the three films that are dealt with here—*Sleep, My Love* and *Shockproof*—have occasionally been linked to film noir, primarily because of their plots: the former is about a husband plotting to dispense with his wife (and failing); the latter about a parole officer who falls in love with a woman who looms as a *femme fatale* (but turns out not to be one).[3] *Mystery Submarine* rarely gets a mention of any kind anywhere, let alone consideration as a film noir.

No place to hide. Parole officer Griff (Cornel Wilde) and parolee Jenny (Patricia Knight) in *Shockproof*.

Certainly, these three films lack the uncompromising, hard-boiled edge and fatalistic gloom that permeates the kinds of works that have come to be regarded as the "classic" films noir (such as *The Maltese Falcon*, *Double Indemnity*, *The Postman Always Rings Twice*, and *Out of the Past*). And all proffer happy endings, which is not usually the case with films regarded as noirs.

Sleep, My Love does this more persuasively than either *Shockproof* or *Mystery Submarine*, where the positive outcomes seem arbitrarily tacked on (and devoid of irony). It's the story of a murderous spouse, but the attitude it invites us to take towards its characters makes it clear that it's not heading towards a *Double Indemnity* denouement.

However, the key to Sirk's inclination towards noir isn't so much in the plotting or the endings. Rather, it's to be found in the way the films have been shot, not only in terms of their use of light and dark but in the visual relationships they establish between individuals or groups and their surroundings. In these three films—and elsewhere in his work (especially in films such as *All I Desire* and *There's Always Tomorrow*)—a crucial constant is the insistent framing of décor to encroach on characters, to impinge on the spaces they pass through, to unsettle them in ways that might not immediately be felt but that accumulate during the course of the films. They were shot by different cinematographers, all of them American—Joseph Valentine (*Sleep, My Love*), Charles Lawton Jr. (*Shockproof*), and Clifford Stine (*Mystery Submarine*)—but the compositional strategies they deploy are the same.

Consider the use of the grand staircase opposite the front door in the Courtland mansion in *Sleep, My Love*: shot from the ground floor looking up, it's like a monster waiting to devour all who pass through the door, evoking a realm of darkness and danger and serving as a visual analogy for the threat waiting for the central character. Or in the lovers' oil-rig refuge *Shockproof*: the complete absence of privacy there seems to be as much a manifestation of their fear that everyone is watching them as it is a living space. Or the cluttered interior of the U-boat in *Mystery Submarine*: the crew's survival is at stake and the cramped interiors make it seem as if the world is closing in on them.

This deployment of decor mightn't be as visually arresting as the gloom or chiaroscuro lighting that feature in films traditionally classified as noir, but it follows similar lines. Call it Sirk-noir, if you like.

SLEEP, MY LOVE (1947)

> "To gaslight: a verb meaning 'to manipulate someone by psychological means into doubting their own sanity.'"
> —OXFORD ENGLISH DICTIONARY

Probably the closest to traditional noir of the three films under discussion in this chapter, *Sleep, My Love* belongs to a group of 1940s and early '50s Hollywood films that has been labeled as "the persecuted wife cycle"[4] or, more speculatively, as "Freudian feminist melodramas."[5] Probably the best known film of the cycle is George Cukor's *Gaslight* (1944), based on Patrick Hamilton's 1938 play, made for MGM and set in London.[6] Over the years, it's even gone from being a film title to a verb.

However, the cycle's beginnings can be traced back to Hitchcock's *Suspicion* (1941), based on Francis Iles's 1932 novel and also set in England. That film and those that followed—including *Jane Eyre, Experiment Perilous,* and *When Strangers Marry* (all 1944), *Conflict* (1945), *Undercurrent* (1946), *The Two Mrs. Carrolls, Monsieur Verdoux,* and *Secret Beyond the Door* ... (all 1947), *Sorry, Wrong Number* (1948), *Caught* (1949), *Sudden Fear* (1952), and *Dial M for Murder* (1954)—are all at least partially indebted to Charles Perrault's four-page seventeenth-century folktale about Bluebeard.

Viewed from a certain angle, it's as if the same elements are circulating through all of these films, some remaining constant, others shifting into differing concatenations: the husband with an agenda (often played against type by romantic leads such as Cary Grant, Charles Boyer, and Robert Taylor); the put-upon wife, often a complete innocent, frequently an heiress (it's through her initially disbelieving eyes that we usually see events unfold); the Gothic house filled with shadows and secrets and shot and lit in a noirish way; the house staff who usually serve as silent witnesses but are occasionally implicated in the action; the other man, sometimes a friend, sometimes a romantic alternative to the husband; the regular household beverage that comes to seem like a weapon (a glass of milk or hot chocolate, a coffee or a cocktail, perhaps a dose of medicine); the doctor/psychiatrist (who's either treating the wife's "condition" or in league with the husband); and, of course, the policeman/men who are called upon to investigate.

The entire cycle could, in fact, simply be tagged "the gaslight films" were it not for the fact that the husband isn't always trying to make his wife think she's crazy, or to kill her. In *Suspicion*, for example, Johnnie (Cary Grant) behaves very dubiously towards Lina (Joan Fontaine), but the film's ending tries to provide reassurance about his intentions.[7] In *Undercurrent*, although events reveal that Alan (Robert Taylor) was a murderer even before his first appearance in the film, it's only towards the end that he decides to murder wife Ann (Katharine Hepburn). And, in *Secret Beyond the Door* . . . , Celia (Joan Bennett) is drawn to the dangers posed by her husband (Michael Redgrave) in ways that make her less of an innocent victim than a knowing participant.

Based on a pulp novel by Leo Rosten, who also wrote the early drafts of the screenplay before *New Yorker* writer St. Clair McKelway became involved,[8] *Sleep, My Love* is very much a "gaslight film." The key elements are all there, with a couple of others tossed in for good measure. Richard Courtland (Don Ameche) is trying to get rid of his wealthy wife Alison (Claudette Colbert) both for her money and because he's besotted with another woman, the *femme fatale*-ish Daphne (Hazel Brooks). Daphne, who hails from the wrong side of town, isn't subtle: "We've got a lot," she tells Courtland, "but we haven't got everything. I want what she's got."

He's been drugging his wife's bedtime hot chocolate with a substance that puts her into a hypnotic state and allows him to steer her into dangerous situations. The film opens in the midst of one of them: in the dark of night, with a piercing whistle on the soundtrack, a train is speeding straight towards the camera; Alison awakes in a daze in her compartment with no idea of how she got there or how a gun got into her handbag. Among those who come to her aid is an old busybody (Queenie Smith), who, we later discover, is there on Courtland's instructions.

Meanwhile, back at their riverside mansion, which looks out on Manhattan's Fifty-ninth Street Bridge, he has reported Alison missing to the police. And, while playing the role of the concerned husband for the benefit of a visiting detective (Raymond Burr), he's actually working to ensure that her recent behavior appears unhinged. Both are lies. He's also nursing an injured arm that he says, but doesn't want anybody to believe, is a self-inflicted wound acquired while he was cleaning his gun.

However, despite his careful planning, he's not completely in control and, after Alison runs into the amiable Bruce Elcott (Robert Cummings) when she gets off the train, an unexpected player joins the fray.[9] Describing himself as "a bachelor in the bleachers," he becomes her knight in shining white armor, eventually learning enough to warn her to beware Courtland's hot chocolate nightcap. While the film begins by setting us alongside Alison, the lens widens soon afterwards.

The film's visual style is in the noir mold, with low-angle lighting in the Expressionist manner. The Courtland mansion appears more like a museum than a home in the way it has been furnished, and dark corners lurk in virtually every frame. The large staircase inside the front doorway seems to reach on upwards forever, and the house's often vertiginous settings seem "perfect for an accident" (as Jack Palance's murderous husband in 1952's *Sudden Fear* says of wife Joan Crawford's summer house with its perilous cobblestone stairs down to the beach).

A "B-movie" made for Mary Pickford's Triangle Productions, *Sleep, My Love* is an engaging crime thriller that features the usual kinds of twists and turns that one has come to expect from the genre. At the same time, it's also more than that. It allows plenty of room for Sirk to maintain his recurring concern with life as an ongoing performance where no one really appreciates the bigger picture that they're part of—in this case, it's as much defined by the rules of the genre as it is by the vagaries of human existence—but everyone has a role to play.

What ensues once Bruce arrives on the scene is a series of competing scenarios that have two men flexing their theatrical muscles with Alison as the spoils. With a cast of well-rehearsed actors at his disposal—including a fake psychiatrist (George Coulouris), whose assigned task is to help persuade Alison that she really is going off her rocker—Courtland spends much of his time trying to recruit others as supporting players (even if they remain unaware that this is what he is doing), summoning them into service as witnesses who will testify to Alison's derangement. He even sets up a scene in which she's supposed to shoot the fake psychiatrist once he's outlived his usefulness.

For his part, Bruce adopts several disguises as he builds an alternative scenario to the one that Courtland wants to put in place. He becomes a regular visitor to the Courtland home, submerging his romantic feelings for Alison by playing the part of her "very, very good friend" and conjuring up his own "alternative facts" (not a quote from the film) to compete with the ones Courtland has been providing. Even though he's become very suspicious of Courtland, he doesn't change his manner towards him. And he variously adopts the roles of a reporter "from the *Times*," an investigator from North Atlantic Fire Insurance, and a man in search of a passport photo in order to uncover Courtland's duplicities.

Sirk seems to have been engaged by *Sleep, My Love*, whatever he had to say about the film when he looked back on it in interviews. It's often funny in a way that isn't usual either in gaslight films or those that exhibit noir influences. In particular, Bruce's daffy sister, Barby (Rita Johnson), is a delight. But the setting of two contrasting styles of leading men opposite each other—Ameche with his smooth charm, Cummings with his fast-talking repartee—is engrossing. It indicates some extremely canny casting and Sirk's distinctive grasp of a very American style of filmmaking.

SHOCKPROOF (1949)

> "My next yarn was called *The Lovers*. (My agent) sold it to Columbia . . . The great Douglas Sirk directed (it) in 1949. Apparently they didn't like my title, so the studio renamed it *Shockproof*. One of my postwar scripts had finally been made into a movie, so I didn't give a damn what they called it."
> —SAMUEL FULLER, 2003[10]

In 1949, Sirk's general sense of displacement—as a European intellectual stuck in a cultural wasteland—and his inability to find out what had happened to the son from whom he'd been estranged during the war, led him back to Germany. And the fate that had befallen *Shockproof* a few months earlier clearly didn't help his state of mind.

He'd originally taken on the project on the basis of a screenplay by Samuel Fuller entitled *The Lovers*. But during the course of the shoot, significant changes had been made, largely instigated by writer Helen Deutsch, whom Columbia had attached to the project and had given the power of oversight. As a result, the film that Sirk had believed he'd been making was seriously compromised.

The plot is simple enough. After spending five years in prison for shooting a man in defense of her lover, Jenny Marsh (Patricia Knight) is paroled into the official care of tough but sympathetic Griff Marat (Cornel Wilde, Knight's then-husband). However, disobeying the rule that forbids parolees to mix with anyone with a "bad reputation," she continues to see her lover, Harry Wesson (John Baragrey), a disreputable gambler bent on insinuating his way back into her life.

At the same time as Griff falls for her, she is drawn to his straight-down-the-line folksiness and to the everyday world he represents, and finds herself torn between her old ways and the chance to start afresh. But Harry isn't prepared to let go easily. He threatens to expose the double life Jenny has been leading since her release. After he is shot during a confrontation with her, she and Griff find themselves on the run from the law.

In the film, a flashback is inserted to ensure that there's no doubt about what actually happened, that Jenny hadn't tried to kill Harry. Given how Fuller has spoken about his screenplay and, inasmuch as it's possible to glean Sirk's dramatic strategies from the finished film, the presence of the flashback appears to indicate an intervention by the studio or Helen Deutsch rather than a Fuller- or Sirk-driven decision to remove any such ambiguities.

In an extended 1963 interview with French critic Jean-Louis Noames, Fuller spoke enthusiastically about *The Lovers*, which he'd written shortly before embarking on his own directing career. "I wanted it to be an A-film because [it] had a very tragic end and I had a fantastic sequence for it; the lovers run away but they don't realise that for the greater part of the film, no one is in fact chasing them . . . The great thing is that the chase is going on inside them."[11]

Fuller's fingerprints are still visible on the finished film: yet another protagonist named Griff,[12] the pared-back plot line, the rough-edged storytelling style that constantly leaves one on edge, the collision between a normality and the forces that drive individuals to break its rules, the characters' headlong rush towards what seems to be an inevitable fate. There are also several scenes in the film's latter stages clearly meant to point to how "the chase is going on inside them." And an exchange between Jenny and a female police psychiatrist (Ann Shoemaker) about the reasons for her state of mind seems to have been ripped from Fuller-penned headline-style dialogue. "Heredity!" Jenny declares. "Environment!" the psychiatrist snaps back.

But many of the elements that we have come to customarily associate with Sirk are also in evidence in *Shockproof*. The notion of life as an ongoing performance is, again, a recurring feature here. The film begins with the camera tracking behind Jenny on her way first to a department store (to buy a dress) and then to a hairdressing salon (where she is transformed from a brunette into a blonde). After the purpose of her makeover becomes clear—she has an appointment with her parole officer, Griff—it's as if she's been backstage preparing herself for a role she's about to play.

She knows the rules of the game and she's been making herself presentable to him, feigning a new identity. She hides her intention to return to her relationship with Harry but, soon afterwards, she's picked up in a police raid on a bookie joint to which she's gone with him.[13] It's only when Griff throws her a lifeline by giving her another chance to demonstrate that "she has character" that she becomes more open to the opportunity being offered to her.

Just as the title character in *The Girl from the Marsh Croft* goes to work for Gudmund's invalid mother, Jenny becomes carer to Griff's blind mother (Esther Minciotti), taking up residence in the family home and being made privy to another way of life. She seems too comfortable pursuing her duties there—which even include reading poetry to Mrs. Marat (including Emerson's "Give All to Love")—for her to be entirely in "performance" mode.

Yet her motives remain ambiguous, and later scenes when she agrees to do Wesson's bidding suggest her duplicity. But she's clearly been warmed by the compliments and friendship heaped upon her by Griff's kid brother, Tommy (Charles Bates), and his mother, whose blindness allows her to see more than those who have the use of their eyes. She recognizes Griff's feelings for Jenny perhaps even before he does.

Jenny's hard edge is also softened when she becomes aware that Griff is falling in love with her. When Mrs. Marat tells her about this, she says, "It isn't possible." But, without ever articulating how she has been transformed, she finds that what had begun as a knowing performance is gradually becoming one that is becoming increasingly difficult for her. "You deserve better than me," she tells Griff.

For his part, Griff too is engaged in a performance. The decision he takes in his role as a parole officer to give Jenny a break, despite the obvious reservations of his superior (Howard St. John), is as much a sign that he's falling for her as it is a humane gesture. At work, his professional demeanor becomes a disguise for his private feelings. He maintains this when he takes her home for dinner with his family. There's another parolee (Russell Collins) there too, so this isn't the kind of thing he's doing for the first time.

If other films of the time about relationships between parole officers and their charges are any indication, such a hands-on approach isn't unusual. For example, Griff's methods are similar to those Lizabeth Scott's idealistic parole officer adopts when she invites the recently released Mildred (Jane Greer) to join her for "a night on the town" near the start of John Cromwell's *The Company She Keeps* (1950).

But Wilde's nicely controlled performance also quietly suggests that, while Griff is denying personal involvement, he's also bent on establishing it. And when, soon afterwards, he declares his feelings to Jenny, it comes as no surprise. His mother has already suggested to him that he doesn't know his own mind. Just as Jenny's public persona serves as a disguise for the turmoil within, so it is with Griff.

His hostility to Harry from the first time he encounters him seems to stem at least as much from his personal feelings as it does from his professional disapproval. "He doesn't love anybody but himself," he insists, despite the fact that Harry is there to greet Jenny and to declare his loyalty to her after her initial release. It's not too much of a stretch to read Griff's reactions to Jenny's reluctance or inability to cut her ties with Harry as those of a jealous lover.

There is also the sense with many of the characters around Jenny and Griff that everyone is engaged in a performance of one kind or another. The man who is a dinner guest at the Marats' is introduced to Jenny as a friend, but later tells her the truth about who he is: "I don't like pretending to be someone I'm not." In order to get past Jenny's guard, the police psychiatrist assessing Jenny pretends to be a doctor tending to the ankle she had sprained during her arrest. Sirk shows the psychiatrist arranging her office beforehand like a stage set. Like backstage hands going about their business, characters often arrange décor in Sirk films to create sought-after impressions (see, for example, *No Room for the Groom*). And numerous exchanges between characters occur with others watching or listening as if they are the members of an audience.

Beyond these familiar Sirk strategies, there is also the way in which *Shockproof* inclines towards noir without fully succumbing to its fatalistic pull. If cast in the genre's classic mold, Jenny would be the *femme fatale* whose siren song draws the male towards his doom, as Jane Greer's Kathie does in Jacques Tourneur's *Out of the Past*, made a couple of years earlier. And the noir aspects of Sirk's film—the shadowy interiors of both the parole office and the Marat home (reminiscent, in the way it has been shot and lit by Charles Lawton Jr., of the home in *All I Desire*); the sense of forces beyond the characters' control conspiring against them—open the door on the possibility that Griff will be destroyed by his feelings for Jenny.

But, even though their relationship does lead them on to the wrong side of the law and they become increasingly paranoid about their situation, Sirk ensures that we don't blame Jenny for this or see Griff as having been, in any way, duped by her and brought undone.

What one can glean from Fuller's comments about the screenplay he submitted and from *Shockproof* itself indicate that, whatever fate is to befall Jenny and Griff, they're in it together. They might have broken the rules—which forbid any romantic relationships between parole officers and parolees—but, in their different ways, they're both innocents.

In Fuller's screenplay, as both he and Sirk have outlined,[14] the story's denouement is tragic. However, under the influence of Helen Deutsch, whose credits include the screenplays for *National Velvet* (1944) and *Lili* (1953), as well as the lyrics for a featured song, "Hi-Lili, Hi-Lili, Hi-Lo," and despite Sirk's protests, things changed. As a contract director at Columbia, where the autocratic Harry Cohn was at that time the president and production boss, Sirk had little power. And when the studio added a very clumsy happy ending before the film's release, he wasn't even informed.[15]

In it, the villainous Harry has a complete change of heart when he tells the authorities from his hospital bed that his near fatal wounds were the result of an accident. "I'm a good enough gambler to know when I've lost," he tells the relieved lovers. "It took a bullet to convince me." The film's steady descent into mayhem is thus halted and order is restored.

Ironically, this ending is virtually duplicated by the one that Sirk shot five years later, albeit reluctantly, for *All I Desire* where the embittered Lyle Bettger, who had been wounded in a struggle with the film's protagonist (Barbara Stanwyck), suddenly turns nice guy and tells her husband (Richard Carlson) that she shouldn't be held responsible. Just as ironically, Deutsch's career came to a close with her complaints about how a "meddling" novelist and studio pressures had ruined her screenplay for *Valley of the Dolls* (1967), based on the Jacqueline Susann novel.[16]

Shockproof was the second film Sirk made under the Columbia banner, and it's no surprise that it was also the last.

MYSTERY SUBMARINE (1950)

> "Although I was hired to do comedy, the first [film] I did was that submarine picture . . . I got it, I suppose, because I had been in the navy. It was alluring to shoot in a submarine, with hand held cameras and so forth. But it was a miserable little story. Here the auteurship of the studio comes in."
> —DOUGLAS SIRK, 1977[17]

Sirk's first film after he signed with Universal, *Mystery Submarine* is both a pedestrian adventure yarn and a fascinating example of the director trying to bend seemingly intractable material into something of interest—and failing.

An espionage drama set during the early years of the Cold War, and very much a B-movie, it pivots on the actions of two central characters. The first is Madeline Brenner (Marta Toren), a widowed German American. She is accused of treason for her part in the kidnapping of Dr. Adolph Guernitz (Ludwig Donath), a German scientist who has offered to help the US, and the murder of the US citizens who had been looking after him. The second is Brett Young (Macdonald Carey), a US Navy doctor who attempts to rescue Guernitz from his captors.

"Suggested by a story by Ralph Dietrich," who was the film's producer, *Mystery Submarine* also credits George W. George and George F. Slavin (*Week-End with Father*) with the story and screenplay. The duo became historically noteworthy the year before for contributing the story for Robert Stevenson's *The Woman on Pier 13* (1949), a notorious film originally entitled *I Married a Communist*. Howard Hughes famously used the script for Stevenson's film, made during the height of the investigations by HUAC (the House Committee on Un-American Activities), as a political litmus test to weed out writers, directors, and actors whose politics were regarded as suspect.[18]

Mystery Submarine has no such colorful history, and it suggests a slightly less simplistic view of the world than *The Woman on Pier 13*. Perhaps it's even possible to argue that it represents a retraction of a kind for George and Slavin, at least in its opening sequence. Set in the New York office of the US Attorney, it hardly offers a stinging rebuke to the HUAC investigation, but it does paint a notably unflattering portrait of the two male attorneys appointed to pass judgement about whether or not Madeline is guilty of treason. What's more, its sympathies are clearly with the accused.

The men's manner is unequivocally predatory. Looking at a newspaper photograph of Madeline, salivating assistant attorney Rodgers (Steve Pendleton) describes her as "a real beauty." "So was Mata Hari," he's told by his smug superior, Hagan (Thomas Browne Henry), who adds that he thinks they can successfully indict Madeline. "Too bad," leers Rodgers. "She has such a pretty neck."

After Madeline is shown into the office and sits down, Hagan assumes an aggressive position, leaning on his desk, looking down at her, thrusting his chin forward, and immediately going on the offensive. "Miss Brenner, do you understand the meaning of treason?" he barks. She responds firmly that she does, going on to say that she will tell the truth about what happened, before turning, directly addressing the camera and adding, "And I know the meaning of loneliness."

What ensues traces her actions before, during, and after the kidnapping. The sequence of events is outlined chronologically via depositions from Madeline, Captain Elliott (Howard Negley), a navy officer who had visited Dr. Guernitz and his hosts before the kidnapping, and Young. All are presented in the form of flashbacks (although the visualization of Young's testimony repeatedly moves beyond what he's actually seen). The narrators are reliable, their voice-overs perfunctory.

Madeline explains how she was duped by a stranger on the Cape Cod beach who turned out to be Eric von Molter (Robert Douglas), the commander of a German U-boat. He had promised her a reunion with the husband she'd thought was dead if she agreed to shut down the radio on the yacht carrying Dr. Guernitz. She'd agreed to the deal, with disastrous consequences. Not only had von Molter been lying about her husband, but she'd only survived the sinking of the yacht because von Molter, like the US investigators, found her "beautiful and desirable."

Captain Elliott offers brief testimony about the wreckage of the yacht and the ballistics of the torpedo which sank it, before Young takes over. His description of what happened during his efforts to rescue Dr. Guernitz takes up most of the film and incorporates his account of Madeline's attempt to make reparation for her involvement in the attack on the yacht. Thereafter, it's left to the attorneys to decide whether that is sufficient to make up for her earlier betrayal.

The drama is largely devoid of tension and the resolution is tame. Hagan apologizes to Madeline and tells her she's free to go, although he never outlines the reasons for his decision. In fact, at the start of the closing scene, he appears ready to convict her. "The facts are interesting, revealing," he tells Young, who has just completed his testimony. "And, I must add, somewhat prejudiced." All the film offers to transform his skepticism into sympathy is Young's brief intercession, pointing out that Hagan has overlooked what she did to redeem herself.

Strictly speaking, Madeline *is* guilty as charged, whatever her reasons and whatever she did afterwards by way of compensation. But Hagan makes no mention of this or of there being any tension between what the law decrees and what might be required for a verdict in which compassion has a part to play. As a result, his judgment simply seems like a mechanism to enable a happy ending, and a potentially interesting clash of values—along with a debate about what might constitute loyalty to a cause—is sidestepped.

Sirk regarded the film as one of those that were "best forgotten"[19] and it's not hard to see why. Yet there are glimpses of his engagement with the material beyond the hint of hostility to HUAC in the characterization of the government investigators. Shot by Clifford Stine (who went on to work with him again on *Week-End with Father*, *No Room for the Groom*, and *Has Anybody Seen My Gal*), *Mystery Submarine* fills its interiors with a clutter of detail that seems to be competing for prominence with the characters and, especially in the sequences set inside the submarine, evokes a potent sense of claustrophobia. The confined spaces press in on the inhabitants, and the low angles make it seem as if the roof is bearing down on them.

Furthermore, as in much of the director's other work, the sense of life as an ongoing theatrical performance is evident throughout *Mystery Submarine*. In the opening sequence, when the various witnesses are in the room, the attorneys behave in a much more formal and measured way than they have beforehand. When he's trying to persuade Madeleine to help him, von Molter pretends to be a clam digger on the beach near the beach house where she's been staying. In order to infiltrate von Molter's hideaway in South America, Young passes himself off as a German doctor who's escaped from a Texas prisoner-of-war camp. That hideaway is an elaborately camouflaged cove off the Argentine Sea, designed to conceal the presence there of the U-boat.

Much of the action during the latter stages of the film pivots on the strategies deployed by the submerged submarine to avoid detection from the US planes and warships trying to locate it: switching off the engines and adopting the mode known as "silent running"; then, after the navy drops depth charges, sending up furniture, loose clothing, life jackets, and an oil slick in order to feign wreckage. And the final confrontation with the US Navy finds the Americans assuming the guise of their enemy, having taken over the boat where a bag of money is to be exchanged for Dr. Guernitz and laid a trap for the submarine crew.

It's not as if Sirk has had to smuggle all of this into the film: endemic to crime dramas, thrillers, and many adventure films are characters hiding their identities and burying realities behind disguises. None of it makes *Mystery Submarine* anything more than a tepid espionage drama, but the attention to detail does show Sirk at least trying to shape the material in line with his wider concerns.

Postscript

THE STRANGE WOMAN (EDGAR G. ULMER AND, UNCREDITED, DOUGLAS SIRK, 1946)

> "Beautiful picture. It nearly got Hedy Lamarr an Academy nomination. It's the only picture where she ever had to act. A beautiful picture—very beautiful, very difficult."
> —EDGAR G. ULMER, 1970[20]

After finishing *A Scandal in Paris,* but before beginning production on *Lured,* Sirk was asked to do some reshoots for *The Strange Woman,* which was being directed by Edgar G. Ulmer. The Czech-born filmmaker had worked in Germany during the 1920s before moving to Hollywood, where he worked without official credit on *Hitler's Madman* in various roles (on writing and production design, and as a second unit director), before going on to become famous as a B-movie master.

The Strange Woman's executive producer Hunt Stromberg was already committed to *Lured* and, along with stars Hedy Lamarr (who was also an executive producer) and Sirk's good friend, George Sanders, asked him to become involved in his current project. It's not clear why it was felt necessary to ask Sirk for help.

Most sources indicate that he only reshot *The Strange Woman*'s prologue, dealing with the childhood of the film's central character,[21] although his comments in passing to Jon Halliday[22] seem to suggest that he was responsible for more of the Ulmer film than other citations indicate. Whatever the truth of this, it's worth noting how *The Strange Woman* might have interested Sirk.

Based on Ben Ames Williams's 1941 novel of the same name, the film is set in Bangor, Maine, distinguished cinematographer Lucien Andriot's noirish imagery casting the New England town as a dangerous, shadowy place dominated by dimly lit streets and candle-lit interiors. The action begins in 1824 and features a protagonist who could easily be taken as a blend of Olga (Linda Darnell) in *Summer Storm* and Marylee (Dorothy Malone) in *Written on the Wind*. In his excellent commentary on the film, Gary Morris[23] also likens her to Ellen (Gene Tierney) in John M. Stahl's *Leave Her to Heaven*, made the previous year (and also based on a novel by Williams). And there's even something of *Imitation of Life*'s Lora Meredith (Lana Turner) in the way Jenny is constantly playing a role in order to get what she wants.

Jenny Hager is played by Lamarr, who brought the project to Ulmer and had been a longtime friend.[24] Jo Ann Marlowe, who had just appeared as Mimi de Pierremont for Sirk in *A Scandal in Paris*, plays the character as a little girl. The opening sequence lays the foundations for all that is to follow and firmly anchors Jenny's troubled existence in the social tensions that surrounded her during childhood: an alcoholic father (Dennis Hoey); a mother who's abandoned her; a dockside town riven by class tensions, its residents torn between the need to keep business lively and a contempt for the riff-raff who pass through and ensure that it is.

Young Jenny is a kid from the wrong side of town, a precocious brat and a bully. The first person to suffer at her hands is Ephraim (Christopher Severn, later Louis Hayward), the son of wealthy businessman Isaiah Poster (Gene Lockhart), who is eventually to become Jenny's husband. Asserting her superiority to Ephraim, she insists that he jump off a bridge and into the river below despite his protests that he can't swim. When he hesitates, she shoves him in, then pushes his head under water.

At which point, the arrival of an adult, an authority figure, Judge Henry Saladine (Alan Napier), provides an interruption and sees her go into full performance mode. Putting on her sweet face, she accuses someone else of pushing Ephraim into the water and explains that she'd simply been trying to save her friend. She's even able to convince Ephraim that this is what happened. Yet when the judge, also persuaded by her performance, offers to help her out by taking her into his home, she refuses, asserting her loyalty to her father.

The manipulative tendencies displayed by the young Jenny persist into adulthood. A consummate actress, she's well-equipped to get what she wants from everyone with whom she comes into contact. A sexual temptress, she becomes a classic *femme fatale* figure for all the men of the town. Like Cora (Lana Turner) in *The Postman Always Rings Twice* (1946), she offers herself as bait as she incites Ephraim, now her stepson, to kill his father. And, like Daphne in *Sleep, My Love*, she's a lower-class siren who wants whatever an upper-class woman—her best friend, Meg (Hillary Brooke)—has, including her handsome fiancé (George Sanders). At the same time, Jenny is subversively outspoken, becoming a spokeswoman for the repressed women of the town when she asserts herself against its patriarchal order.

Yet, for all this, she's never fully in control, and Ulmer and Lamarr's subtly nuanced melodramatics manage to make her simultaneously monstrous and vulnerable. This is clearly an Ulmer film, and Jenny has much in common with many of his protagonists (in films as various as *Bluebeard* and *Detour*). John Belton puts it perfectly: "Ulmer's characters, living on the brink of insanity, constantly run the risk of making that one mistake and of unleashing fantastically chaotic forces that will hound them to their own destruction."[25] But it's also not hard to see Sirk himself embarking on such a project and making it his own.

CHAPTER FOUR

The Uncomfortable Comedies

"My idea at this time, which was slowly developing, was to create a comedie humaine with little people, average people—samples from every period in American life."
—DOUGLAS SIRK, 1977[1]

MELODRAMA WAS LURKING IN THE WINGS THROUGHOUT SIRK'S CAREER, even when he was working in genres conventionally beyond its parameters. What distinguishes these four comedies is how often they seem to be sliding towards it. Even as the plots move their characters in different directions, towards different kinds of resolutions from those one generally expects from melodrama, an undercurrent of unease persists. In them, when the curtains close, one is left with the sense of an order very unpersuasively restored and characters unconvincingly content with their newly acquired lot.

It's probably true of all comedy, to greater or lesser degrees, that a slight shift in plot or character could produce an entirely different dramatic outcome. What is melodrama but comedy clad in a different costume? Think, for example, of the films of Frank Capra—especially the social comedies from *Mr. Deeds Goes to Town* (1936) through *Mr. Smith Goes to Washington* (1939) to his masterpiece, *It's a Wonderful Life* (1946)—in which only a twist of fate allows a happy ending to prevail, that "emergency exit" Sirk used to talk about.[2] Or of Preston Sturges's comedies in which total mayhem is only just avoided by what amounts to the filmmaker's knowing choice to step back from the quandaries facing his characters, as in the denouement he conjured up for *The Palm Beach Story* (1942), simultaneously a brilliant parody of the *deus ex machina* strategy and a routine deployment of it.[3]

The twist in Sirk's comedies is that their emphasis is on the situation rather than the resolution, on the problems that divide the characters rather than on the contrivances that suggest that all will be well after the final credits have rolled. All four films are romances of one kind or another and these problems are invariably posed as personal: in *The Lady Pays Off*, Evelyn Warren (Linda Darnell) wants to be seen as a *woman* rather than a woman who looks after children; in *Week-End with Father*, Brad (Van Heflin) wants to be seen as a *real* man rather than a sensitive father. But the tensions that envelop the characters are generally also depicted as the result of social pressures and, especially in Evelyn's and Brad's cases, the ideological positioning of women and men in American society.

At least in part because of this, the films—aside from *Week-End with Father*—aren't especially funny, and most of the laughter they provoke is of an uncomfortable kind. The way they strain against the conventions of the genre also contributes to the sense that what's happening to the characters is no laughing matter. Call them "problem comedies," if you like.

Sirk told Jon Halliday that he had little feeling for them. "I restructured to some extent some of the rather impossible films I had to direct," he says. "Of course, I had to go by the rules, avoid experiments, stick to family fare, have 'happy endings,' and so on."[4] The director's inability to recall much about the details of the films isn't helped by the fact that Halliday hadn't seen them at the time—they were even more difficult to track down in the 1970s than they are today—and so isn't in a position to prompt the director's memory. Six years later, by the time of his interview with Michael Stern for *Bright Lights*, Sirk had re-seen *The Lady Pays Off* and *No Room for the Groom*, and was much more forthcoming about and pleasantly surprised by them.

It perhaps tells us something of his intentions here that all four films were shot in black-and-white: *Slightly French* at Columbia by Charles Lawton Jr., *The Lady Pays Off* by William Daniels, *Week-End with Father* and *No Room for the Groom* by Clifford Stine, all at Universal after Sirk changed studios. Color was clearly available to him had he wanted to use it: he made his first film in Technicolor during this period, *Has Anybody Seen My Gal* (1951). Instead, these are comedies filled with shadows and shot in hues that are akin to film noir, which is arguably more appropriate to the oppressive circumstances in which the characters find themselves than any traditional notion of the comic.[5]

Tragedies routinely end in disaster, melodramas can go either way, but comedies conventionally arrive at happy endings. The ritual closures of romantic comedy perform several functions at once, simultaneously setting up marriages, integrating protagonists into the social order, and generally restoring a sense of balance to the universe (illusory or otherwise). Superficially, Sirk's comedies adhere to these conventions. But he always had his own ways of bending the rules and these films are no exception.

SLIGHTLY FRENCH (1949)

> "*Slightly French* is what the trade calls a program picture, which is another way of saying that if your expectations are not too great your disappointment won't be either."
> —T. M. P., *THE NEW YORK TIMES*, MAY 27, 1949

Underrated and misread by virtually everyone who's written about it, Sirk's playful but unsettling *Slightly French* is a remake of David Burton's *Let's Fall in Love* (1933), named after the famous Harold Arlen and Ted Koehler song that features in both films. A relatively straightforward romantic comedy, Burton's film stars Edmund Lowe, Ann Sothern, Miriam Jordan, and Gregory Ratoff (before he moved into a career behind the camera), and lists screenwriter and Tony Award-winning playwright Herbert Fields (*Du Barry Was a Lady*) as the author of the original story and the screenplay. Fields also receives a "story by" acknowledgment for *Slightly French*, which is written by Karen DeWolf (who worked on nine *Blondie* films for Columbia in the late 1930s and early '40s).

Populated by people who are forever putting on a show, both versions are Hollywood satires about Hollywood, making much of the behind-the-scenes wheeling-and-dealing and the ego-driven duplicities that underpin other films of their ilk (*A Star Is Born* in all its incarnations, *The Bad and the Beautiful*, *The Legend of Lylah Clare*, *The Player*, and so on).

But Sirk's has a much harder edge. Its director protagonist, John Gayle (Don Ameche), is full of bravado and bluster. In the opening, his on-set bullying is infuriating the star of his current project, Yvonne La Tour, also known as "the French fireball" (Adele Jergens). (In the original, played by the Romanian-born Tala Birell, she is Swedish.) When she collapses during the shoot of his very noirish-looking musical, Ten Days in Paris, the studio isn't happy and his future looks precarious.

Gayle's attempts to restore his reputation intersect with the plot's star-is-born trajectory as he sets out to persuade carnival dancer Mary O'Leary (Dorothy Lamour) (a) to replace Mademoiselle Fireball as the lead in his film, and (b) to assume the identity of French star Rochelle Olivia off-screen, for the benefit of the studio honchos and the press. Playing Henry Higgins to her Eliza Doolittle, he woos the working-class girl, who's gauchely mistaken his palatial mansion by the water for a hotel, with promises of "fame and fortune and your name in lights."

He is arguably the most dislikeable character ever to serve as a so-called romantic lead. To the accusation from his sister Louisa (Janis Carter) that he's unbearably self-centered, he replies, "Just tell me, whoever does think of anybody but himself?" When she later cautions Mary/Rochelle that "falling in love with him is like falling in love with a refrigerator or an adding machine," adding that both she and her brother are "incapable of love," her warning seems totally apposite. And when producer Doug (Willard Parker), apparently duped by Mary's disguise, begins to fall for her and she for him, Gayle isn't concerned about the emotions that have crept in. "Remember, you like him," he tells Mary/Rochelle, reminding her of the role she's playing. "Well, I *do*," she replies, confessing her feelings. To which he responds, "That doesn't matter. The important thing is that he *thinks* you do."

Slightly French is like a game of mirrors in which what is real and what is a performance become indistinguishable to the point where they're inseparable. When, in a private moment at a party, Mary finally explodes at Gayle's shallow charades, her reproaches born of her carnival background—"You're lower than a midget and colder than a snake-pit and your head is so big you couldn't get it in the lion's mouth"—she's dismayed to find an audience of tuxedo-clad men applauding her outburst as if it too is a performance.

And when, despite all the evidence indicating that she shouldn't believe a word Gayle says, she finally and inexplicably surrenders to his charms, their exchange happens on the set of the movie they're making with him directing her as if she's playing another scene in it.[6]

Gayle is so unpleasant for so long that when he has the change of heart required to navigate the film towards the conventional happy ending, it becomes impossible to believe (Lowe's transformation in the earlier version from cocky windbag to humble suitor is much smoother). The male lead of the romantic comedies of the era (and beyond) is conventionally a smooth-talking wolf who needs to be tamed, persuaded by the realization that the woman playing opposite him is the damsel of his dreams. He's perfectly embodied by the characters Cary Grant played in films such as *The Awful Truth* (1937) and *His Girl Friday* (1940); but even if Grant had been transplanted into *Slightly French*, it's still hard to see how it would have made Gayle any more sympathetic. Ameche was a convincing romantic lead elsewhere (*Midnight*, *Heaven Can Wait*), but Sirk makes him such a Satanic figure that his eventual conversion isn't likely to convince anyone.

It's as if *Slightly French*'s plot is moving in one direction while Sirk is skeptically guiding it in another that is entirely at odds with the spirit of the Hollywood romantic comedy in general (and *Let's Make Love* in particular). His strategically subversive approach is not just evident in the film's refusal of the genre's customary ordering of our sympathies, but also in the uncompromising depiction of the Hollywood that was to be Sirk's workplace for a further decade. Additionally, and just as important, the high-key lighting which characteristically thrusts away the possibility of darkness in most other films of the genre is here replaced by high-contrast lighting and shadow-fraught settings that work to disconcert rather than reassure.

In contrast, *Let's Make Love* is content to gently satirize the workings of the film business and to focus attention on the romance between director Max (Lowe) and ingenue Jean (the irresistible Sothern). Ratoff's performance as film producer Max is very funny, and the film's highlight is a winningly ridiculous party scene in which native Swedes assess whether or not she passes muster as "Sigrid Lund." But Sirk's film is having none of this, its sardonic edge designed to unsettle.

Intriguingly, as pointed out by indefatigable blogger Michael E. Grost, the structural similarities between *Slightly French* and Sirk's *Written on the Wind* (1956) are noteworthy.[7] What emerges from the comparison is a classic case of a story arriving at one kind of a denouement as a comedy and a very different one as a melodrama. Both films revolve around a wealthy brother and sister with serious emotional problems (Ameche and Carter here; Robert Stack and Dorothy Malone in *Written on the Wind*), a sympathetic working girl who falls for the brother (Lamour/Lauren Bacall), and a handsome nice guy who lends support to the brother, is in love with the working girl, and also involved with the sister (Parker/Rock Hudson).

Their interactions work out differently, determined as much by the internal operations of the genres that have brought them to life as by the dramatic directions launched by their particular circumstances. But it's also fascinating to contemplate what might have become of the characters in the two films had they been interchanged.

THE LADY PAYS OFF (1951)

> "I wanted there [to be a] contrast to all those silly women you see in pictures. Now this pre-dated women's lib. I wanted to draw a picture of a woman who is free to the extent that she wasn't even likeable . . . Unfortunately all this was tamed down by the studio—even before I started on the script."
> —DOUGLAS SIRK, 1977[8]

Sex roles are to the fore in this unsettling romantic comedy about an award-winning school teacher, Evelyn Walsh Warren (Linda Darnell), who wants to be seen as a woman, not just as someone whose skills have come to define her as "a mother away from home." Written by Frank Gill Jr. and the film's producer Albert J. Cohen—who also produced *Meet Me at the Fair* for Sirk in 1953, as well as *Never Say Goodbye* (1956), with which Sirk was also involved[9]—the film follows her quest to remedy the situation.

As in Sirk's other films with female protagonists, Evelyn's identity is shaped by social circumstances that define what it means to be a woman. She is a respected professional, but one whose perceived skills are deemed to be inseparable from the needs of the home. She is being lauded because she's good at playing mother when her students' real mothers aren't around.

She's uncomfortable with her place in the world, her exchange with the woman who gazes back at her from the mirror pointing to her confusion about who she is, how she should act, and what she should want from her life. The debate she conducts with herself lays the foundations for her subsequent actions and suggests a dark Other lurking somewhere inside her as she makes her way through the film's noirishly lit settings.

Her story begins as she's being celebrated at a luncheon award ceremony for her talent as "a teacher in the great tradition." Her employers at the Howell School for Girls in Pasadena are especially delighted that she's made the front cover of *Time* magazine, where she's been nominated as "the universal mother," and are happy to bathe in her reflected glory. However, she's distracted from the proceedings by her threadbare love life, which we know about because we're seeing her lackluster options through her eyes. She's hallucinating them in the food spread out in front of her, while the host (Paul McVey) prattles on about how wonderful she is.

With the roomful of enthusiastic guests ready to hang on her every word, he invites her to contribute "some little pearl of wisdom." "What do you think a woman today needs most in dealing with the problems of motherhood?" he asks. Her reply isn't what he'd been expecting. "A bottle of whiskey and a psychiatrist," she declares. Chaos breaks out in the room, and nothing that follows does anything to contradict her prescription.

Advised by the school dean (Katherine Warren) to take a holiday, she heads off to Reno, to "someplace where I can forget I'm a teacher," and ends up in a casino run by Matt Braddock (Stephen McNally). She drinks more than she can handle, loses $700 on the roulette wheel, naively believing that her chips had been worth one dollar each rather than $100, and insists that she has no intention of paying. Adopting her sternest stuffed-blouse manner, she announces, "I'm not the carousing type who frequents places like this. I'm a woman of some substance in my community, and eminently respectable."

She's also someone who needs to get down off her high horse, and Matt clearly believes that he's equipped to manage that maneuver for her. He has plenty of cards up his sleeve too, the first of which happens to be that issue of *Time*. He knows exactly who she is and tells her he's prepared to go public with her misdemeanors in the casino if she declines to help out his troubled nine-year-old daughter. "Find out what's wrong," he commands, "snap her out of it, and I tear up the IOU."

Reluctantly, Evelyn accepts the deal and agrees to spend the summer fulfilling her end of the bargain. Matt takes her to his plush beachside house in Carmel, where she meets Diane (Gigi Perreau, a winningly precocious child actor in the first of her four films with Sirk) and his earthy French housekeeper, Marie (Ann Codee), and maintains her standoffish manner. However, while she's initially horrible to the little girl, she eventually takes her under her wing, telling Matt that "there's nothing wrong with Diane that a mother's affection wouldn't cure." However, when he humiliates Evelyn by tricking her into thinking she has a choice about her end of the bargain, she plots her revenge.

She pretends to fall in love with him, planning to dump him once she's succeeded in winning him over. While the tone has been largely comic to this point—albeit with an edge—her ruthlessness in pursuing her ends sends it veering towards melodrama. After he sells off his business to spend his future with her and to provide Diane with the mother she's been lacking, Evelyn reveals all, pulls the rug from under his feet and leaves. Mission accomplished? Not quite.

What she hasn't been aware of is that there's another plan afoot, running counter to hers and hatched by young Diane with Marie as her co-conspirator. In an attempt to create a crisis that will return Evelyn to the fold and bring her and Matt back together, Diane goes missing. It's a cruel strategy that points to a lesson she'd learned long before Evelyn came into her life: how to arrange circumstances to get what she wants. The outcome is the surrogate wedding ceremony with which film ends. Matt's daughter serves as celebrant. "I now pronounce you mummy and daddy," she intones as she finally brings them together in a scene reminiscent of the closing one in Vincente Minnelli's *The Courtship of Eddie's Father* (1963).

For all intents and purposes, order has been achieved, along with the characters' ostensible goals. A couple has been formed and a family has been restored. Evelyn has found an eligible man, and pays attention when Matt tells her that she shouldn't be compartmentalizing her life, that she is a woman made up of many parts. He has given up his dubious profession as a casino owner: we've seen that the people he's been doing business with might easily have been extracted from a gangster movie and could be in the process of dragging him back into it with them. And Diane's troubles, all related to the empty space in her life, have been removed by Evelyn's decision to join the family.

Yet one doesn't have to look too closely to feel uneasy about all of this. Given the terms in which the future has been laid out, it's hard to see that what lies ahead for Evelyn is going to be especially liberating for the frustrated matron we'd encountered at the start. The notion that a woman is a person of many parts seems to be contradicted as she steps into the conventional roles of wife and stepmother, manipulated there primarily by the perceived needs of a little girl rather than by any choice, or force of romantic destiny. Matt has obviously fallen for her and has stepped out on a limb on her behalf, but, at least until Diane and Marie's intervention, she's also been willing to leave him stranded there.

All along the way, in the various wheelings and dealings that drive the narrative forward, all of the characters play dirty. "Never give a sucker an even break," says Matt early on after, in a feigned display of trust, he had pretended to burn Evelyn's IOU. Believing he had actually done that, she had headed for the door, only to be rudely returned to reality by his production of the still-intact IOU. It is this betrayal as much as anything else that motivates her to dig into her box of tricks to make him fall for her.

For her part in the proceedings, Diane is as wretchedly manipulative as anybody. The arrival of Kay Stoddard (Virginia Field), whom the little girl sees as Evelyn's rival for Matt, leads to a flurry of activity to push her out of the picture. This reaches its lowest point when, on a walk into the hills alongside the beach, the little girl sets the unfortunate woman on to the path of misery by deliberately piloting her into contact with a poison oak. As if to hammer home how badly Matt has been missing the point about his daughter's duplicity, he sympathetically says of poor Kay, as she lies in bed with painful rashes, that "she's just not the motherly type." It might be true, but her punishment by far outweighs her alleged crime.

The Lady Pays Off eventually arrives at what can only superficially be seen as a happy ending. Just as Sirk's melodramas frequently close by rubbing against the grain of audience expectations, pointing to what the characters have lost with the return of order to their lives rather than what they've gained from it, so do the comedies. Evelyn's "happy ending" finds her back where she began—playing mother—and the means by which she and Matt are transformed into a couple leave a very sour taste.

WEEK-END WITH FATHER (1951)

> BRAD (VAN HEFLIN): I'd like to come home at night and find a person I love waiting for me.
> HOUSEKEEPER (ELVIA ALLMAN): So would I and I've been married for twenty years.

Made back-to-back with *The Lady Pays Off* and written by Joseph Hoffman (who also wrote *No Room for the Groom* and *Has Anybody Seen My Gal*), George W. George, and George F. Slavin (who both also worked on *Mystery Submarine*), the witty *Week-End with Father* deals with a developing relationship between two widowed parents.

Like Evelyn and Matt in *The Lady Pays Off*, which is mainly set at his summer home by the sea, the characters here travel to a place far from the routine stresses that afflict their everyday lives. Except that, in both films, they're not really. A sense of dislocation follows both of them wherever they go.

New Yorkers Brad (Van Heflin) and Jean (Patricia Neal) meet at Grand Central Station as they're saying farewell to their children, who are going to summer camp in Maine. He has two girls, Anne (Gigi Perreau again) and Patty (Jeanine Perreau, Gigi's real-life sister); she has two boys, Gary (Jimmy Hunt) and David (Tommy Rettig). The other man in the story is camp counselor Don Adams (Richard Denning);[10] the other woman is TV star Phyllis Reynolds (Virginia Field again, in a role similar to the one she plays in *The Lady Pays Off*).

While Sirk's use of two shots binds Brad and Jean together visually, events in general and the couple's children seem committed to pushing them apart. And, as tensions arise, the camera repeatedly assumes low angles during indoor sequences to claustrophobic effect: the ceilings above the characters seem to be pressing down on them and the architecture around them acquires an almost threatening aspect.

Sexual and social stereotypes are again the focal point. During the opening sequence at Grand Central, Don reassures the concerned Jean that she shouldn't worry, that the camp is just what her sons need, that "it will make men out of them." And most of Brad and Jean's subsequent conversations with each other and others are peppered with references to the pressures on them about how they're supposed to behave as male and female parents and their fears of failing to live up to their responsibilities. It's as if they're enslaved by the expectations that have been imposed on them from without and that they have assimilated.

Bumbling Brad's timidity proves to be in sharp contrast to cocky Don's red-blooded ways when the two parents visit their offspring at the camp for "brother and sister day." "He's nothing to cry over," Gary tells his mother in order to comfort her during a moment of crisis in her relationship with Brad. "He can't follow a trail, can't fight, can't jump, can't run. He can't do anything. What good is he?" In their eyes, muscle-bound Don is much more worthy of their mother's attentions. He's a man's man, a collection of the kind of attributes that make a man a *real* man, one who, in Brad's words, "would make Tarzan look anemic."

On the other side of the gender equation, warm and caring Jean is the living antithesis of Phyllis's career-woman coldness. As poor, emasculated Brad points out to Phyllis late in the film (echoing the chief accusation made against Field's Kay Stoddard in *The Lady Pays Off*), "The problem is that you don't know how to be a mother. And I do." However, his daughters are impressed by "Auntie Phyllis" because she's a celebrity, and they do their darndest to ensure that she stays around, even after she's worn out her welcome with their father. They can't see her failings, or the unfairness of the social expectations oppressing her too, and, like Brad's sons, wield far too much influence on their parent's choice of partner.

Frequently in the melodramas, Sirk's children become warriors against the best interests of their parents (as in *There's Always Tomorrow* and *All That Heaven Allows*). They manipulate circumstances to achieve what they see as appropriate outcomes. And, more often than not, they become instruments of social oppression, acting on behalf of social mores that function as obstacles between their parents and the possibility of happiness.

Here, their eventual change of heart about their parents' potential partners doesn't affect their modus operandi, just the ends to which it is applied. Rather than leaving Brad and Jean to sort out their own lives, they continue to conspire to achieve their goals (not unlike Diane in *The Lady Pays Off*, even using a variation on that film's "lost child" ploy). And their motivations have less to do with what their parents might want than their belated realization of how they might themselves be inconvenienced by the partners they'd originally endorsed (like being compelled to eat health food rather than hamburgers).

One of the film's wryest touches is its depiction of parents rather than children as the ones in need of protection. Brad and Jean's offspring might officially be regarded as dependants, but they actually operate as an occupying force in their parents' lives, denying them their privacy (the interruption motif so central to Sirk's films is again prominent here), and plotting to undermine their relationship.

The pressures subverting the parents' attempts to find some physical and psychological space for themselves lend the film a constant sense of disquiet. The children are a key source of this, but they're not the only one. During the parents' visit to the camp, the two families all go riding together, their route to the top of a mountain and back guided by markers. While Brad boasts about his prowess at manly adventures like this, he's also well aware of the dangers: "I'd hate to think of where we'd wind up without those markers," he says.

The scene provides a handy metaphor for his situation in relation to the social rules that proscribe not just his but all of the characters' lives. And, in such a context, the chaos that ensues after David removes the markers indicates how reliant everyone is on guidelines to show them the way.

Essentially agreeing with Gary's criticism of his inadequacies, Brad comes to believe that he's a failure, that his inability to take charge of a situation—a horse-ride up the side of a mountain, a bag race, a relationship—are signs of his inadequacy as a male. His fears aren't dissimilar from those that afflict Stanley Banks (Spencer Tracy) in Vincente Minnelli's equally discomfiting family comedies, *Father of the Bride* (1950) and *Father's Little Dividend* (1951), both made around the same time.

Another unsettling force at work in the film is the undercutting of the customary happy ending which brings the couple together by way of validation of the lessons they've learned during their passage towards each other. Here, there's little sense that anyone has achieved any real understanding of anything. Brad and Jean drive off with the "Just Married" banner across the boot of their car, but the notion that he's become some kind of hero—by finding the boys who'd been "lost"—is an illusion. Furthermore, there's no suggestion that he or anyone else has really learned anything about themselves or each other during the course of the film.

NO ROOM FOR THE GROOM (1952)

> "I have just seen this film and I am surprised that it still holds up. It still seems sharp to me. It never becomes doctrinaire. It never preaches values. It is always dissolving itself into funny situations."
> —DOUGLAS SIRK, 1977[11]

Remarkably forthright and even Capra-like in its critique of capitalism's encroachment on traditional values, *No Room for the Groom* is both a tale about the trials facing returned servicemen and a canny variation on the romantic comedy of remarriage. Adapted by Joseph Hoffman (*Week-End with Father*) from novelist and former army intelligence officer Darwin L. Teilhet's 1945 book *My True Love*, the film begins with soldier-on-leave Alvah (Tony Curtis) and his sweetheart, Lee (Piper Laurie), as they arrive in Las Vegas at a wedding parlor that promises "Dignified Weddings" but delivers anything but. From the beginning—a shot of the couple behind a bus window, barely visible inside its glittering reflections of the City of Sin—they're at odds with their surroundings.

Subsequent events conspire to keep them apart. Alvah contracts chicken pox on their honeymoon night, before being shipped off to Korea for ten months. When he returns, he finds his home, a vineyard near small-town Suttersville, has been taken over by an occupation force made up of Lee's relatives. Their general is her mother, Mama Kingshead (Spring Byington), who doesn't approve of Alvah and has embarked on a campaign to have Lee marry her boss, cement magnate Herman Strouple (Don DeFore). Mama is accurately described by Bruce Babington and Peter William Evans in their commentary as "a monster of comic hypocrisy"[12] for the way in which she feigns ill-health in order to manipulate those around her to give her what she wants.

Making the situation even worse, Lee's reluctance to tell her that she's already married to Alvah means that he's cast as an unwelcome outsider

Alvah (Tony Curtis) and his sweetheart, Lee (Piper Laurie), lost amid the glittering reflections of the City of Sin in *No Room for the Groom*.

in his own home. He's compelled to share a bedroom with Donovan (Lee Aaker), a child who's so hyperactive that it would come as no surprise were it revealed that he was possessed by the devil. Every time Alvah and Lee try to find a private moment, let alone consummate their marriage, they're interrupted. And even after the truth is revealed, nothing changes as Mama tries to persuade her daughter to have the marriage annulled. *No Room for the Groom* might be a comedy, but it's undeniably tinged with horror.

When Alvah urges Lee to take a day off work to be with him, Mama sees it as an affront to the war effort and his duty to his country. "I'm beginning to think you should be investigated by a congressional committee," she accuses. Delivered by such an unsympathetic character, it's a line which, in 1952 at the height of the HUAC hearings, was clearly meant to provoke. And it appears to have been successful to the extent that, according to Stern, the FBI questioned Sirk "about morality in *No Room for the Groom*."[13]

With unfolding events acquiring a manic edge, and the indoor action frequently being shot from a low angle (as in *Week-End with Father*), Alvah and Lee appear to be trapped and powerless to do anything to sort out

Always somebody watching. Alvah (Tony Curtis) trying to make a point to Lee (Piper Laurie) with cement magnate Herman Strouple (Don DeFore) lurking, in *No Room for the Groom*.

the problems facing them. It becomes worse, especially for Alvah, when Strouple proposes a scheme to build a train line through his vineyard in order to speed up the transport side of his business. Lee not only supports her boss's offer of remuneration to Alvah, but even believes that it's a generous one.

Alvah's refusal is couched in terms that classify his stand as a defense of traditional values and an American dream that is in danger. "I love this town the way it used to be," he declares. And with a portrait of George Washington on the wall behind him, he goes on to describe the kind of mindset that has changed it. "Moral values, principles, sentiment," he says, "Chuck 'em all out for a quick buck." His passionate attack on "dollar and cent values" and on how "people have forgotten what it's like to be human beings" not only leads to Mama's "I knew he should be investigated," but is also very prescient.

In his discussion of the film, Alan Miller proposes that it "depicts wartime patriotism as it is imperceptibly demobilized into unreflective support for the most top-down, paternalistic version of capitalist progress," going on to describe the mob of relatives who occupy Alvah's home as "Tea Party invaders."[14]

For Stern, the film's critique of capitalism and the pursuit of progress at all costs is "shrill," and he notes his disappointment that "the film's characters and situations have little of the ambiguity or vulnerable charms that characterize even the worst of Sirk's people in the other comedies."[15] Such criticism need not be the only measure of the film's worth, but it is clear that a debate about America's future lies at its heart, and the characterizations certainly leave little room for doubt about where Sirk's sympathies lie.

Yet there is also much more that needs to be said about *No Room for the Groom*. It's a boldly paranoid comedy set in a time of paranoia, when any social criticism was deemed an act of disloyalty. Its style might be broad inasmuch as it operates as farce—a "savage farce," as Stern correctly notes[16]—but its methods are as subtle and quietly subversive as those of the other comedies. In the same way that Alvah and Lee are "unconsciously infected by the surroundings"[17] right from the start, so too are all the other characters. Just as Alvah and Lee are barely visible behind the reflected lights of Las Vegas in the opening shot, everyone in the film is enveloped by their milieu. "I don't blame you," Alvah tells his domestic oppressors. "If there's anything to blame, it's the times." And the times are embodied as concisely by the flashing Strouples Cement sign that looks down on Suttersville as they are by the neon hell of Las Vegas.

Like Sirk's other "uncomfortable comedies," *No Room for the Groom* conjures up a happy ending that is unlikely to convince anyone that all is well. After realizing that her boss has been using her to trick Alvah into allowing the vandalizing of his property, Lee seeks a reconciliation with her husband, who's abandoned all hope. Reworking an earlier scene in the film in which, with romancing her on his mind, he'd carefully arranged the décor in the apartment he'd borrowed from his wartime buddy (Jack Kelly), she makes her own adjustments to the apartment to woo him back. Life is very much a stage here as elsewhere in Sirk. Her stage-managing sets the scene for a conventional happy ending, but the Strouples Cement sign can still be seen through the window and no truce has been made with Lee's vindictive mother. The only thing that's changed is Lee's viewpoint.

Like Sirk's other comedies, *No Room for the Groom* is, in its own way, dissembling the happily-ever-after American dream that has the characters looking inward rather than turning their gaze on the rules by which the world around them operates.

CHAPTER FIVE

Sirk and God
"The Pure Ambiguity of Experience"

"The problems of religion have, in fact, always fascinated me,
even though I'm not a believer"
—DOUGLAS SIRK, 1967[1]

SIRK'S FILMS AREN'T CONCERNED WITH WHETHER OR NOT THERE IS A God. Rather, whenever the issue arises, as it does occasionally, the focus is on those who believe in some Higher Power or who don't. What matters is their humanity, or lack of it, and the existential crises they might face, whatever their beliefs.

However, men and women of the cloth generally receive respectful, sympathetic treatment. In *Boefje*, for example, a kindhearted pastor is the young protagonist's savior, his generosity and wisdom providing the boy with an escape route, "an emergency exit," which would otherwise remain unavailable. And the refuge turns out to be a Catholic haven for children who have strayed and whose only alternative is a less comfortable detention.

Sometimes, Sirk's viewpoint is less cut and dried. In *Hitler's Madman*, Lidice's parish priest represents the failure of the Catholic Church as an institution to recognize the danger posed by the Nazis. However, he eventually shows courage in the face of Reich Protector Heydrich's madness and, when he is shot in cold blood for his refusal to bow to the evil German's authority, his murder is presented as a genuine martyrdom. His death and the executions of Lidice's adult males in the village churchyard are depicted as a monstrous betrayal of humanity.

Set in a rural township in Tsarist Russia, *Summer Storm* is more quietly ambivalent about the role of religion. In a scene early in the film, the Russian Orthodox church serves as a communal gathering point, where the aristocracy rubs shoulders with the peasantry and where a beggar woman waits by the front door for offerings from the worshippers as they leave. Elsewhere in the region, though, Count Volsky's private chapel works differently, catering to a more select congregation: commoners Urbanin and Olga can be married there, but only at the count's pleasure, the same approval required for "the riff-raff" who are part of the wedding party.

The local priest (Gabriel Lenoff), who presides over both the church and the chapel, isn't a prominent presence in the film but appears to represent all equally. He delivers the last rites to Olga and seems to make no distinctions between the members of his congregation. But nor does he take a position about the ways in which the aristocracy automatically assumes its right to rule, despite the social changes occurring all around.

Although *A Scandal in Paris*'s ironic tone hardly invites such a judgement, the same could be said of the parish priest based at the church that features in the film's rural setting, not far from Paris. His main role appears to be the planning of the St. George and the dragon mural which is to adorn the church's exterior. But he also acts as chief confidant for Therese, the film's lead female character. And the film presents her as a kindly aristocrat more interested in understanding what makes people tick than in exploiting anybody.

Will Hall—Sterling Hayden's widowed lumberjack-preacher in *Take Me to Town*—is a very different kind of cleric. The film is set in the Old West, and its tone is amiable, content to invite a wry smile. So, immediately following Will's two-fisted riposte to a parishioner who has insulted the woman of the world who has become his housekeeper, Sirk appears to be amused by rather than judgmental of his subsequent move to the pulpit immediately afterwards to offer a rationale for his actions. And even if Will's mostly conservative congregation doesn't fully approve of his Old Testament ways, they show no inclination to oppose them.

The division of roles underpinning Will's place in his community becomes much edgier with Sirk's depiction of the Reverend/Colonel Dean Hess (Rock Hudson) in *Battle Hymn*. An air force officer and a "man of God," he is seeking redemption after the accidental bombing of an orphanage during World War II.

And, while acknowledging their all-too-human flaws, Sirk presents the priests in *The First Legion* and the nuns in *Thunder on the Hill* as men and women trying to do the right thing, even if their reach exceeds their grasp. The magisterial Pope Leo in *Sign of the Pagan* is another matter.

In Sirk's films, a belief in a Higher Power can provide a source of awe and inspiration for his characters (as in *Magnificent Obsession*), or a rationale for righteousness (as it does for the puritanical townsfolk in *The Girl from the Marsh Croft* and the tight-lipped section of Will's followers in *Take Me to Town*). Or it can create a fragile refuge against the possibility that human existence has no meaning beyond itself.

That possibility becomes a point of discussion in *A Time To Love and A Time To Die*. The film's foot-soldier protagonist, Ernst Graeber (John Gavin), is a believer who finds himself unable to understand how a Higher Power could sit by while the world destroys itself. He and Professor Pohlmann (Erich Maria Remarque), who effectively becomes his mentor, debate the issue, Pohlmann serving the same narrative function here as the priest in *A Scandal in Paris*, albeit in a far more probing way.

Surrounded by the rubble of their former lives, Graeber questions the professor's continued belief in God: "How can anyone believe in God with all that's happening here?" The professor replies, "God is not responsible to us. We are responsible to God for all that's happening here," underscoring both his way of maintaining hope—his belief in the existence of a God—and the film's primary thematic concern: that mankind has created its own destiny and that the forces which obstruct the possibilities of happiness are all-too-human. Pohlmann points out to Ernst that all must decide for themselves what is right and what is wrong.

Without ever offering any endorsement of what the characters in the three main films under discussion in this chapter believe, Sirk's attention is on where their beliefs lead them, the courage they show, and the attributes that make them human as they try to decide what is right and what is wrong.

THE FIRST LEGION (1951)

> "Technically, the picture was interesting to me because of its being completely away from the studio. Where and how you shoot a film is a technical matter, but it is also something wider than that: it is integral to its whole conception; it gives an unmistakable character to the picture."
>
> —DOUGLAS SIRK, 1970[2]

Sirk's first film after returning to the US following his brief postwar visit to Germany, *The First Legion* finds him working under much more amenable circumstances than he'd experienced at Columbia. This time, he acquired control over the project, an independent production on which he was officially credited as co-producer alongside Rudolph S. Joseph, a German Jew who'd originally fled Germany in 1933 and with whom he'd previously worked harmoniously on *Hitler's Madman* and *Summer Storm*. According to Sirk, lead actor Charles Boyer was originally planning to produce the film himself, but, after viewing *Summer Storm* and *Lured*, placed his trust in the director.[3]

The source is a play of the same name by Emmet Lavery[4] which was first performed on Broadway at the Forty-sixth Street Theatre (now the Richard Rodgers Theater) on October 1, 1934. A powerful portrait of a community of Jesuits at St. Gregory's Novitiate "in a small town somewhere in the United States—or for that matter in any country,"[5] it leaves one with the impression that it has been very much written from the inside. Offering a sympathetic account of the ways in which the men's faith gives them a reason for living, the story pivots on two miracles that occur within the walls of the seminary and deals with their ramifications for the occupants. One of the miracles is seemingly a hoax; the other is apparently for real.

For Lavery, a practicing Catholic, the setting is essentially a nurturing one. Tensions might arise there between the conservatively inclined Jesuits and the more liberal thinking ones, and self-doubts might regularly surface. But the solidity of the location and the rituals conducted within its walls provide a safe harbor from the world beyond and a secure vantage point on it.

The play's title and the dialogue—much of it reproduced in the film—insist on an analogy between the Jesuits and a military unit.[6] The disaffected Father Fulton explains that he joined the Order in the first place "like some men beg to be in the front line trenches."[7] A wavering Fr. Rawleigh (whose Christian name is, pointedly, Thomas), declares that "it's pretty lonely being a soldier of God all the time."[8] And, skeptical about what others regard as a miracle, the play's central character, former lawyer Father Ahern, described in the play's script as "the romantic intellectual of the Society,"[9] vents his despair at what he sees as his colleagues' betrayal of reason: "We are only a regiment of straw men marching out to a sham battle," he tells the rector.[10]

But, however else they regard themselves, the Jesuits share a sense of the Order to which they've given their service as a family and of the novitiate as a home away from home. They might criticize each other, express doubts about belonging, and debate the ways in which they go about engaging with the world, but the seminary is place from which they begin their mission and against which they measure themselves. And the sense that it embodies a force bigger than all of them is rendered in the play's deployment of a simple décor and in its use of the "Te Deum" hymn and other music of worship as a force of unification. As the stage directions for the close of Act I have it, "Against the chant of the happy voices in the 'Te Deum,' (the broad sweeping chords of the 'exaltation' motif of a Beethoven symphony) grow with majestic beauty and dignity. They soar quickly to a mighty peak and as the curtain comes down the candles burning so brightly beneath the portrait of St. Ignatius make of the piano a veritable altar."[11]

Sirk's film more or less adheres to the general thrust of the play, pursuing the same plot trajectory and, with one minor variation, assembling the same group of characters. The chief difference is that, unlike the play, but without ever sacrificing any sympathy for the characters, it creates the impression that it has been directed from the outside.

In Sirk's hands, as elsewhere in his work, the way the settings are deployed becomes the key. In contrast to the play's depiction of St. Gregory's as a supportive environment, the film presents it as more like a Gothic prison than a haven. Insistently shot from low angles, the novitiate's roofs, arches, and pillars seem to weigh down on the characters, while statues constantly intrude upon the spaces they occupy, and stained-glass windows and portraits of saints hover almost menacingly over them. Whenever the priests move back and forth along the corridors and up and down the staircases, the setting even comes to seem maze-like. And, as John Belton observes in his brief but seminal commentary on the film's visual style, it's generally as if Sirk is "trapping them in the clutter of objects or obscuring them in slabs of darkness."[12]

And the soundtrack of chorales and regularly chiming church bells—what, in another context, might be taken as a form of celebration—only adds to the sense of the characters being dwarfed by the circumstances in which they find themselves. They are there by choice, but that only makes them seem even more helpless in their entrapment.

One could draw a direct line between Sirk's depiction of the characters' surroundings here and the point of view he brought to the domestic settings in his subsequent work, most notably *All I Desire* and *There's Always Tomorrow*. The parameters of the inhabitants' existence are mapped out by their physical surroundings, the settings and decor not only giving a specific shape to their lives but enclosing them in the values that they embody. All shot in black-and-white (by different cinematographers), these films are filled with the chiaroscuro lighting and the shadowy spaces that one is accustomed to finding in conventional films noir of the time.

And, even if Sirk's work contains few of the other elements that one has come to expect from the genre, the tension that emanates from his approach is palpable.

In such a context, the Jesuits' pursuit of their faith becomes a matter of considerable urgency, a way of bringing order to an otherwise meaningless existence. So, when it appears that a miracle has occurred, they regard it as an act of God designed to reassure them of their vocation. The bedridden Fr. Jose Sierra (H. B. Warner) has suddenly arisen, declaring that he'd done so on the instructions of "the Blessed Joseph," the founder of the seminary whose statue stands in the hall outside Fr. Sierra's room.

Only Fr. Arnoux (Boyer), "Marc" to his friends—his surname changed from the play's "Ahern" in order to accommodate the actor's Frenchness—remains skeptical, pondering alternative explanations. All around him is rejoicing, everyone unaware of the role that Dr. Peter Morell (Lyle Bettger), an agnostic, has played in this miracle. "I felt at the start it was a nervous condition," he eventually confesses to Fr. Arnoux. "I gave him an injection and his imagination did the rest." There's no mention of an injection in the play, which thus casts a greater degree of ambiguity over the source of the ailing priest's recovery than is present in the film.

Dr. Morell goes on to explain that he saw the deception as a chance to have some fun at the Jesuits' expense, not realizing the consequences it might have. Sirk's focus here is on those consequences, for the Jesuits and for the general public that gathers outside the novitiate after the news breaks. Lavery's play includes some of these details, but they're much more strongly felt in the film.

For some, it provides a marketing tool for the Order and a means of achieving beatification for "the Blessed Joseph"; for others, it serves as a personal message, an indication that God must be watching over their every move; for the newspapers, it opens the door on a series of sensationalist headlines. "What does it all mean?" asks Fr. Fulton (Wesley Addy). "Why should a miracle happen to Fr. Sierra just as I was getting ready to leave?" Terry (Barbara Rush), the young crippled woman who is a friend of Dr. Morell's, arrives in the hope of a cure and the belief that "it just stands to reason that there must be something somewhere that holds the world together."

Observing the people flocking to the gates of St. Gregory's, some simply to be near an act of God, others to hawk their wares, Morell is abrasively contemptuous. Describing them to Terry as "a bunch of sensation seekers chasing a fire engine," he explains that "you find them everywhere: floods, tornadoes, murder trials."[13] Nowhere does he acknowledge that they're also good for his business, but it's not by chance that Sirk shows them queuing at his door. He also includes a scene, not in the play, where a "pilgrim" whose son has just died (Dorothy Adams) expresses her fury at what she sees as a betrayal by all involved.

Both the play and the film offer a final twist, a second miracle for which neither offers any rational explanation: it is, literally, a *deus ex machina*. In the play, Morell's nephew, Jimmy, who has been suffering from anterior poliomyelitis since he was five, arrives in the hope of a cure. He plays no part in the film; Terry is his replacement. Her spinal cord had been completely broken but, like him, she rises from her wheelchair and takes a few tentative steps.

For both play and film, there's no question that a miracle has occurred this time and it points to the limits of human understanding, suggesting that there are forces at work that lie beyond human comprehension. For Lavery, who also wrote the screenplay for the film, it is unquestionably an act of God. The stage directions make this clear: "The sunlight is strong on the boy who is looking up with eyes shining; the doctor is sitting with bowed head at side of child and Father Ahern looks up into the sunlight as a man will when he meets his Maker or as Thomas must have looked up to the Lord. A wind rustles through the room and you feel definitely that Something has brushed your shoulders."[14]

For Sirk, however, the turn of events is more about how little humanity is able to grasp of the complexities of its existence. Or, as Belton puts it, "Sirk gives no clear answers; he merely celebrates the pure ambiguity of experience."[15] For the characters, there is no doubt. While Morell looks on in disbelief and wonder at the foot of the altar in St. Gregory's chapel, Terry says, "God doesn't forget us," and Fr. Arnoux, cradling her in his arms, agrees: "No, he doesn't." And then, again, looking up, with the chords introducing the "Te Deum" chorale on the soundtrack, he reaffirms his faith: "He doesn't."

Both endings are equally moving, even uplifting, but for different reasons. For the play, it's a celebration of a communion with God; for the film, it's both an embrace of the characters' yearnings and a reminder of their all-too-human limitations. The fact that their doubts have been removed means nothing more than that their doubts have been removed.

Intriguingly, Sirk's declared intentions aren't exactly at odds with this reading, but they add another layer to it. "What I was trying to do," he tells Halliday, "was push [the film] definitely towards comedy. There is a miracle that is not a miracle, but because of it a lot of things happen to this little monastery, and then God says, 'Now I'll send them a real miracle.'

It is as if God is stepping forward saying, 'It seems there has been a false miracle around here, a thing which can make no one very happy, but by God there shall be a real one. I'll show you,' and he rolls up his sleeves."[16]

THUNDER ON THE HILL (1951)

> "I wanted this picture to have *nothing* to do with religion."
> —DOUGLAS SIRK, 1970[17]

Based on *Bonaventure*, a play by British writer Charlotte Hastings which was first performed in London's West End in 1949,[18] *Thunder on the Hill* was the second film Sirk made after signing with Universal. He told Jon Halliday that the studio "didn't interfere with either my camerawork or my cutting," although he noted that his producer on the project, Michael Kraike, "was an ex-writer [who] fiddled around with the whole thing."[19] But while he might have regarded the film as compromised, he was still able to bend it to his concerns.

Officially adapted for the screen by Oscar Saul (who went on to contribute to *A Streetcar Named Desire*, *The Joker Is Wild*, and *Major Dundee*) and Andrew Solt (*Little Women*, *Whirlpool*, and *In a Lonely Place*), working independently of each other, it appears every bit like a companion piece to *The First Legion*. Instead of a Jesuit novitiate in the suburb of Lakeside in New York State, the setting is the convent hospital of Our Lady of Rheims, near Norwich in East Anglia. Like the battalion of priests in St. Gregory's, the community of nuns here is bound together by a shared belief in a higher order and a sense of belonging.

Both films also scrutinize the idea of faith and feature conflicted protagonists: in *The First Legion*, it's Fr. Arnoux (Boyer), a wise, scholarly humanitarian; here, it's Sr. Mary Bonaventure (Claudette Colbert), a force for good who finds herself torn between what she describes as her "deepest conviction" and her vow of obedience to the requirements of the Order to which she belongs.

The settings also have much in common: cavernous Gothic spaces linked by wide bluestone staircases, corridors, and other passageways, with large crosses and other religious statues and portraits at every turn, an environment that presses in on the characters as if framing their lives. The photographs of the somber stage sets that precede the text of the play correspond to the asceticism of the locations used in the film.

Another key character in the films is a visiting doctor whose secret agenda creates a crisis. In *The First Legion*, it's the non-believing Dr. Morell (Bettger), who fabricates the miracle that becomes a point of contention between Fr. Arnoux and his fellow Jesuits. Here, it's Dr. Edward Jeffreys (Robert Douglas), who, prior to the film's beginning, has framed a young woman, Valerie Carns (Anne Blyth), for the murder of her brother. In an echo of the central situation in *Sleep My Love*, he is also sedating his wife, Isabel (Anne Crawford), believing that will ensure her silence about her affair with the dead man by making her think that she is losing her sanity.

The credits at the start of *Thunder on the Hill* unfold over nighttime shots of a group of travelers struggling along a muddy road with rain pouring and lightning flashing. On foot or in bullock-drawn wagons, they are, as soon becomes clear, refugees from the local villages making their way to Our Lady of Rheims. The caption immediately after the credits even lends a biblical note to the scene: "Norfolk County, England. When the floods came."

Whereas Hastings's play features only two settings—the Great Hall and Sr. Mary's room "in the hospital section of the convent"—Sirk's film "opens out" the action, introducing a wider range of spaces both within the convent and beyond. These additional settings allow the inclusion of individuals who don't appear in the play without them seeming out of place. For example, two new characters are introduced as part of the opening sequence, both of them in a car also on its way to the convent: one is the doctor's wife, the other is Abel Harmer (John Abbott). A chemist carrying supplies for the nursing staff at Our Lady of Rheims, he was also—it's later revealed—a key witness for the prosecution in the case against Valerie.

She arrives on the scene soon afterwards. En route to the gallows in Norwich, she is accompanied by two officers of the law (Gavin Muir and Norma Varden). They all find themselves stranded at the convent when contact with the city is cut off by the floods. Initially, Blyth plays her as a young woman constantly on the edge of hysteria, loudly asserting her guilt and refusing any gestures of comfort from the sisters of mercy. When one of the locals sheltering from the storm refers to her as "the Devil's daughter," she seems to readily fit the bill. The play (which names her "Sarat Carn") presents her as withdrawn but with an aura of warmth and calm that places her at odds with the situation in which she finds herself.

In both film and play, Sr. Mary is immediately drawn to her, believing in her innocence. However, Blyth plays her in a way that makes the nun's certainty about this appear to be a very large leap of faith. The actress's uncomfortable performance—or perhaps it's her character's "performance"—has a jarring effect, although Sirk's purpose is clear: to ensure that Sr. Mary's assessment of Valerie runs contrary to external appearances. In the play, however, there's little room to doubt Sr. Mary's judgment: like her, we "just know" that the condemned woman is innocent.

Sr. Mary's only real support comes from the amiable Sr. Josephine (Connie Gilchrist), who is as much a wise observer of events as a participant. Ever the practical one—"Never burn a newspaper or throw away a piece of string," she advises anyone who cares to listen—she is able to assist Sr. Mary's investigation of Valerie's case with key press reports about the trial. It's almost as if she's playing Watson to Sr. Mary's Holmes.

In fact, the plots of both film and play have much in common with the strand of detective fiction known as "locked-room mysteries," which is probably best illustrated by Agatha Christie's writings. And they both maintain the same trajectory—towards Valerie's/Sarat's exoneration—even if they follow very different routes to this destination. The film's alterations to various details along the way aren't of any special significance, although they do, for example, provide Dr. Jeffreys with an alternative motive for his crimes and engineer circumstances to bring Valerie's fiance (Phillip Friend) to her side at the convent. He's mentioned in the play but never appears on stage.

For Sirk, what matters in *Thunder on the Hill*—as in *The First Legion* (and elsewhere, from *The Girl from the Marsh Croft* on)—is the nature of belief. Unlike the play, which deals with Sr. Mary's doubts but ends up reconfirming her faith, the film takes no position on this one way or the other. Sirk no more endorses her view of a Higher Order than he does anyone else's. Like all of the other characters in the film, she believes what she believes.

Among the villagers who've come to the convent for sanctuary is a woman about to give birth (Queenie Leonard). On hearing of Valerie's arrival there on the same evening, an old woman (Tempe Pigott) is just as committed in her view of the consequences for the newborn as Sr. Mary is that it is "God's will" that has stranded Valerie at Our Lady of Rheims. "The murder woman will put the mark of Cain upon the child," she opines. Neither the old woman nor the sentiments she expresses appear in the play.

Sr. Mary's beliefs are challenged in various ways during the course of the film. As hospital matron, she is determined to ensure that things are done "the right way," and has very clear views of what that is. But the starchy Nurse Phillips (Phyllis Stanley) resents the nun's bossiness.

"The right way?" she exclaims. "You mean *your* way! . . . It would do your soul good to be wrong once in a while." The tensions between the two women are an undercurrent in the play, but this exchange has been added by the filmmakers.

Towards the latter part of *Thunder on the Hill* (in a scene which also has its equivalent in the play), the convent's mother superior (Gladys Cooper) appears to endorse Nurse Phillips's criticism when she challenges what she sees as "the stubborn fanatic manner" in which Sr. Mary clings to her belief in Valerie's innocence. But while she's right about Sr. Mary's single-minded determination—what Sr. Mary describes as her "absolute conviction"—she's wrong about Valerie. And *her* hubris leads her towards disaster when she not only forbids Sr. Mary from any further involvement with Valerie—"No more playing Scotland Yard," she declares—but also burns a crucial piece of evidence that could have led to a retrial.

Later in the film, in an exchange which does not appear in the play, the chemist Harmer makes a similar miscalculation when Sr. Mary calls into question his testimony at Valerie's trial. Against his assertion of his professional acumen—"I never make mistakes"—she summons concrete evidence to show him that he's wrong. The point here is not that Harmer should be condemned for his certainties any more than Sr. Mary should be for hers; instead, the message is that fallibility is an all-too-human failing, afflicting everyone.

Again, as in *The First Legion*, Sirk allows for no clear answers. Like Fr. Arnoux, Sr. Mary deserves admiration for her human qualities—for her generosity of spirit, her attempts to help those in need, and her righteousness. But, as the closing sequence makes clear,[20] while this might be a ringing endorsement of her virtues as a human being, it has nothing to do with her faith, with her belief that "God's will" underlies everything that happens.

Sr. Mary believes that her prayers have been answered when Valerie is shown to be innocent. The mother superior admits her errors to Sr. Mary: "You've shown great ingenuity and courage," she tells her. "I'm sorry to have made things so difficult for you." Humbly, Sr. Mary transfers the credit to Sr. Josephine, whose collection of newspapers made it possible for her to conduct her investigation in the first place and who had insisted that she read an item that turned out to be crucial. For her part, Sr. Josephine indicates that she'd only done so because she'd seen Valerie praying to God for help.

Despite the mother superior's "Deo gratias," the film leaves it entirely open as to whether or not this should be taken as a case of "God's will" making its presence felt, or simply as a series of human exchanges in which people have helped each other.

SIGN OF THE PAGAN (1954)

> "I was required to shoot so that the film would fit both the new Cinema-Scope screen and the old-size screen. You had one camera, and one lens, but you had to stage it so that it would fit both screens . . . I wasn't happy."
> —DOUGLAS SIRK, 1970[21]

Around the turn of the twenty-first century, four big-name directors—Martin Scorsese, Ridley Scott, Baz Luhrmann, and Oliver Stone—were working separately on plans for (very) big-budget epics about Alexander III of Macedonia, generally known as Alexander the Great. Several studios and producers—20th Century Fox, Universal, Warner Bros., DreamWorks, Dino and Martha De Laurentiis among them—flirted with the idea before, wary of the dangers of the competition, leaving the field open for Stone. The result was, alas, Stone's *Alexander* (2004), budgeted at around $155 million and starring Colin Farrell.

Fifty years earlier, Universal found itself in competition over films about Attila the Hun with an Italy-France co-production overseen by producers and erstwhile rivals Carlo Ponti and Dino De Laurentiis. Both were dealing with Attila's assault in 450 AD on the Roman Empire, but there were, apparently, few concerns about the co-existence of two productions on the same subject. Perhaps the fact that both were being made on relatively small budgets helped.[22]

Universal had a screenplay by Oscar Brodney (who also worked with Sirk on *Take Me to Town* and *Captain Lightfoot*); Ponti and De Laurentiis had a script by Ennio De Concini (who went on to work on Antonioni's *Il Grido* and King Vidor's *War and Peace*), Richard C. Sarafian (almost twenty years before he directed his reputation-making *Vanishing Point*), and Primo Zelio, with Pietro Francisci (*The Queen of Sheba* and, later, three Hercules films) as director.

Sirk had earlier proposed a plan to adapt Marlowe's *Tamburlaine* to Universal without luck—"[T]hey wanted something less colossal, less frightening and with more religion in it"[23]—and then found himself assigned to *Sign of the Pagan* just before it went into production. He'd been working on the *Tamburlaine* idea with the English playwright turned

Hollywood screenwriter Barre Lyndon (*The Greatest Show on Earth, The War of the Worlds*), whom he brought with him to work on this project.

After the already-cast Jeff Chandler indicated that he was only prepared to play the "good guy," Roman centurion Marcian,[24] he chose Jack Palance for Attila and the charismatic actor blasts everyone else off the screen. Nowhere else has the contrast between the bland, decent man and the tortured outsider in Sirk's work been as evident as it is here. Anthony Quinn took the title role in *Attila*.

Production work began on *Sign of the Pagan* soon after *Magnificent Obsession* was completed, and the shoot began a couple of months later than the Italian rendition of the story. Both films were relatively early entries in the then-emerging series of sword-and-sandal epics (known in Italy as "pepla"), but it would have been no loss to cinema history if neither had been made. Sirk rightly described *Sign of the Pagan* as "one of my worst" to Jon Halliday,[25] and it is rarely mentioned elsewhere. In Michael Stern's book, its existence is only acknowledged in the filmography, although it did well enough at the box office, returning $2.5 million. For its part, *Attila* won an international audience and received a splash release in the US and $2 million at the box office there, although the newspaper reviews were generally dismissive.[26]

More than sixty years on, it's difficult to see why Sirk might have agreed to take on *Sign of the Pagan*. There are strong signs of budgetary and other difficulties. While the film was shot by Russell Metty—in Technicolor and CinemaScope—and its interiors are filled with period decor that intrudes on the characters' freedom of movement, the exteriors have the kind of studio-bound artifice that dogged many low-budget Westerns. There's even a campfire scene that has one expecting a couple of gunslingers or cowpokes to ride in from off-screen at any moment. To make matters even worse, some of the dialogue is risibly explicatory and much of the action is clumsily staged.

Sign of the Pagan clearly threw out a challenge to Sirk's declared love for the battle with uninviting material. This was a project he was unable to bend to his will. However, it does hold a particular interest for the ways in which it sets the forces of Christianity embodied in the Roman Empire against the heathen Attila's quest.

The film begins with a collage of the rampaging Hun and his men going about their bloody business while a voice-over narration (by actor Rex Reason, who'd had a supporting role in *Taza, Son of Cochise*) usefully explains that the Roman Empire is split in two between the rival capitals of Rome and Constantinople (now Turkey) and that "like a plague from

Pope Leo (Moroni Olsen) arriving "in a cloud of misty white" in *Sign of the Pagan*.

the North, a fierce race of Mongol horsemen . . . led by the most ruthless conqueror of all times . . . [is] spreading fear and bloodshed under the pagan sign."

The remainder of the film moves back and forth between the progress towards Rome of Attila's army and events unfolding in Constantinople, which is governed by the duplicitous Emperor Theodosius (George Dolenz, father of Monkee Mickey), who has formed an unholy alliance with the Huns. Treachery abounds there: Theodosius is preparing to turn his back on Rome; his sister, the princess Pulcheria (famed prima ballerina Ludmilla Tcherina), and General Paulinus, the leader of his army (Jeff Morrow), are ready to do what's required to ensure that the city remains loyal to Rome; and Attila, who arrives in Constantinople as if he owns the place, is planning to betray the emperor as soon as his usefulness expires. The noble centurion Marcian, an envoy from Rome, escapes from Attila in the opening sequence and joins forces there with the princess and the general.

While essentially telling the same story, *Attila* comes at it from a slightly different angle. Marcian is effectively replaced by Etius (Henri Vidal), a Roman general (in both films, the character earning Attila's admiration for his courage); the internal politics of Constantinople is replaced by the internal politics of Rome, giving us the contemptible weakling of Valentinian, emperor of Rome (Claude Laydu), instead of thoroughly disreputable Theodisius; and Pulcheria is replaced by the eminently dishonorable Honoria (Sophia Loren, soon to be married to producer Ponti), who foolishly sells her soul to the devil by delivering herself into the hands of Attila.

Attila gives priority to the political ramifications of the conflicts, especially the one between Rome and the Huns. A key scene has Attila and

The shadow of the sword used to stab him forming a cross beside the body of Attila (Jack Palance) at the end of *Sign of the Pagan*.

Etius debating the merits of the Empire: for the Roman, it stands for "law and order, freedom and justice"; for Attila, it represents "corruption, intrigues, slavery." What ensues forcefully suggests that Attila has a point, even if our sympathies lie elsewhere.

However, Sirk's telling of the story hones in on the way that the forces of both Christianity *and* Attila ascribe to systems of belief attached to the supernatural. The latter might not believe in God, but he recognizes—like the priests in *The First Legion* and the nuns in *Thunder on the Hill*—that there are forces at work in the universe way beyond his knowledge. Throughout the film, he is emotionally, if not always strategically, dependent on his seers' advice about what lies ahead for him.

When Marcian tries to warn him that Rome should be off-limits, that it has already been conquered "by Christians who carry a cross" and is now beyond reach "because man can never conquer God," he scoffs. But when the portents begin to augur ill for him, he becomes increasingly fearful. Although he doesn't immediately acknowledge it, the beginning of the end takes place when he raises his sword in a declaration of war only to have a bolt of lightning strike dead one of his prophets. At this point, he sees God as a powerful enemy—"I have no wish to anger God," he tells his followers—but he's not yet ready to abandon his mission.

This professed non-believer turns out to be very much a believer, fleeing the sight of a cross raised in "the temple of Christians," haunted by a childhood memory of an old slave woman's vision of him as a dying man with the shadow of a cross falling alongside him, and increasingly paranoid about what his future holds. His Persian astrologer (Eduard Franz) warns him to stay away from Rome, but he presses on until yet another prophecy becomes a reality.

In the film's most striking scene—presenting the same events that actually bring *Attila* to a close—a man dressed all in white and carrying a staff, Pope Leo (Moroni Olsen), arrives at Attila's camp on a boat "in a cloud of misty white," fulfilling an earlier prophecy and accompanied by a Frank Skinner-Hans J. Salter score reminiscent of the one that Skinner wrote for *Magnificent Obsession*. Describing himself as "the servant of the servants of God," Leo declares that his fate is in the hands of God and departs, leaving Attila to descend into madness.[27]

When he dies, with the shadow of the sword that had been used to stab him forming a cross beside his body, the scene is akin to the one in *The First Legion* in which the second miracle occurs. Just as Boyer's Father Arnoux cradles Terry in his arms after witnessing the miracle, so too does the astrologer hold Attila's lifeless body. To borrow Belton's phrase again: there is no confirmation that anyone's belief here is right, just an acknowledgment of "the pure ambiguity of experience." This is in sharp contrast to the ending of *Attila* in which, atop a hill, the Hun brandishes his sword before riding away as a giant white cross is superimposed on the scene. Here, God has indeed made His (or indeed Her) presence felt.

CHAPTER SIX

Pastoral Yearnings
Sirk and the Musical

> "The musical is essentially a genre that concerns itself with the romantic/rogue imagination and its daily battle with a restraining, 'realistic,' social order."
> —MARTIN SUTTON[1]

ON THE ONE HAND, THERE IS THE DOUGLAS SIRK WHOM FIFTY YEARS of film commentary has cast as the supreme master of the ironic melodrama. On the other, there is the Sirk who, after directing an operetta and three music-infused melodramas in Germany, made a trio of smart, knowing musicals during the early 1950s. He used to call them "half musicals,"[2] although their tone and style suggest they deserve full membership in the club.

All feature titles referencing songs and were made over a period of thirteen months, between October 1951, when shooting began on *Has Anybody Seen My Gal*, and November 1952, when production was completed on *Take Me to Town*. (*No Room for the Groom* was also made during this period, immediately after *Has Anybody Seen My Gal*.) And, at the same time as they maintain Sirk's general concerns and his critical embrace of American culture, they also exude an infectious sense of fun that isn't customarily associated with his work in the US.

Part of that fun is the playful knowingness that Sirk brings to them, consistent with the ironic distance that underpins the melodramas but also of a different order. It's as if he's taken on these musicals with a bemused smile rather than a troubled frown, allowing their characters room to move amidst the constraints that shape their lives.

Made in bright storybook colors, rather than the often noirish black-and-white shadings of the "uncomfortable comedies," they strategically evoke a make-believe world. Part of Sirk's wider plan for "a group of stories about small-town life,"[3] they were all set in the past. And their warm Technicolor palette affectionately evokes a fairy tale dimension in sharp contrast to the ambiguity-laden imagery of his melodramas and comedies.

Offering barely a glimpse of any disruptive darkness, the films are lyrical in style, with their vitality and visual flair and the winning charm of the performances taking priority over all else. Their worlds are made up of pretty Technicolor towns populated by people who officially ascribe to the American way and espouse the values of home, hearth, and free enterprise. The film's critiques of how these values can go wrong are gentle, their resolutions reassuring if not exactly comprehensive. Villains appear—greedy malcontents, corrupt town officials, puritans, anyone who believes that the money they've acquired or the beliefs they hold makes them better than their fellow citizens—but they're swept aside by happy endings, either repenting their ways or being forced to face public humiliation.

These musicals have been surprisingly undervalued by chroniclers of the genre. In their simultaneous seriousness of purpose and lightness of touch, they are to the rest of Sirk's work what Shakespeare's festive comedies are to his dramas. Informed by an appreciation of the fact that music changes everything and that it speaks a language of the emotions, they provide an abundance of pleasures. And they're made up of musical numbers that liberate the participants from their everyday lives and provide them with the opportunity to rejoice in the simple fact of their existence. Or that simply serve as a celebration of companionship: the singing and dancing at the soda joint near the start of *Has Anybody Seen My Gal*; the "Oh! Susanna" duet which opens *Meet Me at the Fair*; the first saloon number in *Take Me to Town*.[4]

The protagonists in these films are outsiders, individuals who don't play by everybody else's rules. In *Has Anybody Seen My Gal*, Samuel Fulton (Charles Coburn) might be a millionaire, but when he assumes the identity of John Smith and takes a trip to his home town of Hilverton, his eccentricities and apparent social transgressions set him apart from the locals. Home for *Meet Me at the Fair*'s "Doc" Tilbee and Enoch Jones (Dan Dailey and Scatman Crothers) is the medicine wagon that transports them from town to town, so they don't really belong anywhere. And when, in *Take Me to Town*, saloon singer Vermillion O'Toole (Ann Sheridan) attempts to assume the role of housewife and stepmother on the outskirts of a Western town, most of the God-fearing folk there greet her with resentment and distrust.

The films' visual style is consistent with the approach taken in Sirk's other work, inasmuch as it creates a tension between images in which the characters are framed by their surroundings (such as doorways, windows, and hallways) and "free" shots, in which they appear unencumbered by the settings. The overall effect is to suggest that, while their lives are, to an extent, preordained by their social situations, they are also able to exercise a certain freedom of choice.

The pervasive air of theatricality that is intrinsic to the musical also sits perfectly with Sirk's customary mise-en-scene, both in the ways in which his characters are forever putting on a show—performing on-stage, or adopting airs and pretending to be other than they are in their everyday lives—and in the fact that they're rarely alone: almost always, someone is watching, either from the wings or from the point of view of an audience.

Finally, the idea of family is central to all three films, an idealized state for which all of the characters yearn. But whereas that is generally depicted as an illusion in Sirk's other films, overridden by ambiguities, all three musicals end with a family or its equivalent happily united after the threats to it have been overcome.

HAS ANYBODY SEEN MY GAL (1952)

> "As to who will prove to be the wisest handler of the hundred thousand, and thus my eventual heir, I haven't the least idea . . . Time will tell . . ."
> —MULTIMILLIONAIRE STANLEY G. FULTON PONDERING WHAT MONEY MIGHT DO TO PEOPLE IN ELEANOR H. PORTER'S *OH, MONEY! MONEY!*[5]

The first of Sirk's Hollywood musicals and his first film in color is based on the 1918 novel *Oh, Money! Money!* by Eleanor H. Porter, who is best known as the creator of the *Pollyanna* series and as the author of its first two books (there were fourteen). Adapted by Joseph Hoffman, who also worked with the director on *Week-End with Father* and *No Room for the Groom*, it retains the broad narrative arc of its pedestrian source but very much goes its own way.

In Porter's novel, fifty-something multimillionaire Stanley G. Fulton bestows a gift of $100,000 on three cousins he's never met by way of testing their suitability as heirs.[6] In order to keep an eye on their progress, he assumes the name of John Smith and makes an extended visit to Hillerton, the small town where they live (in the film, it's Hilverton;

go figure). Once installed there, he has to watch in dismay as their lives gradually fall apart, with the money they've received exacerbating their worst tendencies. On the positive side, he falls in love.

In the film, the grandfatherly Fulton (Charles Coburn, who was seventy-five at the time) becomes the benefactor of the Blaisdell family, the one that might have been his had things turned out differently with the now-deceased Millicent, the love of his life. "Turned me down for a bookkeeper," he sadly tells his lawyer (Frank Ferguson), "a man earning $30 a week." Money and class mattered to Fulton back then, and still do.

So he returns to Hilverton incognito and moves in as a boarder with Millicent's snooty-nosed daughter, Harriet (Lynn Bari), and her family: pharmacist husband Charles (Larry Gates), who runs a soda fountain (in the novel, his equivalent is a grocer); amiable but pretentious son Howard (William Reynolds, who plays Jane Wyman's uptight offspring in *All That Heaven Allows*); vivacious daughter Millie (Piper Laurie, Tony Curtis's wife in *No Room for the Groom*); and her kid sister, Roberta (once again, Gigi Perreau, this time playing a sweetheart).

Fulton's money provides Harriet with the means to climb the social ladder to the rung where she believes she belongs, and she's determined to drag her family along, regardless of what they might want. As a mother, she has much in common with Spring Byington's monster matriarch in *No Room for the Groom*, her social aspirations and domineering ways becoming a destructive force within the family, especially when combined with the opportunities provided by Fulton's gift.

The family moves to a home more indicative of its "proper place in society"; visitors are greeted at the door by a butler (Ray Flynn); husband Charles gives up the business he loves to better maintain the façade of a man of means; son Howard falls in with the wrong crowd; Roberta watches helplessly as the beloved family mutt is replaced by two French poodles. "But I don't *speak* French," she protests.

Even worse, Harriet manages to manipulate Millie away from her engagement to handsome soda jerk Dan (Rock Hudson), who works at her father's store, and towards the son of a more socially suitable family (Skip Homeier), who says groovy period things like, "Hot diggity, Millie. You're the cat's meow." As literate and eloquent as he was, Sirk must have struggled with the finely wrought nuances of lines like this.

However, while money might serve as a catalyst for plot development here, as it does in the book, it's clear from the start that neither its presence nor its absence is responsible for the characters' dissatisfactions. What makes Sirk's musical different from its source is its inflection of the situation to highlight the characters' lack of understanding of their circumstances: they might believe themselves to be free, making independent decisions, but they're actually subservient to forces they can neither see nor understand.

This applies to everyone, including Dan, who sees himself through the same distorted filter as Harriet, believing he's a lesser person because he's not rich like his rival for Millie. Fulton, our ingratiating guide to the unfolding story whose way with a one-liner keeps him at a distance from his hosts, is also largely unaware of the motives for his generosity.

Longing for what has been lost to him, longing to be ordinary (to be John Smith), he has returned to Hilverton in what eventually becomes an attempt to engineer the happy ending that had been blocked by past choices. By playing Cupid for Dan and Millie (whom Roberta tells us looks like her grandmother), he creates a poignant echo of what happened between him and Millicent years earlier, when she had to choose between the humble bookkeeper and the man whom everybody knew was on his way to becoming a millionaire. This time, however, he's endorsing the equivalent to his rival from years before.

Elements like these are the stuff of a Sirk melodrama, in which the characters' lack of self-knowledge is evoked in the way they're constantly acting out parts, their existence a constant roundabout of role-playing. But in this film, Sirk cuts his characters some slack and the possibilities inherent in the genre in which he's working allow them a reprieve. Borrowing the title of the 1920s song "Has Anybody Seen My Gal?,"[7] the film not only embraces the performative aspects required for its musical numbers but also the transformative potential they offer.

When Fulton/Smith first visits the soda joint, he encounters a teenage chorus line exuberantly immersed in the title song. He's not yet ready for such communal frivolity, but he eventually takes a job there[8] and even comes to enjoy a Charleston kick-step or two. When Dan and Millie are about to go for a drive in his dashing green convertible, the tune being played by an organ grinder (Gino Corrado) for a group of kids in the park—"Gimme a Little Kiss (Will Ya, Huh?)"—infuses her with the spirit of serenade.

When Fulton/Smith and Roberta happen upon Harriet doing her household chores and singing along to the record she's put on a turntable, "When the Red, Red Robin Comes Bob, Bob, Bobbin' Along," they see a different person from the stressed, anxious social climber of her other exchanges, and they even sing along with her. When circumstances conspire to put Fulton/Smith in jail, he becomes somebody else too: known by his

"Gimme a Little Kiss (Will Ya, Huh?)" Millie (Piper Laurie) encourages Dan (Rock Hudson) to join in the fun in *Has Anybody Seen My Gal*.

fellow inmates as "Johnny," he discovers a genuine sense of camaraderie with them via a rousing verse of "It Ain't Gonna Rain No Mo'."

Here, performance can lead to liberation, excavating previously stifled instincts, something that never happens in a Sirk melodrama. And in his musicals (as elsewhere in the genre), characters are largely defined by their attitude to music: Millie's piano occupies pride of place in the Blaisdells' living area; humorless Howard complains about her playing; anxious Charles cautions Roberta, "No singing at the table"; the new Scrooge-like owner of the soda fountain complains to the organ grinder outside in the snow, "Do you have to make so much noise playing 'Silent Night'?" And when Harriet throws parties in the Blaisdells' new home, they're like lavishly costumed musical numbers in comparison to the preferred blue-collar ones that prevail elsewhere.

Furthermore, spontaneity, the heart and soul of the musical world in general ("Shpontanuity, always shpontanuity!"), represents a positive force here too, incarnated in Roberta's instinctive rejection of her mother's pretensions as well as in the way characters take to song to give voice to their inner lives. And when they put on a show, the outcomes are usually positive—as they are conventionally in musicals—rather than self-deceiving, as they are so often in Sirk's melodramas. Harriet's transformation at the end, as the family gathers to express relief that their problems are behind them, that the money was a distraction they hadn't needed, might not be entirely convincing. But her inclination to sing and her readiness to join in the closing family celebration to the strains of "Auld Lang Syne" suggests that all is not lost.

MEET ME AT THE FAIR (1953)

> "Dan Dailey was good. He even, I thought, had some elements of Sanders' way of acting in his performance: cool, a little cynical, selling his medicines which at the same time caused diarrhoea; he maintained a nice and merry pace."
> —DOUGLAS SIRK, 1970[9]

Set at the turn of the twentieth century and taking its title from a song written for the film by Milton Rosen (music) and Frederick Herbert (lyrics), *Meet Me at the Fair* is based on *The Great Companions*, an enjoyably folksy yarn by Gene Markey which was published as a "complete-in-one-issue novel" in the *Ladies' Home Journal* in 1951.[10] The adaptation is by Martin Berkeley, a journeyman screenwriter best known as HUAC's "number-one friendly witness who provided the committee with the most names, names that were later authenticated by the investigative panel and other witnesses."[11] And novelist Irving Wallace (the author of the books upon which films such as *The Chapman Report*, *The Prize*, and *The Man* were based) did revisions of Berkeley's screenplay.

Like *Has Anybody Seen My Gal*, *Meet Me at the Fair* maintains the overall direction of its source. Traveling around the countryside in their wagon, "Doc" Tilbee (Dailey, on loan to Universal from 20th Century Fox) and his loyal assistant, Enoch Jones (Crothers), make their living hawking the Doc's "Wonder Tonic." In the novel, Doc describes their vehicle as "part-bus and part-opera house." Their lives are changed when they pick up young Tad Bayliss (Chet Allen), an orphan who has escaped from the Dickensian Springville Detention Home. While Markey overtly links Enoch's insistence that they take Tad with them to his empathy for runaway slaves, the film doesn't raise it as a motive.

With the authorities in pursuit, the trio makes its way across country with the boy discovering the delights and the dangers of life on the road. At first, their nemesis is idealistic State Orphanage Board member

Zerelda Wing (Diana Lynn, in a role for which Ann Blyth was originally announced), the fiancée of spineless District Attorney Chilton Corr (Hugh O'Brian). But, from the moment she first sees Doc strutting his stuff, her engagement is clearly destined for disaster, even if it takes her a while to acknowledge her feelings for Doc.

At this point, Corr takes control of the campaign against him. In the novel, his vendetta is all personal, but in the film, he's in the pay of crooked politician Pete McCoy (Rhys Williams), who is preparing for an election and has been embezzling funds intended for the orphanage.

All of the film's characters are linked by their associations with make-believe, pretense and putting on a show. They're Doc's stock-in-trade as he makes his pitch to those who gather by the wagon's makeshift stage, as well as his way of relating to people in general. Tad is captivated by the yarns his newfound friend spins about his colorful past, fanciful imagination-stretches that are celebrated in the trio's irresistibly bouncy three-way song "I Was There."

> DOC: "I used to cook for King Richard the Third."
> ENOCH: "And for his son, July the Fourth."
> ALL THREE: "Anyplace, anywhere, when it happened, I was there . . ."[12]

Part of the pleasure of the number comes from Tad and Enoch's shared appreciation that, while Doc's exuberant storytelling is hardly believable, his blarney is precious. Pretense need not always be deceptions of the kind perpetrated by McCoy and Corr.

In *Meet Me at the Fair*, people are forever disguising themselves and/or their motives, sometimes for good, sometimes for evil, sometimes just because it's fun. In order to hide from the authorities, Tad dresses up as a girl and becomes Millicent. In order to retrieve him, Corr employs an old couple to pretend to be prospective adoptive parents. Showbiz people put on costumes—and, in one case, blackface for a rendition of "Won't You Come Home, Bill Bailey?"[13]—and perform for audiences' enjoyment. And, in the second half of the film, the action moves to Capital City, where the entire town seems to be in performance mode: an Election Jamboree is in progress, brass bands parade in the street, crowds wave flags, and audiences flock to sideshows.

As in *Has Anybody Seen My Gal*, Sirk's deployment of the conventions of the musical allows his characters—or at least those of them who sing and dance or take pleasure in the art of performance—to transcend the limitations of their world. While Doc is revealed as a man of culture

"Anyplace, anywhere, when it happened, I was there . . ." "Doc" (Dan Dailey), runaway orphan Tad (Chet Allen), and accompanist Enoch (composer Crothers) are caught up in the spirit of the song in *Meet Me at the Fair*.

(his asides taking in Thomas Hood, Gray's "Elegy," Brigham Young, and Oscar Wilde), his and the film's chief reference point is Shakespeare, in particular *As You Like It*.

A scene drawn from Markey's story places Zerelda by herself in Doc's wagon. She looks at his books, selects the play from the shelf (in Markey's version, it's Walt Whitman's *Song of the Open Road*), and reads a marked passage. Shakespeare's Phebe is reflecting on her feelings for the character whom she believes to be the handsome Ganymede, but who is actually Rosalind in disguise.

> Think not I love him, though I ask for him.
> 'Tis but a peevish boy. Yet he talks well.
> But what care I for words? Yet words do well
> When he that speaks them pleases those that hear . . .

Like Zerelda, Phebe is sought by another man (Silvius), but drawn to an individual whose true identity is much harder to pin down. The quoted passage applies to Doc as well as to Ganymede/Rosalind, and links Zerelda and Phebe's state of mind, both caught up in a whirlwind of attraction and resistance to the object of their desire.

Just as disguises and characters putting on shows playfully drive Shakespeare's plot, so do they underpin *Meet Me at the Fair*. Furthermore, as the happy ending approaches, Doc woos Zerelda by spinning a yarn about the time that he assumed the role of another Shakespeare character and played his own variation on the balcony scene in *Romeo and Juliet*. It's also not stretching a point too far to suggest that his meditation on the stage near the end about what has preceded echoes Rosalind's at the end of *As You Like It*.

Sirk's knowing celebration of theatre and film as positive forces is clear in the scene where the villains are forced to answer for their crimes with the governor (George Spaulding) in attendance. The setting is the Wonderland Café and Museum, where vaudeville rubs shoulders with "the newest thing in the entertainment field: the moving picture." On stage, a barbershop quartet, the Kansas City 4, is singing "Sweet Genevieve," while color slides of a courting couple boating on a river are projected on to a primitive screen alongside them.

Suddenly, the romantic flow is interrupted by shots of the Springville Detention Home, noting the misappropriation of funds that were supposed to have been directed to it. "Who's responsible for this?" shouts Corr, rushing from his seat. "I am," says Doc, stepping forward from the singers and removing his large-moustache disguise.

Thus, theatre and film become weapons in the battle against the villains, exposing their misdeeds. As Michael Stern observes in his book on Sirk, the auditorium is suddenly transformed into a courtroom, and the sequence usefully illustrates Sirk's appreciation of the power of popular cinema to make political points, "the social message being 'snuck in' as the audience is held captive by the cinematic entertainment."[14]

As in *Has Anybody Seen My Gal*, the forces responsible for the disharmonies in the film's world remain in place: the governor's expression of horror at the crimes that have been committed on his watch doesn't erase the lingering concern that he too is simply putting on a show for public consumption. But the happy ending that is generally anathema to Sirk and constantly undermined elsewhere in his work here overrides the doubts.

The title of *As You Like It* is like a playwright's knowing wink to an audience—"This is designed with *you* in mind!"—and one of its characters speaks directly to that audience when he says, "We begin these rites / As we do trust they'll end, in true delights." *Meet Me at the Fair* goes exactly the same way.

TAKE ME TO TOWN (1953)

> "This is early America, and therefore it is almost a fairy tale.
> The women of the establishment are the evil queens, and the hero,
> he is completely stalwart. A preacher!"
> —DOUGLAS SIRK, 1978[15]

Marking Ross Hunter's debut as a producer, Sirk's final musical is officially based on a "story and screenplay" by playwright Richard Morris (*Thoroughly Modern Millie*), with uncredited contributions by Oscar Brodney (who also worked with Sirk on *Captain Lightfoot* and *Sign of the Pagan*) and Lou Breslow.[16] However, there's little indication that Morris's story, entitled *Flame of the Timberline*,[17] was ever much more than a plot on a page.

Whatever form it took, that plot is an uncomplicated one. Unjustly accused of a crime, saloon singer Mae Madison (Sheridan), also known as Vermillion O'Toole, escapes the law, embodied by Marshal Ed Dagget (Larry Gates, from *Has Anybody Seen My Gal*), flees the unwanted attentions of her partner-in-crime (Phillip Reed), and makes her way to the small Western town of Timberline where she falls in love with the local hunk, towering Will Hall (Sterling Hayden), a widowed lumberjack and father of three who also serves as the town's preacher on his day of rest.

As the witty song behind the opening credits informs us, *Take Me to Town* is "the tale of Vermillion O'Toole."[18] And Sirk's film is one of the few Westerns that feature a female protagonist, made even rarer by the fact that, unlike her screen peers, who include Calamity Jane, Annie Oakley, Belle Starr, and Hannie Caulder, she doesn't wear a gun. She might have been born ordinary, as Mae Madison, but she's now a showgirl through and through. She knows her way around a number or two and her life is an ongoing performance.

The dictionary might define vermillion as "a brilliant scarlet red," but she sees it, more provocatively, as "just one step hotter than a redhead." And her outgoing ways and bright outfits testify to her difference from the somber demeanors and staid dress of the puritanical Timberline townsfolk. Her presence especially upsets Mrs. Edna Stoffer (Phyllis Stanley), a widderwoman who has Will in her sights and, in conversation with the town gossips, huffily dismisses Vermillion as "that creature." Lumberjack Chuck (Robert Anderson) is similarly judgmental, describing her as "the Devil wrapped in a maiden's form."

Lumberjack Will (Sterling Hayden) and showgirl Vermillion (Ann Sheridan) joining forces in *Take Me to Town*.

On the other hand, after they see her singing "I'm a flamin' redhead" from their backstage vantage point at the local opry house,[19] Will's stable of kids—Corney (Lee Aaker, who was the devil-child in *No Room for the Groom*), Petey (Harvey Grant, also in *Magnificent Obsession*), and Bucket (Dusty Henley)—regard Vermillion differently. They ask her if she'd like to be their Mom.[20] Like the children in the other Sirk musicals—Roberta in *Has Anybody Seen My Gal* or Tad in *Meet Me at the Fair*—but distinctly *unlike* children in the rest of Sirk's work, Will's offspring are creatures of instinct, innocents who see to the heart of the matter in ways that the adults around them can't.

To avoid the long arm of the law, Vermillion agrees to take on the job of "housekeeper" and look after the kids while Will is away at work. The role fits her like a glove—her Mae Madison persona re-emerging?—and she finds herself right at home. The kids are happy, she's happy, and only Will needs to be persuaded. To their insistence that he likes her, she asks disbelievingly, "How do you know?" To which, by way of reply, Corney, the eldest, summons irrefutable proof: "The way he looked at your meat pie."

Sirk's summoning of the iconography of the Western is also a knowing one which transforms the setting into the equivalent of an outdoor stage: the opening shot of the train chuffing across a barren landscape; the small town where locations and characters have double functions (the general store that is also a post office, the "opera house" that is actually a saloon/brothel, the fighting man of the West who is also the town preacher); a place where an often-oppressive civilization collides with what Sirk has called "the American ideal of the simple, outdoor life."[21]

The point is mirrored in the use of the forested location where Will delivers a sermon about how one must defend love "not by words alone, but by all the strength that God has given us." This comes immediately after, and by way of offering an amusing justification for, his brawling with Chuck, who has insulted Vermillion. The same open-air setting later becomes an impromptu theatre of a different kind, providing the stage for the "melodrama in three scenes" that Vermillion directs to raise funds for the building of the church. The play is intercut with the adventure scenario that draws the film to a benign close. It also neatly intersects with it, as the play's piano score and sound effects simultaneously (and comically) serve the action both on- and off-stage.

As in Sirk's other musicals, the characters are more or less "free to recreate their lives," as Stern observes in his commentary on *Take Me to Town*.[22] Whereas in his other work, innocence is an illusion, communities are divided, and entrapment is everywhere, here those elements are present but shaded differently. The plot permits the characters to come together, free of the ironies that fracture their unions elsewhere. The happy ending that is cast as an "emergency exit" in the melodramas and the uncomfortable comedies here becomes possible. Critic Michael Walker perceptively notes that *Take Me Town* and *All I Desire*, which was made immediately afterwards, are "essentially the comedy version and the melodrama version of the same structure."[23]

According to Ross Hunter, Sirk argued vehemently against the happy ending in the screenplay, but eventually surrendered to it.[24] His memory of their exchanges may or may not be accurate—if ever two people were on different wavelengths, Hunter and Sirk were—but *Take Me to Town*'s ending is unequivocally a happy one.

Along the way, though, the director manages to have some reflexive fun with stories whose endings adhere religiously to the happily-ever-after principle. Vermillion takes to reading fairy tales to Will's children at bedtime, and, when she gets to the inevitable "and they lived happily ever after," young Petey asks, "What's ever after?" He's a kid of very few words, so the ones he uses matter.

Sirk's deployment of what is effectively the central theme of the Hollywood musical, the way singing and dancing draws people together, merges here with a key preoccupation of the Western, the building of communities in the wilderness. And it's through Vermillion that we come to see *Take Me to Town*'s community, for all its flaws, as a positive thing. Along with the ballad-like song that evokes a mythology around her, the film casts her as a vibrant life force, celebrates her powers and rewards her with the kind of happiness achieved by few Sirk characters.

CHAPTER SEVEN

Hollywood, Rock Hudson, and the Idea of the Hero

"In all my films, you have a sense of the vanishing hero."
—DOUGLAS SIRK, 1979[1]

MOST OF THE WRITING ABOUT SIRK—IN BOOKS, MAGAZINE ARTICLES, and scholarly essays—has bypassed any close examination of his adventure films. But to ignore them is to take a blinkered view of his career. Indeed, it wasn't only in the melodramas on which his critical reputation largely rests that one could see him testing his creativity against the well-known constraints suffered by all who toiled inside the studio system during the 1950s.

Like his better-known work, these lesser-known films point to his love affair with American populist art, which he took very seriously. In his later years, looking back over his time in Hollywood, he would talk repeatedly about how much he enjoyed the challenge of working there. The obstacles he faced might have been "ridiculous" (his word), but they became catalysts for his creative juices. "You have to bend your material to your style and purpose," he said. "And, when somebody tells you that you can't do something, then you have to find another way of doing it. And you usually do it better as a result."

In part, these films went missing in earlier critical overviews of Sirk's work simply because they were so difficult to track down. Perhaps because of this, they were presumed not to be worth pursuing. But they are crucial to any examination of Sirk as an auteur, their flaws frequently as illuminating about his working methods and his circumstances in Hollywood as are the films upon which his standing rests.[2]

In all three of these adventure films, it's possible to identify Sirk's attempts to bring material into line with the vision that informs his best films, working against the grain of the generic conventions they deploy, casting shadows in places that elsewhere might be filled with light, introducing ambiguities where others would find clear moral purpose.

They all deal with real-life characters and draw, albeit loosely, on historical events. *Taza, Son of Cochise*, written by George Zuckerman (who later collaborated with Sirk on both *Written on the Wind* and *The Tarnished Angels*) and adapted by Gerald Drayson Adams from his own story, is a Western about the struggles of a chief of the Chiricahua Apache tribes on behalf of his people.

Captain Lightfoot, based on the exploits of two actual nineteenth-century highwaymen and perhaps the most successful of the trio, is adapted from a 1954 novel by W. R. Burnett, who also co-wrote the screenplay with Oscar Brodney (who'd worked with Sirk the year before on *Sign of the Pagan*). A rollicking yarn set in Ireland with some light comic flavoring, it's about an aspiring highwayman trying to walk in the footsteps of his hero.

Battle Hymn, a psychological drama set during wartime, tells the story of Colonel Dean Hess, an Ohio minister who flew with the United States Air Force in the Korean War during the early 1950s. Although it shares its title with Hess's autobiography, which was published at the same time as the film was released,[3] it is not an adaptation. Instead, it's based on an original screenplay by Charles Grayson (*The Barbarian and the Geisha*, *The Woman on Pier 13*) and Vincent B. Evans, a real-life bombardier on the Memphis Belle during World War II whose only other screen credit was for *Chain Lightning* (1950).

While the three films offered Sirk the chance to work on location, which he loved to do—he said that the main reason he agreed to direct *Captain Lightfoot* was that it gave him and Hilde a chance to visit Ireland for the first time—they were all plagued with production problems. *Taza* was shot entirely on location in Utah, during an oppressive summer, with a cast that included "real Indians," as he told Jon Halliday, "ones who hadn't been spoilt by Ford," most of whom he could communicate with only through an interpreter.[4] Universal also decreed that it should be made in 3-D, "which was no help to me."[5] *Captain Lightfoot* was shot during the summer of 1954 but almost entirely in drizzle, with all the attendant problems, even if it ended up looking splendid.

For *Battle Hymn*, Arizona played Korea reasonably effectively, although Sirk remained unhappy with the finished film for a variety of reasons. As he told Halliday,[6] he found Hess's constant presence on the set inhibiting, broke his (own) leg during the shoot, was subsequently confined to a wheelchair, had to deal with studio intrusiveness—such as its addition of the opening statement on behalf of the US Air Force, made direct to camera by General Earl Partridge[7]—and blamed himself for what he saw as the miscasting of Rock Hudson. While the actor's presence as an immovable force lends weight elsewhere, Sirk believed that it was ill-suited to the kind of "split character" that he wanted here. "An actor like (Robert) Stack would have been much more fitting," he said.

All of this is exacerbated by how Sirk appears to be uncomfortable filming action sequences and not the least bit interested in fleshing out the excitement. In *Taza*, in particular, perhaps as a consequence of the language barrier, his extras often stand around in the background looking lost, frequently fixed in place in a way that suggest figures posing for portraits, given nothing more to do than occupy space in the frame.

That said, though, these films are important additions to the Sirk oeuvre, each in its own ways. What appears to have caught his interest in them are the political and/or personal tensions that drive their stories. All are about men who find themselves in positions of leadership in times of turmoil, characters whom one might conventionally regard as heroes. Yet Chief Taza, Captain Lightfoot, and Colonel Hess remain divided, pushed this way and that by their circumstances, declaring their certainty about what they're doing and why they're doing it, and yet somehow blind to the realities around them. There are no conventional heroes (or heroines) in Sirk's work, just individuals stumbling around in the dark searching for some light.

The films' protagonists are each played in a straight-down-the-line way by Rock Hudson, a young actor under contract to Universal who first worked with Sirk as a relative unknown on *Has Anybody Seen My Gal* (1952). But, by the time of *Battle Hymn* four years later (the same year he made *Giant*), he had become a star. It has often been said, by Sirk and others, that he provided a solid, reliable presence—tall and handsome, with a resonant voice and a commanding disposition—but wasn't good in parts requiring characters to be divided.

"I was very fond of him," Sirk said of Hudson in the 1970s. "He was a lovely young man and very eager to learn. And the camera loved him. But I could never make a split character out of him. Certainly not like I was able to with Robert Stack in *Written on the Wind* and *Tarnished Angels*." *Battle Hymn* suffers in part because of this. However, it also needs to be said that, in addition to the gentle but powerful authority Hudson brings to the men he plays in these three films, his performances also lend them a distinct and very human vulnerability.

TAZA, SON OF COCHISE (1953)

> "The tragedy in the figure of Taza, son of Cochise, the great Indian revolutionary, lies in the dilemma he faced: to end the revolution in order to ensure the survival of his race."
> —DOUGLAS SIRK, 1973[8]

Taza is the final installment of an unofficial Cochise trilogy, whose parts are bound together by the casting of Jeff Chandler as the legendary Apache chief in all of them and by a sequence of historical events which occurred over a period of eight years. Jay Silverheels plays the film's chief antagonist, Geronimo, in the first two films, to be replaced by Ian MacDonald in the third. The trilogy was made out of order, but in terms of the chronology of the events depicted, *The Battle of Apache Pass* (George Sherman, 1952) comes first, set in 1862 (and also written by Gerald Drayson Adams), followed by *Broken Arrow* (Delmer Daves, 1950), set in 1870, and then Sirk's film, set four years later.

All three follow more or less the same narrative trajectory that was a regular feature of the Western.[9] Excepting those films where all Native Americans are presented unambiguously as the Enemy, whooping wildly as they swoop on wagon trains or massacre innocent settlers, a clear opposition was established between good Indians and bad Indians, defining those co-operating with the "white eyes" as good and those refusing to as bad. It's a dichotomy in clear evidence here.

A further opposition is frequently created in the genre between a hawk-like cavalry martinet committed to oppressing Native Americans and a lesser officer more sympathetic to the Indians' situation (classically in *Fort Apache*), a tension which is generally accompanied by a blood-brother kind of relationship between the officer and a good Indian. This too is present here.

A key issue in the trilogy, first for Cochise, and then for Taza, is to decide whether Apaches should maintain control over Apache affairs or pass all legal responsibility for them over to the whites. Alongside this is the depiction of the mismanagement of the situation by the US authorities, also a recurring feature of many Westerns.

In the first two films in the trilogy, Cochise is befriended by a sympathetic white man—an honorable cavalry officer, Major Jim Colton (John Lund), in Sherman's film; an army scout with clout, Tom Jeffords (James Stewart), in Daves's—and persuaded that it would be best for his people if he sought a peaceful rapprochement with the white forces. In *Taza*, Cochise dies soon after the start and his son replaces him as the chief of the Chiricahua Apache, but the story arc remains the same, with the well-meaning white man being inhabited by another cavalry officer—this time, Captain Burnett (Gregg Palmer).

In all three of the films, rebellious Apaches and xenophobic whites become obstacles to peace: cavalry officers rigidly citing orders from Washington as their guide; racist settlers summoning God as theirs. But Geronimo is presented the key stumbling block, a leader who refuses to make peace with those he regards as oppressive forces of occupation and vows to drive them out.

Each of the films depicts him as the chief villain. The poster line for *Taza*, in fact, declares of its protagonist, "He led the Apache nation against Geronimo's pillaging hordes." And when Taza (Hudson) is made chief, an army scout's assessment of him—"He's got it in him to be a greater chief than Cochise or a worse devil than Geronimo"—appears to speak for the film.

Despite this, in their sympathetic presentation of peace-loving Indians, the three films can reasonably be described as "liberal Westerns" for their time.[10] But, equally, they're also fundamentally conservative in their depiction of Geronimo as an unapologetic warmonger and his refusal to compromise with an enemy that has taken his land in the name of "manifest destiny" as a moral flaw.

What distinguishes *Taza* from its predecessors is the way it places its title character at the center of the action, shifting the focus away from the white blood brother. It's unlikely that the films were made with this in mind—except, perhaps, in the case of *Taza*—but there appears to be a logical progression in their structure that steers the Indian protagonist more and more into the foreground.

The narrative problems requiring resolution in *The Battle of Apache Pass* and *Broken Arrow* all relate to the whites sorting out their differences with the Indians, with Major Colton and Tom Jeffords, respectively, in the driver's seat. Captain Burnett is a key figure in *Taza*, but, whereas Cochise

Taza, Son of Cochise. "He is my most symbolic in-between man," Sirk said of Taza (Rock Hudson), a status signaled by the outfits he wears.

is a significant but secondary character in the earlier pair of films, here Taza's struggle is central as he finds himself caught between his desire to maintain peace and the need to assert his people's rights in his negotiations with the whites.

Although considerable weight is given to the increasingly isolated position in which Cochise finds himself in *Broken Arrow*, it's a struggle that's more fully fleshed out in *Taza* than in the earlier films. To start with, Geronimo is shown to be speaking for others intimately acquainted with Taza as well as himself and this lends the new chief's quandary a potent emotional dimension.

After the leadership is thrust on him and he accepts the terms of the peace brokered by his father, others in the tribe—his brother, Naiche (Rex Reason, under the pseudonym of Bart Roberts); Grey Eagle (Morris Ankrum), the father of the woman he loves, Oona (Barbara Rush); and Geronimo—regard Taza as a traitor to the Apache cause. They are discredited by the film, but the personal consequences of their hostility towards Taza leave him especially torn.

"He is my most symbolic in-between man," Sirk said,[11] and this is clearly signaled in the way Taza's divided sympathies are embodied in the outfits he wears. Even if Hudson's performance never quite lends Taza's torment the intensity it requires, the film's script and costume design make it unmistakable.

"It will easier fit my body than my mind," Taza says regarding the uniform of the reservation police that Captain Burnett gives him to wear in line with the responsibilities he has assumed. It's effectively a cavalry uniform, with only a bandana worn under the hat and a shell necklace as reminders of Taza's identity as a Chiricahua. Significantly, he casts it off after Burnett's short-sighted superior, General Crook (Robert Burton), breaks the agreement that had been made to allow Apaches to punish Apaches for any transgressions.

Sirk identifies the world in which Taza moves as a divided one, even structurally pairing him with Captain Burnett in the way that both men find themselves in conflict with those who wear the same uniforms as they do. Indian customs are contrasted to those of the white man, pointing to the ways in which both cultures are born of differing and sometimes irreconcilable ways of viewing the world. Sirk pays close attention to the rituals that shape their existence, to the different ways in which they communicate, and to how they conduct themselves in battle: the Indians' whoops and flexible strategies in combat are in sharp contrast to the more orderly approach taken by the cavalry with its bugles and rigid troop formations.

Intriguingly, as if pointing to what the Apaches are missing in the way they conduct their lives, and underlining another aspect of this divided world, Sirk constantly films sequences so that women's business occupies the foreground of the images while the bellicose activities of the men are, visually at least, pushed into the background.[12]

Along the same lines, the film's narrative rhythms, as well as the shifts from one sequence to the next, evoke a cycle of peaceful activities constantly being interrupted by warlike ones and never reaching a resolution. This strategy echoes the one persistently used in Sirk's romantic and domestic melodramas where intimate exchanges between characters are forever being interrupted and left unresolved.

In its immersion of its central character in a vortex of contradiction and compromise, Sirk humanizes a Native American chief in a way that few Westerns have managed. At the same time, he links Taza to all of those other characters in his films who are trying to make sense of their lives but are forever being thwarted by their circumstances and their uncertainties. It's not hard to see how Robert Stack, or another actor more malleable in his method than Hudson, might bring a different kind of emotional urgency to Taza's situation and to the film's narrative momentum. But Hudson's Taza nonetheless manages to evoke the poignancy of the situation in which he finds himself, a man hemmed in by circumstances which history has created for him.

At the same time as one can recognize what Sirk was able to do with such a heavily formularized genre, it's instructive to see what he failed to do. On the one hand, his decision to make a Native American his protagonist was an adventurous move, in the wake of Anthony Mann's *Devil's Doorway* (1950) and in the same year as Robert Aldrich's *Apache*. On the other, his failure to move beyond the clichéd genre opposition of the good Indian and the bad Indian[13] prevents *Taza* from offering the same kind of social critiques that he pursued elsewhere.

That he might have taken a far more subversive approach is evident in *Captain Lightfoot*, which he made two years later.

CAPTAIN LIGHTFOOT (1954)

> "Mrs. Sirk and I liked to travel as much as we could and the main reason I took on *Captain Lightfoot* was the opportunity to spend time in Ireland. I'd already had a long love affair with Irish writers and playwrights and the chance to visit their country was too good to refuse."
> —DOUGLAS SIRK, 1981

Although *Captain Lightfoot* is equally ruled by convention, it seems less constrained by it. The film sits comfortably among those tales of men (and, occasionally, women) who lived outside society and its laws before the twentieth century, stealing from the rich and, occasionally, passing on the proceeds to the poor. Sometimes they're depicted as free spirits, adventurers who've simply cut themselves loose from society and its proprieties and gone their own way; sometimes they're cast as villains; and occasionally their motives are given a political edge.

In Europe, they're generally known as highwaymen, in America as outlaws, in Australia as bushrangers. Robin Hood, Jesse James, and Ned Kelly might come from different continents (to name three of the most famous), but they're spiritual brethren. And Captain Thunderbolt (real name: John Doherty), as played by Jeff Morrow, and Captain Lightfoot (real name: Michael Martin), as played by Hudson, the two heroes of Sirk's film, belong in their company.[14]

The clever strategist and his earnest admirer. Captain Thunderbolt (Jeff Morrow) and Captain Lightfoot (Rock Hudson) in *Captain Lightfoot*.

The setting is Ireland in 1815, fifteen years after the country found itself being ruled from Westminster rather than Dublin. An opening scroll announces that what follows is a story about "the Ireland of deep, black rivers, and red-coated dragoons riding through a land bitter with resistance against foreign rule, the Ireland of secret societies and highwaymen on the Dublin road, the Ireland of dark deeds performed with a light heart." And the "bad, good old Ireland" which Sirk depicts in *Captain Lightfoot* proves to be a divided world with more than a few similarities to the one depicted in *Taza, Son of Cochise*.

Michael is a reckless young man who lives in awe of the famous Captain Thunderbolt, a leader in the struggle to oust the occupying British forces. After he discovers that the man whom he's befriended on the road and has come to know as John Doherty is actually Captain Thunderbolt, he joins forces with him. When Doherty is injured, Martin reluctantly accepts the invitation to fill in for him as a rebel leader, the transaction echoing the passing of the leadership of the Chiricahua Apache from Cochise to Taza.

In Burnett's novel,[15] which is divided into three sections, Doherty/Thunderbolt dies at the end of part one, whereas in the film, he's wounded and withdraws from the action but is alive and well until the end. In both cases, though, as a result of his injuries, he passes the baton of command on to Martin/Captain Lightfoot.

In its depiction of the attitudes of the Irish towards the British interlopers, *Captain Lightfoot* also makes for a fascinating contrast with *Taza*. Our sympathies here are unquestionably with the two Irish rebels, their fellow freedom fighters, and their struggle against the unwelcome intruders. Any inclination to negotiate with the enemy is regarded as a betrayal of the cause. When the uptight Regis (Denis O'Dea), a fellow member of "the Society," speaks in measured terms about how best to maintain a spirit of rebellion, Michael is contemptuous of him. "Words, words, words," he scoffs. "A mask for a coward to hide behind." And the British also regard Regis as malleable.

However, all is not as it seems and Regis is subsequently revealed to have an abundance of cards up his sleeve. Towards the end, it appears that he has betrayed "the Society," but that turns out to be a ruse to allow him to help Michael to safety after he's been captured by the dragoons. Which is entirely consistent with the film's thematic pattern that appearances are not to be trusted. As Doherty explains to Michael, "We live in a world of phantasmagoria, fake forms and fake faces. Each man wears a mask against his fellows . . ."

Nevertheless, the film implicates us in Michael's view of Regis's apparent failings, its case clearly loaded to favor the men of action. This is to take a very different view from the one *Taza* offers about how best to deal with occupying forces. The discredited ideological position which Regis seems to occupy makes him the film's equivalent of Taza, while Michael and Doherty are more like Geronimo in their refusal to roll over and play nice.

That said, though, Michael is repeatedly shown to be misguided, allowing himself to be led by his instincts rather than his intellect. He might be nominally the film's hero, but the colorfully romantic name he acquires—"Captain Lightfoot"—is bestowed on him ironically by Doherty's daughter, Aga (Barbara Rush), in honor of his social awkwardness. In the novel, he's described as a "young rustic barbarian,"[16] and the book presents its story as an account of the education of an innocent, a narrative map also roughly sketched out by the film.

Michael is headstrong, impulsive, and not especially bright. A policeman unkindly but correctly observes of him that he sees "with befuddled eyes." Moreover, his exploits fit neatly into the film's general cycle of misadventure which has the major characters repeatedly embarking on missions that prove to be counterproductive. Naïve Michael gets by overall on a wing and a prayer rather than sound strategies, and it remains unclear throughout—even to Michael himself—whether he's driven by a genuine concern for the future of Ireland in its struggle against an occupying force or simply by an impatience for adventure, an inability to sit still and contemplate life's complexities. The film might appear to be charting the course of his education, but it's finally hard to see what exactly he's learned.

Doherty is a much smarter operator, although it's not easy to grasp what exactly he sees in Michael that makes him believe that the young man he found by the side of the road would be a suitable leader for the rebel movement. They're both on the same side, but Doherty's Captain Thunderbolt is a clever strategist who knows how to use the enemy's failings against it, whereas Michael, without ever becoming unsympathetic, seems to be simply going along for the ride. Hudson makes him terribly earnest, awfully foolish, and poignantly unsophisticated.

The most successful of the three films under discussion here, *Captain Lightfoot* has an appealing playfulness that makes it very different in tone from the others. Eschewing the melodramatic potential of the material, it instead metaphorically winks at us, unfolding as an ironic comedy, with Hudson's performance much more in tune with its wry outlook. Rather than being required to carry the film's emotional weight, the actor is allowed to loosen up a little, his statuesque heart-throb looks at odds with his less than heroic stature. "Hudson was playing comedy and I realised his talents might lie there," Sirk said of his contribution.[17] As a result, the director was able to bring a festive dimension to the film, a mischievous sense of fun that one might not always associate with his work.

BATTLE HYMN (1956)

> "The title in a picture is like the prologue in a drama . . . *Battle Hymn* . . . not bad . . . It's full of duplicity—the relationship between war and Christianity . . . It is the combination of 'hymn' and 'battle' that really counts."
> —DOUGLAS SIRK, 1970[18]

Ostensibly about the psychological consequences of inflicting what has now become known as "collateral damage" during wartime, *Battle Hymn* tells the story of Dean Hess, or at least a part of it. Hess was an Ohio-based Disciples of Christ minister who joined the US Air Force during World War II and later fought in the Korean War, although the film begins "in the summer of 1950, five years after the end of World War II and one month after the invasion of South Korea," as General Partridge's opening statement informs us. He also adds that what we're about to see is a tale about "the essential goodness of the human spirit," which is not exactly untrue, although it's something of a simplification of the impact of war on Hess and his responses to it.

The preacher and the air force pilot. The Reverend Dean Hess and "Killer" Hess (Rock Hudson) in *Battle Hymn*.

The film proper starts with the Reverend Hess (Hudson) at his Ohio pulpit, delivering a sermon about guilt and its consequences. Hudson's solidity oozes decency and good intentions, although subsequent scenes indicate that he's a deeply troubled man. "Nice sermon, Dean," Deacon Edwards (Carl Benton Reid) tells him, "though, if you don't mind me saying so, you might dwell less on guilt and more on the hope that Heaven holds for us." In one form or another, Hess receives the same counsel twice more during the course of the film.

The source of his discontent is an incident he was involved in during World War II when a malfunction in the missile trigger of his single-pilot fighter plane resulted in him accidentally bombing a German orphanage and killing thirty-seven children. His wife, Mary (Martha Hyer), has been living with his guilt about this and is sympathetic to his efforts to deal with it. A brief flashback presents the incident and reveals that Hess's nickname, apparently bestowed on him by his pilot buddy, Dan Skidmore (Don DeFore), is "Killer."[19]

Then, for reasons that seem unaccountable, Hess returns to the air force as a volunteer. Mary wonders why he would return to combat since that was where his problems began, and he has no answer for her. "One doesn't always have to have a clear reason for the things he does," he tries to explain. "It's just how I feel, that's all. This is what I have to do." The suggestion is that he's placing his trust in God, or at least his own instincts, to guide him, and surrendering himself to whatever destiny holds in store for him.

Advice offered by two other characters stresses the point. One is an African American pilot in Korea, Lieutenant Maples (James Edwards), who strafes a truck filled with refugees, believing it to be a North Korean convoy, and is traumatized by his actions. Hess goes to comfort him, his empathy colliding with Maples's determination to deal with it. "Sir, it's . . . the way of things, I guess," Maples says. "I figure it's all God's making and will. . . . Doesn't the book say it: 'No sparrow shall fall to earth unless He first gives his nod'? Well, He must've given his nod to what happened out there today too. He must have . . . He's the almighty, isn't He? We have to trust Him, sir. How can we live without that?"

The second is Lun-Wa (Philip Ahn), an old South Korean craftsman who reassures Hess about the decision he's made to return to war, implicitly endorsing America's entry into it after the North Korean invasion of its neighbor. "What must one do when a choice between two evils is all that is offered? To accept the lesser sometimes can be our only choice. In order to save, at times we must destroy and, in destruction, create new life."

By returning to the air force, Hess gives himself a second chance, taking the opportunity to clear the way for the building of an orphanage in South Korea (celebrated in the final sequence). That allows him to make at least some kind of reparation for the earlier "collateral damage," for the bombing that continues to haunt him.

But complicating the matter are the very "Sirkian" suggestions that, like many of the director's protagonists, Hess is blindly flailing around trying to come to terms with his troubles. Central to this is the uniform motif which pervades the film and provides the characters with a cloak of identity. It gives them a sense of who they are, but that reassurance is persistently undermined and a continuing sense of dividedness is crucial to the film.

The opening shot lays the foundations: a stained-glass window connoting a church is to the left of the frame, a pilot's helmet and goggles is to the right; on the soundtrack, a chorale of "heavenly voices"—evoking memories of *Magnificent Obsession*, with which *Battle Hymn* has much in common—is set against the stirringly patriotic "Battle Hymn of the Republic." It's also taken up in Hess's move from a preacher's suit to an air force uniform, a shift naturalized by the flow of events—as are the costume changes in both *Taza* and *Captain Lightfoot*—but made especially potent by the significance attached to dress in what follows.

A Korean woman (May Lee) who has brought some orphaned children to the base where Hess's Air Base unit is stationed turns out to be a saboteur when she's shot with a grenade in her hand by a South Korean officer (James Hong). The point that appearances are not to be trusted is underlined: the woman had used the children as her disguise, pretending to be caring for them in order to inveigle her way into the camp and do her dirty work. It's the reverse of the situation in which the truck that had appeared to Lt. Maples from the air as another of the enemy vehicles they'd been attacking turned out to be filled with passengers the US forces had been deployed to defend.

Then, in the following sequence, Hess and Sgt. Herman (Dan Duryea) are driving through the countryside when they come upon Lun-Wa and a group of children who flee the jeep's approach. "They mistrust anyone in uniform," the old man explains. To which Hess replies, "They'll have to learn that there's many different kinds of uniforms."

He thinks that the uniforms he and Herman are wearing provide some guarantee to the locals that they're trustworthy. Yet, earlier at the base, we've seen the US flyers patronizing the Koreans and chasing the children away, in palpable examples of their racism. Hess might be trying to change this, but it makes his claim that the children should place their trust in anyone wearing the US uniform naïve at best.

Later, in a sequence included to provide some conventional "comic relief," uniforms are again cast as unreliable guides to the truth about those wearing them. Herman has been sent by Hess to Seoul to fetch candy for the children. An impossible mission, he thinks, until he spies a US Navy depot, doffs a shore patrol officer's jacket as a disguise, and uses the navy man's jeep to requisition the requested supplies.

Earlier, Hess had returned to service without letting his unit know of his prior life as a minister. With his air force uniform as his disguise, he'd remained silent when a fellow officer asked if there was anyone better able to offer grace at a Thanksgiving celebration at the base. When a letter from the deacon arrived addressed to "Reverend Dean Hess," he'd been exposed, the officer expressing anger that Hess had said nothing. And when the minister/colonel challenges Skidmore for disobeying orders, his former friend asks, "Whatever happened to 'Killer' Hess?"

These details do much to subvert any straightforward notion that, with Hess, what we see is what we get. Appearances can be deceptive and, while he might be presented as a decent man trying to do the right thing—and to salve his stricken conscience—there's also a suggestion that he's reaching out for a mirage and deceiving himself. His beliefs about what he's doing and why, embodied in the uniforms he wears during the course of the film, might be what make him human but offer no guarantee regarding "the essential goodness of the human spirit."

Structurally, *Battle Hymn* has much in common with *Magnificent Obsession*, shot three years earlier. Both deal with an accident and its consequences, the course of Hess's attempt to redeem himself matching the one followed by Bob Merrick (Hudson again) in *Magnificent Obsession*: from overwhelming guilt through involvement in a course of action designed to make reparation for his mistake. Pervading this is a strategic uncertainty attached to the characters' motives, the film casting a shadow of ambiguity over the "magnificent obsession" that guides them both towards redemption.

Alongside this, a recurrent motif in *Magnificent Obsession* has Merrick bursting into the frame, as if afraid of being left out of the life going on inside it. For Hess, though, the movement is in the opposite direction: Sirk repeatedly presents him moving out of the frame, as if in retreat from the unfolding action, as if seeking a kind of oblivion.

CHAPTER EIGHT

Sirk, the Family Melodrama, and the Production Code

"The sanctity of the institution of marriage and the home shall be upheld . . . Adultery, sometimes necessary plot material, must not be explicitly treated, or justified, or presented attractively."
—FROM THE MOTION PICTURE PRODUCTION CODE, 1930[1]

"At the time, all that nonsense was a nuisance. But, in retrospect, I think it made me work harder to get what I wanted, and the results usually turned out better than they otherwise might have."
—DOUGLAS SIRK, 1975

EDWARD BUZZELL'S MARX BROTHERS FILM *AT THE CIRCUS* (1939) FEAtures a series of very funny exchanges between Groucho (playing J. Cheever Loophole) and Eve Arden (as "Peerless Pauline"). During one such scene, Groucho discovers that she's picked his pocket, stealing his wallet in order to retrieve $10,000 he'd taken from her. But before he can do anything, she thrusts it down the front of her dress, leaving him to ponder how difficult his task has now become: "There must be some way of getting that money without getting into trouble with the Hays Office."

It's a film in-joke only made possible by the existence of the Motion Picture Production Code, also known as the Hays Office. Without it, Groucho—or at least the film's writer, Irving Brecher, or whoever was responsible for putting the line in Mr. Loophole's mouth—might have got by with some characteristic Groucho eyebrow-raising to the camera about the assignment. But such a wink-to-the-audience gag would have lacked the teasing political edge added by the reference to a Code designed to keep Groucho and others in line and to maintain so-called community standards regarding "goodness, honor, innocence, purity (and) honesty."[2]

Similarly, for Sirk all that the Code disallowed served as a stimulus to his creativity, a challenge he didn't exactly welcome but that turned out to be beneficial. Like the other prohibitions in place under Hollywood's studio system, its repressive requirements unexpectedly served as a source of inspiration rather than frustration. "At that time, we Europeans called Hollywood a prison," he recalled in 1973. "And that it was. But, although it appears paradoxical, the system had its advantages. An artist needs walls against which to fight, even if they are prison walls. Total freedom is only for the genius, and even that is open to doubt. Attacking these walls makes a man cunning and inventive. It strengthens the muscles of his talent."[3]

Nowhere was this process more in evidence than in the family melodramas Sirk made when the Code was in place, officially at least. Since the early 1950s, filmmakers had been chafing against it—most notably with *The Moon Is Blue* (1953), *I Am a Camera* (1955), *Baby Doll* (1956), and *Island in the Sun* (1957), the last the only one of the four to be produced within the studio system (by 20th Century Fox)—but its guidelines were still generally treated as gospel. Sirk's *Imitation of Life*, which, like *Island in the Sun*, pivots on a matter of miscegenation, was made after many of its restrictions had been unofficially lifted. But *All I Desire*, *There's Always Tomorrow*, *All That Heaven Allows*, and *Written on the Wind* were shot in the shadow of the Hays Office, each dealing with traumas directly attributable to the family lives of their protagonists.

That said, the family melodrama as a genre, stretching back to the time when the Code was first strictly enforced—in 1934—frequently, and perhaps inevitably, fluctuated between what was permissible and what wasn't. For the authors of the Code, the issue of how individual films situated viewer sympathies was deemed to be critical. One of its cautionary clauses makes this explicit: "Out of regard for the sanctity of marriage and the home . . . the love of a third party for one already married, needs careful handling. The treatment should not throw sympathy against marriage as an institution." However, the allocation of sympathies in fictions can be notoriously difficult to pin down and, because of this, many non-compliant films slipped through the Hays Code's net.

And it is clear, as numerous commentators have observed, that Sirk's family melodramas structure viewer sympathies by linking his characters' domestic and wider social circumstances to their plight. These are films which, as Thomas Elsaesser puts it, "manage to present *all* the characters convincingly as victims" with "the questions of 'evil,' of responsibility ... firmly placed on a social and existential level, away from the arbitrary and finally obtuse logic of private motives and individualised psychology."[4]

From a vantage point of more than sixty years later, it seems inconceivable that Sirk's films' critiques of what he described as a "decaying and crumbling American society"[5] could escape the Code's scrutiny. Yet, if we're to take them as any guide to the tenor of their times, the contemporaneous reviews of the films suggest that their social critiques weren't at all evident to audiences in the 1950s.

New York Times critic Bosley Crowther might not have been the most insightful of commentators during his twenty-seven years as the paper's film critic, but his views of Sirk's films are surprisingly representative. Two samples. He reduces *There's Always Tomorrow* to a plot description which is full of certainty but devoid of any appreciation of the film's workings, writing, "Fred MacMurray is comfortably wed to Joan Bennett. He has a nice business, three blossoming children and a tidy home. But his family takes him for granted—treats him slightly worse than a dog. Then along comes Barbara Stanwyck, an old sweetheart—successful, unattached. She is nostalgic, sympathetic. Naturally, Dad falls. What happens next is cut to order—routine procedure, as they say. The two older kids get suspicious and give Dad a further blast of frost. He takes his hurt to Miss Stanwyck and begs her to marry him, but she gets wind of what's cooking and tells the kids to show some love toward Dad. They do (in a random fashion) and this pleases him very much. All's right again in our blue heaven. Miss Stanwyck goes away."[6]

Then he renders *Written on the Wind* virtually unrecognizable. "The trouble with this romantic picture," he writes, "is that nothing really happens, the complications within the characters are never clear and the sloppy, self-pitying fellow at the center of the whole thing is a bore. Outside of that, it is luxurious and the color is conspicuously strong, even though it gets no closer to Texas—either geographically or in spirit—than a few locations near Hollywood."[7]

What Crowther and the administrators of the Code missed in their respective assessments of the films is the way in which Sirk guides us towards understandings that require more than plot outlines and character descriptions. Like other Hollywood directors working in the realm of the family melodrama—Max Ophuls, Vincente Minnelli, and Nicholas Ray prominent among them—Sirk brought to the genre smartly nuanced scripts and a visual intelligence that stamped his films as about as far from "routine" as you could get and encouraged audiences to look more closely at the social worlds he was creating.

As filmmaker Allison Anders puts it, Sirk's use of composition, color, and lighting is "constantly a commentary on what you're seeing."[8] And, in the four films under discussion here, the narrative situations in which the characters are placed and the director's striking *mise-en-scene* eloquently define the parameters of their existence.

Nominating his models as "the countless *Home and Garden* magazines of the mid-'50s, crammed with glossy coloured pictures,"[9] Sirk turned everyday domestic environments and workplaces into metaphorical prisons. This is evident in the way they're filmed: as spaces in which characters are framed by the bars of staircases and surrounded by threatening shadows.

As Victoria L. Evans points out, even the architecture of the settings conveys a history of its own and tells a story of entrapment. In her brilliant study, she outlines how the widowed Cary Scott (Jane Wyman) in *All That Heaven Allows* is a veritable prisoner of the physical design of the place she calls home: "A repository of dead conventions," she writes, "[is] built into [her] family's suburban dwelling, inhibit(ing) freedom of thought as well as movement."[10] She might own it, but, in far more profound ways, it owns her.

This sense of entrapment is also directly referred to in the dialogue. In *There's Always Tomorrow*, a desperately unhappy Clifford Groves (MacMurray) comes to see his home and family circumstances as "a tomb of my own making." In *All That Heaven Allows*, Cary's daughter, Kay (Gloria Talbott), tells her about the Egyptian custom "of walling the widow up alive in the funeral chamber of her husband, along with his other possessions," and expresses her relief that it doesn't happen any more. To which Cary's response is simple, direct, and telling: "Doesn't it?" she quips, adding, "Well, perhaps not in Egypt."

Along the same lines, and consistent with much of his other work, Sirk is also persistently drawing attention to the theatricality of his characters' lives. They're usually unaware of this. As Sirk put it, "Your characters have to remain innocent of what your picture is after. [They] shouldn't be what in German is called *eindeutig* [that is, having only one meaning]."[11] But the suggestion is that they're also hemmed in by the roles they're playing. Compositions constantly catch them posed in doorways or framed by windows, or making entrances through areas inside the frame or simply from somewhere beyond its edges.

As elsewhere in Sirk's work, there's a pervasive sense—especially in the endless interruptions that plague the characters' interactions—that someone's always watching. The persistent suggestion is that, once anyone steps on to the stage of his or her life, an escape to a private space, somewhere off that stage, becomes impossible. Their scripts have been written for them by their social circumstances, and while—like Clifford or Cary—they might struggle to escape them, there's really nowhere else for them to go.

Their identities are intricately bound up with their sense of the place they occupy in a wider order, one whose traditions, customs, and rules have been drawn up elsewhere. It's an order over which they have no control. Seemingly free to make choices within the social spaces they occupy, they're also constrained by an ideology they cannot see but that's manifested everywhere around them. Thus the pervasive air of frustration and thwarted hope that hangs over all of the films.

Much of the drama in them arises because of the arrival of outsiders: Naomi Murdoch (Barbara Stanwyck), the prodigal wife who returns home in *All I Desire*; Norma Miller (Stanwyck again), the lost soul who arrives at Clifford's door in *There's Always Tomorrow*, mistakenly believing that her salvation somehow lies with him or the life he's been leading; Ron Kirby (Rock Hudson), the gentle arborist in *All That Heaven Allows*, who's deemed acceptable as Cary's gardener but an unsuitable prospect for a husband by her children and her social set; Lucy Hadley (Lauren Bacall), the working girl in *Written on the Wind*, who's initially seduced by the allure of the Hadley oil empire but subsequently discovers a kingdom in a state of collapse.

"There is always in the films a dialectic—between the imprisoned group and the one who wants to come inside," Sirk told Michael Stern.[12] But whereas a dialectic conventionally points to a resolution growing out of contradictory viewpoints, the ambiguities embedded in the films' resolutions undermine the process. "All my endings, even the happy ones, are pessimistic," he insisted.

It makes no difference to our perceptions of the homes in the films whether or not the vantage points on offer come from our being placed alongside a character who is a member of the "imprisoned group" or an outsider. In *All I Desire* and *All That Heaven Allows*, the female protagonists serve as our guides: Naomi, who arrives in the small town of Riverdale as an outsider, although she lived there years earlier; and Cary, who begins as an insider in Stoningham, but eventually comes to see the place as an outsider. In *There's Always Tomorrow*, we're primarily alongside Clifford, an insider yearning for something else. In *Written on the Wind*, the situation is more complicated.

However, all of these characters appear to be doomed passengers on the same merry-go-round. Reaching out for an escape from the limitations of their circumscribed lives, they find themselves trapped on a route that seems destined to take them back to where they began without any real insight into what's happening to them.

This applies not only to the characters in the foregrounds of the family melodramas but also to their offspring. As Sirk told Rasner and Wulf, "These children, brought up with conservative opinions by the social system and the examples it holds up to them, will become like their parents and live in imprisonment."[13] And these tales about American families conjure parallels between the generations, suggesting that they're all stuck in the same cycle.

Such generalizations about Sirk's work point to its continuity, but the specific details are where its richness lies, in its evocation of the aching humanity that results from individuals struggling with the mold in which they've been cast. In these four films, it's bracingly evident in the urgency that Stanwyck, MacMurray, Wyman, Stack, and others bring to their performances, but it's also palpable in the way Sirk shapes their world and their stories.

ALL I DESIRE (1953)

"*Stopover* would have been such a good title to have kept for *All I Desire*, which is very flat. *Stopover* would have been not just a sign, but an ironic one."
—DOUGLAS SIRK, 1970[14]

Right from the start of his seventeenth US film, set around 1910, Sirk plunges us into a world of performance. The opening shot introduces the Bijou Theatre in Chicago, where Naomi Murdoch (Stanwyck) is the support act. Backstage in her dressing room, she's contemplating a return to Riverdale, the Wisconsin township which she'd abandoned more than a decade earlier, leaving behind her husband and children, and dreaming of a new life and fame as an actress. Now her teenage daughter, Lily (Lori Nelson), who's about to graduate from high school, has written, urging her to come home to see her in the senior play.

Although Naomi's dreams have been dashed and she's been slogging her way around the circuit, she'd given her family the impression that she's been doing well, performing in "legit" theatre, and currently on a European tour playing Shakespeare. Aging Belle (Lela Bliss), the veteran vaudevillian with whom Naomi shares the dressing room and in whom she confides, insists that she should accept the invitation. "Let your hair go back to natural," Belle advises her. "Act real classy. Why, you'd be their idea of a perfect lady and a big star." Naomi has her doubts: "I don't think the town approved of me," she tells Belle, revealing that she'd left in disgrace after an affair with the local gunshop owner, Dutch Heineman (Lyle Bettger). Nonetheless, she sets aside her qualms and prepares for her homecoming performance.

Whether the film's characters are on-stage or -off, whether they're deliberately setting out to deceive—as Naomi has been doing—or simply being themselves, they're playing roles, as indicated in the following sequence which begins with an overhead establishing shot of the neighborhood where Naomi used to live.

Her oldest, Joyce (Marcia Henderson), is riding down the street in a sleek horse-drawn carriage driven by her fiancé, Russ (Richard Long). They stop in front of the two-story family home where she lives. Joyce is in a rush, haughtily explaining the maternal role she's taken on because of Naomi's absence. Russ wants her attention for himself. "Shall we scandalize the neighbors?" he asks mischievously, before planting a chaste kiss on her cheek.

The well-bred Joyce feigns shock at such a public display of affection, before sweeping indoors and downstairs to the scullery, where Lily is deep in conversation with the maid, Lena (Lotte Stein). Joyce immediately takes over, instructing Lena about her expectations—the props she's going to require—for the forthcoming graduation party, which she's hosting. Preoccupied with proprieties, she also turns her attention to Lily's manners. "One doesn't eat honey without bread," she explains to her sister, who's seated at the kitchen table and has been chatting to Lena. And Joyce doesn't stop there: "Lily, you shouldn't have your feet up like that. It's not ladylike."

After the bossy lady of the house rushes off upstairs to conduct further family business, Lily tells Lena how important it is to have her mother in the audience—"If she were here tonight, my performance would be like Mr. Halley's comet streaking across the sky"—and outlines her plans to follow in Naomi's footsteps. There's an air of hand-to-brow theatricality in her delivery as she walks to the window and gazes longingly through it, as heroines are wont to do in melodramas, before turning back to Lena and making her intentions clear. "They're not going to bury me in this provincial burgh," she proclaims.

Both the actors' performances and Sirk's staging of the opening sequences suggest that everything these characters do is for an audience, real or implied. It's not that anybody sees Russ kissing Joyce, or that Lena could care less about what Lily is eating or how she is sitting, or that there's anybody other than her in the room to hear the aspiring young actress's oration. The issue is how people go about presenting themselves within their own lives, whether anybody is watching or not.

Naomi's appearance later that day—reminiscent of Vermillion O'Toole's in *Take Me to Town*—is not welcomed by anyone in her family, other than Lily. Her ex-husband, Henry (Richard Carlson), the school principal, has become comfortable in the role of the injured party, just as Joyce has as the surrogate mother. Naomi's discomfort at this is clear, but she's determined to maintain an air of calm for Lily's sake, and she commits to leaving as soon as the play is over. Lily, however, has a different scenario in mind.

This performance motif is sustained throughout the film. When, oozing glamour, Naomi goes to see Lily's play, she becomes the star of the show. Word has spread about her attendance, the place is full—"The whole town seems to be here," laments Joyce—and every eye is on Naomi when she makes her entrance. Dutch makes his later than everyone else, focusing his attention on her too, rather than on "Baroness Barclay's Secret." It has been quietly suggested by this point that he might also be the father of her son, Ted (Billy Gray), who was born shortly before she left Riverdale.

Along with detailing the way in which Naomi becomes a spectacle for various members of the audience, Sirk's cutting of the sequence incorporates an alternation between shots from the audience's point-of-view of the stage and from the actors' point-of-view looking out over the audience (including pre-performance as Lily peeks through the as-yet unopened curtains). Everybody has their part to play.

At the same time, however, the emotional heart of the sequence is Naomi's response when Lily makes her entrance on to the stage. With the opening bars of Franz Liszt's concert etude "Un Sospiro" on the soundtrack (also used as the main theme in Ophuls's *Letter from an Unknown Woman*), and a glowing close-up of a tearful Naomi, the sequence abruptly shifts into a dreamlike mode. "It was just an amateurish high school play, until Lily came on stage," the awestruck mother confides in voice-over. "She looked beautiful . . . Everything else seemed to melt away and, for me, there was only Lily."

Disillusion lies ahead for both mother and daughter, their disappointments made even more potent and poignant by this seemingly transcendent moment. And if Stanwyck's previous career hadn't already established it, the actress achieves greatness here as Naomi realizes that her daughter has a presence beyond her wildest dreams. What she's yet to

Naomi (Barbara Stanwyck) in *All I Desire*, awestruck by her daughter's performance in the senior high school play.

appreciate, however, is how manipulative Lily can be: it's subsequently revealed that she's encouraged her mother's return to Riverdale in order to facilitate her own departure with her.

Written by James Gunn (*Harriet Craig*) and Robert Blees (Sirk's *Magnificent Obsession*), with the adaptation (from Carol Ryrie Brink's 1951 novel, *Stopover*) credited to Gina Kaus (*The Robe*), *All I Desire* pivots on the sense of a cycle turning: of history repeating itself as Norma rediscovers the reasons why she left town in the first place (in the novel, it is called Placid Lake); of Lily planning to follow in her footsteps. Filled with echoes of the past and incidents repeated with variations, the film seems to be moving inexorably towards Naomi's departure at the end, which is what happens in the novel and what Sirk had wanted to occur in the film. Its working title was, in fact, *Stopover*, until producer Ross Hunter stepped in, and its dramatic logic and cyclical structure strongly suggest that, given the malevolence of the town gossips, there's no place for Naomi in Riverdale.

Doctors in Hollywood melodramas set in small towns are frequently fonts of wisdom, and so, when the one here (Thomas E. Jackson) describes the tongue-waggers as "maggots," it's effectively a confirmation. And, in that context, his warning to her to go back to Chicago, "for Henry's sake and the children's," seems to make good sense. Yet, seemingly against the grain, the film ends with her decision to stay, welcomed back into the family and given a chance to break the cycle that seemed to have enclosed her.

"[T]hat's the happy end,' so called," Sirk told Halliday. "Ross Hunter was iron. We had to have it. But that was a further reason I wanted to keep *Stopover* as the title for the picture. It was a much darker title."[15] The director, in fact, actually filmed the ending he wanted, but was compelled to do away with it. "In it," he told me, "Barbara Stanwyck leaves, just as she does at the end of *There's Always Tomorrow*. She goes back to where she began, to her tawdry theatrical career, and we leave her there, crying in despair, in the film's final shot." Interestingly, at the same time Sirk revealed that, after seeing the film again, he'd come to feel less aggrieved about how it ends.

Michael Walker's elegant 1990 commentary on the film in *Movie*[16] also offers a persuasive case for it as it is. He points to the transformation that the family undergoes during the course of the film, in particular the changes that take place in Joyce and Henry, as a strong motive for Naomi's decision to stay. With her encouragement, the uptight Joyce we see at the start, concerned about what the neighbors might think, discovers a part of herself that she had been repressing: as Walker puts it, "In effect, Naomi de-puritanises Joyce."[17]

He proposes that it's also because of Naomi that the socially conservative Henry eventually stands by her against the town gossips, identifying how the seeds for this are planted early on in his keeping of Sara (Maureen O'Sullivan), the school's drama teacher, at arm's length: "It is Henry's inability to 'settle down' with Sara, his secret yearning for Naomi, which disturbs the equilibrium of his social position."[18] Henry's suppressed feelings for Naomi are also evidenced by the fact that he's kept her framed photo in a desk drawer.

All I Desire ends, as Hunter preferred, like "Baroness Barclay's Secret," in a way that audiences would have wanted (or so we've long been told), and in line with the principles of the Production Code. Since Naomi and Henry have been wife and husband, it's not as if their union could provoke any disquiet. The film's resolution also evokes the sense of a cycle *knowingly* broken: instead of history repeating itself, Naomi stays in Riverdale, and Lily is denied the opportunity to escape the place she's earlier described as "this provincial burgh."

So, on the one hand, there is a "happy ending." On the other, though, the future remains uncertain: aside from what's occurred inside the Murdoch family, nothing has really changed in Riverdale. The forces that drove Naomi to leave her family in the first place are still in place. And if it's Naomi who has changed, what kind of future lies ahead for her? As Sirk commented, "It is impossible. Pretty soon she'll be one of those housewives, inviting the academic crowd for tea and cake."[19]

Yet, as Walker points out, life inside the walls of the Murdoch home *has* changed, and both Naomi and Henry have made the choice to take a stand against the odds. Theirs is a courageous act of defiance and worthy of celebration. But their final embrace takes place in deep shadow on the front veranda and there's an irresistible irony in the fact that their kiss echoes the stage one shared by Lily and her lead actor (Brett Halsey) at the end of the school play: a performance (even if Lily accuses her co-actor of taking it a little too seriously).

Are we to take this as suggesting that Naomi and Henry are still immersed in roles that have been laid out for them (and that we shouldn't take them too seriously)? And what should we make of the way that the high-contrast lighting of the interiors of the Murdoch home in the penultimate scene evokes a noirish sense of danger rather than a feeling of paradise regained?

All I Desire is not without its flaws: Dutch, for example, seems more like a plot device than a coherent character. But its ending is preferable to the despairing alternative which Sirk had shot but was prevented from using. As poignant as it is powerful, it is a perfect illustration of the director's belief that the prohibitions inside the Hollywood "prison" often encouraged creativity rather than limiting it. Sirk is correct to describe the closure as "an unhappy happy end,"[20] but it's also a deeply and richly ambivalent one.

ALL THAT HEAVEN ALLOWS (1955)

> "My pictures are critical of a certain class of American—whom I do not like. The American in transition from a little guy to a not-yet big guy, so to speak; the small-town, country club Americans, the ones you find in *All That Heaven Allows*, for example."
>
> —DOUGLAS SIRK, 1978[21]

In January 1955, a few months after the release and box-office success of *Magnificent Obsession*, *All That Heaven Allows* went into production, again pairing Wyman and star-on-the-rise Hudson. Apparently, Sirk agreed to the project after producer Ross Hunter presented him with an adaptation of Edna and Harry Lee's 1952 novel and agreed to a partial rewrite. "I liked your script," Sirk told Hunter, "though it was much too romantic for me . . . But after working with you and screenwriter Peg Fenwick, we came up with a solid script that gave me an opportunity to use beautiful, bright 'false' colors and surfaces."[22]

Largely filtered through the experiences of its protagonist, wealthy New England widow Cary Scott (Wyman), the film tells a straightforward tale about her affair with gardener-arborist Ron Kirby (Hudson), which flies in the face of the expectations of her two children and her snooty social circle. Its critique of the complacency and social prejudice that surrounds Cary is unrelenting, and its depiction of the upper-crust world of Stoningham, Connecticut, provides strong evidence to support German filmmaker Rainer Werner Fassbinder's declaration that "after seeing this film, small town America is the last place in the world I would want to go."[23]

At first glance, though, Stoningham looks like a peaceful orderly place, the opening overhead shot taking in a church steeple, a quiet street, manicured lawns, comfortable homes, and autumn leaves gently falling—not unlike a Technicolor version of Riverdale in *All I Desire*. A car moves along the street and pulls up in Cary's driveway, her best friend, Sara (Agnes Moorehead), behind the wheel. Ron is trimming a tree in the background as the visitor walks towards the house to tell Cary she can't stay for lunch. She leaves, Cary invites Ron to share the meal she has prepared, and, after he asks if she'd like to see his "silver-tipped spruce," all hell breaks loose, at least metaphorically.

For the most part, until she runs afoul of the gossips, the prevailing snobbery, and a lurking lecher (Donald Curtis) at the local country club—who are akin to the audience at Lilly's play in *All I Desire*—politeness is the order of the day. But the battle lines are clearly drawn. Her children, Princeton student Ned (William Reynolds) and his younger social-worker sister, bespectacled, Freud-quoting Kay (Gloria Talbot), want her life to continue along the same lines it had been following before she was widowed.

For them, her role as a wife and mother was scripted long ago and improvisations are frowned upon. Even her style of attire has been decided—somber greys and blues—and that's the way it's supposed to stay. And her future should be with the fatherly Harvey (Conrad Nagel), a man of the same social class who is no longer in his prime and aware of it. As far as Kay is concerned, he's perfect for her mother: "As Freud says, 'When we reach a certain age, sex becomes incongruous.' I think that Harvey understands that."

She's right about this. In a poignant scene at Cary's door after Harvey drives her home from a party at the country club, he sweetly and sadly admits that he's not "romantic or impetuous," and then cuts her to the quick by adding, "But you'd hardly want that sort of thing: companionship and affection are the important things."[24]

For her, the alternative that Ron has to offer is exciting and challenging: he lives in the countryside, in an idyllic setting close to nature and far from the comforts of her existence in Stoningham, comforts that she is now seeing through different eyes. According to one of his friends, Alida (Virginia Grey), Ron is the living embodiment of Thoreau's *Walden*: "I don't think Ron's ever read it," she tells Cary. "He just lives it."[25]

The issue of class is everywhere felt. Even if she says she's not "a club woman," her membership of Stoningham's upper crust is part of her mindset and Ron is not just an outsider but, to make matters worse, doesn't even care that he is. "You can't be serious!" Sara tells Cary, going on to enumerate the gossip points that will follow: Ron is younger than she is; he's actually after her money; and, because he had worked for her husband, their affair must date back to before she became a widow. Furthermore, there's the problem of the children's reaction to the interloper.

When Cary tells them of her plans to marry, they're happy for her, until they discover who's to become their stepfather. Ned appears to be horrified by the realization that his mother is not only a woman who looks good in a red dress but is also ready to sell the family home. "Don't expect me to come and visit you," he petulantly tells her. "I'd be ashamed." Kay is more sympathetic (and eventually apologetic), but just as upset, and her *j'accuse* is no less hurtful because it bespeaks a naivete: "You love him so much you're willing to ruin all our lives?"

What Kay fails to notice—although, given her interest in the art of psychoanalysis, she should have—is that her mother's attraction to Ron is also a clear case of the return of the repressed. *All That Heaven Allows* isn't exactly *Lady Chatterley's Lover*, but mentioning these two tales about an upper-crust woman and her gardener/gamekeeper in the same breath isn't entirely fanciful.[26] And, given the operation of the Production Code, how else might D. H. Lawrence's at-the-time infamous novel have been adapted to Hollywood screens?

Without making that link specific, Molly Haskell notes in her rightly celebrated 1974 book *From Reverence to Rape* that "*All That Heaven Allows* is as advanced and, without an explicit word or image, as sexually aware as any film made since."[27] There were objections from the PCA about the time-lapse dissolves that make the "unacceptably suggestive" implication

Cary (Jane Wyman) torn between desire and social expectation in *All That Heaven Allows*.

that Cary and Ron are lovers rather than just good friends,[28] but the implication remains in the finished film. And there was pressure from inside Universal to ensure that the film should not run afoul of the censors.

In 1970, Conrad Nagel recalled a representative from the studio front office raising objections to a dialogue exchange between his Harvey and Wyman's Cary. "We have a scene where we are decorating the Christmas tree, and I say to her, 'Oh, I got this wonderful doctor . . . '—kind of an intimate little scene. Well, so help me, they cut it out because they claimed the censors would interpret it as our having an affair." Such a notion is totally at odds with the details of the film: "She could barely tolerate me. I'm dull. To claim there was anything remotely suggestive there was absurd."[29] But no amount of arguing could change the studio's mind.

Many commentators about the film have proposed that its social critique is "just below the surface," as Halliday puts it.[30] In fact—despite Crowther's contemptuous put-down of the film as nothing more than a "frankly feminine fiction"[31]—it's all there *on* the surface: there's simply no other way to make sense of what's happening on the screen and in the dialogue.

The contrast between the sense of entombment created by Cary's home[32]—as full of shadows as the Murdochs' in *All I Desire*, and frequently lit like the interior of a mausoleum with those "bright, 'false' colors"—and the natural lighting and welcoming closeness to nature of Ron's is striking. And the difference between the stuffy party at Sara's (where Cary introduces Ron to her social set) and the relaxed one (where she meets his friends in the countryside) couldn't be starker.

What *is* less than readily apparent is how happy the "happy ending" imposed on Sirk actually is. After a period of estrangement provoked by the various forces working to keep them apart, Cary and Ron are reunited in the closing sequence. Reassured by Alida that he still cares, she goes to visit him. Since he's out hunting with his friend, Mick (Charles Drake), Alida's husband, their paths fail to cross. He returns just as she is leaving, and calls after her, but she doesn't hear. Rushing to reach her, he falls down a slope, badly injuring himself. After Alida explains what happened, Cary returns to look after her injured beloved, telling him she's "come home" to stay.

Sirk recalled wanting a different ending, calling a halt to proceedings with Ron's tumble and leaving open the question of his survival. But producer Ross Hunter once again stepped in and explained to his director that this would be too "depressing" and "disturbing" for audiences. The closing sequence now has her assuring him of their future together and assuming responsibility for his care. It's an exact reversal of the one at the end of *Magnificent Obsession* in which Hudson's and Wyman's characters are reunited, with her recovering from the operation that he has performed and him promising to care for her.

The key question becomes: to what extent does the sequence resolve the problems that have kept the couple apart in the past and provide a signal that all will be well? Some commentators take the ending straight. Haskell, for example, sees it as evidence that, like the Murdoch family in *All I Desire*, Cary has been transformed by what she has learned from her encounter with this outsider. "[I]n terms of the middle-class security and conditioning with which Sirk makes us understand her, her choice could not be more radical."[33]

Brandon French, on the other hand, while agreeing that Cary has been liberated, views the ending as a negation of the film's "protest against fifties bourgeoisie," as "ultimately reactionary, betraying a nostalgia for the past rather than a hunger for a better future."[34] Missing the point that the title of the film is *All That Heaven Allows* (which suggests that what is allowed is *limited*) rather than *Heaven Allows All*, she argues that "Haskell fails to acknowledge that this choice is not all that heaven allows, as it pretends to be."[35]

For Sirk, interviewed two decades later, the inevitable compromises which lie ahead for the couple should already be evident. "The man who is close to nature [Naturmensch] is shown by the end of the film to have been changed by middle-class ways: in his dress as in his attempts to alter his Spartan barn into a fashionably rustic home for himself and the wife who loves him. There are grounds for anticipating that he will eventually integrate himself into that very society which he had despised and rejected."[36] Certainly, within a generation, the value of his land and property will increase well beyond that of the suburban real estate owned by the likes of Cary's social set.

Over the years, filmmakers like Fassbinder, with *Fear Eats the Soul* (1972), and Todd Haynes, with *Far from Heaven* (2002), have openly acknowledged their debt to Sirk's work. That, and the critical respect given to the film from the 1970s onwards is, I believe, at least in part, based on the way it ends. The ambivalence of the film's closure seems clear, even if the plotting enabling it seems clumsy. It's impossible to ignore the fact that Cary and Ron's reunion occurs only after he is injured and bedridden, effectively helpless, and that she appears to have been "liberated" back into the role of a wife and nurturer. At the same time, the film's empathy for its female protagonist certainly touches the zeitgeist of the '70s, and its endorsement of the stand she takes against the social forces arrayed against her makes her a noteworthy heroine for an evolving feminism.

Yet one is left wondering if *All That Heaven Allows* is fully deserving of the degree of adulation it has received. The unadulterated schmaltz of much of the popular commentary which has grown around it over the years is perfectly illustrated by critic and filmmaker Mark Cousins's 1998 introduction of the film for BBC2's *Moviedrome* series (available on YouTube). Incorrectly identifying it as "a film based on *Walden*," he declared his belief that the cocktail party sequence is "as devastating an indictment of middle-class inhumanity as anything by Bertolt Brecht, but wrapped in mink," directing viewers to "feel free to weep at the awfulness of the world and the beauty of the movies."[37]

What has been ignored at the same time as the film's reputation has been enhanced, however, is the debt it owes to its source, originally published as a story in *Woman's Home Companion* in 1951, then soon afterwards as a novel. From the first page to the last, Edna Lee's compelling story, written in collaboration with her son—who reportedly assisted his mother with her depiction of Cary's children[38]—never strays from Cary's point of view. Locking the reader inside the feelings of its widowed protagonist as she struggles to escape the constraints of her comfortable middle-class existence, it's a sharply observed, psychologically astute account of the complacency of 1950s America and the dangers concealed behind its placid surfaces.

Crucial to its purposes is that the reader should understand how Cary sees the unfolding events. She's not all-knowing, but her insights allow a fuller understanding of her children's reactions after she tells them of her plan to marry Ron. The plotting problems with the film's last act, in fact, might have been avoided had it adhered to the narrative structure of its source, rather than venturing into incidents that lie outside Cary's knowledge (Ron's hunting excursion with Mick).

Whereas in the film, Ned and Kay are introduced as selfish brats, Cary's empathetic response to their shocked response to her news about her impending marriage guides our view of them in the book. In the film, they're not entirely unsympathetic, but they're primarily used as mouthpieces for a loathsomely oppressive class system. That's still present in the novel, but we're also made to appreciate why they might be so unnerved by their mother's declared intention to take her life in a different direction.

In one of the film's most striking and oft-discussed incidents, Ned proudly presents her with a Christmas present from him and Kay: a television set. The scene ends with an image of a forlorn Cary's reflection on its screen, seemingly a prisoner of its frame. The same scene, minus this sinister image, carries similar connotations in the book, but also acknowledges Ned's attempt to do something nice: "She was made a little sad and a little rueful by his supreme faith that the set would assure her a full and satisfactory life."[39]

More crucially, prior to the happy ending and at a time when all appears to be lost with Ron, Cary accidentally locks herself in the basement of her house when she goes downstairs to try to fix a gas leak. With her life in danger, she remembers how "in ancient and barbaric lands, when their lord and husband died, women were sealed into the tomb where his body lay."[40] After she escapes, she begins to wonder about her motives for going into the basement in the first place, remembering Freud's belief that there are no such things as accidents. Lee leaves it implicit, but firmly plants the idea that, unless Cary follows where her heart is guiding her, she might well do harm to herself.

Whereas the film dissipates the dramatic intensity of Cary's plight by abruptly transferring our attention away from her—to Ron, out hunting with Mick—the enclosure inside Cary's perspective in the book not only enriches her character but is formally more consistent and satisfying.

Curtis Bernhardt's stylishly noirish *My Reputation* (made in 1943 but not released until 1946) adheres more or less to the same plot path as *All That Heaven Allows*, but doesn't make the same mistake. And the result is dramatically more effective because of it, even if the film arrives at a similarly ambivalent closure, awkwardly disguised as a happy ending.

All the same elements are there. Barbara Stanwyck plays a grieving widow whose two adolescent sons are sympathetic characters but become spokesmen for a monstrous patriarchy. "You belong to Dad," says the younger boy (Scotty Beckett). "It doesn't make any difference whether he's dead or not." The family lawyer (Warner Anderson) is the equivalent to Harvey; Ron is replaced by a likable womanizer (George Brent), who tells the widow, "You've been hermetically sealed most of your life." Ginny (Eve Arden) assumes the role taken by Sara in Sirk's film, while another male predator (Jerome Cowan) hovers around the edges of the action, and so on.

Although there's a greater sympathy in *My Reputation* for the agents of repression, at least within the family, town gossips again target the film's protagonist and there's another confrontation at a party. And, centrally, the film etches a portrait of a widow struggling with her grief, with the social expectations of her family and friends, and with the stultifying conventions that seem to have turned her superficially comfortable life into a prison.

That said, *All That Heaven Allows* should not be underrated even if the credit often ascribed solely to Sirk for it should be spread more widely. And, although I can find nothing from the director on the subject, one commentator has even identified an especially personal side to it, seeing in his "drama of a couple oppressed by a society that persecutes difference . . . an allegory for Sirk's own experience in Nazi Germany."[41]

THERE'S ALWAYS TOMORROW (1955)

> "*There's Always Tomorrow* is another fair title. An ironic one too. Tomorrow is the yesterday, and MacMurray will still be playing with his toys (the only reservation I had about that was that there have been too many 'tomorrow' titles)."
> —DOUGLAS SIRK, 1970[42]

Just as *All That Heaven Allows* references *Magnificent Obsession*, *There's Always Tomorrow* draws on *All I Desire*. In both films, Barbara Stanwyck plays women estranged from their former lives and revisiting their pasts. Here, she's New York dress designer Norma Vale, nee Miller. The initials that she and *All I Desire*'s Naomi Murdoch share can hardly be coincidental (in Edward Sloman's original version, released in 1934, her name is Alice Vail). Her destination is suburban Los Angeles, where her former employer, toy manufacturer Clifford Groves (Fred MacMurray), lives with his wife, Marian (Joan Bennett), and their three children, Vinny (William Reynolds), who is the eldest, Ellen (Gigi Perreau), and Frankie (Judy Nugent). And we find ourselves mainly but not exclusively alongside him throughout the film.

In the earlier film, Stanwyck's character is an estranged wife and mother visiting her family. Here Norma is a businesswoman, separated from her husband but now, she says, "married happily to 738 Madison Avenue," although, like Naomi, she is drawn to the possibilities of a life she'd left behind years earlier. A conference at the nearby Palm Valley resort is the official reason for her visit, but more personal reasons for her presence gradually become clear.

As in *All I Desire*, the home is the key setting and the family is the focus. Norma, who'd secretly been in love with Clifford when she left—it's suggested that her unrequited passion was the reason for her departure—is full of admiration for both. When he answers the door to her, it takes a moment for him to realize who it is, but she identifies his surroundings immediately. "Oh, the house is beautiful," she enthuses. "Warm and cheerful, just as I had imagined it. The kind you always wanted." And after she meets his family, she's equally admiring of them. "I'd trade every New York celebrity for a family just like this," she tells them.

On both counts, though, she's wrong. She looks at but appears to make nothing of the family photo from which Clifford is notably absent. And her assessments of his circumstances are more revealing of her dissatisfaction with the life she's been living than of Clifford's. Before her arrival, we've been introduced to his nightmare: arriving home from work, he's treated as an irrelevance by his children, and his invitation to take Marian out to the theatre for her birthday is rebuffed because Frankie's ballet club debut is deemed far more important. Again, as in most of Sirk's other films, interruptions abound. "Every time we plan on doing anything together, something gets in the way," Clifford complains to Marian.

His home is about as far from a haven as it's possible to get; like the Murdochs' house in *All I Desire*, Clifford's is shrouded in shadow and depicted in a way that perfectly illustrates what Stanwyck biographer Dan Callahan describes as "Sirk's icy visual style that traps people in architectural cages."[43] And the film creates a telling parallel between Clifford's toy factory, filled with lifeless automatons, and the doll-house structure of his home. As it unfolds, in fact, *There's Always Tomorrow*—written by

Domestically stressed. Clifford (Fred MacMurray) as Norma (Barbara Stanwyck) arrives in *There's Always Tomorrow*.

Bernard C. Schoenfeld (*Phantom Lady, The Dark Corner*)—comes just about as close to being a film noir as a family melodrama can get without someone dying, or at least pulling a gun.

A key difference between the two films is that this time we're introduced to events through the eyes of the male. We also see a lot more than he does, although it's his emotional life that is prioritized. When Clifford opens the door to Norma, who materializes like a glamorous apparition, he's wearing an apron, carrying a just-boiled-over coffee pot, and feeling stressed.

Apologizing for his appearance, he belongs to the same school of castrated masculinity as Spencer Tracy in *Father of the Bride* (1950) or *Father's Little Dividend* (1951), Tom Ewell in *The Seven Year Itch*, or James Dean's father (Jim Backus) in *Rebel Without a Cause* (both 1955). And, indeed, in a few years, one can imagine him ending up like Harvey in *All That Heaven Allows*—a "sweet and thoughtful" man, as Norma describes him to Vinnie and Ellen, but one who's given up on most of what life has to offer.

The parallel between the surrealist nightmare suffered pre-wedding by Tracy's character in *Father of the Bride* and what befalls Clifford during the opening passages of *There's Always Tomorrow* is a strong one. The only significant difference is that Clifford's anguish is grounded in a conventional narrative realism, even if its excess suggests a stylistic straining at the leash, at the same time as it lends his sense of displacement a potent paranoid edge. He appears to be as disengaged from his family as it is from him. For example, shouldn't he have been aware that Frankie was making her ballet debut?

Outside looking in. The prodigal wife (Barbara Stanwyck) returning home in *All I Desire*.

Like *All I Desire*, *There's Always Tomorrow* is also grounded in the idea of life as a kind of social theatre. Characters are constantly putting on a show while others pass comment or draw conclusions about what they're watching.

Like the Murdoch household in *All I Desire*, the Groves home becomes a ready-made theatrical setting, especially in the way it allows for entrances and exits through doorways and for proscenium-arch-like framings, and the idea of performance becomes a part of the inhabitants' everyday life. When Frankie hurts her ankle and overplays the pain she experiences, Marian slips comfortably into the role of the understanding mom—"Children are apt to dramatize"—by way of explaining to Clifford why she now can't go away with him as planned for the weekend.

Other locations perform the same function as the characters construct scenarios about their lives. When Norma joins Clifford at the theatre after Marian becomes unavailable, they leave before the second act of the show, replacing it with a visit to his workplace and a shared journey down memory lane. First, he introduces her to his new invention, Rex, the walking-talking robot—"I'm Rex the robot, the mechanical man. Push me and steer me wherever you can"—a creation with which he subsequently comes to identify. Then, provoked by "their" song, "Blue Moon,"

Trapped inside. Clifford (Fred MacMurray), "desperate in [his] own living-room" in *There's Always Tomorrow*.

the tune Clifford has had recorded for a toy barrel-organ—he describes it as "that old relic"—they sentimentally look back on incidents from earlier times. The soundtrack subsequently takes up the tune as a motif for their nostalgia-laden reprise of the past.

MacMurray plays Clifford as a man trapped in the soap opera of his mind.[44] He's not a tragic figure because he never comes to the point of understanding what's happening to him: that he's grasping blindly at another life, not a better one.[45] The histrionics of his children's phone calls to friends and their conversations in general spill over into the melodramatic highs and lows of his escalating feelings for Norma. Like his offspring, he's preoccupied with himself, and it's as if he's been reborn as a teenager in the way he dramatizes his life. "I feel like I just made a touchdown," he tells her excitedly, "Not a day older." And then, when he finds himself miserable, "desperate in my own living room," he moans to Marian, "I'm becoming one of my own toys."

Seemingly incapable of finding comfort, Clifford struggles in vain to make sense of what's happening to him. So too do the other characters as they assume the role of an audience, interpreting what's going on around them. Apparently oblivious to the fact that she's a character in a marital drama, Marian reacts to the signs of Clifford's increasing malaise by wondering if he's catching a cold. And to his increasing desperation about "the rut" he's in, she responds like a mother talking to her child: "Darling, if life were always an adventure, it would be very exhausting."

Bennett's nuanced performance carries the suggestion that Marian's failure to understand what's happening to her husband is a knowing one, a front designed to keep any problems between them at arm's length, her armor against reality. If she doesn't admit to them, she won't have to deal with them. Her observations to Clifford, after he invites Norma home for dinner to meet the family, that their guest is "lonely" and unhappy with her life indicate an unexpected alertness to others' circumstances.

When I put this reading to Sirk in 1978, he had mixed feelings—he's referred to her elsewhere as "mindless" (see below)—but he conceded that the actress's contribution to the complicated undercurrents at work in the sequence could allow for such an interpretation. "They point to a tinge of anguish," he said, "and leave open the possibility that she knows what's going on and is committed to handling it in her own way."

After Marian again fails to join Clifford on a date—this time, a weekend away at a Palm Valley resort—she insists that Clifford should go without her. He does, largely because he's arranged a business meeting there, and he and Norma run into each other, seemingly by chance. In the scene at his workplace, she had told him that she would be there for a conference, although he appears not to have taken in the information. Here, as before, it seems, in line with a convention of romantic melodramas and comedies—that destiny is pushing Clifford away from Marian and towards Norma. As it turns out, their liaison at the resort remains platonic, perhaps because the Production Code was still operative at the time, perhaps not.

However, the leering bellboy (Paul Smith) has his own take on what's going on. He's seen it all before and, after all, the place is known as "the bachelor's paradise." And when Vinnie, girlfriend Ann (Pat Crowley), and two friends (Race Gentry and Myrna Hansen) decide to drive to the resort to visit his father, he draws the same conclusion after he sees Clifford and Norma together. Like a spy in an espionage thriller, Vinnie sneaks around conducting surveillance, compiling evidence—it leads to a false conclusion at this point, but, ironically, one that later becomes true—and eventually filing a report with Ellen.

He declares his reference point for what's going on: Theodore Dreiser's *An American Tragedy*. Ann, however, interprets the situation differently: she becomes Clifford's defender, expressing her belief in his "innocence" and telling Vinnie that he's being childish by "suspecting [his] father of a cheap back-alley romance."

As in both *All I Desire* and *All That Heaven Allows*, children are summoned into service as social police keeping their intransigent elders in line. To *Filmkritik* magazine, Sirk observed that the children in his films "act as moral, status-preserving forces which keep the adults in the cages which society has prepared for them."[46] To Jon Halliday, he explained their role slightly differently: "Children are put into pictures right at the end to show that a new generation is coming up. In my films I want to show exactly the opposite: I think it is the tragedies which are starting over again, always and always ."⁴⁷

Sirk's comments point to a not entirely unsympathetic view of the children in his films. As already noted, Michael Walker has persuasively argued that the characters of the children in *All I Desire* are fleshed-out in a variety of ways,⁴⁸ and the same points apply here, at least to Vinnie and Ellen. Frankie remains very much on the fringes of the action, involved but unaware. The two older offspring, however, are initially self-centered and insensitive to their father's plight. Only when the possibility of him leaving arises are the blinkers removed from their eyes.

When they go to see Norma in her hotel to make their misjudged protest about her behavior, Vinnie advises her to go back to New York while Ellen uncomfortably follows his lead. Vinnie's expressed concern is the impact it will have on their mother, but after Norma speaks up for Clifford and points out how his family has been taking him for granted, the young man's smug hostility disappears. And, as Norma comes to appreciate, Ellen isn't so much passing judgement as tearfully pleading with her not to take their father away.

Once again, Sirk attaches one of his so-called unhappy happy endings to *There's Always Tomorrow*. Norma leaves, telling Clifford to go home to his family, which he does. As he tells Marian, "You know me better than I know myself," their offspring look on, Frankie observing, "They make a handsome couple, don't they?" The children make up an audience that completely misses the point of what they're seeing. Sirk's description of the scene is evocative: "We see at the end . . . the toy manufacturer and his mindless, garrulous wife walking arm in arm through the house which protects them from destructive emotional threats," he told his *Filmkritik* interviewers. "As they do, the pair is observed through the bars of the banisters by their curious children, like imprisoned animals in a zoo."⁴⁹

In the interview with Stern, Sirk indicated that he was happy with the scene he eventually came up with: "I like that ending. It's ironic. But the way it was before I reshot it was even more direct." And, perhaps, less effective because of that. "Groves goes back to his office and watches the plane fly away," he recalled. "The shot's still there now, as the robot walks towards the camera. But now it cuts. I had it keep walking, walking, then fall off the table. The camera pans down, whoom! And there's the robot, on the floor, spinning, rmmm, rmmm, rhmm, rhhmm . . . rhmmm, slowly spinning to a halt. The End. That is complete hopelessness."⁵⁰ It's clear, and not for the first time, that there were times when producer Hunter did save director Sirk from his darker inclinations.

The ending that Sirk eventually shot deepens the sense of a cycle continuing—the film is full of repetitions and echoes of the past—and, as it happens, is at least superficially a straightforward reworking of the one in the original version, directed by Edward Sloman and adapted for the screen by William Hurlbut (who also wrote the first version of *Imitation of Life* as well as *Only Yesterday*, both for John M. Stahl). Released shortly after the Code had come into force, it was variously known as *There's Always Tomorrow* and *Too Late for Love*. The original source was a story by Ursula Parrott, whose name is above the opening title.[51]

Furthermore, Sloman's film as a whole tells more or less the same story. From the moment that Joe White (Frank Morgan) returns home from work to find no room for his coat on the stand inside the front door, it's clear that he's experiencing the same sense of displacement as the one afflicting Clifford. Wife Sophie (Lois Wilson) has forgotten their wedding anniversary and the children are just as careless with his feelings as are Clifford's. There are five of them, "all grown up" except for Margie (Helen Parrish), with Robert Taylor playing Vinnie's equivalent, Arthur.

During a disquieting family dinner-table sequence, they reveal that they're only too aware of their failings, although nobody is making any apologies for them. "I'm not going to be like Mom, loaded down with a house full of five brats," says the eldest, Janet (Louise Latimer). "I'm with Janet," declares Fred (Maurice Murphy). "I'm modern too. You won't catch me putting my head in any noose like poor Pop."

There's a darkness lurking around the edges of the White family, one that ensuing events never quite manage to remove. Struggling to find somewhere to read his newspaper in peace, Joe comes across a potentially pertinent article: "Father Slays Wife and Children with Axe. Claims family drove him to it." The news story goes on to reveal that the killer had surrendered himself to police and "offered no other motive." Clearly all is not well in the White household even before Joe's former employee, the beautiful Alice (Binnie Barnes), steps back into his life.

When they discover he has been secretly visiting her, the children's perceptiveness about their parents' circumstances vanishes and they prove to be just as suspicious of their father as Vinnie and Ellen are of theirs, at least until the dignified Alice sets them straight. "I found out that he was lonely amidst all that big family," she tells them. And when she informs Joe she's leaving and that he can't come with her, "because you belong to them," a conventional facade of propriety collides with his sense of loss to conjure a tearjerker of an ending.

The chief difference between the two films is that Sloman's is devoid of the kind of irony that moves Sirk's into a different realm. The 1934 version is a well-made romantic melodrama, boasting strong performances and a potent air of melancholy. Sirk's is that, but much more too, an incisive critique of the superficially comfortable suburban existence that characterized America during the Eisenhower era, a telling appraisal of the traumas of family life, and an empathetic meditation on the fragile illusions that underpin human existence. As Andrew Sarris observed of the film in 1977, "Sirk's compassionate disenchantment has never been more exquisitely fashioned."[52]

WRITTEN ON THE WIND

> "I like this title too . . . It conveys the feeling of frustration, which is certainly one of the themes of the picture."
> —DOUGLAS SIRK, 1970[53]

Based on the 1945 novel by Robert Wilder, *Written on the Wind* begins in the midst of chaos and in a way that is markedly different from the other films under discussion here. With night falling, the wind blowing, and a storm brewing, a yellow sports car speeds past rows of derricks and pumpjacks and signs for the Hadley Oil Company and through the town of Hadley—population 24,844—on its way to the Hadley mansion. Behind the wheel is Kyle Hadley (Robert Stack), chugging on a bottle of whiskey and driving erratically, seemingly a man bent on his own destruction.

As his car swings into the driveway and skids to a halt, Frank Skinner's dramatic opening music fades into the Four Aces' harmonious version of the melancholy title song (music by Victor Young, lyrics by Sammy Cahn). Guided by this soundtrack shift, an air of regret replaces the earlier doom-laden build before it reaches a crescendo. Kyle climbs out and takes a final swig from the bottle before angrily throwing it against the front wall of the house, as the inhabitants peer through windows: upstairs, his ailing wife, Lucy (Lauren Bacall), friend Mitch Wayne (Rock Hudson), and sister Marylee (Dorothy Malone); and, at basement level, the manservant, Sam (Roy Glenn), and his wife (Maidie Norman). He staggers inside the house, the camera eventually assuming a position outside, looking through the doorway, with leaves swirling across the entrance. A shot rings out. A man stumbles out of the house, a gun in his hand, before falling to the ground.

Indoors, Lucy faints by the window from which she'd been watching, the camera looking past her and a billowing curtain to a desk calendar. Accompanied by a series of dissolves, the wind blows the pages from November 5, 1956, back to October 24, 1955, in the process, taking us to the calendar on Lucy's desk in the Hadley Company's New York office. What follows is an extended flashback that eventually leads to an elaboration of what occurred inside the house after Kyle's entry at the start.

The effect is to enclose him and all the other characters inside a course of events over which they have no control. Whatever happens during the course of the film, the ending that awaits isn't going to change. It's as if they're prisoners from the start, ruled by the decrees of the house of Hadley, powerless to make any changes to the course that destiny—or the machinations of their social world—has charted for them.

The flashback begins by introducing Lucy as the newly appointed executive secretary in the company's marketing department. This is the day on which she first meets Mitch, a geologist working for the Hadleys, who's just flown in from Texas with Kyle. As in the opening, the Hadley business operation is a dominant presence: bright banner advertisements on stands are prominently lined up in a row in her office.

When they meet, Mitch and Lucy immediately begin the kind of amicable sparring that makes them seem like lovers-to-be in a romantic comedy. They bond as down-to-earth folks who aren't susceptible to people like Kyle who insist on putting on a show. But after being shoved aside by Kyle and confused by the way Lucy allows herself to be ensnared by him—"Nothing like this has ever happened to me before," she says. "It's an adventure; it's exciting"—Mitch becomes a walking time bomb. He might never explode, but he's constantly there in the background, watching, his discomfort palpable, as Kyle uses the power of his money to turn Lucy's head.

Whereas *All I Desire*, *All That Heaven Allows*, and *There's Always Tomorrow* all largely attach our sympathies to a single protagonist, *Written on the Wind* keeps us at an emotional distance from all its characters. While it might initially seem as if Mitch and perhaps Lucy are to be our guides to the film's world, each subsequently acts in ways that make them less than reliable. As Christine Saxton argues, "Despite [Mitch's] strength and virtues in the midst of weakness and degeneracy, he does not come out clean," and nor does Lucy, along the same lines.[54] Sirk endorsed such a view, describing Mitch as "a negative figure" and, perhaps overly harshly, referring to both him and Lucy as "rather coldish people and not very interesting."

Mitch (Rock Hudson) as outsider, watching Lucy (Lauren Bacall) and Kyle (Robert Stack) in *Written on the Wind*.

In what ensues, the past becomes a potent force that leaves no one unscathed. Its effects are filtered through conversations between the characters, but also through the haunted look that Kyle brings to his every moment on screen. Reminiscent of Hudson's Bob Merrick in the early scenes of *Magnificent Obsession*, Kyle is human wreckage in urgent need of repair, Stack's film-stealing performance making his plight heartbreaking. And no reprieve is in sight for him, at least until he meets Lucy.

As a boy, Mitch had been unofficially adopted by the Hadleys in accord with the wishes of his father (Harry Shannon). He's become the kind of son that Jasper Hadley (Robert Keith) had yearned for and the kind of man that Kyle has always wanted to be. On the surface, he and Kyle are friends, but their relationship is full of simmering resentments and Kyle's treatment of Mitch as an errand boy and his successful wooing of Lucy only add to the unresolved tensions.

During Kyle and Lucy's whirlwind courtship, Kyle pilots the Hadleys' private plane to Miami, filling her in on his past, describing the world below as "the big poker table" for which he has been given too many chips. "Throw them up in the air," he says, "and a few land on my shoulders." Written by George Zuckerman (*Taza, Son of Cochise*, *The Tarnished Angels*), this is a film that boasts an abundance of sharply written dialogue.

The past is significant in other ways too. For Kyle and sister Marylee, it represents the lost paradise of their childhood, one that they believe they've shared with Mitch, although he clearly sees it differently from them. Marylee is largely defined by her unrequited yearnings for him. She tells Mitch that she's always hated Kyle because, as she saw it, her brother had taken him away from her (a motive which remains unspoken, but is nonetheless implicit, in the novel).

Everything Marylee does is cast as a reaction to Mitch's refusal to treat her other than as a sister: the air of restlessness that she exudes everywhere she goes; her pursuit of lovers at the local bar; her masturbatory fantasy as she dances in her bedroom to a recording of "Temptation" in front of a framed photo of Mitch. As Robin Wood puts it, "The dance is an extraordinary device for suggesting all those things that couldn't be shown on the screen in 1956, and which perhaps gain greater force from the partial suppression."[55] And, under Sirk's guidance, Malone's overheated performance makes Marylee like a demon unleashed inside the Hadley home.

The living embodiment of a disquieting excess, she exhibits the kind of intemperance that, in another context, might lead to calls for an exorcist. A veritable monster from the Id, she constantly threatens to rupture the film's naturalistic surfaces. While Kyle manages to keep his alcoholism at bay for a while during his marriage to Lucy, Marylee's cravings appear to be entirely out of her control.

Mitch and Lucy are the "ordinary people" in the film, at least in comparison to Kyle and his sister. Both, however, suffer as a result of their contact with the Hadleys, and it's as if their lives have been poisoned by it. Mitch's job, essentially, is to hold the family together, but he finds himself implicated in its failures and unable to do anything to restore order. Lucy, a beacon of hope for Kyle, also becomes a reminder of his perceived inadequacy when he comes to believe that it's because of him that she's been unable to conceive. Then, when she does become pregnant, he jealously suspects that Mitch is the father and, in a brutal irony, assaults his wife, causing her to miscarry.

In *Written on the Wind*, the children have reached adulthood, even if they long for the past, for "the river." For Marylee, this represents a time when everything seemed possible, and she urgently pleads with Mitch to go to the river with her. As does Kyle in the scene which is abbreviated at the start, and then repeated in fuller detail, confirming him as the man who has been shot. Dying, he desperately pleads with his friend, "What are we doing here. Mitch? Let's go down to the river, where we belong." Even their surrogate brother, resentful of the way he's been devoured by the Hadley past, appreciates the significance of what has been lost, sadly reflecting to Marylee, after she threatens to blame him for Kyle's death, "How far we've come from the river."

Unlike the children in *All I Desire*, *All That Heaven Allows*, and *There's Always Tomorrow*, though, Kyle and Marylee aren't the judgemental guardians of the future, frowning at the misdemeanors of their parents, keeping them in "the cages which society has prepared for them." Instead, they're both fleeing the past that has determined their future and hurtling towards disaster.

The Hadley empire represents something very different from the small-town or suburban families of the other family melodramas. Led by patriarch Jasper, until his death towards the end of the film, the Hadleys are conventionally regarded as the kind of people who sit atop the pinnacle of the social hierarchy. Their empire is a manifestation of the power of capital, their story a tale that goes to the heart of the American way. Along with George Stevens's sprawling *Giant* (based on Edna Ferber's 1952 novel and also released in 1956), *Written on the Wind* laid the foundations for the TV soap sagas, *Dallas* (1978–91; with a sequel, 2012–14) and *Dynasty* (1981–89; remade in 2017). Yet, Sirk's film couldn't be more different from them, its critique traversing a similar terrain but offering a very different perspective on it.

Its tone and approach is, at least in part, inspired by Wilder's novel, which is not unlike a feverish Tennessee Williams melodrama about a Southern family in a state of implosion. Effectively, the book tells the story of a house, "The Hill," which is owned by the Whitfield family (the equivalent of the Hadleys in the film), and what it signifies for the town that has grown up in its shadow. A malevolent force haunted by the past, the property features a mausoleum alongside the house, the final resting place for its original owner and an ever-present reminder of the fate that awaits the whole family.

There are numerous differences between the film and its source in terms of plot details, characterizations, and narrative structure. The film's setting is a town in Texas; the novel's is in North Carolina. The Whitfield family fortune comes from tobacco rather than oil. Several key characters are absent from the screen adaptation, in particular, the family matriarch and her husband's brother, through whose eyes we gain a perspective on the family story. He's mentioned in passing in the film, but cast there as a "black sheep" who'd died years earlier. However, with variations, the film's four key characters and the situations in which they find themselves can be found in the book.

An extended flashback makes up its middle third—dealing with their childhoods together—but the earlier passages move freely between the past and the present, with the past reaching back to the Whitfield family's ancestry as well as incorporating the more recent assimilation of Reese (who becomes Mitch in the film) into its current generation. The structure is a relatively conventional one pointing to intricate connections between past and present, but the impact of the film's journey back to its beginnings is dramatically much more forceful, and devastating.

A further key difference is the ending. Cary (Kyle in the film) dies, but an ambiguity remains over how it happens. In the film's epilogue, it seems as if Marylee is planning to implicate Mitch at the inquest into Kyle's death, but we already know that he's innocent (because we have, by this stage, seen what took place in the film's penultimate sequence). In the novel, Reese and the pregnant Lillith (Lucy in the film) go their separate ways to avoid gossip about whether or not the child-to-be is Cary's or Reese's. The father *is* Cary, just as it is Kyle in the film, but in the novel there is no miscarriage.[56] And Reese and Cary's sister, Ann-Charlotte, unexpectedly end up together, a development that brings the novel to a moving close.

Sirk appears to have had much greater degree of freedom over the direction this film took than on the other three dealt with in this chapter. He later recalled that producer Albert Zugsmith would regularly defer to his judgement in ways he'd not previously experienced in America. Nevertheless, he still had to deal with the routine demands for a happy ending.

According to Sirk, the original plan was that the last shot would be of Marylee sitting at her late father's desk with the model of the oil derrick in her hand and her father's portrait looking down on her.[57] What we have now, reportedly because Hudson's agent insisted on it, is a reversal of the opening in which Kyle arrives at the house: a series of shots crosscutting between Mitch and Lucy getting into a car and driving away—as if free at last from the cursed Hadleys—and Marylee watching from a window and then moving to the desk.

In the final shot, Sam ushers the car out the front gates and then closes them, the house behind their bars as the credits roll. As before in Sirk's films, a hint of hope is set against the devastation of Marylee's fate: dressed in a business suit, she has inherited the Hadley empire and now occupies her father's chair.

There were also pressures from elsewhere. The novel was originally believed to have been based on events surrounding the death of tobacco heir and playboy Zachary Reynolds in 1932. He'd pursued Broadway musical comedy actress Libby Holman and married her, the news that she had become pregnant setting off a confrontation that led to his death. Suicide was one possibility; the involvement of a friend of Reynolds another.

Victor Fleming's *Reckless* (1935), written by David O. Selznick and starring Jean Harlow, William Powell, and Franchot Tone, was also inspired by the case.

The novel has the routine disclaimer that "no character in it is drawn from or relates to any living person," but, according to Sirk's writer, George Zuckerman, its potential as a film project had initially been quashed because of a threatened lawsuit by the Reynolds family and objections from the Hays Office.[58] But Zuckerman's enthusiasm and the changing times breathed new life into the project and it suddenly became a hot property. As Barbara Klinger notes, "*Written on the Wind* and other films with adult themes were produced within a climate of growing sexual permissiveness . . . with advertising serving the purpose of foregrounding those elements that would support such a frame of reference."[59]

Whatever the pressures, though, *Written on the Wind* is a film of remarkable power, from its visceral opening to its heavily qualified "happy ending." Once again, a family melodrama holds up a mirror to a world in a state of disarray and a way of life from which, for these characters, and for Kyle and Marylee in particular, there is no escape. For theorist and critic Laura Mulvey, "the strength of the melodramatic form lies in the amount of dust the story raises along the road, a cloud of overdetermined irreconcilables which put up a resistance to be neatly settled in the last five minutes."[60] Nowhere is the validity of her claim better evidenced than in *Written on the Wind*.

Postscript

NEVER SAY GOODBYE (JERRY HOPPER, 1956)

> "Although Sirk is uncredited on *Never Say Goodbye* and disowned the movie, he did work on it, and there are so many similarities and points of reference in it to other Sirk movies, both thematically and emotionally, I feel it should be counted [as part of his work]."
> —MARK RAPPAPORT, 2009[61]

In Jon Halliday's book, Sirk appears not to remember *Never Say Goodbye* especially well, but concedes a degree of involvement. "I did some work on preparing it," he says, also acknowledging that, after he'd finished *Written on the Wind*, he was "brought back to finish it as best I could," which, apparently, included reshooting scenes with George Sanders. "It was only because the head of the studio begged me that I did it."[62]

Still, it's not hard to see what might have attracted him to the idea of the project. The source is Luigi Pirandello's 1919 play *Come prima, meglio di prima* (*As Before, Better Than Before*), which was first adapted for the screen in 1945 as *This Love of Ours*, also made for Universal, directed by William Dieterle ("by arrangement with David O. Selznick") from a screenplay by Bruce Manning, John Klorer, and Leonard Lee, and starring Merle Oberon, Charles Korvin, and Claude Rains.[63]

Pirandello's play tells the story of a search for identity: its female protagonist abandons her surgeon husband and infant daughter, adopts the life of a libertine, despairs and attempts suicide, is saved by her husband and returns home, but is rejected by her now-teenage daughter who can't stand the idea of anybody attempting to assume the role of the mother she believes had died years earlier. The play ends with the wife/mother's spiritual rebirth, the restoration of her sense of self and of the family that had been fractured by her initial departure.

The Dieterle adaptation adheres reasonably closely to the outlines of Pirandello's plot, but the perspective on it differs. Obviously, under the Production Code, libertinism was a no-go zone. Anyway, given the tenor of the times, any kind of marital infidelity becomes an issue if we're to view a character sympathetically later on. So, when we first meet her, Karin (Oberon) is a nightclub singer in the employ of a sketch artist (Rains).[64] After a chance meeting with Michel (Korvin), whom she has known before, she attempts suicide. During her recovery, he reads her diary, cueing an extended flashback to their first meeting—when she'd been working as an actress and he was already a doctor—followed by the birth of their child and their separation. In Dieterle's film (and in the remake), he'd been responsible for the marital breakdown, his misplaced jealousy rather than her dissatisfaction with her life the key factor.

An element of this mix that might have stirred Sirk's interest is the similarity between aspects of it and *All I Desire*. He sometimes appears to be revisiting characters and the situations in which they find themselves in order to rework and revise them. *This Love of Ours* presents Michel's relationship with their daughter, Suzette (Sue England), as very like the one in *All I Desire* between Naomi's abandoned husband and their daughter, Joyce. Both daughters play the role of surrogate mother entirely platonically, at least on the surface. "My father and I never say goodbye," Suzette explains, underlining their closeness, as Michel heads off to a conference.

Later, during the second half of the film, after he has persuaded his estranged wife to return home—"It's not for my sake," he urges, "It's for Suzette's"—Karin steps into a situation very similar to the one in which Naomi finds herself soon after the start of *All I Desire*. Suzette's hostility to her is just as overt as Joyce's to Naomi, and the suggestion is strong in both cases that the two daughters want their father to themselves and aren't ready to brook any interference, especially from rivals for his attention. The Electra complex simmers away strongly in both films, whatever implications one draws from its presence.

This Love of Ours arrives at a happy ending of sorts. This is at least partially enabled because the problems that led to the initial breakdown of Michel and Karin's marriage—his failure to trust her and his possessiveness—simply vanish somewhere along the way, subsumed into his regret at having lost her. In *All I Desire*, the happy ending, as discussed earlier in this chapter, is at least a qualified one, the problems that led to Naomi's departure in the first place casting shadows across Naomi and Henry's final embrace.

Changes of heart and mind—like Suzette's and Naomi's—can't simply be dismissed as dramatic conveniences. They matter, as does the response of all the other characters around them to the choices they're making, and they *can* be dramatically plausible—as long as they're seen to be earned.

Never Say Goodbye adds little that is new to the template provided by *This Love of Ours*. The bond between the father here, Michael (Rock Hudson), and his little Suzy (Shelley Fabares, soon to play America's favorite teenage daughter in *The Donna Reed Show*, and become a pop star) is equally close. "It's an unusual and beautiful relationship between a father and daughter," Miss Tucker, the adoring housekeeper (Helen Wallace), knowingly explains at the start. And with Hudson bringing an unexpectedly brooding intensity to the part, Michael's jealousy is once again the chief factor causing the rift with wife Lisa (Cornell Borchers).

An additional edge is given to her relationship with the sketch artist who employs her (Sanders), although that's almost entirely because of his unconsummated desire for her. She exhibits no interest in him other than as a loyal friend. And rather than attempting suicide after she runs into Michael, Lisa flees from him into the street, where she's hit by a car.

Updates to the first screenplay are by Charles Hoffman, who'd worked for Sirk uncredited on *Here Comes the Groom* a few years earlier, but the original film's characters and the dialogue, or minor variations of them, remain. *Never Say Goodbye* begins, like *All That Heaven Allows*, with a car being driven along an orderly suburban street to the home Michael shares with Suzy (and with the staff that serves them). It's a sitcom suburbia—green lawns, pretty flower beds, lushly leafed trees, white-lace window curtains, paving-stone paths, everything in its proper place. In other words, it's an idyllic '50s dream of a privileged and impossibly peaceful way of life. And the ending sees the restored nuclear family, their arms around each other, walking inside the house and closing the door behind them on the traumas that have threatened their paradise.

What's missing here, however, are the rich ironies that cast Sirk's remakes of earlier Universal properties in such a different light from their originals and suggest that there might be more to what we're seeing than what immediately meets the eye. Like those films and the others discussed in this chapter, *Never Say Goodbye* deals with the stresses that go hand-in-hand with everyday life. But it does so without the nuances that give an extra dimension to Sirk's melodramas, nuances that point to the all-too-human complications that exist beneath, or alongside, their glossy surfaces and that belie their fairy tale colorings.

CHAPTER NINE

Sirk and John M. Stahl
Adaptations and Remakes

"I used to call them love stories; his phrase was 'if only' movies."
—ROSS HUNTER, 1988[1]

THERE IS A CLEAR COMMERCIAL IMPERATIVE FOR THE ADAPTATION OF novels, plays, TV shows, and comic books for the screen, and for film remakes and sequels. Producers and investors, in fact everyone involved in the process, will inevitably have their eyes on the financial prize at certain points along the way, even if their motives might sometimes also relate to the cultural import of a proposed project. And while the revisiting of a "property" with a proven track record may not be a guarantee of box-office success, history suggests that the familiarity factor can certainly provide a useful marketing component.

My concern here, however, is not with the business side of Sirk's films, but with what can be revealed by looking beyond that, by probing the differences between a source and its adaptation(s). What can we learn about the various creative forces at work in all incarnations of, say, *Magnificent Obsession*, through a comparison of Lloyd C. Douglas's novel, John M. Stahl's adaptation and Sirk's remake? To what extent can one identify variations in their creators' artistic sensibilities through them? How do the social and cultural frameworks in which each came to see the light of day impinge on the meanings they produce? And in what ways is the sense that each makes shaped by the medium that brings it into being?

Although serendipity clearly played a part, it's not entirely by chance that Sirk remade three Stahl films: first, *Magnificent Obsession*, then *When Tomorrow Comes* (which became *Interlude* for Sirk), and finally *Imitation of Life*. The studio for which the two directors worked—known as Universal Pictures in the 1930s and Universal-International Pictures from the

1940s—owned the film rights, and both men had shown an inclination towards and a talent for so-called women's pictures.

This chapter focuses on how the various intersections and divergences between the three versions of "the same story" amount to an implicit dialogue, even a three-way debate, between a novelist and two filmmakers (and their other collaborators) about how best to tell that story. And it is important to remember from the start that, although the stories they're telling can be summarized to seem the same, the novels and the films that bear their creators' signatures aren't *really* telling the same story. The similarities between them might be readily evident, but they're arguably outweighed by their differences: primarily in their contrasting styles, in the shifting details of plot and characters, and in the overarching views of the world brought to them by their creators.

Adaptations from page to screen and from one screen version to another are never simple or straightforward processes: any story always reveals itself in the telling. Aside from the obvious contrasts between a novel and a film, between words on a page and moving images on a screen and between the accumulation of words, sentences, paragraphs, and chapters in a book and the progress of images, scenes, and sequences on a screen, there are other equally complicated and complex differences to be explored.

Perhaps most important of these, especially for our examination of Sirk's films, is the tone of voice adopted by the storyteller, consciously or otherwise, in the telling of the story. Just as a novelist deploys all the elements at his/her disposal to guide us towards a way of regarding plots, characters, and the world around them, so too does a filmmaker's *mise-en-scene* shape the kinds of sense we make of his or her work.

There are also many other points of variance: to do with the omission of characters and incidents, the addition of new ones, the changes made to the dialogue the characters speak, the actors who bring distinctive personas as well as acting skills to their performances, and so on. In what follows, I've attempted to trace the ways in which the various versions of the three stories are similar to and different from each other with an eye to what they finally have to tell us about Sirk, his working methods, and his artistry.

MAGNIFICENT OBSESSION

"Magnificent in all that made the book a memorable best seller . . . and in all that can make a motion picture an unforgettable experience."
—MARKETING LINE FOR *MAGNIFICENT OBSESSION*, OCTOBER 1954

In the beginning there was the word, embodied in then-Protestant minister Lloyd C. Douglas's debut novel,[2] published in the immediate wake of the 1929 stock market crash. In 1935, the word became a film, directed by John M. Stahl and starring Irene Dunne and Robert Taylor, which, in turn, begat Douglas Sirk's 1954 remake with Rock Hudson and Jane Wyman.[3]

All three versions follow more or less the same plot line. Resuscitated after a boat accident on a lake, self-centered playboy Bobby Merrick learns that the emergency team which had come to his aid had, as a result, been unavailable to the widely respected Dr. Wayne Hudson, who'd suffered a heart attack on the other side of the lake. Merrick's guilt over Dr. Hudson's death and his quest for redemption lead to both his assumption of the late doctor's role in the community and his discovery of a formula for how to lead a constructive life.

The keys to this kingdom are provided by the late Dr. Hudson: in the novel, it's via the mysterious diary he's left behind, which Merrick is required to decode; in both films, it's via the counsel of an artist who knew the doctor. Along the way, Merrick falls in love with his widow, and her initial resistance finally gives way as various obstacles are overcome and his moral worth is proven.

LLOYD C. DOUGLAS'S *MAGNIFICENT OBSESSION*

While Douglas's novel has generally been regarded with condescension, it is reasonably engaging pulp, fueled by its author's committed belief in the rewards on offer from a Higher Power and occasionally leavened by a dry humor. A parable-like tale loaded with biblical allusions, it's both a love story and a mystery, with Merrick as the protagonist, Helen Hudson as his beloved, and her late husband's coded journal as a puzzle which, once solved, will provide the means for Merrick's redemption.

However, Merrick isn't introduced until more than twenty pages in. The opening chapter instead takes us inside Dr. Hudson's life before the cardiac arrest that ends it, establishing him as both a decent man and "the most important figure in the field of brain surgery on this continent."[4] And his legacy remains a driving force throughout the rest of the book, Merrick's eventual deciphering of his diary steering him towards a personal transformation.

The epiphany that represents Merrick's road-to-Damascus moment is his realization that Hudson's commitment to "a higher altruism,"[5] his magnificent obsession, had been the secret source of his power. In his diary, Hudson cites *his* inspiration as a sculptor named Randolph, now dead, describing him as not only "a consummate artist" but also "a miracle-man."[6] From him, the doctor has learned about the rewards of performing good deeds and revealing them to no one.

Douglas draws a clear parallel between Hudson and Merrick in the way they discover these rewards and what they do as a result. Merrick becomes Hudson's spiritual heir, committing himself to a future in medicine, assuming responsibility for others, and inspiring them to follow his example. Those he helps, even Helen's cousin, who exploits his position as a broker to steal from her, find a new purpose by doing as he does.

Even as she rebuffs Merrick's romantic overtures, Helen too comes to understand through him that a key obligation to her late husband is to take care of Joyce, Hudson's adult daughter from a previous marriage. If Merrick is a Christ-like figure, then she and everyone else who falls under his spell are surrogate disciples.

Douglas indicates early on that the lesson that his protagonist has to learn is that money isn't the solution to his problems. In the aftermath of the accident that leads to Dr. Hudson's death, he makes Merrick's irresponsible mindset explicit. "There would always be some way to settle it. There always had been. Was he not accustomed to paying for smashed fenders, broken china, splintered furniture, outraged feelings, and interrupted business? If anybody had a grievance, let him make a bill of it, and he would draw a check."[7]

Yet Merrick's transformation also comes as a consequence of financial transactions that see him effectively buying his way into a new deal. Merrick's wealth (like Hudson's before him) not only funds his donations to those in need but also gives him the wherewithal to invest in his own spiritual future. In other words, he's now greasing God's palm.

And Douglas ensures that he's always rewarded with the proper payoff, most significantly when he gets to use his skills as a surgeon, as well as a revolutionary scalpel he's invented along the way, to save Helen's life and sight after she's injured in an accident. The novel might have been designed as a modern-day parable, but it appears to have little in common with an earlier one about how hard it is for a rich man to enter the Kingdom of Heaven.

JOHN M. STAHL'S *MAGNIFICENT OBSESSION*

Stahl's adaptation of *Magnificent Obsession* is much more measured than its source. It's as if he has set out to drain the material of as much of its melodrama as possible. Comic bits of business are frequently deployed to provide a counterpoint to the emotional intensity of unfolding events; aside from behind the opening and closing credits, there is no non-diegetic music, and "musical director" Franz Waxman has designed a soundtrack that is largely devoid of the emotive force that was *de rigueur* for dramas of the 1930s;[8] and Stahl's visual style rigorously eschews the big, glowing close-ups that are characteristic of the melodramas of the time.

Instead, working with cinematographer John J. Mescall, Stahl relies heavily on master shots, with exchanges between the characters repeatedly filmed as unbroken two- and three-shot exchanges. The effect is to draw our attention to the flow of an interaction rather than to individuals' particular contributions to it—to make it not about one or another, but both or all—a visual approach which is subtly distancing and, arguably, at odds with any melodramatic impulse.

The presentation of the almost vignette-styled plot—made up of relatively brief "chapters" separated by fades to black—is readily recognizable as an adaptation of the approach taken by Douglas's novel (the Sirk film also deploys the same strategy). However, numerous details have been changed that also make it a very different kind of story.

Gone are numerous establishing elements and secondary characters as the filmmakers trim back the plot detail and create a different tone for the telling of the tale. Whereas the novel's first twenty pages deal with Dr. Hudson's life and his work running Westchester's Brightwood Hospital, Stahl's film begins as Hudson's wife, Helen (Dunne), picks up his daughter, Joyce (Betty Furness), at the New York waterfront at around the time of his off-screen death. Only on their arrival at the hospital do they hear about it and about the unavailability of the life-saving equipment because it was being used to tend to Merrick (Taylor). All that we come to know of the doctor emerges through what the other characters in the film have to say about him.

Randolph, the famous sculptor who was Hudson's spiritual mentor in the novel, is dead before the novel's story begins. Here, however, played by Ralph Morgan, he's alive and well and, in fact, indebted to Hudson for the access he's gained to the secret power, rather than the other way around. As a result, there's no need for any diary to be decoded in order for Merrick to discover how "to make contact with a source of infinite power." It's a simple solution for the filmmakers, who were faced with having to find something visually interesting in a man poring over a book for lengthy stretches of time and launching into philosophical dissertations about its contents.

While the novel builds a back story regarding the automobile empire that has provided the foundations for the Merrick family's riches, the film changes the source of their wealth to an electrical power company, which is merely noted in passing. The grandfather who founded it is only referred to in a throwaway line: near the end of Merrick's first visit to Randolph's studio, he says that his grandfather owns stock in a nearby powerhouse. His aside comes as Randolph compares how Hudson taught him to rise above himself with the turning on of a switch to make a stove work, a much more concise analogy than the one Douglas had come up with in the novel.[9]

The adaptation also eschews the novel's reference to an earlier romantic attachment between Merrick and Helen's stepdaughter, Joyce, the filmmakers clearly regarding it as an unnecessary complication. And it removes any reference to the unconsummated yearnings which hospital superintendent Nancy Ashford (Sara Haden) had for the late Dr. Hudson in the novel.

Furthermore, it changes the character of Tommy (Charles Butterworth), Joyce's boyfriend. In the novel, he's an old friend of Merrick's with a drinking problem that threatens his relationship with Joyce, and he needs help to get his act together. Cue another Merrick intervention. In the film, however, he's simply depicted as a good-humored lapdog, nicknamed "Poopsy," who traipses along behind her like a transplant from a screwball comedy. He appears primarily in the interests of light relief, only briefly crosses paths with Merrick, and doesn't have a drinking problem.

As in the novel, Merrick again works secretly to repair Helen's and the hospital financial affairs, which are in a mess as a result of her late husband's deployment of its funds for his charitable acts. But there's no duplicitous broker cousin around in the film to take advantage of Helen.

There are further changes between novel and film in their depictions of what happens to her, some of them minor, some crucial. Most significantly, the accident that blinds her and puts her life at risk occurs late in the book (only sixteen pages before the end), but takes place at the halfway mark of the film. Here it's presented as a direct result of her attempt to escape Merrick's advances, making it seem as if there's nothing he can do right as far as the Hudson family is concerned. In the novel, it occurs while Helen is away overseas.

At the same time, however, its placement in the film has far-reaching effects on what follows. One is that, supported by some citing of *Hamlet* that isn't in the book, the Oedipal implications of Merrick's mission and his pursuit of Helen come more clearly into focus. Put simply, the reshaping of the plot leads to them spending more time together, to her adjusting to her blindness, and to him ingratiating his way into her trust incognito (she's blind and doesn't recognize his voice). Furthermore, what happens between them is no longer thrust into the background by his musings about Hudson's diary or by his discussions about religion with a minister friend on whom he's operated (and who doesn't figure in the film).

In both novel and film, Helen travels to Europe, but for very different reasons. In the book, it's strongly suggested that her trip is a flight from her feelings for Merrick. Further disillusionment sets in when she realizes that he's manipulating her life from afar—with the best of intentions, of course—helped by a friend whose husband he's assisted with his medical studies back home (neither she nor her husband appear in the film). It's only after word of her accident reaches the now famous Dr. Merrick that he and Helen are brought together again, with him performing the operation that saves her.

In the film, however, her trip to Europe occurs *after* her accident when, unbeknownst to her, Merrick arranges for a consultation with the world's leading eye specialists in Paris. However, when they tell her that nothing can be done, the film's tone darkens considerably. Facing the rest of her life without her sight—"Joyce, you don't know how lonely it is in the dark," she tells her traveling companion (who doesn't accompany her in the book)—she contemplates leaping from her apartment window in Paris to her death. Only Merrick's unexpected arrival from America prevents her from doing so. He takes her out for the evening, but then she mistakes his subsequent proposal for pity and flees early the next morning.

The film's rearrangement of the narrative not only pushes the relationship between Merrick and Helen more fully into the foreground, but also grounds his efforts to step into Hudson's shoes in his feelings for her and his wish to do something to help her condition rather than in his belief in some Higher Power.

After her accident, Helen vanishes, and six years pass before he receives news of her (even though it's only a few minutes of screen time). In the interim, he's acquired some grey around the temples, become a brilliant surgeon, funded clinics, donated to medical research, been rewarded for his efforts with a Nobel Prize, and has become a fully fledged and officially accredited hero. Furthermore, as he explains to Randolph, his good deeds haven't been "to better myself in any way" but to assist Helen, "hoping she might be one of those helped without my knowledge."

The film thus replaces the novel's insistence on the material benefits available for benefactors—its Merrick likens them to "earn[ing] compound interest"[10]—with an emphasis on its protagonist's altruism. And it raises a knowing eyebrow at the happy ending which it confers on the lovers with its reference to the Sleeping Beauty fairy tale in its closing sequence. Merrick's operation on Helen serves as the equivalent of a waking kiss.

Stahl's reshaping of the material has resulted in a very different kind of story from the one told in the novel. The results are sometimes to the film's detriment: the screwball elements, for example, at times seem awkward, as if out of touch with the serious events unfolding around them. But the general rearrangement of Douglas's plot, the distinctively different viewpoint the film brings to its characters and their motives, and the marked shift in tone make it clear that Stahl and his collaborators are taking a creative step away from the limitations of their source.

DOUGLAS SIRK'S *MAGNIFICENT OBSESSION*

If Stahl set out to drain much of the melodrama out of Douglas's novel, Sirk's goal appears to have been to put it all back in, and then some. Much of the commentary on his version over the years has correctly drawn attention to its use of the stock features of melodrama: the exaggerated use of coincidences in the plotting, the broadly drawn characters, the full-on score (by Frank Skinner), and so on. Sirk drew extensively on these elements throughout his career, but it's probably accurate to say that, of all the films he made, *Magnificent Obsession* is where he takes them over the top.

Perhaps as a result of this, as Jean-Loup Bourget points out in his fine commentary, "even some of Sirk's devotees have trouble in accepting [it]."[11] The melodramatic excess might also explain why Victoria L. Evans, in her refreshingly original reading, introduces it as "this infamous film."[12] And why, in *Sirk on Sirk,* Halliday opens their exchange about it by confessing his discomfort with it: "I'm rather perplexed how you came to make something like this," he says, describing the film as "an out-and-out melodrama, to put it mildly"[13] and "an appalling weepie."[14] Even Sirk himself describes the material he's dealing with as "a combination of kitsch, and craziness, and trashiness."[15]

The project was initially brought to his attention by producer Ross Hunter[16] as one Jane Wyman wanted to do. With her career in the ascendancy after she won an Oscar for *Johnny Belinda* (1948), as well as nominations for *The Yearling* (1946) and *The Blue Veil* (1952), the actress had achieved a considerable degree of credibility for her wounded-women roles.

Just as Sirk said he tried in vain to read Lloyd C. Douglas's novel, he also claimed never to have seen Stahl's adaptation. "I didn't know it even existed," he told Halliday. "I think that what happened was that Ross Hunter had a treatment made of the Stahl script . . . I took it home and read it. I thought, my god, and then I showed it to Mrs. Sirk and she read it and said, 'Detlef, if you make this you're dead—and so am I.'"[17]

With these comments Sirk would appear to be disassociating his version of *Magnificent Obsession* from both the novel and the Stahl adaptation, the implicit suggestion being that his film owes little to them. But this is clearly not the case, even if, finally, its indebtedness is far outweighed by its reinvention of the material. At the same time as Sirk's film *is* very different in tone, various aspects of its predecessors' character profiling, dialogue, and narrative shape have found their way into it. Some of the similarities stem from the original novel; others from the changes Stahl's film makes to its plot details, or, perhaps, from the treatment Hunter passed on to Sirk.[18]

Adapted by Wells Root, with a screenplay by Robert Blees, who also co-wrote Sirk's *All I Desire* (1953), Sirk's remake more or less traces the same story arc as Stahl's. Wyman replaces Irene Dunne (and also receives top billing), Rock Hudson replaces Robert Taylor, and the late Dr. Wayne Hudson becomes the late Dr. Wayne Phillips, apparently to avoid any confusion between the character and the film's male lead—although it remains difficult to work out who exactly might have been confused by this: the actors on the set? the film's audience? As in the 1935 version, even though he's never seen, Sirk's equivalent for Hudson still exerts a significant influence over what occurs. His intermediary, as in Stahl's film, is Edward Randolph (here played by Otto Kruger), a painter this time rather than a sculptor.

There are numerous other minor changes, although their accumulation lends them significance. The film opens with Bob Merrick hurtling

Playboy Bob Merrick (Rock Hudson) and widow Helen Phillips (Jane Wyman) soon after they've met in *Magnificent Obsession*.

dangerously across a lake in his speedboat, an accident waiting to happen, rather than with Helen picking up Joyce and Tommy at the pier in New York, as in the Stahl version. Sirk's film introduces the two women in the following sequence, as they're driving home after a Manhattan shopping excursion (with Barbara Rush as Joyce) and just before they hear about Dr. Phillips's death.

Soon afterwards, as the boorish Merrick, wearing stylish silk pajamas, complains about the service in the hospital where he's recuperating after the accident, superintendent Nancy Ashford (Agnes Moorehead) makes passing mention of the source of his wealth: "the Merrick Motor Company," as in the novel (Sirk might not have read it, but clearly someone contributing to the screenplay had).

Stahl's version has Merrick coming across Helen and her broken-down car on a country road, whereas Sirk's brings them together when she's driving home from the hospital. He's fleeing an enforced convalescence, but only too willing to pause to make a pass at an attractive woman. As in the novel, he realizes who she is during their conversation; as in Stahl's film, she doesn't discover who he is until his return to the hospital.

The Oedipal thrust evident in the Stahl film is again noteworthy here, as Michael Stern points out.[19] It's made even clearer by having the action start with a symbolic execution, Merrick's bravado inadvertently leading to Dr. Phillips's death. Chronologically the age difference between the two leads—Wyman was thirty-six at the time of filming, Hudson, twenty-eight—might have been marginally less than the eleven years separating Irene Dunne and Robert Taylor. But the younger-man-older woman dynamic that was made explicit in Sirk's recasting of Wyman and Hudson for *All That Heaven Allows* (1955) is also in evidence here. Wyman, who earned another Oscar nomination for the film and who gives a performance that is both dignified and heartbreaking, always looked older than her years and seemed well-equipped to deal with whatever crises befell her characters.[20]

Both film versions are propelled by coincidence. In the Stahl film, Merrick ends up at Randolph's studio-home after he and screwball Tommy have been out on the town, with a sozzled Tommy driving as they pull up at a "Road Closed" sign. In Sirk's film, where Tommy is transformed into the much more upright Tom (Gregg Palmer), lawyer to the Phillips family as well as Joyce's fiancé, a drunk Merrick is alone and behind the wheel when his sports car crashes into a "Danger" sign, only a short stagger from Randolph's front door. Merrick's recklessness and irresponsibility is the point here, as it had been on the lake, and as it is in a subsequent sequence when his arrival at an outdoor restaurant is marked by squealing tires.

This is linked to his insecurities about his place in the world, which Sirk establishes visually by having him constantly trying to force his way into spaces occupied by others, as if afraid of being left out of the life going on inside them. He's forever knocking on people's doors, demanding to be let in, or barging into the frame, insisting that people pay attention to him. Seen in this context, his decision to make reparation for the wrongs he believes he's done to Helen and to be the best doctor he can are as much a consequence of his insecurities, his need to find acceptance, as they are a way of providing for those in need.

During Merrick's initial exchange with Randolph, the artist/guardian angel tells him that Phillips, his best friend, had explained how one might contact a Higher Power by using a lamp (rather than the stove of the earlier version) to illustrate the point. In the Stahl film, Randolph makes the point and it's not referred to again; in the Sirk, it resonates visually throughout the rest of the film, the subsequent switching on of lamps and other lighting devices, and the opening of blinds a way of bringing light into a prevailing darkness. A simple detail in the 1935 film is transformed into a key motif in the 1954 version.

In most of Sirk's work, the décor defines the characters' world. His interiors often suggest prisons without bars (as in *There's Always Tomorrow*). And, here, the characters seem to be struggling with forces they can no more see than we can: the forces of fate and happenstance that lie beyond human awareness or understanding. Beautifully shot and lit in a mostly non-naturalistic style by regular Sirk collaborator Russell Metty,[21]

Magnificent Obsession creates a world in which the characters seem forever encroached upon, constantly being embedded in pools of shadow.

The impression is further highlighted by the recurring visual contrast between shadow-dominated interiors and bright exteriors visible through windows, or by the vibrant colors of objects frequently prominent in the frame (most often flowers). In such a context, the switching on of a lamp, or even the mere presence of one in a shot, serves as an ongoing reminder of the characters' attempts to cast light on their surroundings, both metaphorically and literally. It's not only Helen who finds herself groping around in the dark.

As in Stahl's version, the insensitive Merrick's attempts to win over the still-grieving widow leads to her being blinded in a car accident. This happens about a third of the way into Sirk's telling of the story. And, again as in the Stahl, during her recovery, Merrick inveigles his way into her company by hiding his identity from her. Here, though, he secretly pays for her to travel to Switzerland, rather than Paris, to consult the eye specialists.

Their bad news once more leads her to despair. "It's funny, but the nighttime is the worst time," she tells Joyce, "It does get darker, you know. And I know that, when I wake up in the morning, there won't be any dawn." As if to push away Helen's suffering, Joyce turns on the lamps in their apartment, but they make no difference and soon afterwards Helen is contemplating suicide.

This time, though, she's *already* made the decision not to jump to her death by the time Merrick rings the doorbell to the apartment they've rented. Reaching out blindly on the balcony, she knocks a pot plant over the edge, its crash to the ground halting her movement towards the railing.

As in Stahl's version, Merrick then takes Helen out for the evening. But instead of the romantic Lubitsch-style evening in a glittering Paris that Stahl allowed them, Sirk has the lovers driving through the Swiss countryside (back-projected) to a small village where a festival is in progress and where they dance the night away together. Their dialogue as they drive underlines the fairy tale aspects of their escapade. "There's a moon, as there should be," Merrick tells her, describing what she can't see. "And, just ahead, the lights of a little old town." "Just as there should be," she finishes for him. They're both knowingly engaging in the fantasy, itself serving as a light in their darkness.[22] As Bourget points out,[23] the sequence is filled with echoes of Max Ophuls's *Letter from an Unknown*

Woman (1948): their drive through the back-projected countryside recalls the sequence in which Stefan (Louis Jordan) and Lisa (Joan Fontaine) visit a scenic railway in a Vienna park, their romantic exchange there set against a background defined by its artifice; and their dancing past midnight, oblivious to the restaurant staff's wish to head home, references a similar scene in Ophuls's film.

To Merrick's proposal that, from tomorrow, they'll never be apart, Helen wistfully sighs, "Tomorrow," as if wishing away the knowledge that she's already planning to disappear from his life so as not to burden him with her disability. Their exchange here is echoed by the last scene of the film, after Merrick has operated on her and successfully restored her sight. Sirk is both giving us the fairy tale ending and reminding us that we shouldn't be deceived by it. "Starting tomorrow, we'll never be apart," he tells her. As the music soars, ostensibly signaling a happy ending, she sighs again, "Tomorrow . . . tomorrow . . . ah, tomorrow."

In casting a shadow of ambiguity over the "magnificent obsession" that guides the film's characters towards hope and, in Merrick's case, redemption, Sirk's *Magnificent Obsession* moves us far from the mission-accomplished, rewards-received, life-goes-on resolution to Douglas's novel and from the more nuanced happy ending to Stahl's film, with its strategic summoning of a fairy tale reference. And although reference is made to the noble man who "went to the cross at the age of thirty-three," the religious underpinnings of Douglas's novel and, to a lesser extent, Stahl's adaptation are all but done away with here. Sirk's Merrick is a man who does good deeds, but he never achieves self-awareness.

A key aspect of Sirk's work is that the stories he has to tell are always (and knowingly) complicated by the ways in which he tells them. In particular, they emerge through the dichotomy he's able to create between their visual design and their characters' understandings of their circumstances. His *Magnificent Obsession* perfectly illustrates this. While its surfaces might suggest "a ferociously straight face,"[24] they also point to other ways of understanding the drama unspooling before our eyes.

And they achieve a moving balance between an empathy for the plight of the characters—Hudson's powerful contribution as Merrick is often undervalued, as is Wyman's performance—and the ironic distance which allows us to see them all in a different light. As noted in my analysis of *Battle Hymn*, Merrick's persistent efforts to thrust himself into the center of the action have as much to do with his sense of insecurity as they do with his attempts to find a moral redemption.

INTERLUDE

> "Yet my heart can smile a little while
> Because I knew this interlude with you."
> —FROM THE TITLE SONG FOR *INTERLUDE*[25]

Douglas Sirk shot *Interlude* in 1956, between *Battle Hymn* and *The Tarnished Angels*. Starring June Allyson and Rossano Brazzi and implicitly acknowledged in the credits as a remake of John M. Stahl's *When Tomorrow Comes* (1939), it's rarely discussed in critical commentaries about the director's work. In fact, in my research on Sirk's career, I found only passing reference to it in the books and numerous journal articles written about the filmmaker.

In his notes on Sirk, Fassbinder observes that it's "hard to get into" and essentially ignores the particulars of the film in order to insert more general perceptions about the director's concerns. "After seeing Douglas Sirk's films," he writes, "I am more convinced than ever that love is the best, most insidious, most effective instrument of social repression."[26] He doesn't explain how *Interlude* might have further persuaded him about the dark side of love. And, in comparison to Sirk's generally acknowledged major works, *Interlude* effectively exists in the shadows.

Before *Interlude*, though, there was Stahl's *When Tomorrow Comes* and, before it, James M. Cain's *The Root of His Evil*,[27] a short novel that wasn't published until long after Stahl's film had been made. According to David Madden and Kristopher Mecholsky,[28] its plot was dreamed up over a lunch in 1928 with Kenneth Littauer from *Collier's* magazine who'd said he wanted "a modern Cinderella story" to serialize. *The Modern Cinderella*, in fact, became the working title for Stahl's film. In his cited comments to Halliday about *Interlude*, Sirk appears unaware of any of this and is in error about the source material for Stahl's film: "I was given an outline based on the Stahl picture, which had originally been extremely loosely based on *Serenade* by Jimmy Cain."[29]

JAMES M. CAIN'S *THE ROOT OF HIS EVIL*

Divided into four parts and eighteen chapters, Cain's hard-edged 168-page novel features as its untrustworthy narrator a twenty-something working-class woman. "I am Carrie Selden, the Modern Cinderella," she announces on the first page, before outlining a series of events that chart her rise in social status.

The first is a chance meeting with the initially mysterious Grant Harris at Karb's Diner, the Lower Broadway restaurant where she works. The second is an equally chance encounter with Evan Holden, a charismatic union leader, who flatters her after she is unexpectedly thrust into the forefront at a waitresses' strike meeting. He subsequently becomes Grant's rival for her affections.

To the reader, she casts herself as a hard worker and a planner: "When I came to New York and saw the night deposit boxes maintained by the banks there," she tells us, "I came to the resolution that has been an important part of my life: Let no working day go by which does not represent an amount saved."[30] But there are hints along the way that her characterization of herself as a conscientious innocent making her way in the world might be misleading. "Everything about you seems delicate and flowerlike," Grant tells her early on, "except that really you're very cold and knowing."[31] She protests, but it proves to be a sharp observation, Cain economically establishing her as a young woman with her eyes firmly on the prize and a carefully calculated strategy about how best to acquire it.

As she commences her climb up the social ladder, he depicts her as keenly alert to the nuance of a situation and able to turn even unexpected circumstances to her advantage. Her socially polished methods of getting ahead are placed alongside her waitress friend Lula's crass manipulations. Their goals might be shared, but the contrast between them and the complications that envelop Carrie's personal life become signposts to the brutal rules governing the world she has entered.

It also becomes clear before the end of Part One that, while Carrie might be a canny operator, events are controlling her rather than the other way around. Only when Grant takes her boating on Long Island does she come to realize that, in social terms, he might be out of her league. Evan tells her later, "You can't get away with it. You aren't of his class,"[32] but she already knows she's taking a risk, even if, as the story's narrator, she hasn't kept us fully informed of this.

Grant understands the lie of the land in a way that she can't. Just as he's able to identify the squall that arises when they're out on the Sound long before she has any sense that something is amiss, he also recognizes that both of them are slaves to a "system" that determines their social place. And the metaphorical implications of the squall are immediately clear.

Like *Mildred Pierce* (1941), Cain's more fully fleshed-out novel about a woman attempting to rise above the social station the world has determined for her, *The Root of His Evil* deals with its protagonist's dawning awareness of the impossible odds confronting her. Carrie's chief rival for Grant is his mother and the "silver cord" that binds them, which a sympathetic ally from the moneyed class explains to her is "an intangible but terrible bond, that sometimes exists between mother and son, and invariably spells trouble for them both."[33] But an even more insidious threat to her well-being is the class system whose rules define her as an outsider in Grant's world.

Carrie's quest is to unravel the secrets of this world and to find her place in it. However, any victory she might think she has achieved as she ends her story is qualified by the cold-blooded methods she's used to achieve them. She might present herself as a fairy tale heroine in modern dress, but Cain makes us see her reflection in the mirror very differently from the way that she does. "You take things any way you can get them," she tells Grant on the last page of the book. "That's what *I* always do."

JOHN M. STAHL'S *WHEN TOMORROW COMES*

"This movie bore no relation to the original story," Cain told Peter Brunette and Gerald Peary.[34] And it's not hard to see why he'd make such a claim. In Stahl's film, Carrie Selden becomes Helen Lawrence (Irene Dunne), still a working girl and a leader among women, but any ambiguity about her character and the way she moves into a more glamorous world has been methodically removed. Alongside her, poor little rich boy Grant has become famous classical pianist Philip Chagal (Charles Boyer).

The renovation the character has undergone is in line with the Hollywood romantic melodrama's commitment to the notion that classical musicians automatically exude a charm other men lack, especially when they have a foreign accent.[35] Furthermore, the film replaces the "silver cord" elements of Cain's plot—which would never have found approval under the Production Code in place in 1939—with a different kind of female problem for Monsieur Chagal.

Here the woman in question is his wife, Madeleine (Barbara O'Neil), rather than his mother. Although the Code routinely forbade any sympathy for men engaging in extramarital affairs, the film structures the scenario so that any condemnation of his adultery is at least partially qualified by the fact that—in a variation on the mad-woman-in-the-attic plot device in *Jane Eyre*—Madeleine is presented as psychologically disturbed. Unofficially at least, this apparently provides proper cause for some flexibility as far as the "for better or worse" clause of the marriage vows is concerned.

The source of Madeleine's problems, it's proposed, is that, five years earlier, their baby had been born dead and, according to her mother (Nella Walker), "she never got over it." As a further buffer to any hasty censuring of his infidelity, the film has Chagal go on to explain to Helen how it is for Madeleine: "Doctors say she's not unhappy," he says. "She lives in a world of her own." However, a later scene where an almost sinister Madeleine pays a visit to Helen and warns her to stay away from her husband suggests that the diagnoses by Chagal and her mother might not be entirely accurate.

In Cain's novel, union leader Evan Holden competes with Grant for Carrie's affections. In the film, he becomes Jim Holden (Onslow Stevens) and is perfunctorily downgraded by the plotting. It's clear that he is interested in Helen, but, in a divergence from the set-up in the novel, he's never depicted as a serious rival to the charming Chagal. And after she agrees to go out to dinner with him but then finds herself otherwise occupied, with Chagal, he disappears altogether from the film.

Finally, Carrie's artless friend Lula here becomes Helen's good-natured workmate and flatmate, Lulu (Nydia Westman). A ditzy blonde along the lines of the characters played by Billie Burke or Judy Holliday, she serves as a likable comic foil to the much smarter and more glamorous Helen.

All this said, though, even if it is understandable that Cain saw nothing of *The Root of His Evil* in *When Tomorrow Comes*, it's also clear that the film has drawn heavily on it. The fluidly directed opening sequence, set in Karb's diner where Helen works, not only deals with her meeting with Philip but also provides the foundation for a supportive depiction of the waitresses' strike for better wages and work conditions. And here the film's depiction of a heartless capitalism at work seems in accord with Cain's critique. A strike is the only option, Jim explains, when workers feel "crushed and helpless."

Furthermore, in a telling scene, after the strike meeting where the women have delivered a rousing rendition of the union anthem "Solidarity Forever," Helen and Chagal find themselves walking along a street in the poor part of town. They're passed from behind by two young boys, one seated on a cart, the other pushing it along with one hand and holding his pants up with the other. She turns their activity into an acerbic metaphor, describing it as like "capitalism taking a ride and labor pushing with its pants falling down."

After this, however, the film turns its attention to the romance between Helen and Chagal, which largely displaces any further concern with the strike. Aside from a brief scene towards the end of the film where its success is noted, it's effectively excised from the proceedings. Only a gentle hint of the class differences between the two lovers remains.

Following the plot line of the novel, the film has Helen discovering when she goes boating with him on Long Island that the suave Frenchman who's been serenading her isn't just any old piano player. After the squall finds them fleeing for shelter, like Carrie and Grant in the novel, they take refuge from the storm in his mansion, which is where she learns his true identity.

But while the dialogue suggests she's thunderstruck by her surroundings, she seems very much at home in them. This is in sharp contrast to the ways in which the class issue is sustained throughout the book. Even if the social differences between the working woman and the man she falls in love with remain in play here, they're de-emphasized, replaced by other more immediately personal obstacles.

When Tomorrow Comes is widely referred to as an attempt to cash in on the successful pairing of Dunne and Boyer in Leo McCarey's *Love Affair* (1939), which was released shortly before Stahl's film went into production. Reports suggest that shooting began without a completed script, indicating that it was made in a rush and, perhaps, explaining its failure to follow through with some of the plot details and themes that it introduces.

Nevertheless, in line with motifs in other romantic melodramas of the era (and beyond), the film consistently draws attention to the way in which the passage of time seems to be forever ruling the characters. The first words uttered in the film introduce this via a message being passed around the team of waitresses at Karb's Kitchen, summoning them to a strike meeting: "Eight o'clock tonight at Unity Hall." Soon afterwards, their boss is bustling them back on to the job, reminding them that everyone's day is arranged according to time: "Space is money at lunchtime," he barks.

Not long after Helen meets Chagal, he tells her that he has to go back to France in seventy-two hours. Even before she knows about Madeleine, the limit on their time together serves as a reminder of the transience of anything that might occur between them. The film's title, effectively a declaration that tomorrow *always* comes, underlines her understanding of this in the sequence where he takes her to Long Island. With the storm raging outside his house, their tryst becomes an escape from reality, as both of them understand, even if they have different attitudes towards it. At first.

"I'd better be getting back to town," she tells him. "By the looks of the storm, it's now or never." Kissing her at the door, he says, "Let's make it never." She kisses him back, then replies, "Let's make it now," pulling away from their embrace and indicating that the time has come to leave.

On the drive back to New York, they find the highway has been washed out. A roadblock diverts them on to a side road and it seems as if destiny is guiding them to the refuge of a church. There she falls into his arms, and everything is set up to indicate that they should be together, with the deft use of two-shots, the cutting, and the setting itself conveying their increasing sense of togetherness and lending a special transcendence to their union. Stahl's direction of the actors and the conviction they bring to their roles persuasively suggests that fate has guided these two people towards each other. For various reasons, as we will see, it's not an impression that one gains at all from Sirk's remake.

When Philip pauses, announcing that there's something he has to tell her, she stops him, having already become aware that he's been hiding something from her. In the Long Island house, she's seen the photograph of the woman we subsequently learn is his wife and wants to ensure that, at least for one night, the cruel passage of time is not going to get in the way of their happiness.

The sequence in the church led to Cain taking the filmmakers to court in 1942 for infringement of copyright. The incident doesn't appear in *A Modern Cinderella* and, it was alleged, had been borrowed by the writer(s) of *When Tomorrow Comes* from Cain's *Serenade*. Since Universal had only paid Cain for the rights to *A Modern Cinderella*, he sued Stahl, writer Dwight Taylor, and the production. The court eventually decided in favor of the defendants.

However, beyond any specific borrowings from Cain, one could argue that the chief inspiration for the film is the set of conventions by which the Hollywood romantic melodrama operates. And that the choices made by the filmmakers—from the casting of the leads, through the plotting to the soft lighting, methodical framings, and use of music (the score is, again, especially restrained)—are dictated by their flair for the genre and the intelligence that informs their response to it.

DOUGLAS SIRK'S *INTERLUDE*

The same point applies to Sirk's film (aside from the deliberately florid score Frank Skinner composed for it). Made almost twenty years later, it was, according to the credits, adapted by Inez Cocke, "based on a screenplay by Dwight Taylor and a story by James Cain," and written by Daniel Fuchs (*Love Me or Leave Me, Jeanne Eagels*) and Franklin Coen (*Johnny Dark, Alvarez Kelly*). But while Cain is still acknowledged, the connection with *A Modern Cinderella/The Root of His Evil* has become even looser than it was in *When Tomorrow Comes*.

The film is set in and around Munich and Salzburg rather than New York and Long Island, the shoot providing Sirk with the opportunity to revisit some of the places of his earlier years for the first time since the end of World War II, albeit with his leg in a cast after the accident during the closing stages of the *Battle Hymn* shoot. The plot pivots on an affair between Helen Banning (Allyson), a young American woman working as a librarian at Amerika Haus, the US information agency in Munich, and a famous conductor, Tonio Fischer (Brazzi), who is married to the psychologically disturbed Reni (Marianne Koch).

Dr. Morley Dwyer (Keith Andes), an old family friend of Helen's who has been doing an internship at a Munich hospital, is also romantically interested in her, but she regards him without passion, as a friend and confidant rather than a lover. He's the equivalent of both union leader Jim Holden in *When Tomorrow Comes* and the decent but dull Harvey (Conrad Nagel) in Sirk's *All That Heaven Allows* (1954).

Interlude's equivalent for Carrie's Lula in *The Root of His Evil* and Helen's Lulu in *When Tomorrow Comes* is Gertrude (Frances Bergen), a neighbor in Helen's apartment block, who also works at Amerika Haus. She is much more knowing in the ways of the world than Helen, taking it upon herself to counsel her friend not to expect anything serious to come of her relationship with Tonio. "This is Munich, not home," she reminds her. "Men act differently here." Another American living abroad, she's Helen's opposite in her freewheeling approach to the opposite sex, her expectations and flamboyance standing in marked contrast to Helen's self-effacing modesty.

The sexual triangle linking Helen, Tonio, and his wife in *Interlude* is more or less identical to its equivalent in *When Tomorrow Comes*. However, the film as a whole has moved far from Cain's original design, which can be glimpsed (like a palimpsest) through the structure and plotting of *When*

Tomorrow Comes, but is barely discernible here. The union business of *The Root of His Evil* and the notion of its characters as "slaves" of a system have been entirely done away with. Cain's Carrie Selden and Grant Harris have, instead, been transformed into an American innocent abroad and an allegedly charming European musician who sweeps her off her feet.

It's not difficult to identify how the thinking underpinning this shift was determined by a longstanding recipe for screen romances in general. In fact, *Interlude* has just as much, if not more, in common with David Lean's 1955 Venice romance *Summertime* than with Stahl's film. In the Lean, a middle-aged English visitor (Katharine Hepburn) is drawn out of her solitude by a charming antiques dealer (Brazzi again, much more effective here), only to discover that he already has a wife and children.[36]

More broadly, Sirk's film is a generic relative of an abundance of other sexual-triangle films about travelers finding romance away from home, away from what they know as "reality": from cruise-ship romances like *The Lady Eve* (1941) and *Love Affair*, remade as *An Affair to Remember* (1957) and then again under its original title (1994), to more recent tales about travelers abroad such as *Before Sunset* (2004), *Vicki Cristina Barcelona* (2008), and *Midnight in Paris* (2011). Halliday is also right to observe that, thematically, "there seems to be a good bit of Henry James in *Interlude*."[37]

So, instead of a drama about the workings of capitalism and the class divide, Sirk's film—like Stahl's before it—focuses primarily on the romantic (and, implicitly, sexual) triangle. Its lead is followed by the 1968 remake of *Interlude* by British director Kevin Billington, even if that film's only acknowledgment of Sirk's film is that it shares its title. Cain's name has totally vanished from the credits, which, curiously, nominate the source as "an original screenplay" by Lee Langley and British TV writer Hugh Leonard.

Like *When Tomorrow Comes*, Sirk's *Interlude* is only loosely based on Cain's story. As always, the director goes his own way with the material, "bending" it according to his particular inclinations. Yet, at the same time and despite the very different surfaces of their works, it's possible to see Cain and Sirk as kindred spirits in their subversions of genre. Rather than simply inviting us to go along with the events they depict, both create an ironic distance between their protagonists and their readers/viewers. This is not to say that Cain's Carrie and Sirk's Helen are cut off from our sympathies but rather that they don't know themselves as well as we come to know them.

Time after time in Cain's novels, the protagonists' moral compromises and self-deceptions only gradually become apparent, by which time it's usually too late for us to step back from our empathy for them and avoid being at least a little bit implicated in their actions. Unreliable narrators are everywhere in his work, from *The Postman Always Rings Twice* (1934) through *Serenade* (1937) and *Double Indemnity* (1943) to *Rainbow's End* (1975). His description of his prose style is disarmingly simple: "I merely try to write as the character would write." But only when it's linked to his interest in "the art of letting a story secrete its own adrenalin"[38] does one gain a more precise impression of the way his novels work on the page.

As I have argued throughout this book, Sirk's films embrace their characters' yearnings at the same time as they scrutinize the circumstances that provoke those yearnings more knowingly than the characters are able to. And the extended warmth of that embrace is, to a degree, enabled by the fact that, unlike most of Cain's protagonists, they're generally trying to do the right thing.

Along these lines, even if she's not always the best judge of what might be good for her, Helen is depicted as honest, decent and likable. She's certainly not a user like Carrie. She's an individual who unexpectedly finds herself swept along by the romance of the moment. When Tonio tells her that she's "so sure of [her]self, so direct," linking this to the cliché about how uncomplicated Americans are, she vehemently rejects the description.

In fact, everything we see of her after her arrival in this unfamiliar city far from her Washington home points to how unsure of herself she actually is: entranced by Tonio's otherness, yet also fearful of where their relationship is leading her; in awe of the grandeur of her surroundings, yet also dwarfed by them and the sense of history they embody. As her friend Morley tells her, she's "on foreign soil in more ways than one."

Soon after *Interlude* begins, the picture postcard montage that accompanies Helen's taxi-ride from the train station in Munich to the apartment where she's going to be staying is a familiar setting-the-scene trope for films of this ilk. Nonetheless, in the context Sirk's film provides for it, it also serves as a precursor of what's to come, providing a hint about how she's about to be smothered by the unfamiliar place she's entering, a bewitching emotional trap that will take her breath away but also threaten her sense of who she is.

When Tonio drives her to Salzburg later in the film, the couple go sightseeing, pausing on a stone bridge overlooking the city and the mountains and castles beyond. "It's just like a fairy tale!" she exclaims. She's referring to the setting, but the line also applies to the entire image Sirk has composed, which includes her and her Prince Charming in the foreground.

"It's just like a fairy tale." Helen (June Allyson), her Prince Charming (Rosanno Brazzi), and Salzburg in *Interlude*.

On the one hand, Sirk is working to immerse us in the romance, while on the other he's deconstructing it for us with his CinemaScope compositions. While Helen is torn between her desires and her perception of the constraints imposed by her reality, the film's *mise-en-scene*, full of mirrors and reflections, proposes that what is real can be difficult to differentiate from an illusion.

Furthermore, Sirk's cutting and compositions constantly evoke the sense of life as a performance, otherwise straightforward dialogue scenes repeatedly framed so that doorways and other items of architecture suggest a proscenium arch.

Much in *Interlude* can be seen to have drawn its inspiration from *When Tomorrow Comes*: the couple from different worlds; the mentally ill wife (revealed much earlier here); the lovers who find themselves trapped in the aftermath of a storm and drawn together, almost as if they're the last two people on earth; the unsettling confrontations between the wife and her rival; the characters' expressed wishes to escape the realities that oppress them; the broken dinner date; the references to time constraints that underline the transience of their lives.

However, *Interlude* lacks the affective power of its predecessor, in large part as a result of the casting. Both Allyson and Brazzi play it straight, but while she is suitably earnest, he simply seems uncomfortable. They embody the same opposition as Dunne and Boyer—setting American ordinariness opposite European allure—but much less effectively. What makes Sirk's film engaging is the delicate and immensely poignant balance it sustains between what the characters believe about themselves and what the audience knows about them. As always, Sirk skilfully molds the material to his purpose, to the wider vision that informs most of his work.

IMITATION OF LIFE

> "The characters of melodrama are signifiers of social forces . . . templates for the tracing of society's invisible or ideologically dissembled ministers of power, while the narrative unwinds the psychological machinery of their enforcement. Personality becomes the crucible of the culture's contradictions."
> —JOHN FLAUS, 2002[39]

A bestseller when first published, Fannie Hurst's 1933 novel *Imitation of Life*[40] has spawned two American screen adaptations.[41] The first was released the following year, directed by Stahl, the second in 1959, directed by Sirk in what was his last Hollywood production before he returned to Europe.

The plots of all three versions have much in common: they deal with the developing relationship between two mothers, both widows, one white, the other black. In each case, the latter not only serves as a nanny and live-in housekeeper for the white woman but also becomes a personal confidante and a professional colleague. And, despite their obvious differences, they're further linked by their struggle—often a contentious one—to do right by their offspring, daughters who live in the shadow of their mothers' fears and flaws as they venture out into the world around them.

At the same time, the three tellings of the tale are melodramas about race relations, echoing the structure and the thematic concerns of fictions as various as Mark Twain's 1884 classic *The Adventures of Huckleberry Finn*, Stanley Kramer's *The Defiant Ones* (1958), and Jeff Nichols's *Loving* (2016). In each of these stories, a Caucasian and an African American are emotionally, or even literally, handcuffed together and forced to deal with their personal differences and confront external challenges together.

Yet, while similarities between the three versions of *Imitation of Life* are readily evident, they are outweighed by their differences: in their contrasting styles, in the shifting details of plot and characters, and in the overarching point of view brought to each recounting of the story.

FANNIE HURST'S *IMITATION OF LIFE*

After first appearing in serial form in the women's magazine *Pictorial Review*, in November, 1932, Hurst's shamefully undervalued novel became a bestseller, although much of the commentary about it has ignored its style, structure, and tone, and accused it of failing to accurately represent the realities of the lives of women and the race relations of the time. In the process, its social critique and progressive politics have largely been ignored.

An epic American tale, the novel strategically subverts both the classic Horatio Alger story and clichéd depictions of what it means to be female and living in the US in the early years of the twentieth century. Almost universally overlooked has been the subtly nuanced way in which Hurst's story makes the white protagonist, Bea Pullman (nee Beatrice Fay Chipley), its ruling consciousness. The novel isn't written in the first-person, but Hurst is concerned to stress that events are being presented through the perceptions of a well-intentioned, upwardly mobile white woman, who is relatively naïve about the ways of the world.

It begins and ends with a death that leaves Bea anguished and alone. In its first sentence, she's a teenager grieving the loss of her mother and grappling with the fact of her absence. All that follows is overshadowed by her ongoing fears of abandonment. As she travels from her humble childhood home on Arctic Avenue in Atlantic City to the Manhattan mansion which comes to signify her success as a businesswoman, these anxieties persist.

In the book's closing passages, which take place around twenty years later, she is distraught over the death of the African American woman whom she employed as her daughter's nanny and her housekeeper and who ended up as her business partner, along the way also serving as *her* surrogate mother.

Delilah Cillah Johnston had been the force behind and the public face of Bea's professional achievements, making waffles and maple-sugar hearts with "her great fluted white cap and great, fluted white smile on each box," and, in the process, Aunt Jemimah-like, becoming "mammy to the world."[42]

She'd also always fussed over the things that had been lacking from Bea's life, such as "man-lovin,'" instinctively understanding that this had been an absence even before Bea's husband was killed in a train crash. When Delilah dies, Bea again becomes like a lost child, a ship without a rudder.

The novel is, in fact, haunted by death, most forcefully exemplified by Delilah's constant obsessing over what awaits her. "When I drives up to dem pearly gates," she tells Bea, "Saint Peter's gwina say, here comes Delilah payin' glory to de Lawd who she served on earth an' will serve in heaven. Dat's me, Miss honey-Bea, as I sees mahself every night of mah life when I lays dis here hulk down to sleep. Ridin' up to heaven in a snow-white hearse wid de Lawd leanin' out when he hears de trumpets blowin' to see if I's comin' in a white satin casket pulled by six white horses."[43]

Hurst's *Imitation of Life* is, then, a tale of two women which condenses the world around Bea and Delilah into their actions, reactions, and interactions. In her eventual realization that she can enter a world that she'd thought was forbidden to her, Bea finds herself becoming an embodiment of the New Woman of the times. But there's no missionary zeal in her aspirations or her struggle, just a determination to make ends meet for her daughter and her ailing father, who lives with them.

Her experiences teach her how difficult it is for a professional woman to satisfy the wider demands made of her and, perhaps most difficult of all, her expectations of herself. When she eventually comes to recognize "man-lovin'" as a significant absence, she looks to her business manager, Frank Flake, eight years her junior, in hope of finding a Prince Charming. Hurst's representation of her feelings for him stresses her naïvety and lends a strategic ambiguity to her yearnings. But then Bea's dreams are shattered when she discovers that, while remaining loyal to her, he and her now-adult daughter, Jessie, have fallen in love.

On the other hand, Delilah pays little heed to business matters. Just as much a product of her times and particular social circumstances as her employer, she defines herself primarily according to her roles as a nurturer: to her own daughter, Peola, a mulatto whose late father Delilah refers to as "a white nigger . . . that you'd never think would have had truck with the likes of me";[44] to Jessie; and indeed to Bea. The fact that an entrepreneurial white woman is able to build her success on the foundations Delilah has provided remains as irrelevant to her as forging new frontiers for women is to Bea.

Hurst creates an impeccable dramatic logic by linking Bea's youthful dream of a domestic haven to the diners selling Delilah's delights: the mood created by these is "akin to the kennel warmth and brightness she so passionately wanted to pour around herself and [the] little family in the house on Arctic Avenue."[45] At the same time, though, she laces this logic with a brutal irony. Bea's escape from the physical constraints of domesticity is real, but it's also psychologically illusory, and her professional relationship with Delilah is a benign variation on the way her race has routinely exploited black labor.

Hurst embraces Delilah as an enormously sympathetic character trapped in a world that is not of her own making and, through her, offers a critique of the Aunt Jemima/"Black Mammy" stereotype.[46] Delilah's tragedy is that she mistakes the racist society that has spawned her for

God's will. "Every day of my life," she tells Bea, "I's gonna rear mah young un to know de glory of bein' born one of de Lawd's lowdown ones."[47]

For her, paradise is always linked to whiteness, and her skin color is the cross He's given her to bear. Peola grows up in the shadow of this well-meaning mother who has internalized the sense of inferiority inflicted on her race. She has become a witness to the oppression born of such a self-loathing. As Hurst puts it, for Delilah "in every matter of precedence, including teeth, was the priority of Bea's child most punctiliously observed. The duet of their howling might bring her running intuitively to her own, but the switch was without hesitancy to the white child, every labor of service adhering rigidly to that order."[48]

In order to escape the invisible chains that shackle her, Peola seizes the passport provided by her skin and, rejecting her African American roots, sets out to pass herself off as white. The consequences for her and for her relationship with her mother are harrowing. At the same time, her "passing" links her to Bea, whose entry into the business world has been enabled only by the "B. Pulman" on her business card that conceals her gender.

Hurst never lets us forget the social context in which these personal dramas unfold. Pointing to the parallel between Peola's identity crisis and Bea's ongoing anxieties about who she is, Daniel Itzkovitz draws attention to the novel's "interest in the broad implications of American 'self-making,' heretofore generally a male domain," and to how, as "the novel's central figure of rebellion against an oppressive social order, Peola attempts to find a way, like Bea, to transcend the identity into which she is born."[49] Doubtless, the Jewish Hurst's own upbringing in America gave her special insight into how an individual's craving for social assimilation can lead to an attempt to abandon the outward signs of difference.

One strand of the negative criticism that has been directed against the novel argues that it is "punishing" the two women by denying them success in their strivings. "In today's terms, both mothers suffer unjustly," writes Freda Freiberg. "The novel seems to punish working mothers and to suggest that they cannot mother properly if they work full time."[50] And even Itzkovitz's admiring introduction to the 2004 edition allows that "the novel's grim finale might easily be read as a punishment for Bea's ultimate choice of ambition over motherhood."[51]

Yet such approaches entirely miss the significance of Hurst's social commentary and the perspective that she's able to bring to the characters and the world they inhabit, ignoring the ways in which readers' sympathies can be used to provide the foundations for a social critique. Presenting its characters as prisoners of the ideology of their times, *Imitation of Life* no more punishes mothers for working than it punishes Delilah and Peola for being black. On the contrary, rather than providing them with a fairy tale ending that ignores the social realities all around, it invites us to be angry about those realities on their behalf.

JOHN M. STAHL'S *IMITATION OF LIFE*

Stahl's adaptation was a box-office hit, although it might never have been made if the PCA had got its way. Early in 1934, Joseph Breen, its recently appointed chief, refused to register the project because Peola was of mixed race: as a mulatto, she signified the occurrence of "sex association between the white and black race" somewhere in her family tree.[52]

Nevertheless, despite the official disapproval, the film went on to earn three Oscar nominations, including one for Best Picture. And its place in history is assured for its bold introduction of a commentary about race relations into a realm of popular American cinema which, as Breen's reaction indicates, was unaccustomed to dealing with such matters. It's one thing to look back at the film from the safe harbor of contemporary sensibilities; it's quite another to see it as a product of the time in which it was made and to reflect on the constraints under which its makers had to work.

The process of adapting Hurst's novel to the screen included a rigorous streamlining of the plot and reduction of its scope, as well as some revision of the characters. As the film begins, Bea is a widow, living in Atlantic City with three-year-old Jessie (Juanita Quigley) and dealing with the frustrations of being a working mother. "Mama's so late and she's got so much to do," she tries to explain to her daughter, who's vehemently protesting from the bathtub about having to go to day nursery.

In the midst of the chaos, there's a knock at the door, announcing the arrival of Delilah, who is to watch over Bea and Jessie for the next fifteen years or so. Declining payment, she says that all she wants is accommodation for her and her four-year-old, Peola (Sebie Hendricks), whose white skin belies her racial heritage. "Her pappy was a very light-colored man," Delilah explains matter-of-factly.

In the novel, Bea meets Delilah "across the railway yards [in] the shanty district."[53] She's gone there in desperation to search for a housekeeper to watch over her daughter and her invalid father (who's absent from the film) while she's out working. The film's juxtaposition of the stresses Bea is enduring and Delilah's entrance lends an air of magic to the visitor's appearance on her doorstep, effectively a *deus ex machina* that casts Delilah as something of a fairy godmother or guardian angel whom destiny has assigned to help Bea and take care of Jessie.

Details from the novel about Bea's past are compressed into her conversations with Delilah, who (as in the novel) instinctively identifies what's missing from her employer's life. "Y'oughta have a man takin' care of you, yes'm," she declares as she assumes her role as maidservant and foot masseuse. With the pancakes she prepares for her charges' breakfast, Delilah also inadvertently provides Bea with the key for an expansion of the maple syrup business she has taken over from her late husband.

Riding roughshod over any rights Delilah might have to the fruits of her labor, Bea goes about setting up a pancake business without ever consulting her employee. Whether we're meant to take this as a perfectly reasonable course of action for Bea or as a critique of her behavior remains unclear. Nonetheless, the subsequent scene in which Bea tells Delilah to assume an Aunt Jemimah pose by way of modeling for her sign painter (Henry Armetta) seems to invite laughter. And, soon afterwards, the film opens itself to the charge of racism in the scenes where Bea's business manager, Elmer Smith (Ned Sparks), pokes fun at Delilah's lack of business acumen.

Elmer's chief responsibility in the film appears to be the provision of comic relief, although he remains distinctly unfunny throughout. Sullen of demeanor and scathing in his observations about the world in general, he's a curious presence, a refugee from the Great Depression who becomes helpful to Bea in her business dealings, but is hopeless at anything else. Whereas Delilah advises Bea to lighten up and enjoy life more, he doesn't seem to understand anything beyond what needs to be done to make the business work smoothly, which is one of the reasons why he can't make sense of Delilah, or anyone else, for whom making money doesn't matter.

There's no equivalent for Elmer in the novel. The role there of Bea's empathetic business manager, Frank Flake, whom she comes to fancy, here appears to have been split between Elmer and Stephen Archer (Warren William). Stephen is an old friend of Elmer's (inexplicably!) with whom Bea falls in love the moment she lays eyes on him (equally inexplicably!). By the time he appears on the scene, she's become a successful businesswoman, her home a New York mansion looking out over the Hudson River and the Fifty-ninth Street Bridge. The film bestows on him the profession of an ichthyologist (no, really), but his appearance and demeanor identify him as the kind of playboy who regularly turns up in 1930s screwball comedies.[54] "She's got no time for romance," sourpuss Elmer warns him when he shows an interest in her, although Stephen knows better.

Their affair moves the film in a very different direction from the one taken by the novel. By the time that Jessie (played as an eighteen-year-old by Rochelle Hudson) returns home from boarding school in Switzerland, Bea and Stephen are talking marriage. But then Jessie proclaims her love for him, inadvertently driving a wedge between her and her mother. He sympathetically declines the teenager's advances, but the damage has been done.

The novel ends with Bea left alone and desolate, watching Jessie and Frank move towards their future. "They were so young, standing there . . . so right . . ."[55] The film ends poised somewhere between *Stella Dallas* (1925, 1937, 1990) and *Now, Voyager* (1942), as Bea turns down Stephen's proposal of marriage in order to avoid the perceived disruption which it would cause in her daughter's life. Over his very sensible objection that Jessie simply has a girlhood crush on him and will quickly forget about it, she insists that she's right: "You must see how impossible it is."

It's Delilah and Peola's relationship, though, which lies at the emotional heart of the film, as it did in the novel, even when its attention is officially elsewhere.

Their situation is the stuff of a modern tragedy, driven by a mother's laudable wish for her child to be true to herself—in this case, to accept her racial identity—and the child's perfectly reasonable wish to be free to make her own choices about how she's going to live her life. And the force which creates this tragedy is nothing less than an American way of life, a national ideology that asserts that those whose skin is black are automatically inferior to those who are white. It should come as no surprise to find the PCA raising objections to a work whose emotional power stems primarily from a critique of this.

As Laurent Berlant points out,[56] Delilah's attempt to make sense of her daughter's situation has her uttering "the film's most political sentences": "It ain't her fault, Miss Bea. It ain't yourn, and it ain't mine. I don't know rightly where the blame lies. It can't be our Lord's. Got me puzzled." But these lines also point to Delilah's lack of awareness, to her inability to see beyond the personal to the political, something which the film ensures that we come to understand.

There's a harrowing inevitability to the final exchange between her and Peola. In the novel, agonizingly, Peola never returns. In the film, she does, but only after Delilah's death, for which she holds herself responsible. "I killed my own mother," she wails. In their depictions of Peola's plight, both the novel and the film create a situation for which no happy outcome is possible, short of the civil rights uprising that was still decades away. The film's ending poses a resolution of sorts with Bea noting Peola's agreement to return to the college she'd earlier fled. But whether this represents a sign of Peola's surrender to the oppressive order of race relations or a triumphant reassertion of her identity is left as a question for another day, and another film.

DOUGLAS SIRK'S *IMITATION OF LIFE*

Producer Ross Hunter's initial plan for an *Imitation of Life* remake was to turn it into a musical. He'd acquired the rights to the novel in 1956 and, according to the *Hollywood Reporter*, had wanted Shirley Booth (Oscar-winner for 1953's *Come Back, Little Sheba*) to play the Claudette Colbert role and Ethel Waters (Oscar-nominated in 1950 for Elia Kazan's *Pinky*) the Louise Beavers one.[57] As planning progressed, Pearl Bailey replaced Waters in Hunter's proposed scenario, and then, when she became unavailable, Mahalia Jackson was penciled in. When she declined, Juanita Moore was offered the part, after which, Hunter brought Sirk on board, the director having recently completed filming on *A Time To Love and A Time To Die*.

In interviews, Sirk appeared to know nothing of this background. He told Jon Halliday that he thought Hunter gave him Hurst's novel, but that he didn't get far with it. "After a few pages I had the feeling this kind of American novel would definitely disillusion me," he says. "The style, the words, the narrative attitude would be in the way of my getting enthusiastic."[58] Hunter then gave him an outline based on Stahl's adaptation and work began in earnest on the screenplay. Sirk didn't see Stahl's film until after he'd finished his version. "I liked it, I thought it was very good, but it belonged to the previous generation," he remembered.[59]

The director believed that an update of the material was necessary in order to make it relevant to 1950s audiences, an era which had witnessed not just the decline of the power of the PCA, but also the birth of the civil rights movement: the Montgomery bus boycott in 1955, the struggle over desegregation in Little Rock, sit-ins organized by the NAACP (the National Association for the Advancement of Colored People), and the first stirrings of the "black is beautiful" movement.

Beginning in 1947, Sirk's version retains the four female characters at the heart of both the novel and Stahl's adaptation, but changes their names as well as the profession in which the white mother builds her career. Bea becomes Lora Meredith (Lana Turner), an aspiring actress living in Brooklyn; her daughter becomes Susie (played as a six-year-old by Terry Burnham and as a teenager by Sandra Dee); Delilah becomes Annie (Moore); and her mulatto daughter is Sarah-Jane (played as an eight-year-old by Karin Dicker and as an eighteen-year-old by Susan Kohner).

Lora's rise to Broadway acclaim parallels Bea's success as a pancake entrepreneur, with Annie serving as her nanny, confidante, and personal assistant—looking after the books, answering the phone the way it's supposed to be answered: "Miss Meredith's residence!" In a neat variation on the nice girl/vamp opposition in evidence elsewhere in American cinema (especially), Lora's love life is divided between a nice guy, the kind of man a gal would marry (if her mind wasn't focused elsewhere), and two men whose primary appeal for Lora lies in the professional power they wield. Sharing his name with Bea's beau in the Stahl version, Steve Archer (John Gavin), the photographer whom Lora meets in the opening sequence, represents the former, while agent Allen Loomis (Robert Alda) and playwright David Edwards (Dan O'Herlihy) embody the latter, both serving as means-to-an-end in Lora's quest to become a star.

The family tensions that pervade both Hurst's novel and the 1934 film remain: Sarah-Jane's resentment of her mother (". . . because you keep telling the world I'm your daughter") and her wish to be seen as white ("She can't help her color, but I can and I will"); Annie's anguish at her daughter's rejection ("Tell her . . . if I loved her too much, I'm sorry, but I didn't mean to cause her any trouble. She was all I had"); and Susie's Electra complex (although it's established and resolved differently in each version of the story).

Without any acknowledgment of the earlier adaptation, the official screenwriting credit for Sirk's *Imitation of Life* goes to Eleanore Griffin (*A Man Called Peter*, the 1961 version of *Back Street*) and Allan Scott (a regular writer on the Astaire-Rogers musicals and a contributor to the *Dr. Hudson's Secret Journal* TV series). Sam Staggs also suggests that Sy Gomberg (*The Toast of New Orleans, Summer Stock*) did a final polish on the screenplay.[60]

As already noted, by this time the power of the Production Code had been considerably reduced, Breen had retired and been replaced by the more liberal Geoffrey Shurlock, and the miscegenation matter that plagued Stahl in the early 1930s was no longer perceived as an issue. Still, given that Sirk's version also grapples with questions of racial identity and

Annie (Juanita Moore) watching over Susie (Terry Burnham) and Sarah-Jane (Karin Dicker) in the opening sequence of *Imitation of Life*

the relations between white and black America, there was the inevitable concern at Universal about how best to market the $2 million film since, according to an executive at the time, "white Southerners avoid films that are advertised as dealing with the race problem."[61]

It would appear, however, that such concerns were beside the point, since—despite generally unfavorable reviews—*Imitation of Life* brought in more than $6 million at the US box office and became Universal's top-grossing film of 1959. Both the thirty-six-year-old Moore, who only received seventh billing, and the twenty-two-year-old Kohner (later the mother of filmmakers Chris and Paul Weitz) were nominated for Best Supporting Actress at the 1960 Oscars. And today, more than half a century later, the social significance of Sirk's film has not decreased.

While its telling of the story adheres relatively closely to the courses followed by its predecessors, Sirk's approach makes it very different in substance, emphasis, and tone. Like Stahl's adaptation, Sirk's begins by bringing together the two mothers and their daughters, but minus the impression that Annie's appearance is any kind of a *deus ex machina*. The setting is a packed Coney Island beach, Lora has lost sight of Susie, crosses paths with a camera-wielding Steve, and eventually finds her daughter playing with Sarah-Jane as Annie calmly watches over them.

The sequence lays the groundwork for much that is to follow, binding the five characters together and introducing the tensions that are to simmer away through all that follows: Susie being "lost" to Lora, Annie taking charge when Lora is nowhere to be found, Steve attempting to infiltrate

"He was *practically white.*" Annie (Juanita Moore) remembering Sarah-Jane's father in *Imitation of Life*.

the family unit, Sarah-Jane moving away from under her mother's wing towards Lora and Susie and whiteness.

Plot-wise, Lora is at the center of what happens, but Annie becomes its dramatic focal point as she reveals that she's not Sarah-Jane's nanny, but her mother. "Sarah-Jane favors her daddy," Annie says, looking directly at Lora. Then, looking away as if momentarily lost in a reverie, she adds, almost breathlessly, "He was *practically white*," (her emphasis) as if his skin color was a virtue rather than just a detail. Moore's delivery of the line makes it clear from the start that, whatever Annie might go on say to her daughter about how "it's a sin to be ashamed of what you are," she is yet to discover that black is beautiful or free herself of the sense of inferiority for which she's chiding her daughter.

Annie is a prisoner of the mindset of her times. Like her equivalent in the novel, she even wants a funeral in white, "a white coffin pulled by white horses . . . like I was goin' to glory." The changes wrought on the black consciousness by the civil rights movement of the 1960s still remain more than a decade away. The limitations of her belief that she was "born to be hurt" because of her race, and her acceptance of that because "the Lord must've had his reasons for making some of us white and some of us black," are implicit in her character's equivalents in Hurst's novel and Stahl's film. But Sirk sharpens the focus on them with a distinctive force and clarity. Annie's attempt to impose her will on her Sarah-Jane, insisting that she shouldn't live her life as an imitation, is well-intentioned but catastrophic, a destructive force that shatters their relationship.[62]

Moore's beautiful, heartbreaking performance and Sirk's depiction of the soul-destroying situation in which Annie finds herself place her at the heart of the film's network of mother-daughter/surrogate mother-surrogate daughter stories. And they also make her one of the cinema's great tragic heroines.

As in much of Sirk's work, the idea of performance is central to *Imitation of Life*. For Lora, it is literally a way of life, whether she's trying to make an impression as an actress or do her duty as a mother. Her professional associates expect this of her—they know the rules of the game they're playing—but her intimates want more. Near the end, after Annie has told her that Susie is in love with Steve, she melodramatically tells her daughter that she's willing to give him up, if that's what it takes. Exasperated, Susie sees right through her: "Oh, mother, stop acting," she says. "Stop trying to shift people around as if they were pawns on a stage."

This exchange between mother and daughter recalls the penultimate scene in Stahl's version, where Bea tells Steve that they can't be together because of Jessie's feelings for him. But Sirk proposes a very different reading of the situation, implicitly refuting Stahl's. And Lora's response to Susie's accusation simply proves her daughter's case, her tears drawing an apology from Susie—"Oh, mama, I'm sorry I didn't want to hurt you"—who then kneels at Lora's feet and rests her head in her lap, adopting the role of dutiful daughter. Like mother, like daughter.

For Sarah-Jane, too, life becomes a stage on which she passes for white, and there's a potent irony in the fact that, when she leaves home to find a job, it's as part of a men's-nightclub show in Manhattan. Recalling the rejection scene in Stahl's film where Delilah finds Peola working at a café in Virginia, Annie bursts in on Sarah-Jane, who pretends that she doesn't know the intruder.

The confrontation is replayed with significant variations in a subsequent and unforgettable scene after Sarah-Jane flees to the other side of the country to find work as a showgirl at the Moulin Rouge in Hollywood and Annie again hunts her down, this time to tell her that she's too tired to keep pursuing her and to say goodbye.

The devastating exchange is mostly played out in front of the dancer (Ann Robinson) who is sharing Sarah-Jane's dressing room, with both mother and daughter hiding their real relationship as Annie pretends to be Sarah-Jane's nanny. "So, honey chil', you had a mammy," the dancer observes after Annie has left, not unkindly but with the gently mocking condescension that cuts to the heart of American racism. "Yes. All of my life," Sarah-Jane weeps in reply. The scene is a heart-rending reversal of the one on the beach at the start, where Annie had proudly told Lora that this white-skinned little girl was her daughter.

Imitations are everywhere in the film. Expanding on the implications of the title, virtually every scene has characters adopting roles and helping others to play theirs according to the situations in which they find themselves. Sirk's compositions persistently suggest the everyday as a form of theatre, the characters' surroundings deployed as frames for their performances—cinematographer Russell Metty's imagery observing them through doorways, against windows, in front of mirrors, on landings and stairways, and so on—as if to underline the artifice of their exchanges. The same effect is achieved by having peripheral characters looking on as they unfold, functioning as a built-in audience.

Sirk's adaptation casts *all* of the characters as actors, individuals whose role-playing becomes their means of grappling with the nature of their existence. "No sin in looking prosperous," Annie tells Lora who's been trying to make an impression in the theatre world. When the aspiring actress first meets Loomis, the man who is to become her agent, she pretends to have been sent to him by a Hollywood producer, an act which soon falls apart. Then, impressed by her chutzpah, he invites her to accompany him to a showbiz party, offers her a mink to wear, and some advice about how she should act when she gets there.

Later in the film, by way of protest, a furious Sarah-Jane plays out a brutal caricature of a black maidservant after Lora asks her to help her mother serve food to guests. And when the now-successful Lora rejects a script from her playwright/director/lover Edwards, he dramatically tosses it into the fire in her living room. Annie is shocked, but Lora remains unmoved, explaining that he always makes multiple copies.

Often the nature of the performance isn't as obvious as this, and the fine line between characters' pretenses and their felt responses is blurred, leaving us and them unaware of which side of the line they're on. As I've noted earlier, most of Sirk's films are populated by characters who simply don't know what to make of their lives, who are driven by a sense that "something's missing," their performances becoming a means of filling that gap. Their imitations of life, their representations of themselves, amount to survival techniques that—in this film's supreme irony—leave them dissatisfied and deny them all the kind of comfort that they're seeking.

"Don't you ever get the feeling that you're tired of what you're doing, that it isn't what you've really wanted?" Steve asks Lora late in the film. When she'd met him in the opening sequence, he was a freelance photographer who'd been making ends meet by selling his work to advertising agencies. Now, he's climbed the ladder of corporate success on Madison Avenue, but is yearning to have his work on exhibition. Meanwhile, the trajectory Lora has followed has been the classic star-is-born one,[63] although, having achieved professional success, she's come to recognize what she hasn't achieved as a mother or a lover.

Given that all of the characters' perceptions of their reality have been shown to be, at best, blinkered, it's unlikely that these realizations will lead to any changes in the ways they've been pursuing their lives. The lost-child situation of the opening sequence has become a motif applying to all of them.

What is clear is that any suggestion that the film's ending is a happy one—that a new family has come together in the wake of Annie's funeral—is flying in the face of the ongoing cycle of hurt and reunion that has driven all that has gone before and that afflicts everyone in the film. It's preceded by the bleak finality of Sarah-Jane's return, publicly seeking forgiveness from her mother, as she clutches desperately at the white-shrouded, white-flowered coffin in the horse-drawn hearse outside the church.

Like Peola in the Stahl version, she blames herself for her mother's death: "I killed my mother," she cries in desperation. But whereas Stahl lends some credence to Peola's claim, Delilah's sudden deterioration coinciding with her despair at her daughter's abandonment of her, Sirk calls Sarah-Jane's self-blame into question. Much earlier in the film, not long after they've moved into much more salubrious surroundings,[64] Lora's question to Annie about "those spells you've been getting" points to an ongoing illness. Sirk's point isn't that Sarah-Jane's actions have led to Annie's death but that Sarah-Jane *thinks* they have. Hers is a guilt that isn't easily assuaged.

And the notion that a semblance of order is restored in the film's closing shots—as Steve, Susie, and Lora comfort a shattered Sarah-Jane in the long, black limousine following Annie's hearse—ignores the lack of resolution to all of the previously established problems the characters have been dealing with and the cycles of dissatisfaction and disillusionment that have ruled their lives. As Sirk told Halliday, "[Y]ou don't believe the happy end, and you're not really supposed to."[65]

Peola disappears from the 1934 film after the funeral. Stahl and his writers clearly understood all too well that to have her return would only emphasize the fact that her existential anguish cannot be so simply alleviated, and that the trauma of her relationship with her mother would render the problems that have arisen between Bea and Jessie mere trivialities in comparison. But Sarah-Jane's plight and the death of her mother remain to the fore as the curtains close on Sirk's version.

Over the years, even sympathetic commentary about the film has repeatedly referred to the ways in which it is yet another example of the director being able "to redeem his material." Halliday refers to how the director was able "to use his command over 'style' to transform the awful story."[66] Stern reflects on how *Imitation of Life* ushers us into the comfortable and generically reassuring parlor of the women's film."[67]

Yet there is absolutely no justification for this kind of condescension to stories about the pressures of motherhood or women's struggles with their circumstances, whether they're labeled as "soap operas," "women's films," or "chick flicks." No generic category is worthwhile or worthless per se, and no kinds of plotting or groups of characters can be regarded as automatically superior to any other.

What matters is how a story is told and what it tells us, not the genre to which it belongs. Sirk doesn't "redeem his material" in *Imitation of Life*. As Hurst's novel and Stahl's adaptation attest, it was powerful to begin with. Sirk's achievement is not that he has transcended his material but that he has fashioned from it an American masterpiece.

CHAPTER TEN

Out of the Past

"I believe that happiness exists, if only by the simple fact that it can be destroyed. A happiness without faults would be like a badly written poem."
—DOUGLAS SIRK, 1967[1]

BY THE TIME HE CAME TO MAKE *THE TARNISHED ANGELS* AND *A TIME To Love and A Time To Die*, Sirk had acquired a solid standing at Universal and was relatively free of studio interference. He was especially happy working on *The Tarnished Angels* with producer Albert Zugsmith, with whom he'd also collaborated on *Written on the Wind*. Zugsmith, whose wildly contrasting credits include *The Incredible Shrinking Man* (1957), *Touch of Evil* (1958), and *Sex Kittens Go To College* (1960), saw Sirk as an important filmmaker. Describing him as "the quintessence of elegance, an artiste, a gentleman, a master of camera placement,"[2] he was happy to leave him in charge. Sirk was less flattering about Zugsmith, asiding to Jon Halliday that he was the kind of producer who'd preferred the title *Sex in the Air* to *The Tarnished Angels*,[3] but generally found him very supportive. On the other hand, on *A Time To Love and A Time To Die*, he fell out with producer Robert Arthur, whose credits include films such as *The Big Heat* (1953), *The Long Gray Line* (1955), *The Great Impostor* (1961), and *Lover Come Back* (1961). Describing him as "a fantastic philistine,"[4] Sirk bemoaned the fact that, because he'd fallen ill after the shoot *A Time To Love and A Time To Die*, Arthur had overseen the editing. The result, however, suggests that any damage done was minimal.

Sirk had first read William Faulkner's *Pylon* in translation, soon after its publication in 1935. The title bestowed on it in Germany, he recalled, was *Wendermarke*, "meaning 'Turning Point.'" He prepared a treatment almost immediately, planning to make the film at UFA. However, his

Sirk's son Claus (left).

proposal's detailing of the dark side of a war hero's return to the everyday world was not well-received by studio executives, with Germany moving towards a war for which it was trying to gain popular support. Twenty years later, having discovered that his favorite screenwriter George Zuckerman wanted to do his own adaptation of the book, the director finally got his chance.

For Sirk, *A Time To Love and A Time To Die*, based on a novel by fellow expatriate Erich Maria Remarque and set in Germany during World War II, came out of the past and was also a project that mattered, although for far more personal reasons. In the first place, it took him back to Germany, both literally and metaphorically. The location shoot took place there—in Berlin and Bavaria—and it was his first time in the country of his birth since his frustrating visit almost a decade earlier. But even more important for him was the fact that Remarque's simple story embodied the disillusionment of ordinary people with the history unfolding around them. And the film that Sirk drew from Remarque's story is an affecting state-of-the-nation critique that returned him to the most traumatic time of his life.

The young soldier on his way to the front in A Time to Love and a Time to Die.

In addition to the Nazi atrocities, there was the nightmare of his son's death on the Russian Front. Claus Detlef Sierck had been born in 1925, a few years before Sirk's divorce from his first wife, theatre actress Lydia Brinken, from whom he'd been estranged when she became a Nazi supporter. After their separation, she enrolled Claus in the Hitler Youth program, using a court order to prevent Sirk from seeing him. Her grounds were that his second wife, actress-singer Hilde Jary, was Jewish. Sirk never saw Claus again, except on the screen where he had become a child actor, playing key supporting roles in several German films of the time. He was drafted into the army as a foot soldier in 1942 and was killed in battle in 1944.

For Sirk, all of this was soul-destroying. He would occasionally tell interviewers about what had occurred, requesting that they only make it public after his death. "It is too painful for me to contemplate," he told me, after briefly outlining what happened. All of those he told kept this information to themselves as requested.

Halliday refers to *A Time To Love and A Time To Die* as "not *the* story of his son but *a* possible story."⁵ And the film's characters include several young soldiers at the Russian Front who could be viewed as surrogates for Claus: perhaps the flawed but sympathetic protagonist, Ernst Graeber (John Gavin); perhaps Graeber's Nazi-sympathizing battlefield comrade (Bengt Lindstrom)? No one, of course, can do anything more than surmise about this.

Nevertheless, Graeber's increasing disillusionment with what's being asked of him could reasonably be seen as an optimistic projection of what might have happened to Sirk's son after he went to war. And it's not too fanciful to link him with the Claus lookalike in the sequence near the end of the film where Graeber boards the train for the journey back to the Front.

While he waits by a window, two fresh-faced youths embark with their belongings, the lookalike featured in close-up, a handsome young man who keeps to himself as farewells are exchanged all around. He's never seen again, but it's a moment which perfectly captures an innocence that is about to be destroyed by experiences that are unthinkable.

Screenwriter Wesley Strick's novel *Out There in the Dark* is a thinly disguised fictionalization of Sirk's story, and a key plot point is the anguish experienced by his central character, a film director, over the son who has been lost to him. Born Dieter Seife in Germany, he becomes Derek Sykes after he flees to the US, leaving behind a wife who has become "a favorite of Goebbels" and "a handsome fair-haired son" who has become a film star, his face "plastered all over the Reich, on billboards, posters and banners for the German Youth Festival of 1941."[6] Seife/Sykes's success as a filmmaker does little to compensate for what he has lost, and all that is left for him is the youth's ghost-like presence as a series of screen characters. It's a perceptive, agonizing recasting of the tragedy that Sirk brought with him from Germany to the US and that haunted him throughout his life.

THE TARNISHED ANGELS (1958)

> "I had the sense of coming home to myself, and of having found out what a little circle man's experience is. For Antonia and for me, this had been the road of Destiny; had taken us to those early accidents of fortune which predetermine for us all that we can ever be. Now I understood that the same road was to bring us together again. Whatever we had missed, we possessed together the precious, the incommunicable past."
> —WILLA CATHER, THE CLOSING LINES OF *MY ANTONIA*, 1918[7]

In 1932, William Faulkner went to Hollywood. Soon afterwards, he met director Howard Hawks, with whom he became a regular collaborator. "If I wanted a scene or a story," Hawks told interviewer Joseph McBride, "I'd call Bill up and get it. He could write almost anything."[8] The men had much in common: they drank together; hunted together; and had both trained as pilots during World War I, although neither actually went to war. Aviation was also a favored subject in the stories they told, and, according to Hawks, it was he who guided Faulkner towards writing *Pylon*, the 1935 novel from which *The Tarnished Angels* was adapted almost a quarter of a century later.

"He had kind of a hazy idea about it," Hawks told McBride. "I told him to write it. I got mad at him one day and told him I got so sick and tired of the goddamn inbred people he was writing about. I said, 'Why don't you write about some decent people, for goodness' sake?' 'Like who?' I said, 'Well, you fly around. Don't you know some pilots or something you can write about?' And he thought a while, and he said, 'Oh, I know a good story. Three people—a girl and a man were wingwalkers, and the other man was a pilot. The girl was gonna have a baby, and she didn't know which one was the father.' I said, 'That sounds good,' and he wrote *Pylon* from it. Faulkner was very smart, he told it through the eyes of the drunken reporter."[9]

In 1956, Sirk, who had long wanted to adapt *Pylon* to the screen, discovered that writer George Zuckerman (*Written on the Wind, Taza, Son of Cochise*) shared his passion for the undertaking. According to the director, *Written on the Wind* was the driving force behind their new project: "In a way, *The Tarnished Angels* grew out of *Written on the Wind*. You had the same pair of characters seeking their identity . . . ; the same mood of desperation, drinking and doubting the values of life, and at the same time almost hysterically trying to grasp them, grasping at the wind. Both pictures are studies of failure. Of people who can't make a success of their lives."[10]

At the same time, however, it's not entirely fanciful to speculate that, just as Hawks's conversation with Faulkner led to *Pylon*, and then to Sirk's film, it also left its mark on Hawks's *Only Angels Have Wings* (1939). Dealing with a group of air freight pilots based in a remote part of South America, it's written by Jules Furthman and based on a treatment by Hawks entitled "Plane Four from Barranca."[11] And in terms of both their subject matter and their narrative design, it and *The Tarnished Angels* have much in common.

Both are about tight-knit groups of flyers who are dedicated to their work, not for the money, but, to borrow a line from *Pylon*, simply "because they've got to do it . . . They can't help themselves."[12] Their sense of themselves as an extended family is strong, because they understand each other in ways that others can't, which is why outsiders aren't welcome: like Bonnie Lee (Jean Arthur) in *Only Angels Have Wings*, a chorus girl "with a specialty" who stops over in Barranca on her way to the US; and like Burke Devlin (Rock Hudson) in Sirk's film, a journalist from the *Times-Picayune* who pitches his story about Roger Shumann (Robert

Stack) and his flying circus to his editor (Alexander Lockwood) as "the best human interest yarn I've ever latched on to."

The Tarnished Angels is set in 1932, with the Great Depression at its peak and a regular income hard to come by. A former war hero, Shumann is now a barnstormer, a parody of his former self, trying to make a living (like Buffalo Bill Cody in Buffalo Bill's Wild West circus) by showing off his skills for a paying audience. The plane Shumann flies bears the logo of the Lafayette Escadrille, the unit of American volunteer pilots during World War I who became famous for their reckless bravado.

To both Bonnie Lee and Devlin, the flyers are (in Devlin's words) like "visitors from a strange, faraway planet." She is bewildered when one of the pilots is killed and the others seem to treat his death with disinterest: "Who's Joe?" shrugs Cary Grant's Jeff Carter, deliberately disremembering his fellow flyer. Only gradually does she come to understand that this reaction is a way of dealing with the death that beckons them all, and of moving on while they can. She is then drawn into the group—inasmuch as a woman can ever become a fully-fledged member of a male family in a Hawks adventure—and the film moves inside it with her.

Like her, Devlin is equally fascinated and confused by what he encounters when he steps into the alien world of the flyers. It's winter, and Mardi Gras is in full swing when he arrives on New Orleans' banner-laden Delta Field for the air show. Befriending the Shumanns' son, twelve-year-old Jack (Chris Olsen), he inveigles his way into the company of Shumann and his small team, which is made up of his glamorous parachutist wife, Laverne (Dorothy Malone), and his mechanic, Jiggs (Jack Carson).[13]

Devlin gets a sense of who they are and what they do, but, unlike Bonnie Lee, and despite his best efforts, he remains an outsider. And, whereas *Only Angels Have Wings* moves beyond Bonnie Lee's point of view of the flyers, *The Tarnished Angels* keeps us alongside Devlin. He's either a participant in or a witness to every scene in the film, occasionally arriving a few seconds late. And whereas generic logic suggests that Shumann should become the hero, as Jeff does in Hawks's film, Sirk strategically eschews such an option . . . at least until near the end of the film where, in a bitter irony, Shumann heroically sacrifices his life to save others.

While Hawks's films repeatedly return to the idea of the group as a shelter from the dangers lurking all around, many of Sirk's films can be seen as ruminations on loneliness (from *The Girl from the Marsh Croft* and *Zu neuen Ufern* through *Summer Storm* and *The Lady Pays Off* to *All I Desire*, *All That Heaven Allows*, and *There's Always Tomorrow*, and beyond). And *The Tarnished Angels* is, perhaps, the most moving of all of them.

It's less an adaptation than a reimagining of *Pylon*. Simultaneously modernist and impressionistic, the novel is like an alcohol-fueled blur of prose, its extended sentences, eccentric verbal conjoinings, and erratic punctuations often pushing the borders of clarity. In sharp contrast, *The Tarnished Angels'* narrative architecture and *mise-en-scene* provide a near-perfect model of storytelling precision. It begins in the light, takes us into a deepening darkness, and then ends in bright daylight, leaving us to ponder the theatre of what has passed before our eyes and to count the casualties.

All of the characters exist in an ongoing cycle from which there appears to be no escape. Their pasts enclose them, reminders of dreams they used to have before realities intervened; the alcohol they constantly consume is a way of tranquilizing their disappointments. Devlin tells Laverne of how he was inspired to become a reporter by Richard Harding Davis, the famous American journalist whose legendary exploits serve only to remind Devlin of his own limitations. She confides to him about falling in love with Shumann when she saw his likeness on a Liberty Bond poster and then being prepared to put up with anything to be with him.

Roger is haunted by his past, by nightmares about being "shot down in flames by Baron von Richtofen." When told that he is to be honored at a party for his exploits on behalf of France, he's unsettled by the memory that, when celebrations like this occurred during the war, "the fellows who were honored . . . were those who never came back." It's a memory that also anticipates the posthumous commemoration of his life that replaces the planned party.

Intruding on the soundtrack's prevailing air of melancholy, the recurrent instrumentation of the famous World War I song "Mademoiselle from Armentieres" also serves as a reminder that the past is a constant present for him. As it is for Jiggs, who has long lived in awe of Shumann and been in love with Laverne, all to no avail. He might belong to the Flying Shumanns troupe, and he has a part to play in it, but it's neither as Shumann's confidant nor as Laverne's lover, the roles he really wants.

The sense of the past as a prison even has an impact on Jack, her son. When Devlin first encounters him, the boy is being taunted by an airfield mechanic (Robert J. Wilke). "Who's your father?" the bully blusters, Jack soon afterwards explaining to Devlin how rumors have circulated suggesting that Jiggs might be, gossip that is later definitively quashed by Laverne.[14] Perhaps the most moving image in the film has the boy trapped on an aeroplane carousel, watching Shumann competing in the air show and then realizing that his father's plane is out of control. He could be speaking for everyone in the film as he desperately cries, "Let

An image of "tragic helplessness" (Jean-Loup Bourget). Jack (Chris Olsen) on the aeroplane carousel in *The Tarnished Angels*.

me off." The scene evokes, as French critic Jean-Loup Bourget has noted, "an effect of tragic helplessness."[15]

Even the locations invoke this sense of life as a cycle. Devlin is introduced as he walks on to the tarmac at the Air Field with not only the aeroplane carousel in the background, but, behind and towering over it, a giant Ferris wheel. The fairground attractions feature regularly in what follows, accompanied by shots of the planes following their route round-and-around the pylons that mark the turning points in the races.

Repetitions and correspondences abound, becoming plot turning points that—with differences—return us to what's gone before. Jack takes two rides on the aeroplane carousel: one early in the film as his father competes in a race, then again just before Shumann's death. As he begins the first ride, he waves to Laverne, just as Roger later waves to her from the cockpit as he taxis out for the last time. There are also two scenes in which she's interrupted while reading *My Antonia*, which she's found in Devlin's apartment after he's invited the flyers to stay there.

The first time, he arrives home to find her with it. She explains to him that its appeal for her lies in the way it reminds her of her past life in Iowa. "Nostalgia in Nebraska!" is his cryptic put-down, and, as Michael Stern points out,[16] its function here is the same as that of the river in *Written on the Wind*. The second time she's seen reading the book, her reverie is brought to a halt by the noise from Mardi Gras partygoers in a neighboring apartment. In the film's closing sequence, the book makes a third appearance as Devlin gives it to her as a farewell present before she flies off with Jack into an uncertain future.

There are also two café scenes in which, surrounded by signs listing what's for sale, Shumann bargains about Laverne's future: in the first, a flashback, he throws the dice to decide who will marry her; in the second, he pushes her to prostitute herself with plane magnate Matt Ord (Robert Middleton) in order to get the help from him that he needs. In the first case, Shumann's motives are ambiguous—he only decides *afterwards* whether the winner or the loser will be Laverne's husband—leaving open the possibility that he's unwilling to openly declare his feelings for her. In the second, there's no doubt about the choice that he has made.

Devlin twice visits Ord himself, in order to save Laverne: the first time, after Shumann's attempt to use her to get what he wants; the second, after Shumann's death, when she's gone to Ord to ensure Jack's future. For his part, in a further correspondence, Ord's interest in Laverne is not entirely lascivious and is certainly no less sexual than Devlin's. When, after Shumann's memorial, Jiggs is mourning his death and the fate that has befallen Laverne, it's almost as if the reporter is mocking himself and the role he has assumed in relation to her when he asks the mechanic, "Why don't you get on your white charger and do something about it?"

Devlin's motives remain ambiguous throughout. In the opening sequence, where Jack provides him with an introduction to the flyers, it's clear that he has come to the boy's defense against the bully before he knows who he is. But when he realizes the opportunity that has fallen into his lap, he's happy to take full advantage of it. And it quickly becomes clear that his fascination with the Flying Shumanns has as much to do with the feelings Laverne has aroused in him as with the wish to write a story about them. His interventions in each of their lives underline his loss of journalistic detachment and how he is continually acting in ways that are entirely at odds with the code that demands that he should never make himself a part of the story.

And Devlin's insights are as dubious as his motives. Without ever meeting Shumann and his team, his editor takes a skeptical view that isn't altogether wide of the mark: "Your war hero is probably a cheap, drunken gypsy," he tells his reporter. "And what do you think that air show is? A cheap, crummy carnival of death." On the other hand, beneath the "Is It Interesting?" signs hanging all around the newspaper offices, Devlin's hopelessly romantic mythologizing after Shumann's death might be "preserved in alcohol," as the editor puts it, but it isn't entirely inappropriate either. Grabbing the attention of everyone present, he explains how he's found "truth and beauty where you'd never expect to find it" and a war hero "who was lost until he found those pylons, those three bony fingers of death sticking out of the earth, waiting to bring him crashing down."

In the novel, Devlin's unnamed equivalent is very different from the screen version. Faulkner presents him (perhaps in a self-loathing self-portrait) as an alcoholic and a nondescript irrelevance, likening him to "a

The Rock Hudson characters in *Written on the Wind* and *The Tarnished Angels* reduced to being supporting players rather than the romantic leads they'd like to be. With Robert Stack and Lauren Bacall in the former, and Stack and Dorothy Malone in the latter.

scarecrow in a winter field"[17] and "a corpse roused and outraged out of what should have been the irrevocable and final sleep."[18] Writer George Zuckerman says that, as he read *Pylon*, he saw James Stewart as the journalist,[19] but the film casts a classic Hollywood hunk in the role, gives him a virile name, and makes him flawed but thoroughly sympathetic.

Picking up on a recurring feature of the way in which Hudson characters appear in a number of previous Sirk films, including *Magnificent Obsession* and *Captain Lightfoot*, *The Tarnished Angels* presents him as a man constantly trying—mostly in vain—to push his way into the center of the action. As Adrian Martin points out,[20] "two furiously economical shots" accompanying the opening credits set the scene. In the first, Devlin moves on to the windy tarmac, walking forward from the left of the frame to the center, a position he spends the entire film pursuing. The second takes in Shumann in the cockpit of the Lafayette Escadrille, then pans to include Laverne standing alongside in the swirling white dress she later wears during her parachute jump, before Jiggs steps forward into the frame between them.

Everything that follows plays variations on this scene. In the sequence which begins with Laverne reading *My Antonia* in Devlin's living room, Devlin asks questions of her (fusing his personal interest in her with his professional one) until Shumann interrupts them. He'd been sleeping in Devlin's bedroom and, perhaps possessively, has come to reassert his marital role. Clearly discomfited, Devlin reluctantly retreats. The same thing happens again, as Martin points out in his excellent DVD commentary on the film,[21] in the café sequence where Shumann prevails upon Laverne to go to Ord. Devlin is sitting with her when Shumann and Jiggs arrive. He goes to get coffee, but returns to find that, while Jiggs has assumed his usual place in the background, Shumann has taken the prized seat alongside her. Devlin, reduced to being a supporting player rather than the romantic lead he'd like to be, is visibly put out but doesn't say anything. These scenes deploy the same visual strategy as the one in *Written on the Wind* where Hudson's character is making his play for Lauren Bacall, only to have Stack's (again) arrive and come between them.

Via fluid camera moves and evocative cutting, Sirk shows Devlin in a perpetual state of intrusion, repeatedly entering a scene through a doorway or from outside the edge of the frame, or pushing his way between people in order to get to where the action is happening. Alongside this, other characters keep leaving the frames he'd been sharing with them, nowhere more poignantly than when Laverne flies off at the end, past a pylon, leaving him alone in the final shot, still forlornly hoping for a happy ending: he's told her that he'd like her to personally return the copy of *My Antonia* he's given her.

At its essence, *The Tarnished Angels* is yet another Sirk film about life as theatre. The idea of people putting on a show, is pervasive: the air show, with the banners draped everywhere; the parades in the city streets; the newspaper offices where men (no women in sight) write stories for their public to consume; the partygoers with their masks and drunken carousing (the noise of their partying intrudes on the action has the same impact here as the air raid sirens and whistling bombs do in *A Time To Love and A Time To Die*).

As Martin also points out,[22] the air show can be seen as an apt analogy for the workings of Hollywood spectaculars, the crowd gathered to watch the planes flying around the pylons mirroring film audiences, constantly on the verge of being transformed into an out-of-control mob. For Sirk, Laverne's role as the parachutist is that of the woman in the blinding Hollywood spotlight:[23] "She represents the woman as object—an object for the public who peer and crane for a glimpse of her naked flesh when she jumps and her skirt fans out—a saleable and later exchangeable commodity."[24] There's a hint of this in the novel, where Faulkner refers to her "Harlowcolored hair that they would pay her money for it [sic] in Hollywood."[25]

It's a savage analogy, and, in many ways, despite its measured affection for all of its characters, *The Tarnished Angels* is a savage film. The iconography of the horror movie is never far away as figures in grotesque Mardi Gras masks burst in on the characters, expanding the interruptions that feature everywhere in Sirk's work: forever allowing his characters nothing more than fleeting moments of privacy, these invasions—for that is effectively what they are—deny them the chance to achieve what they most yearn, a sense of completion.

Bourget gets it exactly right when he observes that Irving Glassberg's finely wrought black-and-white 'Scope imagery for *The Tarnished Angels* immerses all of its characters in a carnivalesque *mise-en-scene*, starkly choreographing "a dance of death": "We are being given a vision of Hell," he writes. "Not the dark, dreary Hell into which Roger's plane will sink, but a tumultuous Hell, full of sound and fury, denizened by damned souls with empty laughter and brutal desires."[26]

A TIME TO LOVE AND A TIME TO DIE (1958)

"My death is like a swinging door
A patient girl who knows the score
Whistle for her and the passing time . . .

But whatever is behind the door
Angel or devil, I don't care
For in front of that door . . .
There is you."

—FROM JACQUES BREL'S "LA MORT/MY DEATH," 1959[27]

Nowhere does Sirk's overriding concern with the nature of being alive on planet Earth receive a more eloquent expression than in *A Time to Love and A Time To Die*. His second-to-last feature before he retired from filmmaking, left the US, and moved to Switzerland (at the age of sixty-two), it both crystallizes and intensifies the themes that preoccupied him throughout his career behind the camera. Central to these, as will already be evident, is the notion of human behavior as an ongoing performance that provides individuals with a fragile refuge against the inevitability of death.

For Sirk, life is best seen as a theatre where, for better or worse, individuals assume a variety of roles. They are allowed room to improvise, but the parameters for the parts they play are always determined by the social circumstances in which they find themselves and against which they must define themselves. Here, it's towards the end of World War II, 1944, with Hitler's dream of world domination and the German nation in a state of total disrepair.

However, rather than viewing events through the eyes of the Allies, the perspective which Hollywood customarily provided, Sirk's film locks us inside the viewpoint of a German foot soldier, Ernst Graeber (Gavin), and positions all of its characters according to their responses to the state of the German nation. There are no heroes here, just ordinary men and women—and a few monsters—struggling to deal with what fate has handed out to them.

Based on a 1954 novel by German writer Erich Maria Remarque,[28] who is probably best known for the acclaimed *All Quiet on the Western Front*, written twenty-five years earlier, the film deals with events that took place more than seventy years ago and whose outcome is part of well-known history. So there's no question for the viewer about where the film is headed, and there's no escape for the players trapped upon its stage. Those in the film who fail to acknowledge the inevitable—that the end is nigh—are readily seen to be in denial. Those who have come to see not only that Hitler's cause is lost but also that it was evil in the first place are depicted sympathetically. If the film offers any room for hope, it comes from their ability to take a stand against what their nation had come to represent and to bring some positive meaning to their lives.

Given that Warner Bros. deemed in 1940 that America wasn't ready for Sirk's planned remake of a film he made for UFA—*Zu neuen Ufern*—Universal's investment in a film inviting audiences to be sympathetic to soldiers from "the other side" only a decade or so after the war still seems like a risky business move.[29] And both the critical and box-office responses at the time would seem to endorse this. Most reviews seemed content to take the film to task for its Americanization of German soldiers, its creation of a concept of "the good German," its noisy soundtrack, and, most of all, for its lack of anything solid apart from an "antiwar message."

However, Jean-Luc Godard famously came to its defense in his 1959 essay for *Cahiers du cinema*, enthusing about its "delirious mixture of medieval and modern, sentimentality and subtlety, tame compositions and frenzied CinemaScope," and proposing that the film's young lovers, "by shutting their eyes with a kind of passionate innocence to the bombs falling around them in Berlin, manage to get deeper into themselves than any other characters in a film before them."[30]

Written by Orin Jannings (whose screenplay for 1951's *Force of Arms* tells another World War II story about a couple seeking respite from the battleground), Sirk's third war film, after *Hitler's Madman* and *Battle Hymn*, largely adheres to the narrative route laid out by its source and borrows much of its plot and character detail.[31] It plunges into the nightmare of the Russian Front at the start (the sequence is, effectively, a prologue), then returns with Ernst to his hometown for his three-week furlough, before following him back to the Front (the epilogue). However, Sirk's direction and his unofficial involvement with the writing makes the film very much his own.

The differences between the film's two worlds are superficial. At the Front, all is horror and desolation, the soldiers either fully aware that what was supposed to be "the great advance" has become "the great retreat," or else refusing (or afraid) to believe it. The noble cause of serving their country has given way to the ignominy of executing Russian peasants suspected of being guerrillas. The arrival of spring, heralded by the melting of the snow, might serve as a reminder of another time and "leaves on the trees, flowers . . . ," but all that comes from the earth at the Front are the frozen corpses which had been concealed by the winter falls.

Ernst's furlough had promised him the chance to visit his parents, "delouse, take a hot bath, sleep in a clean bed, and forget for three weeks that there's a war." When he arrives home, it initially appears that nothing has changed from when he was last there and that it will provide him with a safe place away from the Front. As he walks away from the station, past a shop window where a stuffed horse is on display, he observes to a woman sweeping by the door, "The same horse! It hasn't changed since I was seven years old." And the general impression is that the townspeople are going about their normal routines, that their everyday lives remain undisturbed by the war.

However, the dream quickly becomes a continuation of the nightmare when he comes upon the devastation that bombing raids, apparently aimed at the local factories, have wrought upon the town. His home has been turned into rubble, reminders of the war are everywhere, and he becomes a lost soul wandering through the wreckage of his memories. The further it goes, the darker the film becomes, even after Ernst meets Elizabeth (Lilo Pulver). The enemy might remain off-screen, but the shadow of death is omnipresent, enveloping the town as well as the Front. There, the dream was of the furlough and home; at home, the dream is of being somewhere else.

All Ernst and Elizabeth have in common, at first, is the hope that their missing parents are still alive: her father has been arrested and taken to the nearby concentration camp; his parents have simply disappeared. She is staying in the commandeered home that had been her father's in the hope that he will return; he has come there because her father had been his family's doctor and might have been able to provide him with information as to their whereabouts.

It's the war that brings them together and—as in Remarque's book[32]— the film finds a poignant metaphor for their relationship in the unseasonal blossoms gracing a charred tree by the river that flows through the town. Ernst and Elizabeth have gone for a walk along the bank towards a burnt-out boathouse, when she notices it and is astonished. "Half the tree is gone," she exclaims, "but it blossoms as if nothing has happened!" He explains how it has managed to defy the turning of the seasons: "The boat-house took a bomb," he tells her. "The heat of the fire must have forced it to bloom." With the tree in the foreground hanging over them, he and Elizabeth then embrace in what is both a deeply romantic and a

Ernst (John Gavin), Elizabeth (Lilo Pulver) and the unseasonal blossoms in *A Time To Love and A Time To Die*.

profoundly disturbing image, a celebration of their union that is, simultaneously, an acknowledgment of the artificial circumstances that have created it.

What they discover together is a chance to keep the darkness at bay, the golden light of Elizabeth's room replacing the somber tones that prevailed at the Front. However, everything they do becomes inseparable from their knowledge that time will, sooner or later, take it away. Just as Ernst's hope that his furlough will enable him to forget the war is an implicit acknowledgment that it can't be so simply blanked out, so too is Elizabeth's poignant toast on their wedding night: "Let's try to forget everything outside this room"—everything that waits behind the door. And implicit in the fact that his furlough will only last three weeks—and in the film's references to nature's way and the cycle of life, as well as its glorious title's evocation of Ecclesiastes[33]—is the knowledge that their relationship is going to end.

For all of Sirk's characters, life is a metaphorical battleground, an ongoing search for a happiness that constantly seems out of reach. In *A Time To Love and A Time To Die*, the characters are literally enclosed within a *mise-en-scène* of destruction as they confront their fate. The war here replaces the small-town and suburban worlds of Sirk's other films; the only difference is that the dangers are easier to identify. But the characters' methods of dealing with them are the same, consciously seeking ways to escape oppressive realities or to avoid unpalatable truths. For them all, survival is a matter of being able to keep reality at a distance, using whatever methods they have at their disposal. For some, this leads to a denial of their humanity; for others, it becomes a manifestation of it.

While the soldiers at the Front are bound together by the specter of death, the tensions between them stem from the misinformation being provided by their superiors and, in most cases, from how they're being ordered to behave, the roles they're being asked to play. For the sadistic Steinbrenner (Lindstrom), the Nazi plant in Ernst's unit, the call to join the firing squad to execute the suspected guerrillas is an opportunity not to be missed. For his comrades, it's a reminder of the depths to which they've descended in order to survive. Since those who refuse to participate will themselves be executed, it's safer to push doubts away.

"Not our worry!" says the cynical Sauer (Clancy Cooper). "We didn't sentence them. We're not to blame." For Hirschland (Jim Hutton), though, the young soldier who is forced to join the squad (and who doesn't appear in the book), following orders becomes a death sentence: rather than live on with the knowledge of what he has done, he shoots himself. It is an act that haunts the film: not only does it alert the traumatized Ernst to the grave implications of his involvement, but it's an act that provides a final, irreversible escape from reality that all of the characters are seeking.

The German High Command, bent on sustaining national confidence, sends its soldiers home on leave from the Front with tightly scripted roles based on the lie that all is well. Having been given boxes of fruit "from the Fuhrer" to take home to their families as "evidence that the front-line troops are well cared for and can even bring fruit home," they're told that they must reveal "nothing of the Front" and that any revelations or "idle criticism" will be regarded as treason.

Ernst and Elizabeth also repeatedly speak to each other about keeping the reality of their situation at bay—"Let's forget about the war"—but it keeps interrupting their idyll. Their dinner at the elegant Hotel Germania, an underworld nightclub for the German officer class, perfectly illustrates how the film simultaneously allows them to think they're achieving their fantasy and presents it as illusory. Ernst has taken her there on the advice of Lance Corporal Reuter (Keenan Wynn), a self-appointed man-about-town whom Ernst has met at the barracks where he has been staying. Reuter has told him what he needs to do to get the attention of the waiter, even lending him his dress uniform to assist in his performance at the restaurant. And Ernst plays his part to perfection.

He and Elizabeth succumb to the plush setting, the fairy tale atmosphere, and the fine wine, their reflections in the large mirror by their table throwing their interaction off balance, not only linking each alternately with the "image" of the other but also suggesting their other selves

Ernst (John Gavin) and Elizabeth (Lilo Pulver) trying to forget about the war at the Hotel Germania in *A Time To Love and A Time To Die*.

as audiences to the roles they're playing. Their response to the inevitable interruption of the air raid sirens is to ignore them. "Drink it down," Ernst tells Elizabeth as he pours her another glass of wine. "Forget about the sirens." They are a couple in retreat from the world; everything about the sequence serves as a reminder of the distance between their euphoria and the reality in which it exists.

Just as George Sanders's Petroff in *Summer Storm* and Robert Stack's Kyle Hadley in *Written on the Wind* deploy liquor to anaesthetize their psychic pain, so too do they. And it provides for them in the same way that the medication provided to a woman injured in the air raid soon afterwards assists her in dealing with her pain. "This will help till the ambulance comes," the doctor who comes to her aid tells her. Anything to alleviate the anguish.

The soldiers with whom Ernst shares quarters at the barracks had welcomed the news that he was planning to serenade Elizabeth. By way of entertaining them, Reuter theatrically sends Ernst on his way with some old-fashioned male bravado (at the same time offering a brutal reminder of Hirschland's suicide): "Now remember, my boy, it's easier to die than to live. You see that tonight you do us proud." And the other soldiers send Ernst on his way too, with celebratory whoops of good cheer. But then the door closes behind him, the joviality is replaced by silence, and a shroud of gloom falls across the room as they return to their card-playing.

The same scene occurs in the novel, minus what happens after Ernst's departure. Its account is a straightforward description of Reuter's efforts to help Ernst to make the evening a memorable one. Reuter says, "If you take your lady to the Germania, the wine to order is Johannisberger Kochberg 1937, from the cellars of G. H. von Mumm. It's a wine that can raise the dead." And Ernst replies, ending the scene, "Good. That's what I need."³⁴ The difference between Remarque's treatment of the incident and Sirk's is simple but telling. Remarque lays the foundations for Ernst's forthcoming evening, while Sirk places the entire exchange in a far more illuminating context.

Well beyond their dinner at the Hotel Germania, Ernst and Elizabeth's choices about how they want to be, together and separately, and what they want to think serve as their means of survival. When he asks her why she doesn't leave the apartment she'd shared with her father and go somewhere safer, she tells him that she can't. "As long as I'm here, I can hope that my father will come back," she tells him. It's as if she feels compelled to act in a particular way if she's going to avoid surrendering to despair, as if she's tricking herself into hanging on to hope.

She's not alone in practicing this kind of self-deception as a survival strategy. Ernst does it too when he agrees to accept help in his search for his parents from District Leader Oscar Binding (Thayer David), an SS officer with whom he used to go to school. "All I know is that he's the first human being I've seen since coming home who's even willing to help," he argues when Elizabeth challenges him. "Murderers are murderers twenty-four hours a day," she insists. "What happened to you Ernst? Are you blind?" She becomes the voice of his conscience.

For his part, Binding works hard—and not altogether successfully, David's performance subtly suggesting his discomfort with himself—to rationalize his crimes against humanity. Desperate for Ernst's approval, the former milkman's son promises to use his contacts to help him, sidestepping questions about his complicity with the sadistic Heini (Kurt Meisel), the piano-playing commandant of the local concentration camp. Echoing Sauer's words at the Front, he declares, "I don't think about it. I'm not responsible for what other people do." For him, the wish to be one of the in-crowd supercedes whatever better instincts he might have had long ago.

His malicious pleasure in telling Ernst about how he had taken advantage of a woman who had come to him begging for the release of her husband from the concentration camp is Reuter's male bravado pushed over the edge. And the revenge he has taken on their old teacher, Professor Pohlmann (Remarque), for treating him without due respect at school, is reprehensible. But his desperation is as evident as his moral cowardice. His attempts to ingratiate himself with Ernst, his clinging on to empty cliches ("If old school mates don't stick together, who will?"), and his efforts to somehow render himself important ("Who would have thought that I would be an art collector?") point to his loneliness. That said, his descent into a spiritual death places him, like Heini (and the Nazis in *Hitler's Madman*), beyond redemption.

He goes on to remind Ernst that his execution of civilians makes him complicit too—"Drink, you're one of us"—ironically placing his sought-after friend in the same position as Hirschland, who'd earlier committed suicide rather than live with his shame. Ernst has been turning a blind eye to Binding's evil, playing the role of the old friend in order to get what he wants from him. His recognition that Binding's accusation against him is well-founded represents a turning point in his understanding of what it means to wear the uniform—the costume—of a soldier in the German army.

Sirk's film deals with the fall of Germany and the last days of the Nazis. But it is also a compelling drama about Ernst's identity crisis, the route he follows to redemption, and his tragically ironic death at the hands of a Russian prisoner whom he has freed. The final image is of a stream carrying a letter from Elizabeth away from his outstretched hand and out of the frame. In it, he'd learned of her pregnancy.

The agony which finds expression in the film is, finally, less an outraged cry about man's inhumanity to man—though it is that—than a painful detailing of the impossibility of humankind ever finding the happiness which it seeks. The constant and complex juxtaposing of images of death and life, hope and despair, and destruction and celebration make it impossible to consider one without the other, and establish *A Time To Love and A Time To Die* as one Sirk's finest and most affecting achievements and one of the great "lost paradise" films.

CHAPTER ELEVEN

Into the Future
Sirk's Legacy

"Maybe it takes somebody from another culture, maybe an older culture, a more sophisticated culture, to reinvent something that's American and elevate it and show us what's so special about it."
—WESLEY STRICK, SCREENWRITER, 2007[1]

SIRK DIED ON JANUARY 14, 1987, ALMOST THIRTY YEARS AFTER HE brought his career to a premature close and moved to Switzerland with Hilde. During the late 1970s, Rainer Werner Fassbinder somehow persuaded him out of retirement to teach briefly at Munich University, where he made three short films with students there. And those who were fortunate enough to encounter him in person can readily appreciate what a fine teacher he would have been: learned, articulate, patient, and open to ideas other than his own.

Over the years, many who worked with him on both sides of the camera spoke highly of his collaborative spirit and his ability to nurture and inspire. Noting that Rock Hudson was born in the same year as Sirk's son, filmmaker and essayist Mark Rappaport (who made the excellent documentary *Rock Hudson's Home Movies* in 1992) cites the reverence with which the actor spoke of Sirk. '"He was like ol' Dad to me," Hudson said. "And I was like a son to him, I think. When you're scared and new and you're trying to figure out this thing, and suddenly an older man will reach out and say, 'There, there, it's okay,' that was Douglas Sirk."'[2]

But it's the director's films that are now his legacy, and they've already influenced several generations of cineastes. And, although it's not generally seen in this light, much of the material that has been written about Sirk deserves mention here. Among the critics who turned the spotlight on Sirk's 1950s melodramas during the 1960s and '70s, several produced fine commentary and interview material. Jon Halliday's extended conversations with the director are invaluable, but so too are the analyses of specific films by critics such as Jean-Loup Bourget, Fred Camper, and Michael Stern, and the wider analyses of Sirk's style and his importance to American cinema by Thomas Elsaesser, Laura Mulvey, and Paul Willemen. In their wake, further critical work by Barbara Klinger, Michael Walker, Lauren Berlant, Lucy Fischer, Sabine Hak, Linda Schulte-Sasse, Bruce Babington, and, more recently, Kristopher Mecholsky, Adrian Martin, and Victoria L. Evans has both expertly probed the workings of Sirk films and been shaped by them.

Better known to the filmgoing public at large, however, are the filmmakers from around the world who, over the years, have acknowledged their debt to Sirk, celebrating his work and the mark it has left on them. Among them is Mexican writer-director Guillermo del Toro. Accepting the award for Best Director at the 2018 Oscars, he spoke of his astonishment that Fox Searchlight had given him the green light for his tenth feature, *The Shape of Water*, believing that his "mad pitch . . . for a fable about an amphibian god and a mute woman, done in the style of Douglas Sirk, a musical and a thriller, was a sure bet." Later the same evening, after the film won the Oscar for Best Picture, del Toro looked back on those who'd originally inspired him to embark on a filmmaking career, again alluding to Sirk alongside William Wyler and Frank Capra.

He is far from the first director to acknowledge Sirk's influence, and Fassbinder is probably Sirk's best known acolyte. Soon after writing an enthusiastic essay about him for *Fernsehen und Film* in February 1971, he traveled to Lugano to visit the retired filmmaker at his home. Clad in a poncho, carrying a guitar, and accompanied by an entourage, he simply turned up at his door and introduced himself, their conversations impressing Sirk,[3] laying the foundations for an ongoing relationship, and, it would appear, further inspiring Fassbinder.

Released in 1974, his *Angst essen Seele auf/Fear Eats the Soul* (1974) is a clear, if officially unacknowledged, reworking of *All That Heaven Allows*. Shifting the setting to contemporary Munich, it makes the widow (Brigitte Mira) a cleaning woman and her lover (El Hedi ben Salem) a Moroccan immigrant worker, a foreigner looked down upon by the locals. Although their visual styles are distinctively different—Fassbinder's self-consciously posed, tableau-like framings at odds with the conventions of narrative realism, while Sirk's fluid compositions play by the rules—both films meticulously situate their characters within settings that physically and ideologically impact on their behavior. Fassbinder's film is his most direct "borrowing" from Sirk, a perfect illustration of the way in which a filmmaker can simultaneously absorb an influence and still manage to very much go his own way.

Almost thirty years later, Todd Haynes's *Far from Heaven* (2002) also revisited *All That Heaven Allows*. His stylish melodrama is set in 1957, in another leafy New England suburb. And much of the film's lush *mise-en-scène* echoes that of *All That Heaven Allows*. However, in this incarnation, the heroine (Julianne Moore) isn't a widow, although she is estranged from her TV-salesman husband (Dennis Quaid), a sympathetic character who has finally realized that he's gay. Again a gardener comes into her life, but this time he's an African American (Dennis Haysbert).

As in Sirk's film, her superficially idyllic existence is indeed far from heaven, a mirage whose pristine surfaces hide brutal social realities. Again as in the Sirk, Haynes presents the social order they embody as the problem, its deep-rooted homophobia (as well as its inbuilt racism and sexism) a poison that has contaminated all of the characters.

Haynes has spoken eloquently of what he learned from Sirk, having discovered him via Fassbinder.[4] "What Sirk did for Fassbinder," he says, "was show . . . people who you can identify with, not through their free agency . . . but because of their captivity in the rigid society that we all share." And for him, as for Sirk, they "have to be in the dark."

Many reviews of Tunisian writer-director Raja Amari's feature debut, *Satin Rouge*, made in the same year as *Far from Heaven*, have summoned *All That Heaven Allows* as a reference point.[5] And it's not hard to see why. As it begins, a thirty-something widow (Hiam Abbass) is tied to her domestic routines, her home her prison. As her teenage daughter (Hend El Fahem) says to a friend, "Her life is dedicated to my father's memory." Amari's film offers a clear-eyed critique of the constraints that will continue to impinge on the widow's existence in a patriarchal society, while also lending a considerable poignancy to her journey of self-discovery.

Yet what emerges from this is not that Sirk was a noteworthy reference point for Amari. In interviews, she has made no mention of him, and her film deals with a dramatic situation common to many of the so-called "women's films" made in Hollywood during the 1940s and '50s (such as *My Reputation*, as I've proposed elsewhere in this book). But whatever her influences—and her subsequent films also deal with women grappling with oppressive social realities—what is clear from this is the degree to which, for a large body of critical opinion, Sirk's work has now become a touchstone against which to measure the approaches taken by others to films of this ilk.

The "rediscovery" of Sirk might have taken place on the page, in magazines such as *Cahiers du cinema, Positif, Filmkritik, Screen,* and *Bright Lights,* and in the burgeoning film studies courses being taught at colleges and in universities during the 1970s and '80s. But, at the same time, it was being filtered through the consciousness of nascent filmmakers.

Haynes credits his time at Brown University, studying semiotics and feminist film theory, for introducing him to Fassbinder and Sirk (and others) and for the subsequent direction he took as a filmmaker. Kathryn Bigelow recalls being introduced to Sirk's work at Columbia University, where she studied under the tutelage of Andrew Sarris. And it was a formative time for her. "Douglas Sirk was a major, major influence, certainly for the early films that I did and as I began to shape myself as a filmmaker," she recalled in her commentary for German born writer/film historian Robert Fischer's *Fiction Factory* series.[6] Like many others, she visited Sirk in Lugano—with Matthias Brunner and Monty Montgomery for *Interview* magazine—looking back on him as "a rich and indelible inspiration" and referring to the homage to *Written on the Wind* in her debut feature, *The Loveless* (1981).

Also for the *Fiction Factory* series, screenwriter Wesley Strick (*True Believer*, the *Cape Fear* remake) and Allison Anders (*Gas, Food, Lodging, Mi Vida Loca, Grace of My Heart*) sing Sirk's praises. Acknowledging that his familiarity with Sirk's work is limited to a handful of films, all '50s melodramas, Strick provides a firsthand account of how he came to write the novel *Out There in the Dark*, loosely based on Sirk's life.[7] Surrounded by original posters for his films, Anders credits Martin Scorsese for opening her eyes to Sirk, reflecting on the impact his depictions of "the intense anguish in the American family" had on her and submitting the notion that his work wasn't fully appreciated in the US because "Americans don't like irony."[8]

Years before Tim Hunter embarked on a filmmaking career with two fine teen movies, *Tex* (1982) and *River's Edge* (1986), he contributed an astute close reading of Sirk's *Summer Storm* to the book published in association with the Edinburgh Film Festival's 1972 Sirk retrospective. In it, he wrote, "Douglas Sirk is beyond question one of the cinema's great realists. His understanding of people and of the relationship between emotion and action is profound and true, rendering his films often unbearably moving, and inevitably deeply disturbing."[9]

In 2016, Luca Guadagnino, whose *Call Me by Your Name* was also a nominee at the 2018 Oscars, effusively paid his own tribute: "If it weren't for Douglas Sirk, I wouldn't be making the films that I am. He is my most important influence. He means everything to me."[10] Guadagnino's *I Am Love* (2009), in particular, points to his firm grasp of Sirk's use of setting, décor, and composition to evoke character. A decade earlier, Canadian director Guy Maddin told interviewer David Church, "I'm just delighted by Douglas Sirk's greatest works, by the artifice, the visuals, the acting styles, the mannerisms . . . the stories that are both delightfully ludicrous and powerfully tragic at the same time. I couldn't be more delighted when there is that mix of seemingly exclusive feelings going on inside me simultaneously when I'm watching. I get that same feeling from Josef von Sternberg as well, and not that many other directors. So that hybrid feeling of being hit with a wrecking ball while being tickled by a feather really delights me."[11]

Visiting the US in 2014 for a French film festival in Los Angeles, Abidjan-born writer-director Katell Quillévéré also lists Sirk among her key influences. "*Suzanne*," she told the *Los Angeles Times*, "was influenced by Sirk's lush melodramas, such as the *Magnificent Obsession*, *All That Heaven Allows* and *Written on the Wind*."[12] And French writer-director Francois Ozon's films often elicit references to Sirk. Of his *8 Women* (2002), *Variety*'s Lisa Nesselson opined, "Think Douglas Sirk meets John Waters, in France."[13] Ozon acknowledges the link is not accidental, but explains that, like Haynes, he "actually came to Sirk through Fassbinder. Both he and Godard wrote about him at a time when he was considered very old fashioned. People thought that Sirk made silly American melodramas. But Fassbinder and Godard saw something more than guilty pleasures."[14]

As did Pedro Almodovar, who is cited by Roger Ebert as having hyperbolically claimed to have seen *Written on the Wind* a thousand times—"and I cannot wait to see it again," he said.[15] "I love melodramas, especially the most outrageous ones," Almodovar told interviewers Enrique Alberich and Luis Aller. "The Mexican Bunuel, for example, or those by Douglas Sirk, a marvelous director. But personally, I think there are two things that separate me from those who came before me and especially Sirk: morality . . . and humor. As I said, I admire Sirk's films, but one has to recognize that there is a complete absence of humour in his films. The humor that is there is perhaps in the eyes of the one who sees it, but no way is it the intention of the film."[16]

As will be clear to readers of this book, it's my view that Almodovar is entirely wrong about this, although Sirk's shadow still looms large over much of his work. Lucy Fischer argues persuasively that his *High Heels* (1991) is "a postmodern remake" of *Imitation of Life*.[17] And Almodovar also regularly visits Sirk's recurring theme of life being like a series of theatrical performances, perhaps most effectively in his *All About My Mother* (1999).

Ebert also notes that *Written on the Wind* "is a perverse and wickedly funny melodrama in which you can find the seeds of *Dallas*, *Dynasty*, and all the other prime-time soaps," adding that "Sirk is the one who established their tone, in which shocking behavior is treated with passionate solemnity, while parody burbles beneath."[18] And Sam Staggs sees Sirk everywhere in John Waters's films, noting that "although *Polyester* (1981) is Waters's flags-flying homage to Sirk—the suburban dream as upside-down comic nightmare—it's in *Female Trouble* (1974) that Waters runs amok in the atelier of the Sirk psyche."[19]

Then there are the throwaway references to Sirk strewn across a host of later films. On their own, they scarcely indicate *influence*, but in their name-dropping way, they still reference a master. In Quentin Tarantino's *Pulp Fiction* (1994), John Travolta's Vincent Vega orders a "Douglas Sirk steak" from the menu at the Jack Rabbit Slim's diner. Staggs further notes that "it's probably no coincidence that Travolta's Chevy Malibu in the film is as red as Rossano Brazzi's in *Interlude* or Dorothy Malone's in *Written on the Wind*—i.e., Sirk red."[20] Aki Kaurismaki's mostly silent *Juha* (1999) features a Sierck convertible. In its fifth season (2014), the TV series *Pretty Little Liars* introduces a character named Douglas Sirk (Christopher Grove) as chief prosecutor in the murder trial of Alison DiLaurentis (Sasha Pieterse). And so on . . .

It's entirely appropriate, then, that the Oxford English Dictionary introduced the adjective "Sirkian" to its listings in a 2018 revisioning. However, the most extraordinary element of Sirk's legacy is that it appears to be almost entirely focused on scarcely more than a handful of the thirty-nine features he directed during his twenty-five years as a filmmaker. All of the chosen ones were made at Universal, but, while they're certainly major works fully deserving of the attention that has been paid to them, they barely scratch the surface of the qualities that make the director such an important figure in the history of world cinema. It has been the goal of this book to open the door on the rest of his oeuvre, to chart its highs and lows, and to identify the consistency with which he chased his particular concerns throughout his entire career.

FILMOGRAPHY

SHORT FILMS

Zwei Genies/Two Geniuses (1934)
Dreimal Ehe/Three Times Married (1935)
Der Eingebildete Kranke/The Imaginary Invalid (1935)
The Christian Brothers at Mont La Salle (1941)
Sprich zu mir wie der Regen/Speak to Me Like the Rain (1976)
Silvesternacht/New Year's Eve (1978)
Bourbon Street Blues (1979)

FEATURES

April! April! (1935)
Director: Detlef Sierck
Producer: Peter Paul Brauer
Screenplay: H. W. Litschke and Rudo Ritter
Cast: Albrecht Schoenhals, Carola Hohn, Erhard Siedel, Lina Carstens
UFA
(Dutch version: *'T was een April*)

The Girl from the Marsh Croft (1935)
Director: Detlef Sierck
Producer: Peter Paul Brauer
Screenplay: Lothar M. Mayring (based on the novel by Selma Lagerlof)
Cast: Hansi Knoteck, Ellen Frank, Friedrich Kayssler, Kurt Fischer-Fehling
UFA

Pillars of Society (1935)
Director: Detlef Sierck
Producer: Fred Lyssa
Screenplay: Dr. Georg Klaren, Karl Peter Gillmann (freely drawn from Henrik Ibsen)
Cast: Heinrich George, Maria Krahn, Horst Teetzmann, Albrecht Schoenhals
R. N. Film der UFA

Schlussakord (1936)
Director: Detlef Sierck
Producer: Bruno Duday
Screenplay: Kurt Heuser and Detlef Sierck
Cast: Lil Dagover, Willy Birgel, Maria V. Tasnady, Maria Koppenhofer
UFA

Das Hofkonzert (1936)
Director: Detlef Sierck
Producer: Bruno Duday
Writers: Franz Wallner-Baste and Detlef Sierck (from the play *Das Kleine Hofkonzert* by Paul Verhoeven and Toni Impekoven)
Cast: Marta Eggerth, Johannes Heesters, Otto Tressler, Herbert Hubner
UFA
(French version: *La Chanson du Souvenir*)

Zu neuen Ufern (1937)
Director: Detlef Sierck
Producer: Bruno Duday
Screenplay: Detlef Sierck and Kurt Heuser (based on the novel by Lovis H. Lorenz)
Cast: Zarah Leander, Willy Birgel, Viktor Staal, Hilde v. Stolz
UFA

La Habanera (1937)
Director: Detlef Sierck
Producer: Bruno Duday
Screenplay: Gerhard Menzel
Cast: Zarah Leander, Karl Martel, Ferdinand Marian, Julia Serda
UFA

Accord Final (1938)
Director: I. R. Bay (Ignacy Rosenkranz)
Supervisor of the Production: Detlef Sierck
Producers: Georges Lourau, Chiel Weissman, Joseph Weissman
Screenplay: Ignacy Rosenkranz, Max Kolpe
Cast: Kate DeNagy, Jules Berry, Georges Rigaud, Andre Alerme Francinex

Boefje (1939)
Director: Detlef Sierck
Producer: Leo Meyer
Screenplay: Carl Zuckmayer (based on the book by M. J. Brusse)
Cast: Annie van Ees, Albert van Dalsum, Enny Heymans-Snijders, Piet Bron
NV City Film

Hitler's Madman (1943)
Director: Douglas Sirk
Producer: Seymour Nebenzal
Screenplay: Peretz Hirshbein, Melvin Levy, Doris Malloy (suggested by *Hangman's Village* by Bart Lytton)
Cast: Patricia Morison, John Carradine, Alan Curtis, Howard Freeman
MGM

Summer Storm (1944)
Director: Douglas Sirk
Producer: Seymour Nebenzal
Screenplay: Rowland Leigh
Adaptation: Douglas Sirk and Michael O'Hara (from the novel *The Shooting Party* by Anton Chekhov)
Cast: George Sanders, Linda Darnell, Anna Lee, Edward Everett Horton
United Artists/Angelus Pictures

A Scandal in Paris (1946)
Director: Douglas Sirk
Producer: Arnold Pressburger
Screenplay: Ellis St. Joseph (based on *The Life of Eugene Francois Vidocq*)
Cast: George Sanders, Signe Hasso, Carol Landis, Akim Tamiroff
United Artists/Arnold Pressburger Productions

The Strange Woman (1946)
Directors: Edgar G. Ulmer and (uncredited) Douglas Sirk
Producer: Jack Chertok
Screenplay: Herb Meadow (based on the novel by Ben Ames Williams)
Cast: Hedy Lamarr, George Sanders, Louis Hayward, Gene Lockhart
United Artists/Hunt-Stromberg

Lured (1947)
Director: Douglas Sirk
Producer: James Nasser
Screenplay: Leo Rosten (from a story by Jacques Companeez, Ernest Neuville, Simon Gantillon)
Cast: George Sanders, Lucille Ball, Charles Coburn, Sir Cedric Hardwicke
United Artists/Oakmont Pictures

Sleep My Love (1947)
Director: Douglas Sirk
Producers: Chas. Buddy Rogers and Ralph Cohen
Screenplay: St. Clair McKelway and Leo Rosten (from the novel by Leo Rosten)
Cast: Claudette Colbert, Robert Cummings, Don Ameche, Rita Johnson
United Artists/Triangle

Slightly French (1949)
Director: Douglas Sirk
Producer: Irving Starr
Screenplay: Karen de Wolf (story by Herbert Fields)
Cast: Dorothy Lamour, Don Ameche, Janis Carter, Willard Parker
Columbia

Shockproof (1949)
Director: Douglas Sirk
Producers: Earl McEvoy (associate producer), and (uncredited) Helen Deutsch and S. Sylvan Simon
Screenplay: Helen Deutsch, Samuel Fuller
Cast: Cornel Wilde, Patricia Knight, John Baragrey, Esther Minciotti
Columbia

Mystery Submarine (1950)
Director: Douglas Sirk
Producer: Ralph Dietrich
Screenplay: George W. George, George F. Slavin (suggested by a story by Ralph Dietrich)
Cast: Macdonald Carey, Marta Toren, Robert Douglas, Carl Esmond
Universal-International

The First Legion (1951)
Director: Douglas Sirk
Producer: Douglas Sirk
Screenplay: Emmet Lavery (based on his play)
Cast: Charles Boyer, William Demarest, Lyle Bettger, Walter Hampden
United Artists/Sedif Pictures

Thunder on the Hill (1951)
Director: Douglas Sirk
Producer: Michael Kraike
Screenplay: Oscar Saul and Andrew Solt (from the play *Bonaventure* by Charlotte Hastings)
Cast: Claudette Colbert, Ann Blyth, Robert Douglas, Anne Crawford
Universal-International

The Lady Pays Off (1951)
Director: Douglas Sirk
Producer: Albert J. Cohen
Screenplay: Frank Gill Jr. and Albert J. Cohen
Cast: Linda Darnell, Stephen McNally, Gigi Perreau, Virginia Field
Universal-International

Week-End with Father (1951)
Director: Douglas Sirk
Producer: Ted Richmond
Screenplay: Joseph Hoffman (from a story by George F. Slavin and George W. George)
Cast: Van Heflin, Patricia Neal, Gigi Perreau, Virginia Field
Universal-International

Has Anybody Seen My Gal (1951)
Director: Douglas Sirk
Producer: Ted Richmond
Screenplay: Joseph Hoffman (based on the novel *Oh, Money! Money!* by Eleanor H. Porter)
Cast: Piper Laurie, Rock Hudson, Charles Coburn, Gigi Perreau
Universal-International

No Room for the Groom (1952)
Director: Douglas Sirk
Producer: Ted Richmond
Screenplay: Joseph Hoffman (based on the novel *My True Love* by Darwin L. Teilhet)
Cast: Tony Curtis, Piper Laurie, Don DeFore, Spring Byington
Universal-International

Meet Me at the Fair (1952)
Director: Douglas Sirk
Producer: Albert J. Cohen
Screenplay: Irving Wallace (adaptation by Martin Berkeley, based upon the novel *The Great Companions* by Gene Markey)
Cast: Dan Dailey, Diana Lynn, Scatman Crothers, Hugh O'Brian
Universal-International

Take Me to Town (1952)
Director: Douglas Sirk
Producer: Ross Hunter
Screenplay: Richard Morris (based on his story)
Cast: Ann Sheridan, Sterling Hayden, Philip Reed, Lee Patrick
Universal-International

All I Desire (1953)
Director: Douglas Sirk
Producer: Ross Hunter
Screenplay: James Gunn and Robert Blees (adaptation by Gina Kaus, based on the novel *Stopover* by Carol Brink)
Cast: Barbara Stanwyck, Richard Carlson, Lyle Bettger, Marcia Henderson
Universal-International

Taza, Son of Cochise (1953)
Director: Douglas Sirk
Producer: Ross Hunter
Screenplay: George Zuckerman (story and adaptation by Gerald Drayson Adams)
Cast: Rock Hudson, Barbara Rush, Gregg Palmer, Bart Roberts
Universal-International

Magnificent Obsession (1954)
Director: Douglas Sirk
Producer: Ross Hunter
Screenplay: Robert Blees (from the novel by Lloyd C. Douglas, adaptation by Wells Root, based upon the screenplay by Sarah Y. Mason and Victor Heerman)
Cast: Jane Wyman, Rock Hudson, Barbara Rush, Agnes Moorehead
Universal-International

Sign of the Pagan (1954)
Director: Douglas Sirk
Producer: Albert J. Cohen
Screenplay: Oscar Brodney and Barre Lyndon (from a story by Brodney)
Cast: Jeff Chandler, Jack Palance, Ludmilla Tcherina, Rita Gam
Universal-International

Captain Lightfoot (1955)
Director: Douglas Sirk
Producer: Ross Hunter
Screenplay: W. R. Burnett and Oscar Brodney (based on a story by Burnett)
Cast: Rock Hudson, Barbara Rush, Jeff Morrow, Kathleen Ryan
Universal-International

All That Heaven Allows (1955)
Director: Douglas Sirk
Producer: Ross Hunter
Screenplay: Peg Fenwick (based on the novel by Edna Lee and Harry Lee)
Cast: Jane Wyman, Rock Hudson, Agnes Moorehead, Conrad Nagel
Universal-International

There's Always Tomorrow (1955)
Director: Douglas Sirk
Producer: Ross Hunter
Screenplay: Bernard C. Schoenfeld (based on a story by Ursula Parrott)
Cast: Barbara Stanwyck, Fred MacMurray, Joan Bennett, William Reynolds
Universal-International

Written OnThe Wind (1956)
Director: Douglas Sirk
Producer: Albert Zugsmith
Screenplay: George Zuckerman (based on the novel by Robert Wilder)
Cast: Rock Hudson, Lauren Bacall, Robert Stack, Dorothy Malone
Universal-International

Battle Hymn (1957)
Director: Douglas Sirk
Producer: Ross Hunter
Screenplay: Charles Grayson and Vincent B. Evans
Cast: Rock Hudson, Anna Kashfi, Dan Duryea, Don DeFore
Universal-International

Interlude (1957)
Director: Douglas Sirk
Producer: Ross Hunter
Screenplay: Daniel Fuchs and Franklin Coen (adaptation by Inez Cocke from a screenplay by Dwight Taylor and a story by James Cain)
Cast: June Allyson, Rossano Brazzi, Marianne Cook, Francoise Rosay
Universal-International

Never Say Goodbye (1956)
Directors: Jerry Hopper and (uncredited) Douglas Sirk
Producer: Albert J. Cohen
Screenplay: Charles Hoffman (based on a screenplay by Bruce Manning, John Klorer, Leonard Lee, from the play *Come Prima Meglio Di Prima* by Luigi Pirandello)
Cast: Rock Hudson, Cornell Borchers, George Sanders, Shelley Fabares
Universal-International

The Tarnished Angels (1957)
Director: Douglas Sirk
Producer: Albert Zugsmith
Screenplay: George Zuckerman (based on the novel *Pylon* by William Faulkner)
Cast: Rock Hudson, Robert Stack, Dorothy Malone, Jack Carson
Universal-International

A Time To Love and A Time To Die (1958)
Director: Douglas Sirk
Producer: Robert Arthur
Screenplay: Orin Jannings (based on the novel by Erich Maria Remarque)
Cast: John Gavin, Lilo Pulver, Jock Mahoney, Don DeFore
Universal-International

Imitation of Life (1959)
Director: Douglas Sirk
Producer: Ross Hunter
Screenplay: Eleanor Griffin and Allan Scott (based on the novel by Fannie Hurst)
Cast: Lana Turner, John Gavin, Juanita Moore, Sandra Dee
Universal-International

NOTES

INTRODUCTION

1. Jon Halliday, *Sirk on Sirk* first edition (London: Secker & Warburg, 1971), p. 70.

2. Wolfgang Limmer, "The Happy Ending: An Emergemcy Exit," *Suddeutsche Zeitung*, November 17–18, 1973 (translation by Virginia Soukup). Limmer also made a forty-five-minute documentary about Sirk, *Filmarbeit mit Douglas Sirk* (1987).

3. Todd Haynes develops this aspect most effectively in *Far From Heaven* (2002), his dramatized celebration of Sirk's work.

4. Eric Bentley, *The Life of the Drama* (London: Methuen & Co., 1966), p. 202.

5. John Belton, *Cinema Stylists* (Metuchen, NJ, and London: Scarecrow Press, 1983), p. 137.

6. Halliday, op. cit., p. 130.

7. It's worth noting that this interview was done at least three years prior to publication. It is incorrectly ascribed to Jean-Louis Comolli in Michael Stern's *Douglas Sirk* (Boston: Twayne, 1979), pp. 203, 205.

8. Andrew Sarris, *The American Cinema* (New York: E. P. Dutton, 1969), pp. 109–10. Sarris wrote a further appraisal of Sirk's work for *Bright Lights*, Winter 1977–78, p. 5, in an issue devoted to Sirk.

9. Halliday reveals in the introduction to the revised second edition of *Sirk on Sirk* (London: Faber and Faber, 1997) that his interviews with the director weren't recorded but were, rather, written up from notes taken during their exchanges.

10. James Harvey, "Sirkumstantial Evidence," *Film Comment*, July/August 1978, p. 54.

11. See, for example, Sirk's comments about *All That Heaven Allows* in an interview with Kathryn Bigelow in Peter Keogh, ed., *Kathryn Bigelow: Interviews* (Jackson: University Press of Mississippi, 2013), p. 14: "The content of a trite novel could be vivified—you could wake it up—you could put something into it. Take a story like *All That Heaven Allows*, for instance. It's a very trite story basically, it's a nothing story, but . . . I turned it into a meaningful film."

12. *Douglas Sirk: The Complete American Period*, University of Connecticut Film Society, 1974 (program booklet with edited essays).

13. From a series of previously unpublished interviews conducted with Sirk by the author in and around his home in Lugano between April 1975 and May 1981 (all other uncredited quotes come from these interviews).

14. The introduction to the second edition of *Sirk on Sirk* offers a moving account of this period of the director's life.

15. The second edition of Halliday's book replaces his original introduction with a new one, describing Sirk's work in very different terms as "warm-hearted, often humorous and always beautifully crafted portraits of human emotions—especially of difficult choices requiring unusual courage, and of love in extreme circumstances or love thwarted" (p. 2). The general tone of the interview, of course, remains the same, although new material has been included.

16. Peter Lehman, "Thinking with the Heart: An Interview with Douglas Sirk," *Wide Angle*, vol. 3, no. 4, p. 47.

17. Thomas Elsaesser, "Tales of Sound and Fury: Observations on the Family Melodrama," *Monogram*, no. 4 (1972), pp. 2–15.

18. Molly Haskell, *From Reverence to Rape: The Treatment of Women in the Movies* (New York and Baltimore: Penguin, 1974).

19. See, in particular, Laura Mulvey, "Visual Pleasure and Narrative Cinema," *Screen*, vol. 16, no. 3 (1975), pp. 6–18.

20. Lucy Fischer, ed., *Imitation of Life: Douglas Sirk, Director* (New Brunswick, NJ: Rutgers University Press, 1991).

21. Barbara Klinger, *Melodrama & Meaning: History, Culture and the Films of Douglas Sirk* (Bloomington: Indiana University Press, 1994).

22. Most notably by Michael Walker in *Movie*, no. 34–35, pp. 31–47. See also Lucy Fischer, "Sirk and the Figure of the Actress: *All I Desire*" in *Film Criticism*, vol. XXIII, nos. 2–3, pp. 136–49.

23. Jeanine Basinger, "The Lure of the Gilded Cage" in *Bright Lights*, Winter 1977–78, pp. 16–19; Stern, op. cit., pp. 111–34; and Amy Lawrence, "Trapped in a Tomb of Their Own Making: Max Ophuls's *The Reckless Moment* and Douglas Sirk's *There's Always Tomorrow*," in *Film Criticism*, vol. XXIII, nos. 2–3, pp. 136–49.

24. Jean-Luc Godard's review of the film is translated into English in Jean Narboni and Tom Milne, eds., *Godard on Godard* (London: Secker and Warburg, 1972), pp. 134–39.

25. Sabine Hak, "The Melodramatic Imagination of Detlef Sierck: *Final Chord* and Its Resonances," *Screen*, vol. 38, no. 2 (1997), pp. 129–48; Linda Schulte-Sasse, "Douglas Sirk's *Schlussakkord* and the Question of Aesthetic Resistance," *Germanic Review*, Winter 1998, pp. 2–31; and Victoria L. Evans, *Douglas Sirk, Aesthetic Modernism and the Culture of Modernity* (Edinburgh University Press, 2017), pp. 115–46.

26. Marc Silberman, *German Cinema: Texts in Context* (Detroit: Wayne State University Press, 1995), pp. 51–65; Lutz Koepnick, "Sirk and the Culture Industry: *Zu neuen Ufern* and *The First Legion*," *Film Criticism*, vol. XXIII, nos. 2–3, pp. 94–121; and Thomas R. Nadar, "The Director and the Diva: The Film Musicals of Detlef Sierck and Zarah Leander: *Zu neuen Ufern* and *La Habanera*," in Robert Charles Reimer, ed., *Cultural History Through a National Socialist Lens: Essays on the Cinema of the Third Reich* (Rochester, NY: Camden House, 2000), pp. 65–77.

27. Bruce Babington, "Written by the Wind: Sierck/Sirk's *La Habanera* (1937)," *Forum for Modern Language Studies*, vol. xxxi, no. 1 (1995), pp. 24–36; and Eric Rentschler, *The Ministry of Illusion: Nazi Cinema and Its Afterlife* (Cambridge: Harvard University Press, 1996), pp. 124–45.

28. Stern, op. cit., pp. 56–57.

29. Paul Coates, *The Gorgon's Gaze: German Cinema, Expressionism, and the Image of Horror* (New York: Cambridge University Press, 1991), p. 140.

30. Robert B. Ray, *How a Film Theory Got Lost and Other Mysteries in Cultural Studies* (Indiana University Press, 2001), p. 61.

31. Gerd Gemunden, "Introduction," *Film Criticism*, vol. 23, no. 2/3 (1999), p. 8.

32. Gertrud Koch, "From Dietlef Sierck to Douglas Sirk," *Film Criticism*, vol. 23, no. 2/3 (1999), p. 24 (translation by Gerd Gemunden).

33. Eric Rentschler, "Sirk Revisited: The Limits and Possibilities of Artistic Agency," *New German Critique*, no. 95, Spring–Summer 2005, p. 158.

34. Schulte-Sasse, op. cit., p. 3.

35. Fred Camper, "The Films of Douglas Sirk," *Screen*, vol. 12, no. 2 (1971), p. 44.

36. Schulte-Sasse, op. cit., p. 6.

37. Victoria L. Evans, op. cit., p. 4.

38. Lehman, op. cit., p. 46.

39. Heinz-Gerd Rasner and Reinard Wulf, "An Encounter with Douglas Sirk," *Filmkritik*, no. 203, November 1973 (translation by Virginia Soukup).

40. He and Hilde were always eager to hear news of others who had followed the same route to his door that I had. I think the Sirks figured us as a small group of friends who took it in turns to visit them, rather than admirers from different sides of the world who, for the most part, had only them in common.

CHAPTER ONE. DETLEF SIERCK IN EUROPE

1. Jon Halliday, *Sirk on Sirk* new and revised edition (London: Faber and Faber, 1997), p. 29.

2. Marc Silberman, "The Nazi Film Industry," *Jump Cut*, no. 23, October 1980, p. 35.

3. Klaus Kreimeier, *The UFA Story: A History of Germany's Greatest Film Company, 1918–1945* (Berkeley: University of California Press, 1996), p. 286 (translation by Robert Kimber and Rita Kimber).

4. Halliday, op. cit., p. 37.

5. Halliday, op. cit., pp. 41–42.

6. Eric Rentschler, "Germany: Nazism and After," in Geoffrey Nowell-Smith, ed., *The Oxford History of World Cinema* (Oxford University Press, 1996), p. 377.

7. In 1934, two years before she signed with UFA, she recorded "In the Shadow of a Boot," a song written by Karl Gerhard about the Nazi persecution of Jews.

8. *From UFA to Hollywood: Douglas Sirk Remembers* (1991), directed by Eckhardt Schmidt.

9. Bruce Babington, "Written by the Wind: Sierck/Sirk's *La Habanera* (1937)," *Forum for Modern Language Studies*, vol. xxxi, no. 1, p. 28.

10. Antje Ascheid, "A Sierckian Double Image: The Narration of Zarah Leander as a National Socialist Star," *Film Criticism*, vol. 23, no. 2/3, p. 67. It's also worth noting in this context that Hansi Knotech, who plays Helga in *Das Madchen vom Moorhof*, was a member of the German-Austrian underground during the war, and that Marta Eggerth, lead actress in *Das Hofkonzert*, was Jewish, a further indication that the exclusion from UFA of so-called "undesirables" after 1933 was not entirely successful.

11. Moliere, *Five Plays* (Harmondsworth, Middlesex: Penguin Classics, 1958), pp. xv–xvi (translated and with an introduction by John Wood).

12. Grosz (1893–1959) was an important member of the Berlin Dada group during the 1920s, famous for his acidic commentaries about Germany's decadence between the wars. See, for example, his 1926 oil painting, "Pillars of Society." "I considered any art pointless if it did not put itself at the disposal of political struggle," he is famous for saying. "My art was to be a gun and a sword."

13. In particular, *Tartuffe ou l'imposteur*, during his time as the director of the Kleines Theatre in Chemnitz. See Halliday, op. cit., pp. 12, 166.

14. Moliere, op. cit., p. 21.

15. Katie Trumpener, "The Rene Clair Moment and the Overlap Films of the Early 1930s: Detlef Sierck's *April! April!*" *Film Criticism*, vol. 23, no. 2/3, p. 36.

16. Trumpener, p. 34.

17. My viewing of the film was enabled, and enriched, by Evi Nelson, a German friend, who sat by me while I watched it (courtesy of YouTube), translated the un-subtitled dialogue, explained the intricacies of the film's use of accents and language, helped to place the film within the context of the culture of the time, and laughed along with me.

18. Valerie Weinstein, "'White Jews' and Dark Continents: Capitalist Critique and Its Racial Undercurrents in Detlef Sierck's *April! April!* (1935)," in Barbara Hales, Mihaela Petrescu, and Valerie Weinstein, eds., *Continuity and Crisis in German Cinema, 1928–1936* (Rochester, NY: Camden House, 2016), p. 139.

19. Weinstein, p. 132.

20. Weinstein, p. 133.

21. Halliday, op. cit., p. 30.

22. The edition I'm using is Selma Lagerlof, *The Girl from the Marsh Croft* (Boston: Little, Brown, and Company, 1910) (translation by Velma Swanston Howard).

23. Listed on the credits as "Lothar M. Mayring," the writer subsequently worked on Nazi propaganda films and featured on the "God-pardoned List," compiled in 1944, a list of artists deemed to be important to the National Socialist regime.

24. See, for example, Serge Daney et Jean-Louis Noames, "Entretien avec Douglas Sirk," *Cahiers du cinema*, no. 189, April 1967, p. 20; and Halliday, op. cit., pp. 39–40.

25. Lagerlof, op. cit., p. 4.

26. Lagerlof, op. cit., p. 8.

27. Lagerlof, op. cit., p. 13.

28. Lagerlof, op. cit., p. 52.

29. Lagerlof, op. cit., pp. 53–54.

30. Lagerlof, op. cit., p. 89.

31. Here I'm using the term "*mise-en-scene*" synonymously with the notion of "the *dispositif*," as articulated by Adrian Martin in his groundbreaking book on the subject, *Mise En Scene and Film Style* (England: Palgrave Macmillan, 2014). He argues that every work of art "has its own broad *dispositive*—arising from a mix of aesthetic properties and social-historical conditions—and each particular work can create its own rules of the game, its own *dispositif*" (p. 189).

32. See Thomas Elsaesser's postscript to the opening chapter of Laura Mulvey and Jon Halliday, eds., *Douglas Sirk*, Edinburgh Film Festival, 1972, pp. 7–11.

33. Lagerlof, op. cit., p. 43.

34. The perspective on belief systems here is not too far from the one underlying *The Book of Mormon*, Trey Parker, Robert Lopez, and Matt Stone's absurdist musical; or

in Sirk's *Boefje*, when young Jan's mother wonders if he's so mean because he was born on a Friday.

35. There were two earlier feature-length screen adaptations of Ibsen's play, both silent versions, the first directed in the US in 1916 by Raoul Walsh, the second in England in 1920 by Rex Wilson.

36. Intriguingly, one of his schemes is directly mirrored in, or borrowed by, Edward L. Marin's *Forth Worth* (1951), a low-budget Randolph Scott Western, written by esteemed B-movie veteran John Twist. In it, an opportunist businessman (David Brian), who runs the Fort Worth Cattle Exchange, is keen to cash in on the railroad's impending arrival in the town. Like Ibsen's Bernick, he's a man with a shady past, although he casts himself as a visionary working for the community. Again, like Bernick, he's scheming to push the cost of land blocks down so that he can snap them up at bargain prices before selling them off to the railroad companies. But in *The Pillars of the Community*, there's no Randolph Scott to bring him undone.

36. On stage, Sirk had as his lead actor the famous Albert Basserman, a veteran of the theatre and German silent cinema who was revered for his performances in Ibsen's plays. Like Sirk, he was admired by leading Nazi officials but eventually fled the country with his Jewish wife, also ending up in the US where he played supporting roles in films such as *A Woman's Face* (1941), *Once Upon a Honeymoon* (1942), and *Since You Went Away* (1944), and was Oscar-nominated for *Foreign Correspondent* (1940).

36. Also like Sirk, George was a man of the left during the 1920s, although his affiliations moved in a different direction after Hitler came to power. A member of the Communist Party during the years of the Weimar Republic in Germany, he was blacklisted by the Nazis but subsequently revived his career in propaganda films, including a leading role in the notoriously anti-Semitic *Jud Suss* (1940). Arrested as a collaborator, he died in a Soviet concentration camp in 1946.

37. Henrik Ibsen, *Hedda Gabler, The Pillars of the Community, The Wild Duck*, translated and with an introduction by Una Ellis-Fermor (England, Australia, and Canada: Penguin, 1974), p. 134.

38. Ibsen, p. 136.

39. Ibsen, p. 15.

40. Intriguingly, especially given Sirk's original plans for how to end *All I Desire* (see Chapter 8), both Johan and Dina end up staying in the Norwegian town rather than escaping to America (as they do in the play).

41. Eric Bentley, *The Life of the Drama* (London: Methuen & Co., 1969), p. 207.

42. John Mercer and Martin Shingler, *Melodrama: Genre, Style, and Sensibility* (London and New York: Wallflower Press, 2005), p. 2.

43. For a fuller elaboration of the film's use of music in evoking character and furthering the progress of the plot, see Linda Schulte-Sasse's brilliant analysis in "Douglas Sirk's *Schlussakkord* and the Question of Aesthetic Resistance," *Germanic Review*, Winter 1998, pp. 2–31.

44. Sabine Hak, "The Melodramatic Imagination of Detlef Sierck: *Final Chord* and Its Resonances, *Screen*, vol. 38, no. 2 (1997), p. 131. Antje Ascheid makes the same point in Ascheid, "A Sierckian Double Image: The Narration of Zarah Leander as a National Socialist Star," *Film Criticism*, vol. 23, no. 2/3 (1999), p. 49.

45. Gertrud Koch, "From Dietlef Sierck to Douglas Sirk," *Film Criticism*, vol. 23, no. 2/3 (1999), pp. 25–26 (translation by Gerd Gemunden).

46. Gerd Gemunden, "Introduction," *Film Criticism*, vol. 23, no. 2/3 (1999), p. 7.

47. Victoria L. Evans, *Douglas Sirk, Aesthetic Modernism and the Culture of Modernity* (Edinburgh University Press, 2017), p. 136.

48. In Halliday's interview, Sirk tells him that the character of Carl-Otto "was a kind of take-off of a famous clairvoyant who, people said, was advising Hitler, and even running Germany. Can you imagine it? It was ridiculous." See Halliday, op. cit., p. 42.

49. Schulte-Sasse, op. cit. p. 7.

50. During the 1950s, Canadian American sociologist Erving Goffman's study of human behavior drew attention to the ways in which, "when an individual appears before others, he wittingly and unwittingly projects a definition of the situation, of which a conception of himself is an important part." See Goffman, *The Presentation of Self in Everyday Life* (University of Edinburgh, Social Sciences Research Centre, monograph no. 2, 1956), p. 155.

51. Martin, op. cit., pp. 127–54.

52. Daney et Noames, op. cit., p. 20.

53. Halliday, op. cit., p. 45.

54. Directed by Hanns Schwarz and originally planned as a silent, the Pommer-produced *Melody of the Heart* (1929) was the first screen operetta.

55. Kreimeier, op. cit., p. 238.

56. Sirk's fruitful collaboration with cinematographer Franz Weihmayr began with *Das Hofkonzert*. Weihmayr, whose earlier work included *The Blue Angel* (1930) for Josef von Sternberg and the Nazi documentary *Triumph of the Will* (1935) for Leni Riefenstahl, also shot *Zu neuen Ufern* and *La Habanera* for Sirk.

57. Halliday nominates Verhoeven's 1944 film *Das Konzert* as a remake (p. 175). However, that film is an entirely different work, based on a play by Hermann Bahr. Verhoeven's remake is called *Das Kleine Hofkonzert/Palace Scandal* and was shot in 1948. A French version of *Das Hofkonzert*, entitled *La Chanson du souvenir*, credited to Sirk and French director Serge de Poligny, and featuring a different cast—aside from Marta Eggerth—was made side-by-side with the original German one.

58. Although the *Cahiers* interview with Sirk has him claiming to have shot the film on location in Australia—see Daney and Noames, op. cit., p. 20—he later corrected this. "I don't know where they got that idea," he told me. "I never said that and I've never been to Australia. Perhaps one day." *Zu neuen Ufern* was largely shot at UFA studios with exteriors filmed on back-lots.

59. All the songs in the film were written by Austrian-born composer Ralph Bentazky (who, with Robert Stoltz, wrote the operetta, *White Horse Inn*). He had fled the Nazis with his Jewish wife in 1933, ending up in the US in 1940, although UFA was still prepared to hire him to work on *Zu neuen Ufern*.

60. Thomas R. Nadar, "The Director and the Diva: The Film Musicals of Detlef Sierck and Zarah Leander: *Zu neuen Ufern* and *La Habanera*," in Robert Charles Reimer, ed., *Cultural History Through a National Socialist Lens: Essays on the Cinema of the Third Reich* (Rochester, NY: Camden House, 2000), p. 69.

61. Marc Silberman, *German Cinema: Texts in Contexts* (Detroit: Wayne State University Press, 1995), p. 62.

62. Jan-Christopher Horak, http://www.filmreference.com.

63. Lutz Koepnick, "Sirk and the Culture Industry: *Zu neuen Ufern* and *The First Legion*," *Film Criticism*, vol. 23, no. 2/3, p. 103.

64. Much is made in the film of what an unwelcoming place Australia was after settlement, with the film repeatedly drawing attention to the heat and the discomfort it brought to all who reside in the colony, whichever side of the prison walls they're on.

65. Wolfgang Limmer, "The Happy Ending: An Emergency Exit," *Suddeutsche Zeitung*, November 17–18, 1973 (translation by Virginia Soukup).

66. Recurring throughout the film, "The Wind Has Sung Me a Song" was written by Lothar Brune (music) and Bruno Balz (lyrics). It also proved to be Zarah Leander's "most popular recording ever." See Nadar, op. cit., p. 73.

67. The same mindset led to *The Tarnished Angels* after *Written on the Wind*.

68. See Halliday, op. cit., p. 48. Intriguingly, while the opening credits on the prints I have viewed over the years list Sirk as the director, that listing is preceded by reference to *La Habanera* as "A Film by Gerhard Menzel." Perhaps this is an indication of UFA's disapproval of Sirk's departure from Germany within days of the film's Berlin premiere on December 18, 1937.

69. It's worth noting that, at the time, Sirk was still reeling over the battle he'd fought with ex-wide Lydia Brinken over the custody of their son. A similar issue also arises in *Schlussakord*.

70. Paul Coates, *The Gorgon's Gaze: German Cinema, Expressionism, and the Image of Horror* (New York: Cambridge University Press, 1991), p. 234.

71. Coates, p. 236.

72. Eric Rentschler, *The Ministry of Illusion: Nazi Cinema and Its Afterlife* (Cambridge: Harvard University Press, 1996), p. 141.

73. Koch, op. cit., p. 19. The description of Sirk's UFA films as "Nazi features" is mischievously misleading.

74. Geoff Brown, "*La Habanera*," *Monthly Film Bulletin*, January 1981, p. 13.

75. For some, the fact that Juan is blond makes him Aryan—rather than a child of mixed blood—thus, apparently, enabling a Nazi-inspired happy ending when he leaves Puerto Rico with his mother. However, the film could also be seen as suggesting that the Aryan appearance so beloved by the Third Reich reveals little about the actual nature of its source.

76. Linda Schulte-Sasse, op. cit., p. 27.

77. Schulte-Sasse, op. cit., p. 26.

78. Bruce Babington, op. cit., p. 29.

79. Rentschler, op. cit., p 135.

80. Halliday, op. cit., p. 61–62.

81. *Accord Final* remains elusive. My efforts to track it down have been in vain, although I believe that a print does exist. In 1978, Sirk told me that one had been located "in a trash can and put together by a professor from Lausanne." "It was a comedy," he added, "and I made it only because I needed the money" (in order to support his and Hilde's ongoing flight from the Nazis). See also Halliday, op. cit., pp. 59–60.

It is sometimes confused with *Schlussakord/Final Chord*. (See, for example, Jan-Christopher Horak, "Sirk's Early Exile Films: *Boefje* and *Hitler's Madman*," *Film Criticism*, vol. XXXIII, nos. 2–3, Winter/Spring 1999, p. 124.) But they are entirely different films.

82. According to Sirk, these aborted projects included a planned adaptation of Renoir's forty-minute *Une Partie de campagne* into a feature. See Halliday, op. cit., pp. 59–61.

83. As would be clear to anyone who has actually seen *Boefje*, *Wilton's Zoo* is *not* an alternative title, despite the countless reference works online and in print where it has been mistakenly offered as one. In Holland, *Boefje*'s English title is *Little Rascal*. For further clarification, see Halliday, op. cit., pp. 55–58, 178.

84. According to Horak, op. cit., p. 124, "23 of the 31 Dutch films produced between 1933 and 1940 can be considered (German) exile films."

85. F. J. J. W. Paalman, *Cinematic Rotterdam, The Times and Tides of a Modern City* (UvA-DARE, University of Amsterdam, 2010), p. 36 (thesis supervised by Thomas Elsaesser).

86. Tineke Slingerland-Nusink's bronze sculpture of *Boefje*'s protagonist was unveiled on March 14, 1980, in Amman Square, Rotterdam, by the town mayor.

87. Horak, op. cit., pp. 124–25.

88. Paalman, op. cit., p. 37.

CHAPTER TWO. AMERICAN BEGINNINGS: THE EUROPEAN LEGACY

1. *From UFA to Hollywood: Douglas Sirk Remembers* (1991), directed by Eckhardt Schmidt.

2. Heinz-Gerd Rasner and Reinhard Wulf, "An Encounter with Douglas Sirk," *Filmkritik*, no. 203, November 1973 (translation by Virginia Soukup).

3. From a series of previously unpublished interviews conducted with Sirk by the author in and around his apartment in Lugano between April 1975 and May 1981 (all other uncredited quotes come from this source).

4. Rasner and Wulf, op. cit.

5. Jon Halliday, *Sirk on Sirk* new and revised edition (London: Faber and Faber, 1997), p. 64.

6. James Harvey, "Sirkumstantial Evidence," *Film Comment*, July/August 1978, p. 59.

7. Rasner and Wulf, op. cit.

8. Halliday, op. cit., pp. 64–66, 180.

9. Thomas Elsaesser, "Book Review: *Sirk on Sirk* by Jon Halliday," *Monogram*, no. 4, 1972, pp. 41–42.

10. Several further films have been made about the assassination—including *Atentat/The Assassination* (1965, Czechoslovakia), directed and co-written by Jiri Sequens; *Operation: Daybreak* (1975, US), directed by Lewis Gilbert and written by Ronald Harwood; *Anthropoid* (2016, UK), directed and co-written by Sean Ellis; and *The Man with the Iron Heart* (2017), directed and co-written by Cedric Jimenez (2017)—all of which mention Lidice. But they are essentially straightforward espionage thrillers whose focus is on the commandos who kill Heydrich.

11. Alan Lovell and Jim Hillier, *Studies in Documentary* (London: Secker & Warburg/ BFI, 1972), p. 102.

12. Peter Bogdanovich, *Fritz Lang in America* (London: Studio Vista, 1967), p. 60.

13. There has been much controversy over the authorship of the screenplay and Brecht took his case about the credits to court. It appears that he was largely responsible for it with Wexley playing a supporting role. For Lang's comments on the matter, see Bogdanovich, *Fritz Lang in America*. For an insightful discussion about it and other aspects of the film's production history, see Jonathan Skolnick, "28 May, 1942: Bertolt Brecht and Fritz Lang Write a Hollywood Screenplay," in Jennifer M. Kapczynski,

Michael David Richardson, eds., *A New History of German Cinema* (Rochester, NY: Camden House, 2012), pp. 289–93.

14. James Powers, Rochelle Reed, and Donald Chase, "Fritz Lang," *Dialogue on Film*, American Film Institute, April 1974, p. 7.

15. Soon after the massacre, Millay was invited by the Writers' War Board to produce a work about Lidice. On October 19, "The Murder of Lidice" was broadcast across on NBC's radio network and sent by short-wave to Europe. According to a November 13, 1942, *Hollywood Reporter* account, Lang considered using verses from it as a prologue to *Hangmen Also Die!* A 2012 blog by Jan-Christopher Horak reports that it was Sirk's idea to use it in *Hitler's Madman*.

16. Jan-Christopher Horak, "Sirk's Early Exile Films: *Boefje* and *Hitler's Madman*," *Film Criticism*, vol. XXXIII, nos. 2–3, Winter/Spring 1999, pp. 126–28.

17. Mario R. Dederichs, *Heydrich: The Face of Evil* (London: Greenhill Books, 2006), pp. 151–52.

18. The production details in Halliday's book suggest different dates for both the initial filming and the reshoots. See Halliday, op. cit., p. 181. However, Horak's information seems more reliable here.

19. According to Horak, op. cit., p. 128, "the scene where a young student jumps to her death at Prague University, Heydrich's deathbed scenes, and the executions of the men in Lidice were reshot." The first of these is also noteworthy for its inclusion of Ava Gardner in an uncredited performance.

20. Halliday, op. cit., pp. 73–74.

21. Anton Chekhov, *The Shooting Party* (Australia: Penguin Books, 2004; translated and with notes by Ronald Wilks and featuring an introduction by John Sutherland). All further references relate to this edition. Chekhov's story was originally published in Moscow's *News of the Day* in thirty-two installments between August 1884 and April 1885.

22. Although this is the way he spells his name on the manuscript, various credit listings have him as "Fedor" (which is how he's verbally addressed during the film) or even "Fedja." All are Russian forms of "Theodore."

The film changes the names of most of the equivalent characters in the novel. Sirk's Petroff is Sergey Petrovich Zinovyev, Count Volsky is Count Karneyev, Nadena Kalenin is Nadezhda Nikolayevna, and so on.

23. Chekhov, op. cit., p. 67.

24. Chekhov, op. cit., p. 30.

25. Halliday, op. cit., p. 74.

26. Harvey, op. cit., p. 56.

27. Vidocq's memoirs have been published many times, under numerous titles and in a wide variety of forms. They were originally named *The Memoirs of Vidocq* and published in 1828.

28. Eugene Francois Vidocq, *The Memoirs of Detective Vidocq: Convict, Spy and Principal Agent of the French Police* (Enhanced Media, 2015), p. 6.

29. Kristopher Mecholsky, "Narrative Identity and Criminal Ideology in *A Scandal in Paris*," in Rosemary A. Peters, ed., *Criminal Papers: Reading Crime in the French Nineteenth Century* (Newcastle-upon-Tyne: Cambridge Scholars Publishing, 2012), pp. 208–10.

30. Mecholsky, p. 217.

31. Mecholsky astutely observes that they "look like a gallery of ne'er-do-wells from Cesare Lombroso's *L'uomo deliquente*." Mecholsky, pp 207–8.

32. "Flame Song," music by Hanns Eisler, lyrics by Paul Francis Webster.

33. From the official Production Code Administration records on *Lured*.

34. A taxi dancer is employed to dance with club patrons for a fee, calculated according to the amount of time spent on the dance floor (as in *The Taxi Dancer* [1927], starring Joan Crawford). The practice first came to prominence in the US during the early years of the twentieth century.

35. Serge Daney et Jean-Louis Noames, "Entretien avec Douglas Sirk," *Cahiers du Cinema*, no. 189, April 1967, p. 23 (translation by Virginia Soukup).

36. Francis M. Nevins suggests that, in *Pièges*, "the echoes of Woolrich's pulp classic *A Dime a Dance* (*Black Mask*, February 1938; first collected in *The Dancing Detective*, 1946) are as loud as the roar of the sea," going on to point to further connections to *Phantom Lady* (adapted for the screen in 1944 by Siodmak). See http://mysteryfile.com/blog/?p=19316.

Coincidentally, *Lured* lead Lucille Ball stars in a 1994 radio production of *Dime a Dance*, produced and directed by William Spier. And, in 1995, Peter Bogdanovich directed a TV adaptation of *A Dime a Dance* as part of the *Fallen Angels* TV series. See https://www.youtube.com/watch?v=mzLOpBTh4I0.

37. Halliday, op. cit., p. 84.

38. Halliday, op. cit., pp. 79–80.

39. Citations on the TCM website's notes about *Black Magic*; production dates listed in Halliday, op. cit., pp. 183–86.

40. It also features an uncredited Silvano Mangano in a bit part. Soon afterwards, she was to become famous for her role in Giuseppe De Santis's *Bitter Rice* (1949).

41. Mecholsky, op. cit., p. 205.

CHAPTER THREE. IN THE SHADOWS: SIRK AND THE NOIR INCLINATION

1. Paul Schrader, "Notes on Film Noir," *Film Comment*, Spring 1972, p. 8.

2. Sources differ on when films were first labeled "noirs." By Nino Frank in *L'ecran francais* in August 1946, regarding particular American crime films? By French film reviewers in the late 1930s, in reference to particular French films? Either way, it wasn't until well after what is now known as the classic noir period—in Hollywood from the 1940s through the early 1950s—that the term found its way into English-language commentary.

3. See, for example, Frank Krutnik, *In a Lonely Street: Film Noir, Genre, Masculinity* (London: Routledge, 1991), pp. 194, 215–20.

4. Michael Walker, "Film Noir: Introduction," in Ian Cameron, ed., *The Movie Book of Film Noir* (London: Studio Vista, 1992), p. 17.

5. Thomas Elsaesser, "Tales of Sound and Fury: Observations on the Family Melodrama," *Monogram*, no. 4 (1972), p. 11.

6. The original version of *Gaslight* was made in the UK in 1940 and directed by Thorold Dickinson.

7. As Hitchcock told Francois Truffaut, he had a very different ending in mind, a neatly ironic one in which Johnnie does indeed murder Lina and then gets his

comeuppance. Francois Truffaut, *Hitchcock* (New York: Simon and Schuster, 1967), pp. 102–3.

8. Production documents also list Cy Endfield and Decla Dunning as uncredited contributors to the screenplay. According to Brian Neve's *The Many Lives of Cy Endfield: Film Noir, The Blacklist and Zulu* (Madison: University of Wisconsin Press, 2015), p. 59, "Endfield's contributions appear to have been limited to the Chinese wedding scene." Halliday, op. cit., p. 186, also lists esteemed Canadian-born crime writer Ross Macdonald as an uncredited contributor to the script.

9. Cummings played a very similar role opposite Grace Kelly's wife and Ray Milland's murderous husband a few years later in *Dial M for Murder*.

10. Samuel Fuller, *A Third Face: My Tale of Writing, Fighting, and Filmmaking* (New York: Alfred A. Knopf, 2003), p. 240.

11. David Will and Peter Wollen, eds., *Samuel Fuller* (Edinburgh Film Festival, 1969), pp. 98–99.

12. See Gerald Peary, *Samuel Fuller: Interviews* (Jackson: University Press of Mississippi, 2012), p. 75.

13. In the finished film, after Jenny has been arrested, she looks on helplessly as another parolee (King Donovan), fearful of being sent back to jail, jumps out of a window in the halls of justice. In Will and Wollen, op. cit., p. 99, Fuller describes the scene as he'd originally written it: "In my story, when the guy tries to jump out the window, the girl tries to stop him and he begins to drag her with him . . . Then she gets scared and, as he clings on to her, she pushes him to save her own life and he falls out the window. In spite of this, she had at least tried to save him." Like Sirk, but in his own way, Fuller was more interested in shades of grey than in black-and-white readings of characters.

14. Will and Wollen, op. cit., pp. 98–99. Also see Halliday, op. cit., pp. 87–88.

15. Michael Stern, *Douglas Sirk* (Boston: Twayne, 1979), p. 60.

16. Bruce Lambert, "Obituary: Helen Deutsch, 85, Screenwriter of *Lili* and *National Velvet*," *Variety*, March 17, 1992.

17. Michael Stern, "Interview," *Bright Lights*, Winter 1977–78, p. 31.

18. Director Joseph Losey is one of many to confirm this story. After turning down *I Married a Communist*, he says, his RKO contract was terminated. "I later learned this was a touchstone for establishing who was not a 'red': you offered *I Married a Communist* to anybody you thought was a Communist, and, if they turned it down, they were." In Tom Milne, ed., *Losey on Losey* (London: Secker & Warburg, 1967), p. 76.

19. Jon Halliday, *Sirk on Sirk* new and revised edition (London: Faber and Faber, 1997), p. 191.

20. Peter Bogdanovich, *Who the Devil Made It* (New York: Alfred A. Knopf, 1997), p. 598.

21. Noah Isenberg, *Edgar G. Ulmer: A Filmmaker at the Margins* (Berkeley: University of California Press, 2014), p. 165.

22. Halliday, op. cit., p. 121.

23. Gary Morris, "Three Films by Edgar G. Ulmer: *Bluebeard, The Strange Woman,* and *Moon Over Harlem*," *Bright Lights* online, April 1, 2000.

24. According to Ruth Barton's Lamarr biography, she was in fact his "occasional lover." See Ruth Barton, *Hedy Lamarr: The Most Beautiful Woman in the World* (Lexington: University Press of Kentucky, 2010), p. 158.

25. John Belton, *The Hollywood Professionals, Volume 3: Howard Hawks, Frank Borzage, Edgar G. Ulmer* (London and New York: Tantivy/Barnes, 1974), p. 152.

CHAPTER FOUR. THE UNCOMFORTABLE COMEDIES

1. Michael Stern, "Interview with Douglas Sirk," *Bright Lights*, no. 6, 1977, p. 31.

2. Wolfgang Limmer, "The Happy Ending: An Emergemcy Exit," *Suddentsche Zeitung*, November 17–18, 1973 (translation by Virginia Soukup).

3. With the end credits approaching and Gerry Jeffers (Claudette Colbert) torn between her husband, Tom (Joel McCrea), and the Other Man, J. D. Hackensacker III (Rudy Vallee), Sturges hilariously conjures up an identical twin for Gerry and a happy ending/"emergency exit" that not only keeps the good Mr. Hackensacker happy but also satisfied the requirements of the Production Code of the time.

4. Jon Halliday, *Sirk on Sirk* new and revised edition (London: Faber and Faber, 1997), pp. 97–98.

5. In their excellent commentary on the films in *Affairs to Remember: The Hollywood Comedy of the Sexes*, (Manchester University Press, 1989), pp. 234–66, Bruce Babington and Peter William Evans overlook this when they group them with Sirk's pastoral musicals, *Has Anybody Seen My Gal* (1951), *Meet Me at the Fair*, and *Take Me to Town* (both 1952), all shot in Technicolor and very different in aspect and tone from the four black-and-white comedies.

6. I suspect Sirk would have gained considerable amusement from the fact that, while Dorothy Lamour sings her own numbers in the film, a stand-in replaces her for the wide shots of the dance routines in the film within the film.

7. http://mikegrost.com/sirk.htm.

8. Stern, op. cit., p. 31.

9. "I'm not responsible for this picture," Sirk told Jon Halliday in *Sirk on Sirk*. "I did some work on preparing it. But then I had to leave to do *Written on the Wind*, and later I was brought back to finish it as best I could." Halliday, op. cit., p. 121.

10. According to Stephen Shearer's biography, *Patricia Neal: An Unquiet Life* (Lexington: University Press of Kentucky, 2006), p. 119, Rock Hudson—long before his similar role in *Man's Favorite Sport* (1964)—was originally cast in Denning's part.

11. Stern, op. cit., p. 31.

12. Bruce Babington and Peter William Evans, op. cit., p. 254.

13. Stern, op. cit., p. 31.

14. Alan Miller, "Tea Party Invaders! Douglas Sirk's *No Room for the Groom*," *Berkshire Review for the Arts*, December 6, 2010.

15. Michael Stern, *Douglas Sirk* (Boston: Twayne, 1979), p. 79.

16. Stern, p. 78.

17. Babington and Evans, op. cit., p. 254.

CHAPTER FIVE. SIRK AND GOD: "THE PURE AMBUIGUITY OF EXPERIENCE"

1. Serge Daney and Jean-Louis Noames, "Entretien avec Douglas Sirk," *Cahiers du cinema*, no. 189, April 1967, p. 25 (translation by Virginia Soukup).

2. Jon Halliday, *Sirk on Sirk* new and revised edition (London: Faber and Faber, 1997), p. 94–95.

3. Halliday, p. 94.

4. A former president of the Screenwriters Guild of Los Angeles (1945–47), Lavery was a Hollywood liberal who ran into trouble with the HUAC investigation during the mid-1940s. He was labeled one of the Communist Party's "faithful fellow travelers" but eventually exonerated after insisting by way of appeasement that SWG board members should sign an anti-Communist affidavit or be viewed as betraying the guild. He also co-wrote Otto Preminger's *The Court-Martial of Billy Mitchell* (1955) with Milton Sperling and (uncredited) the blacklisted trio of Dalton Trumbo, Michael Wilson, and Ben Hecht.

5. Emmet Lavery, *The First Legion: A Drama of the Society of Jesus* (New York and Los Angeles: Samuel French, 1937), p. 3.

6. This is in line with the Jesuit document, written in 1540, which describes the Order as being for "whoever desires to serve as a soldier of God." The Order's founder was Ignatius of Loyola, a Spanish soldier and theologian who was canonized in 1622.

7. Lavery, op. cit., p. 22.

8. Lavery, op. cit., p. 21.

9. Lavery, op. cit., p. 14.

10. Lavery, op. cit., p. 99.

11. Lavery, op. cit., p. 53.

12. John Belton, *Cinema Stylists* (Metuchen, NJ, and London: Scarecrow Press, 1983), p. 137.

13. His view is not unlike that of the doctor in *All I Desire* (Thomas E. Jackson) who, after Naomi Murdoch (Barbara Stanwyck) is arrested for shooting her former lover, describes the small-town mob gathered outside his surgery as "maggots."

14. Lavery, op. cit., p. 129.

15. Belton, op. cit., p. 137.

16. Halliday, op. cit., p. 95.

17. Halliday, op. cit., p. 96.

18. Charlotte Hastings, *Bonaventure—A Play in Three Acts* (New York and Los Angeles: Samuel French, 1950).

19. Halliday, op. cit., pp. 97–98. Kraike has one official screenplay to his name, as co-writer on *The Wild Scene* (1970), as well as a couple of minor "story by" credits.

20. It's immediately preceded by a scene in the convent's bell tower which notably resembles the final one in Hitchcock's *Vertigo*, made seven years later.

21. Halliday, op. cit., p. 117.

22. *Sign of the Pagan* was made for around $1.3 million; at around $250,000 (450 million ITL), *Attila* was clearly an even less risky proposition.

23. Halliday, op. cit., p. 115.

24. Halliday, op. cit., p. 116.

25. Halliday, op. cit., p. 117.

26. For example: "Hollywood in its most delinquent mood could not improve upon the pointless fudge of violence and piety that the Italian film-makers have poured together in *Attila*. Like the barbarian who dropped down from the fold, the period adventure descended upon the city Saturday with 'saturation' bookings at more than 100 theatres," wrote *New York Times* critic Richard W. Nason, May 19, 1958.

27. While sword-and-sandal epics should never be assessed in terms of their historical accuracy, it's worth noting that the meeting between Attila and Pope Leo I did

actually take place and that Attila abandoned his planned attack on Rome immediately afterwards. However, the reasons for his departure remain a mystery.

CHAPTER SIX. PASTORAL YEARNINGS: SIRK AND THE MUSICAL

1. Martin Sutton, "Patterns of Meaning in the Musical," in Rick Altman, ed., *Genre: The Musical* (London: Routledge/Kegan Paul, 1981), p. 191.

2. Heinz-Gerd Rasner and Reinhard Wulf, "An Encounter with Douglas Sirk," *Filmkritik*, no. 203, November 1973 (translation by Virginia Soukup).

3. Jon Halliday, *Sirk on Sirk* new and revised edition (London: Secker & Warburg, 1997), p. 102.

4. There's nothing especially original in this as an idea. The musical as a genre regularly draws folks together to put on a show, whether it's on a street or in a theatre. More recently, Irish filmmaker John Carney has taken up this music-driven communal impulse as a recurrent theme, in films such as *Once* (2007), *Begin Again* (2013), and *Sing Street* (2016). It also underpins Ben Elton's Australian-made *Three Summers* (2017). But Sirk's knowing deployment of the convention underlines his embrace of music's social function. And those who can't or simply don't join in aren't to be trusted.

5. Eleanor H. Porter, *Oh, Money! Money!* in *The Works of Eleanor H. Porter* (e-book, 2010), pp. 2125–26.

6. Fulton's narrative function is roughly equivalent to that of "miracle man" Randolph in Lloyd C. Douglas's novel, *Magnificent Obsession* (1929), subsequently adapted by Sirk. Randolph is a character who presumes to use his influence and financial power to guide others' destinies.

7. "Has Anybody Seen My Gal? (Five Foot Two, Eyes of Blue)" was written in 1925 by Joe Henderson (music), Sam Lewis, and Joe Young (lyrics), and best known via the version by the California Ramblers. Like many other musicals of the 1930s, '40s, and '50s, Sirk's trilogy draws, in large part, on preexisting musical material (even if the title for *Has Anybody Seen My Gal* inexplicably removes the question mark).

8. One of his customers is played by an uncredited James Dean in his first speaking part.

9. Halliday, op. cit., p. 100.

10. G. Markey, *The Great Companions*, in the *Ladies' Home Journal*, October 1951, pp. 137–200.

11. Robert Vaughn, *Only Victims: A Study of Show Business Blacklisting* (New York: Proscenium, 1972), p. 287. Although Sirk never made any accusations against him, it's worth surmising that Berkeley might have had something to do with the Sirk home being searched by FBI agents during the early 1950s.

12. The song was written by Scatman Crothers (music) and F. E. Miller (lyrics), both African American and neither credited for this contribution to the film.

13. The film was made before such vaudeville tropes were understood not only to endorse the offensive stereotyping of African Americans but also to limit their professional opportunities.

14. Michael Stern, *Douglas Sirk* (Boston: Twayne, 1979), p. 83.

15. Michael Stern, "Interview with Douglas Sirk," *Bright Lights*, no. 6, 1977, p. 31.

16. Universal's official production budget reveals that both Brodney and Breslow were paid at a much higher rate than Morris. According to the *Hollywood Reporter* of

March 1951, Breslow had previously been slated as the original director of *Meet Me at the Fair*.

17. Alan Goble, ed., *The Complete Index to Literary Sources in Film* (Berlin: Walter de Gruyter, 1999), p. 335.

18. "The Tale of Vermillion O'Toole" was written by Frederick Herbert (who also wrote the lyrics for "Meet Me at the Fair") and sung by Dusty Walker (with a final verse over the closing credits). A wide range of instrumental variations on its themes also winds its way through the rest of the film.

19. "Oh, You Redhead," written for the film by Frederick Herbert (lyrics) and Milton Rosen (music). Anita Ekberg makes an early uncredited appearance in this scene as a dance-hall girl.

20. Kids do this a lot in Hollywood films, from Sirk's *The Lady Pays Off* (1951) through *The Parent Trap* (1961) and *The Courtship of Eddie's Father* (1963) to *Sleepless in Seattle* (1993).

21. Halliday, op. cit., p. 114.

22. Stern, *Douglas Sirk*, op. cit., p. 85.

23. Michael Walker, "*All I Desire*," *Movie*, no. 34/35 (Winter 1990), p. 47.

24. Ross Hunter, "Magnificent Obsessions," *American Film*, April 1988, p. 16.

CHAPTER SEVEN. HOLLYWOOD, ROCK HUDSON AND THE IDEA OF THE HERO

1. Michael Stern, *Douglas Sirk* (Boston: Twayne, 1979), p. 157.

2. In a letter to Michael Stern (*Bright Lights*, no. 6, 1977, p. 27), writer George Zuckerman takes a different view: "Sirk, much as I admire the man, wasn't and couldn't have been an 'auteur' the way the studio was run in those days . . . Your 'hero' should be Ed Muhl, who ran the studio. I don't mean to demean Sirk's work. But he had no chance. The budgets were tight, the schedules tighter. A director who went over budget or shooting schedule never worked at U-I again. Sirk knew this. He was rushed, he was harried by the stars. He did what he could—which was better than the other directing talent on the lot."

3. Dean E. Hess, *Battle Hymn* (New York: McGraw-Hill, 1956).

4. Jon Halliday, *Sirk on Sirk* new and revised edition (London: Faber & Faber, 1997), p. 104. While it is true that Sirk used Native Americans as extras, as was the custom in many Hollywood Westerns, all the Indian characters in the film's foreground were played by white actors.

5. Halliday, p. 105. According to IMDb, the World 3-D Expo, which took place in Hollywood during September 2006, premiered a newly restored 3-D print of *Taza, Son of Cochise*, offering the original, high-quality Polaroid version with clear glasses, not the inferior red/blue anaglyph form of 3-D.

6. Halliday, op. cit., pp. 122–26.

7. In the flag-waving style adopted by Hollywood during wartime, officers from the armed forces would, by way of forewords, provide official endorsement of the stories about to be told. The studios responsible were thus seen to be doing their part for the war effort, celebrating the endeavors of the men fighting for the nation and ensuring that their missions were seen by audiences in the correct light. See also, for example, *Bombardier* (1943).

8. Heinz-Gerd Rasner and Reinard Wulf, "An Encounter with Douglas Sirk," *Filmkritik*, no. 203, November 1973 (translation by Virginia Soukup).

9. See Ed Buscombe's excellent *"Injuns!" Native Americans in the Movies* (Great Britain: Reaktion Books, 2006) for an insightful elaboration of this strand of the Western.

10. Based on Elliott Arnold's 1947 novel, *Blood Brother, Broken Arrow* was adapted for the screen by Hollywood Ten member Albert Maltz (under the pseudonym Michael Blankfort).

11. Halliday, op. cit., p. 104

12. Prefiguring the shooting style and thematic preoccupations of Kelly Reichardt's revisionist Western, *Meek's Cutoff* (2010).

13. Forty years later, in *Geronimo: An American Legend* (1993), directed by Walter Hill and written by John Milius and Larry Gross, the title character (played by Wes Studi) is presented with far greater insight and empathy and given a charisma lacking from earlier depictions.

14. Sirk's film, apparently one of director Michael Cimino's favorites of the '50s, provided the initial inspiration for his *Thunderbolt and Lightfoot* (1974), in which the action is transplanted to smalltown America in the 1970s.

15. W. R. Burnett, *Captain Lightfoot* (London: Macdonald & Co., 1955).

16. Burnett, p. 42.

17. Halliday, op. cit., p. 118.

18. Halliday, op. cit., p. 141.

19. In fact, while Hess was a minister when he enlisted in the air force in World War II, he never returned to the pulpit.

CHAPTER EIGHT. SIRK, THE FAMILY MELODRAMA AND THE PRODUCTION CODE

1. http://www.artsreformation.com/a001/hays-code.html.

2. The actual policing of the Code was sometimes less than rigorous. As discussed more fully in Chapter 12, the original screen version of *Imitation of Life* (1934), for example, appears never to have received official script approval from the Production Code Administration. However, it's also worth adding that the fact that Groucho's quandary remained intact in *At the Circus* is an indication that the Code's administrators at least had a sense of humor.

3. Heinz-Gerd Rasner and Reinhard Wulf, "An Encounter with Douglas Sirk," *Filmkritik*, no. 203, November 1973 (translation by Virginia Soukup).

4. Thomas Elsaesser, "Tales of Sound and Fury: Observations on the Family Melodrama," *Monogram*, no. 4 (1972), p. 14.

5. Jon Halliday, *Sirk on Sirk* new and revised edition (London: Faber & Faber, 1997), p. 130.

6. Bosley Crowther, "Domestic Tale: *There's Always Tomorrow*," *New York Times*, January 21, 1956.

7. Bosley Crowther, "Sad Psychosis: *Written on the Wind*," *New York Times*, January 12, 1957.

8. Allison Anders in Robert Fischer's *Perspectives on the American Family: Allison Anders on Douglas Sirk's "There's Always Tomorrow"* (2008).

9. Rasner and Wulf, op. cit.

10. Victoria L. Evans, *Douglas Sirk, Aesthetic Modernism and the Culture of Modernity* (Edinburgh University Press, 2017), p. 166.

11. Halliday, op. cit., p. 77.

12. Michael Stern, "Interview with Douglas Sirk," *Bright Lights*, Winter 1977–78, p. 32.

13. Rasner and Wulf, op. cit.

14. Halliday, op. cit., p. 140.

15. Halliday, op. cit., p. 103.

16. Michael Walker, "*All I Desire*," *Movie*, no. 34/35 (Winter 1990), pp. 31–47.

17. Walker, p. 38.

18. Walker, p. 44.

19. Stern, op. cit., p. 32.

20. Stern, op. cit., p. 32.

21. James Harvey, "Sirkumstantial Evidence," *Film Comment*, July–August 1978, p. 59.

22. Ross Hunter, "Flashback: Magnificent Obsessions," *American Film*, April 1988, p. 18.

23. Rainer Werner Fassbinder, "Six Films by Douglas Sirk," in Laura Mulvey and Jon Halliday, eds., *Douglas Sirk* (Edinburgh Film Festival, 1972), p. 97.

24. Over the years, the vituperation heaped on Harvey makes him seem more like a villain than a decent man living out his years quietly. A sampling of Michael Stern's descriptions of him in his book on Sirk will suffice. In the space of seven pages, the unsympathetic Stern observes that he "represents (and in fact looks like) living death," calls him "dull and boring" and "a tedious old man," sees him as "the incarnation of society's decrepitude, a fossilised, emotionally dead being who represents the sexual lifelessness to which Cary's children and society wish to condemn her," adding that "his is the withered sexuality of the blank, deadly world reflected in the TV screen," captioning shots of Rock Hudson and Conrad Nagel alongside Jane Wyman with the question, "Which man would you choose?" and concluding that, in addition to all the above, he is "a lifeless robot." See Stern, *Douglas Sirk* (Boston: Twayne, 1979), pp. 115–22.

25. Brandon French points out that "Thoreau's message was considered such a threat to conformity that in 1954 [shortly before *All That Heaven Allows* went into production] the United States Information Service banned *Walden* from its libraries on the grounds that it was 'downright socialistic.'" See French, *On the Verge of Revolt: Women in American Films of the Fifties* (New York: Frederick Ungar, 1978), p. 97n.

26. French also draws this connection (French, *On the Verge of Revolt*, p. 92). There's a faint echo here too of the Cathy/Heathcliff relationship in Emily Bronte's *Wuthering Heights*.

27. Molly Haskell, *From Reverence to Rape: The Treatment of Women in the Movies* (New York and Baltimore: Penguin, 1974), p. 275.

28. Letter from PCA director Geoffrey M. Shurlock to Universal-International Pictures, December 29, 1954.

29. Bernard Rosenberg and Harry Silverstein, *The Real Tinsel* (London: Macmillan, 1970), p. 180.

30. Jon Halliday, "Douglas Sirk's *All That Heaven Allows*," *Monogram*, no. 4 (1972), p. 31.

31. Bosley Crowther, "*All That Heaven Allows*," *New York Times*, February 29, 1956.

32. Cary's house, on Universal's Colonial Street backlot, was originally built for William Wyler's *The Desperate Hours* (1955) and was in regular use afterwards, including a

role as the Cleaver family's home after the ABC network's acquisition of that paean to American family life in the 1950s, *Leave It to Beaver* (1959–63).

33. Haskell, op. cit., p. 275.
34. French, op. cit., p. 93.
35. French, op. cit., p. 95. "The studio loved this title," Sirk told Jon Halliday. "They thought it meant you could have everything you wanted. I meant it exactly the other way around. As far as I am concerned, heaven is stingy" (Halliday, op. cit., p. 140).

The title comes from the closing line of "Love and Life," a three-verse poem by John Wilmot, Second Earl of Rochester, 1647–80:

> Then talk not of inconstancy
> False hearts, and broken vows;
> If I, by miracle, can be
> This live-long minute true to thee
> 'Tis all that Heaven allows.

Cited in David Farley-Hills, ed. *Earl of Rochester: The Critical Heritage* (London: Routledge 2002), p. 268.

36. Rasner and Wulf, op. cit.
37. Moviedrome, BBC2, March 1, 1998, 10:20 p.m.
38. Walter Metz, "Pomp(ous) Sirk-umstance: Intertextuality, Adaptation, and *All That Heaven Allows*," *Journal of Film and Video*, vol. 45, no. 4 (Winter 1993), p. 19.
39. Edna L. Lee and Harry Lee, *All That Heaven Allows* (New York: G. P. Putnam's Sons, 1952), p. 260.
40. Lee and Lee, p. 300.
41. Vera Dika, "Strategies of Historical Disruption from Douglas Sirk to *Mad Men*," in J. E. Smyth, ed., *Hollywood and the American Historical Film* (New York: Palgrave Macmillan, 2012), p. 215.
42. Halliday, op. cit., p. 140.
43. Dan Callahan, *Barbara Stanwyck—The Miracle Woman* (Jackson: University Press of Mississippi, 2012), p. 178.
44. According to the *Hollywood Reporter*, Melvyn Douglas and Robert Young were also under consideration for the role of Clifford Groves.
45. Stern, *Douglas Sirk*, op. cit., p. 123, offers an alternative view.
46. Rasner and Wulf, op. cit.
47. Halliday, op. cit., p. 120.
48. Walker, op. cit., p. 38–43.
49. Rasner and Wulf, op. cit.
50. Stern, *Bright Lights*, op. cit., p. 34.
51. I can find no firm evidence of any Ursula Parrott novel or short story named *There's Always Tomorrow* or *Too Late for Love* ever being published. It's possible that she wrote it specifically for Universal to adapt. In the excellent commentary by Adrian Martin and John Flaus on Madman Australia's DVD release of *There's Always Tomorrow*, Martin discusses Parrott's series of stories about professional women struggling with their circumstances. Elsewhere, she has been referred to as "the Candace Bushnell of her day, trafficking in proto-chick lit that examined the trials and tribulations endured by the 'New Woman' of the 1920s and the freshly-minted morals by which she lived." http://www.cladriteradio.com/formerly-famous-ursula-parrott/.

52. Andrew Sarris, *Village Voice*, November 21, 1977.

53. Halliday, op. cit., p. 140.

54. Christine Saxton, "The Collective Voice as Cultural Voice," *Cinema Journal*, vol. 26, no. 1 (Fall 1986), p. 27.

55. Robin Wood, "Film Studies at Warwick," *University Vision*, no. 12, December 1974, p. 36.

56. Among other errors of detail, Peter William Evans's account of the adaptation curiously claims that the novel's Lillith *does* have a miscarriage. See Evans, *Written on the Wind* (London: BFI Classics/Palgrave Macmillan, 2013), p. 16.

57. Stern, *Bright Lights*, op. cit., p. 33.

58. George Zuckerman, "On Sirk," *Bright Lights*, no. 5 (1977–78), p. 27.

59. Barbara Klinger, *Melodrama & Meaning: History, Culture, and the Films of Douglas Sirk* (Bloomington: Indiana University Press, 1994), p. 66.

60. Laura Mulvey, "Notes on Sirk & Melodrama," *Movie*, no. 25 (1977/78), p. 54.

61. https://www.criterion.com/current/posts/935-the-sirk-hudson-connection.

62. Halliday, op. cit., p. 121.

63. The title *Never Say Goodbye* was already owned by Warner Bros. when *This Love of Ours* went into production, thus precluding its use as a title. Directed by James V. Kern, the 1946 Warners film is second-rate screwball, written by I. A. L. Diamond, and starring Errol Flynn and Eleanor Parker as a couple unexpectedly quarreling over custody of a daughter rather than a dog.

64. Under the Hays Code, the choice of alternative professions for those who stray sexually from the straight and narrow is always illuminating about hidden prejudices (in this case about "nightclub and theatre people").

CHAPTER NINE. SIRK AND JOHN M. STAHL: ADAPTATIONS AND REMAKES

1. Ross Hunter, "Magnificent Obsessions," *American Film*, April 1988, p. 16.

2. Lloyd C. Douglas, *Magnificent Obsession*, first published by Willett, Clark, & Colby in New York in 1929. Page references below correspond to the 1952 UK Pan paperback edition.

3. Douglas's *Dr. Hudson's Secret Journal*, a prequel to *Magnificent Obsession*, was published in 1937 and was followed by both an hour-long dramatization in *The Philco-Goodyear Television Playhouse* on American television in 1951 and a TV series in 1955.

4. Douglas, op. cit., p. 8.

5. Douglas, op. cit., p. 125.

6. Douglas, op. cit., p. 96.

7. Douglas, op. cit., p. 26.

8. The restraint in Stahl's use of music is also evident in his versions of *Imitation of Life* (1934) and *When Tomorrow Comes* (1939), as well as in *Back Street* (1932). Elsewhere in his work, though, the scores are deployed far more conventionally.

9. Douglas, op. cit., p. 112: "What did Volta's battery or Faraday's dynamo amount to, practically, until Du Fay discovered an insulation that would protect the current from being dissipated through contacts with other things than the object to be energized?"

10. Douglas, op. cit., p. 171.

11. Jean-Loup Bourget, "God Is Dead, or Through a Glass Darkly," *Bright Lights*, no. 6, Winter 1977–78, p. 24.

12. Victoria L. Evans, "Concerning the Spiritual in Art: *Magnificent Obsession* and the Language of Expressionist Painting," *CineACTION*, issue 91, 2013, p. 34.

13. Jon Halliday, *Sirk on Sirk* revised edition (London: Secker & Warburg, 1997), p. 105.

14. Halliday, p. 202.

15. Halliday, p. 110.

16. Hunter had produced three films for Sirk in the previous year—*Take Me to Town*, *All I Desire* and *Taza, Son of Cochise*—and went on to produce six more after *Magnificent Obsession*. When he visited Melbourne during the 1970s on a promotional tour for Charles Jarrott's musical version of *Lost Horizon*, he described Sirk as "an angel to work with" and "a man of great taste."

17. Halliday, op. cit., p. 106.

18. It was the practice of studios to routinely pass on treatments of earlier box-office successes to producers in the hope of generating interest in remakes.

19. Michael Stern, *Douglas Sirk* (Boston: Twayne, 1979), pp. 105–6.

20. In the voice-over commentary he recorded for the Criterion Collection DVD release, Thomas Doherty refers to her as "matronly."

21. "I would never have been able to make the films the way I wanted to if it hadn't been for Metty," Sirk told me in 1981.

22. The scene is similar to the one in *Interlude* (a remake of Stahl's *When Tomorrow Comes*), where Tonio (Rosanno Brazzi) drives his Helen (June Allyson) to Salzburg. "It's just like a fairy tale," she says.

23. Bourget, op. cit., p. 24–25.

24. Geoffrey O'Brien, "Magnificent Obsessions," liner notes in the Criterion Collection's DVD compilation release of the Stahl and Sirk versions of *Magnificent Obsession*.

25. Written by Frank Skinner (music) and Paul Francis Webster (lyrics), sung by the McGuire Sisters.

26. Rainer Werner Fassbinder, "Six Films by Douglas Sirk," in Laura Mulvey and Jon Halliday, eds, *Douglas Sirk* (Edinburgh Film Festival, 1972), p. 102.

27. James M. Cain, *The Root of His Evil*, an Avon Paperback, 1951. Page references correspond to the 1989 Black Lizard Books paperback edition, California.

28. David Madden and Kristopher Mecholsky, *James M. Cain: Hard-Boiled Mythmaker* (United Kingdom: Scarecrow Press, 2011), pp. 142–44.

29. Halliday, op. cit., p. 127.

30. Cain, op. cit., p. 3.

31. Cain, op. cit., p. 9.

32. Cain, op. cit., p. 59.

33. Cain, op. cit., p. 79.

34. Peter Brunette and Gerald Peary, "Tough Guy: James M. Cain Interviewed," *Film Comment*, May–June 1976, p. 54.

35. As in *Intermezzo* (1939) with Leslie Howard (violinist), *Love Affair* (1939) with Boyer (as a violinist this time), *The Constant Nymph* (1943) with Boyer again (composer), *Deception* (1946) with Paul Henreid (cellist), *Song of Love* (1947) with Henreid again (composer), *Letter from an Unknown Woman* (1948) with Louis Jourdan (pianist), and *Lady Possessed* (1952) with James Mason (pianist).

36. Coincidentally, the set-up also closely resembles the one for yet another Brazzi film, *Dark Purpose* (1964). Set on the Italian Riviera, it has an American tourist (Shirley Jones) falling for Brazzi's Italian count, only to discover that there's another mentally ill wife in the wings.

37. Halliday, op. cit., p. 69.

38. James M. Cain in the preface to *Double Indemnity* (London: Corgi, 1965), pp. 10–11 (first published in 1945 by Robert Hale).

39. John Flaus, "*Back Street* (John M. Stahl, 1932)," *Senses of Cinema*, no. 20, May 2002.

40. Fannie Hurst, *Imitation of Life* first edition (New York: P. F. Collier & Son, 1933). Page references in this article refer to the 2004 Duke University Press reprinting, edited by Daniel Itzkovitz, who also contributes an excellent introduction.

41. There's also a further adaptation/extension of Hurst's novel, Joselito Rodriguez's *Angelitos Negros/Little Black Angels* (Mexico, 1948), which was based on a play by Felix B. Caignet but also acknowledges a debt to *Imitation of Life*. In turn, Rodriguez's film was remade in 1970 in Mexico as a "telenovela" (effectively a TV mini-series), directed by Antulio Jiminez Pons, and then again as *El alma no tiene color/The Soul Has No Color* (1997), co-directed by Pons and Otto Sirgo. Furthermore, according to IMDb, both the Brazilian TV series *Imaticao da Vida* (1960) and the Turkish film *Anneler ve kizlari* (1972) were also based on *Imitation of Life*.

For further commentary on *Angelitos Negros*, see Hiram Perez, "Alma Latina: The American Hemisphere's Racial Melodramas," *Scholar and Feminist Online*, vol. 7, no. 2, Spring 2009.

Also see Lucy Fischer, "Modernity and Postmaternity: *High Heels* and *Imitation of Life*," in Andrew Horton and Stuart Y. McDougal, eds., *Play It Again, Sam—Retakes on Remakes* (Berkeley: University of California Press, 1998), pp. 200–216.

42. Hurst, op. cit., p. 86.

43. Hurst, op. cit., p. 143. The phonetic renderings of Delilah's speech patterns and rhythms are one aspect of how Hurst characterizes her. They point to her personal history—a mammy who speaks in a Southern dialect—while what happens to and around her also makes her a tragic figure rather than the Southern mammy of cliché.

44. Hurst, op. cit., p. 75.

45. Hurst, op. cit., p. 124.

46. Hurst, op. cit., p. xx. Itzkovitz points out in his introduction that "Aunt Jemima products were advertised regularly in *Pictorial Review*."

47. Hurst, op. cit., p. 118.

48. Hurst, op. cit., p. 83.

49. Hurst, op. cit., pp. xxiv–xxv (Itzkovitz).

50. Freda Freiberg, "Fannie Hurst, *Imitation of Life*," *Screening the Past*, no. 20, 2006.

51. Hurst, op. cit., p. xix (Itzkovitz).

52. Report from Joseph Breen to Will Hays, March 22, 1934, official studio documents.

53. Hurst, op. cit., pp. 74–75.

54. In the book, Frank is eight years younger than Bea. Here Stephen is thirty-seven, roughly the same age as Bea. Colbert was thirty at the time of shooting and William, in a part originally slated for Paul Lukas, was forty, although he looks old enough to be her father.

55. Hurst, op. cit., p. 292.

56. Lauren Berlant, "National Brands/National Body: *Imitation of Life*," in Bruce Robbins, ed., *The Phantom Public Sphere* (Minneapolis: University of Minnesota Press, 1993), p. 192.

57. Sam Staggs, *Born to Be Hurt: The Untold Story of* Imitation of Life (New York: St. Martin's Press, 2009), p. 15.

58. Halliday, op. cit., p. 148.

59. Halliday, op. cit., p. 148.

60. Staggs, op. cit., p. 248–51.

61. http://www.tcm.com/tcmdb/title/79029/Imitation-of-Life/notes.html.

62. It is astonishing how many commentators see Annie as an idealized mother figure rather than a lost soul, trying to do the right thing but just as trapped within the maze of mirrors and reflections as all of the other characters. The notes that come with the Madman DVD release package in Australia describe her as a character "who has a clear perspective" on the events unfolding around her. Freiberg, op. cit., accuses Sirk of "heroinizing" her. Marina Heung's thoroughly misguided commentary on the film in Lucy Fischer, ed., *Imitation of Life* (New Brunswick, NJ: Rutgers University Press, 1991), p. 306, asserts that "[t]hrough Annie, the film celebrates a specific maternal ideal."

63. The scene in which Lora and playwright David Loomis look out over Broadway and see it as a kingdom they've conquered is reminiscent of the one in Sirk's *Interlude* in which his central couple (June Allyson and Rosanno Brazzi) go driving to Salzburg and their longings become enmeshed within their romantic surroundings as a fairy tale delusion. As *Imitation of Life*'s title song—sung by Earl Grant, written by Sammy Fain and Paul Francis Webster—puts it, "It's a false creation, an imitation / Of life." The scene between Lora and Loomis also has a Faustian edge, inasmuch as she has sold her soul for this kind of success.

64. For an astute elaboration of how even the settings in the film put on a show, see Victoria L. Evans, *Douglas Sirk, Aesthetic Modernism and the Culture of Modernity* (Edinburgh University Press, 2017), pp. 88–112.

65. Halliday, op., cit., p. 151.

66. Halliday, op. cit., p. 10.

67. Stern, op. cit., p. 19.

CHAPTER TEN. OUT OF THE PAST

1. Serge Daney and Jean-Louis Noames, "Entretien avec Douglas Sirk," *Cahiers du cinema*, no. 189, April 1967, p. 70 (translation by Virginia Soukup).

2. Gary Morris, "Albert Zugsmith on Sirk," *Bright Lights*, Winter 1977–78, p. 27.

3. Jon Halliday, *Sirk on Sirk* new and revised edition (Faber and Faber, 1997), p. 136.

4. Halliday, p. 147.

5. Halliday, p. 212.

6. Wesley Strick, *Out There in the Dark* (New York: Thomas Dunne Books, 2006), pp. 295–97.

7. Willa Cather, *My Antonia* (London: Readers Union/William Heinemann, 1943), p. 217.

8. Joseph McBride, *Hawks on Hawks* (Berkeley: University of California Press, 1982), p. 56.

9. McBride, p. 57.

10. Jon Halliday, op. cit., p. 133.

11. In his Hawks biography, Todd McCarthy adds further color to the possible genesis of *Only Angels Have Wings*—a synopsis by Anne Wigton entitled "Plane Number Four," Hawks's own *Ceiling Zero* (1936), and Lew Landers's *Flight from Glory* (1937)—as well as proposing it as a precursor to Henri-Georges Clouzot's *The Wages of Fear* (1957). See McCarthy, *Howard Hawks: The Grey Fox of Hollywood* (New York: Grove Press, 1997), pp. 266–67.

12. William Faulkner, *Pylon* [The Corrected Text] (USA: Vintage Books, 1987), p. 300.

13. In *Pylon*, there's a fourth member of the team, named Jackson, another parachutist. In *The Tarnished Angels* his function is merged with that of Jiggs.

14. In *Pylon*, the question of Jack's paternity is left open.

15. Jean-Loup Bourget, "Sirk's Apocalypse: *Tarnished Angels* and *A Time To Love*," in Laura Mulvey and Jon Halliday, eds., *Douglas Sirk* (Edinburgh Film Festival, 1972), p. 9 (translation by Peter Wollen).

16. Michael Stern, *Douglas Sirk* (Boston: Twayne, 1979), p. 163.

17. Faulkner, op. cit., p. 24.

18. Faulkner, op. cit., p. 107.

19. Stern, op. cit, p. 156.

20. Adrian Martin, *Last Day, Every Day—Figural Thinking from Auerbach and Kracauer to Agamben and Brenez* (Brooklyn, NY: Punctum Books, 2012), p. 25.

21. In Australian distributor Madman's nine-disc box set *Douglas Sirk: King of Hollywood Melodrama*, released in 2010.

22. Martin, Madman DVD commentary, op. cit.

23. When shooting *The Tarnished Angels*, it's more than likely that Sirk, a Billy Wilder admirer, would have been all-too-familiar with the famous shot of Marilyn Monroe standing over the New York subway grate in *The Seven Year Itch*, made two years earlier.

24. Heinz-Gerd Rasner and Reinard Wulf, "An Encounter with Douglas Sirk," *Filmkritik*, no. 203, November 1973 (translation by Virginia Soukup).

25. Faulkner, op. cit., p. 41.

26. Bourget, op. cit., p. 71.

27. First appearing on the 1959 album *La valse a mille temps*, Belgian singer/songwriter Jacques Brel's "La Mort" has been covered by several other singers, most notably Scott Walker (in 1967) and David Bowie (1983), featuring English lyrics by Mort Shuman.

28. Erich Maria Remarque, *A Time To Love and A Time To Die* (Harcourt, Brace and World, 1954) (translation by Denver Lindley). All quotations from the novel come from this edition.

The book's German title, *Zeit zu leben und Zeit zu sterben*, translates into English as *A Time To Live and A Time To Die*. However, all English-language editions of the novel—from its initial publication in 1954—employ the same title as the film, made three years later. There is no evidence to support Jean-Luc Godard's claim that Universal-International initiated the change (Jean Narboni and Tom Milne, eds., *Godard on Godard* [London: Secker & Warburg, 1972], p. 136). Or Sirk's to Jon Halliday that "we slightly changed the title for the non-German distribution" (Halliday, op. cit., p. 141).

29. During the 1950s, there was an abundance of American films about World War II, many of them dealing with the consequences of war rather than the opportunities

it provides for adventure and what film archivist Clyde Jeavons describes as "aggressive patriotism" (in *A Pictorial History of War Films* [London: Hamlyn Publishing Group, 1974], p. 179). Among the "antiwar" films were *Attack* (1956), *Bitter Victory* (1957), *Paths of Glory* (1957), *In Love and War* (1958), and *Pork-Chop Hill* (1959). Nevertheless, in them the war was seldom seen through the eyes of the enemy. *The Young Lions* (1958), in which Marlon Brando plays a sympathetic SS officer, is another exception.

30. Narboni and Milne, eds., op. cit., pp. 136–39.

31. It has been suggested that Remarque was responsible for the final draft of the film, although I've been unable to confirm this. The novelist, who had fought for Germany in World War I, fled the country in 1933 after the public burning of his books. He and Sirk became friends during the making of *A Time To Love and A Time To Die*, the Sirks retiring to Switzerland soon afterwards, taking up residence in Lugano, less than an hour's drive from Locarno, where Remarque lived with his wife, actress Paulette Goddard.

32. Remarque, op. cit., pp. 146–47.

33. "There is a time for everything
And a season for every activity under the heavens:
A time to be born and a time to die
A time to plant and a time to uproot
A time to kill and a time to heal
A time to tear down and a time to build . . .
A time to love and a time to hate
A time for war and a time for peace" (Ecclesiastes 3).

34. Remarque, op. cit., p. 113.

CHAPTER ELEVEN. INTO THE FUTURE: SIRK'S LEGACY

1. In *Out There in the Dark: Wesley Strick on the Secret of Douglas Sirk* (2007), produced and directed by Robert Fischer.

2. Mark Rappaport, https://www.criterion.com/current/posts/935-the-sirk-hudson-connection.

3. In conversation with the author, April 1975.

4. From *Todd Haynes: From Fassbinder to Sirk and Back*, Criterion Collection.

5. See, for example, David Stratton's review in *Variety*, February 15, 2002.

6. In *Beyond Melodrama: Kathryn Bigelow on Douglas Sirk* (2008), produced and directed by Robert Fischer.

7. *Out There in the Dark* (New York: Thomas Dunne Books, 2006).

8. In *A Tribute to Douglas Sirk by Allison Anders* (2008), produced and directed by Robert Fischer.

9. Tim Hunter, "*Summer Storm*," in Laura Mulvey and Jon Halliday, eds., *Douglas Sirk* (Edinburgh Film Festival, 1972), p. 31.

10. In conversation with the author, March 2, 2016.

11. David Church, "An Interview with Guy Maddin: Dissecting the Branded Brain," *Off/Screen*, vol. 10, issue 1, January 2006.

12. Susan King, "City of Lights, City of Angels Gives French Film an LA Spotlight," *Los Angeles Times*, April 23, 2014.

13. Lisa Nesselson, "*8 Women*," *Variety*, February 5, 2002.

14. Tara Brady, "Francois Ozon: The New New Wave," *Irish Times*, May 16, 2015.

15. Roger Ebert, https://www.rogerebert.com/reviews/great-movie-written-on-the-wind-1956 (January 18, 1998).

16. Enrique Alberich and Luis Aller, "Pedro Almodovar: Cinema in Evolution," in Paula Willoquet-Maricondi, ed., *Pedro Almodovar: Interviews* (Jackson: University Press of Mississippi, 2004), p. 28.

17. Lucy Fischer, "Modernity and Postmaternity: *High Heels* and *Imitation of Life*," in Andrew Horton and Stuart Y. McDougal, eds., *Play It Again, Sam: Retakes on Remakes* (Berkeley: University of California Press, 1998), p. 202.

18. Ebert, op. cit.

19. Sam Staggs, *Born to be Hurt: The Untold Story of* Imitation of Life (New York: St. Martin's Press, 2009), p. 320.

20. Staggs, p. 322.

BIBLIOGRAPHY

Ascheid, Antje. "A Sierckian Double Image: The Narration of Zarah Leander as a National Socialist Star." *Film Criticism*, vol. 23, no. 2/3, Winter/Spring 1999, pp. 46–73.
Babington, Bruce. "Written by the Wind: Sierck/Sirk's *La Habanera* (1937)." *Forum for Modern Language Studies*, vol. xxxi, no. 1 (1995), pp. 24–36.
Babington, Bruce, and Peter William Evans. *Affairs to Remember: The Hollywood Comedy of the Sexes*. United Kingdom: Manchester University Press, 1989.
Barton, Ruth. *Hedy Lamarr: The Most Beautiful Woman in the World*. Lexington: University Press of Kentucky, 2010.
Basinger, Jeanine. "The Lure of the Gilded Cage." *Bright Lights*, no. 6, Winter 1977/78, pp. 16–19.
Belton, John. *Cinema Stylists*. Metuchen, NJ, and London: Scarecrow Press, 1983.
Belton, John. *The Hollywood Professionals, Volume 3: Howard Hawks, Frank Borzage, Edgar G. Ulmer*. London and New York: Tantivy/Barnes, 1974.
Bentley, Eric. *The Life of the Drama*. London: Methuen & Co., 1966.
Berlant, Lauren. "National Brands/National Body: *Imitation of Life*." In Bruce Robbins, ed., *The Phantom Public Sphere*. Minneapolis: University of Minnesota Press, 1993, pp. 173–208.
Bogdanovich, Peter. *Who the Devil Made It*. New York: Alfred A. Knopf, 1997.
Bourget, Jean-Loup. "God is Dead, or Through a Glass Darkly." *Bright Lights*, no. 6, Winter 1977/78, pp. 23–26, 34.
Bourget, Jean-Loup. "Sirk and the Critics." *Bright Lights*, no. 6, Winter 1977/78, pp. 6–10, 19.
Bourget, Jean-Loup. "Sirk's Apocalypse: *Tarnished Angels* and *A Time to Love*." In Laura Mulvey and Jon Halliday, eds. *Douglas Sirk*. Edinburgh Film Festival, 1972, pp. 67–77 (translated from the French by Peter Wollen).
Brody, Richard. "Douglas Sirk's Glorious Cinema of Outsiders." *New Yorker*, December 21, 2015.
Brown, Geoff. "*La Habanera*." *Monthly Film Bulletin*, January 1981, p. 13.
Brunette, Peter, and Gerald Peary. "Tough Guy: James M. Cain Interviewed." *Film Comment*, May–June 1976, pp. 50–57 (also in Patrick McGilligan, ed., *Interviews with Screenwriters of Hollywood's Golden Age* [Berkeley: University of California Press, 1986], pp. 110–32).
Burnett, W. R. *Captain Lightfoot*. London: Macdonald & Co., 1955.

Buscombe, Ed. *"Injuns!" Native Americans in the Movies*. Great Britain: Reaktion Books, 2006.
Cain, James M. *Double Indemnity*. London: Corgi, 1965.
Cain, James M. *The Root of His Evil*. California: Black Lizard Books, 1989.
Callahan, Dan. *Barbara Stanwyck: The Miracle Woman*. Jackson: University Press of Mississippi, 2012.
Cameron, Ian, ed. *The Movie Book of Film Noir*. London: Studio Vista, 1992.
Camper, Fred. "The Films of Douglas Sirk." *Screen*, vol. 12, no. 2 (1971), pp. 44–62.
Camper, Fred. "The Tarnished Angels." *Screen*, vol. 12, no. 2 (1971), pp. 68–93.
Cather, Willa. *My Antonia*. London: Readers Union/William Heinemann, 1943.
Chekhov, Anton. *The Shooting Party*. Australia: Penguin Books, 2004.
Coates, Paul. *The Gorgon's Gaze: German Cinema, Expressionism, and the Image of Horror*. New York: Cambridge University Press, 1991.
Daney, Serge, and Jean-Louis Noames. "Entretien avec Douglas Sirk." *Cahiers du cinema*, no. 189, April 1967, pp. 19–25, 68–70 (translation by Virginia Soukup).
Dederichs, Mario R. *Heydrich: The Face of Evil*. London: Greenhill Books, 2006.
Dika, Vera. "Strategies of Historical Disruption from Douglas Sirk to *Mad Men*." In J. E. Smyth, ed. *Hollywood and the American Historical Film*. New York: Palgrave Macmillan, 2012.
Douglas, Lloyd C. *Magnificent Obsession*. London: Pan Books, 1952.
Dyer, Richard. "Lana: Four Films of Lana Turner." *Movie*, no. 25 (1977), pp. 30–52.
Elsaesser, Thomas. "Tales of Sound and Fury: Observations on the Family Melodrama." *Monogram*, no. 4 (1972), pp. 2–15 (also in Christine Gledhill, ed., *Home Is Where the Heart Is: Studies in Melodrama and the Woman's Film* [London: BFI Books, 1987], pp. 43–69).
Evans, Peter William. *Written on the Wind*. London: BFI Classics/Palgrave Macmillan, 2013.
Evans, Victoria L. "Concerning the Spiritual in Art: *Magnificent Obsession* and the Language of Expressionist Painting." *CineACTION*, issue 91, 2013, pp. 34–40.
Evans, Victoria L. *Douglas Sirk, Aesthetic Modernism and the Culture of Modernity*. Edinburgh University Press, 2017.
Farley-Hills, David, ed. *Earl of Rochester: The Critical Heritage*. London: Routledge, 2002.
Fassbinder, Rainer Werner. "Six Films by Douglas Sirk" (translation by Thomas Elsaesser). In Laura Mulvey and Jon Halliday, eds. *Douglas Sirk*, Edinburgh Film Festival, 1972, pp. 95–107.
Faulkner, William. *Pylon* [The Corrected Text]. USA: Vintage Books, 1987.
Fischer, Lucy. "Modernity and Postmaternity: *High Heels* and *Imitation of Life*." In Andrew Horton and Stuart Y. McDougal, eds. *Play It Again, Sam: Retakes on Remakes*. Berkeley: University of California Press, 1998, pp. 200–216.
Fischer, Lucy. "Sirk and the Figure of the Actress: *All I Desire*." *Film Criticism*, vol. XXIII, nos. 2–3, Winter/Spring 1999, pp. 136–49.
Fischer, Lucy, ed. *Imitation of Life: Douglas Sirk, Director*. New Brunswick, NJ: Rutgers University Press, 1991.
Flaus, John. "*Back Street* (John M. Stahl, 1932)." *Senses of Cinema*, no. 20, May 2002.
Freiberg, Freda. "Fannie Hurst, *Imitation of Life*." *Screening the Past*, no. 20, 2006.
French, Brandon. *On the Verge of Revolt: Women in American Films of the Fifties*. New York: Frederick Ungar, 1978.

Fuller, Samuel. *A Third Face: My Tale of Writing, Fighting, and Filmmaking.* New York: Alfred A. Knopf, 2003.
Gallagher, Tag. "White Melodrama, Douglas Sirk." *Film Comment*, November/December 1998, pp. 16–27.
Gemunden, Gerd. "Introduction." *Film Criticism*, vol. 23, no. 2/3, Winter/Spring 1999, pp. 1–13.
Goble, Alan, ed. *The Complete Index to Literary Sources in Film.* Berlin: Walter de Gruyter, 1999.
Grosz, Dave. "*The First Legion*: Vision and Perception in Sirk." *Screen*, vol. 12, no. 2 (1971), pp. 99–117.
Hak, Sabine. "The Melodramatic Imagination of Detlef Sierck: *Final Chord* and Its Resonances." *Screen*, vol. 38, no. 2 (1997), pp. 129–48.
Halliday, Jon. *Sirk on Sirk.* London: Secker & Warburg, 1971.
Halliday, Jon. *Sirk on Sirk.* London: Faber and Faber, 1997 (new and revised edition).
Handzo, Stephen. "Intimations of Lifelessness: Sirk's Ironic Tear-Jerker." *Bright Lights*, no. 6, Winter 1977/78, pp. 20–22, 34.
Haralovich, Mary Beth. "*All That Heaven Allows*: Color, Narrative Space, and Melodrama." In Peter Lehman, ed. *Close Viewings: An Anthology of New Film Criticism.* Tallahassee: Florida State University Press, 1990, pp. 57–92.
Harvey, James. "Sirkumstantial Evidence." *Film Comment*, July/August 1978, pp. 52–59.
Haskell, Molly. *From Reverence to Rape: The Treatment of Women in the Movies.* New York and Baltimore: Penguin, 1974.
Hastings, Charlotte. *Bonaventure: A Play in Three Acts.* New York and Los Angeles: Samuel French, 1950.
Hess, Dean E. *Battle Hymn.* New York: McGraw-Hill, 1956.
Hodsdon, Bruce. "The Cinema of Douglas Sirk." *Film Alert* (online), 2017.
Horak, Jan-Christopher. "Sirk's Early Exile Films: *Boefje* and *Hitler's Madman*." *Film Criticism*, vol. XXXIII, nos. 2–3, Winter/Spring 1999, pp. 122–35.
Hunter, Ross. "Flashback: Magnificent Obsessions." *American Film*, April 1988, pp. 16–19.
Hurst, Fannie. *Imitation of Life.* Durham, NC: Duke University Press, 2004 (edited with an introduction by Daniel Itzkovitz).
Ibsen, Henrik. *Ibsen: Hedda Gabler, The Pillars of the Community, The Wild Duck.* England, Australia, and Canada: Penguin, 1974 (translation by Una Ellis-Fermor).
Isenberg, Noah. *Edgar G. Ulmer: A Filmmaker at the Margins.* Berkeley: University of California Press, 2014.
Jeavons, Clyde. *A Pictorial History of War Films.* London: Hamlyn Publishing Group, 1974.
Kapczynski, Jennifer M., and Michael David Richardson, eds. *A New History of German Cinema.* Rochester, NY: Camden House, 2012.
Kenesha, Ellen. "Sirk: *There's Always Tomorrow* and *Imitation of Life*." *Women and Film*, no. 2 (1972), pp. 51–55.
Keogh, Peter, ed. *Kathryn Bigelow: Interviews.* Jackson: University Press of Mississippi, 2013, pp. 10–16 (also in Kathryn Bigelow, Matthias Brunner, and Monty Montgomery, "A Visit with the Master of Melodrama: Douglas Sirk," *Interview*, July 1982, pp. 50–52).
Klinger, Barbara. *Melodrama & Meaning: History, Culture and the Films of Douglas Sirk.* Bloomington: Indiana University Press, 1994.

Koch, Gertrud. "From Dietlef Sierck to Douglas Sirk." *Film Criticism*, vol. 23, no. 2/3, Winter/Spring 1999, pp. 14–32 (translation by Gerd Gemunden).

Koepnick, Lutz. "Sirk and the Culture Industry: *Zu neuen Ufern* and *The First Legion*." *Film Criticism*, vol. XXIII, nos. 2–3, Winter/Spring 1999, pp. 94–121.

Kreimeier, Klaus. *The UFA Story: A History of Germany's Greatest Film Company, 1918–1945*. Berkeley: University of California Press, 1996 (translation by Robert Kimber and Rita Kimber).

Krutnik, Frank. *In a Lonely Street: Film Noir, Genre, Masculinity*. London: Routledge, 1991

Kuzniar, Alice. "Zarah Leander and Transgender Specularity." *Film Criticism*, vol. 23, no. 2/3, Winter/Spring 1999, pp. 74–93.

Lagerlof, Selma. *The Girl from the Marsh Croft*. Boston: Little, Brown, and Company, 1910 (translation by Velma Swanston Howard).

Lavery, Emmet. *The First Legion: A Drama of the Society of Jesus*. New York and Los Angeles: Samuel French, 1937.

Lawrence, Amy. "Trapped in a Tomb of Their Own Making: Max Ophuls's *The Reckless Moment* and Douglas Sirk's *There's Always Tomorrow*." *Film Criticism*, vol. XXIII, nos. 2–3, Winter/Spring 1999, pp. 136–49.

Lee, Edna L., and Harry Lee. *All That Heaven Allows*. New York: G. P. Putnam's Sons, 1952.

Lehman, Peter. "Thinking with the Heart: An Interview with Douglas Sirk." *Wide Angle*, vol. 3, no. 4, pp. 42–47.

Limmer, Wolfgang. "The Happy Ending: An Emergency Exit." *Suddeutsche Zeitung*, November 17–18, 1973 (translation by Virginia Soukup).

Madden, David, and Kristopher Mecholsky. *James M. Cain: Hard-Boiled Mythmaker*. United Kingdom: Scarecrow Press, 2011.

Markey, G. *The Great Companions. Ladies' Home Journal*, October 1951, pp. 137–200.

Martin, Adrian. *Last Day, Every Day: Figural Thinking from Auerbach and Kracauer to Agamben and Brenez*. Brooklyn: Punctum Books, 2012.

Martin, Adrian. *Mise en Scene and Film Style*. England: Palgrave Macmillan, 2014.

McBride, Joseph. *Hawks on Hawks*. Berkeley: University of California Press, 1982.

McCarthy, Todd. *Howard Hawks: The Grey Fox of Hollywood*. New York: Grove Press, 1997.

Mecholsky, Kristopher. "Narrative Identity and Criminal Ideology in *A Scandal in Paris*." In Rosemary A. Peters, ed. *Criminal Papers: Reading Crime in the French Nineteenth Century*. Newcastle-upon-Tyne: Cambridge Scholars Publishing, 2012, pp. 201–21.

Mercer, John, and Martin Shingler. *Melodrama: Genre, Style, and Sensibility*. London and New York: Wallflower Press, 2005.

Metz, Walter. "Pomp(ous) Sirk-umstance: Intertextuality, Adaptation, and *All That Heaven Allows*." *Journal of Film and Video*, vol. 45, no. 4, Winter 1993, pp. 3–21.

Miller, Alan. "Tea Party Invaders! Douglas Sirk's *No Room for the Groom*." *Berkshire Review for the Arts*, December 6, 2010.

Milne, Tom, ed. *Losey on Losey*. London: Secker & Warburg, 1967.

Moliere. *Five Plays*. Harmondsworth, Middlesex: Penguin Classics, 1958 (translated and with an introduction by John Wood).

Morris, Gary. "Albert Zugsmith on Sirk." *Bright Lights*, no. 6, Winter 1977/78, p. 27.

Morris, Gary. "Three Films by Edgar G. Ulmer: *Bluebeard, The Strange Woman*, and *Moon Over Harlem*." *Bright Lights* online, April 1, 2000.

Mulvey, Laura. "Notes on Sirk & Melodrama." *Movie*, no. 25 (1977/78), pp. 53–56.

Mulvey, Laura. "Visual Pleasure and Narrative Cinema." *Screen*, vol. 16, no. 3 (1975), pp. 6–18.
Mulvey, Laura, and Jon Halliday, eds. *Douglas Sirk*. Edinburgh Film Festival, 1972.
Nadar, Thomas R. "The Director and the Diva: The Film Musicals of Detlef Sierck and Zarah Leander: *Zu neuen Ufern* and *La Habanera*." In Robert Reimer, ed. *Cultural History Through a National Socialist Lens: Essays on the Cinema of the Third Reich*. Rochester, NY: Camden House, 2002, pp. 65–77.
Narboni, Jean, and Tom Milne, eds. *Godard on Godard*. London: Secker & Warburg, 1972.
Neale, Steve. "Douglas Sirk." *Framework*, vol. 2, no. 5 (1976/1977), pp. 16–18.
Neve, Brian. *The Many Lives of Cy Endfield: Film Noir, The Blacklist and Zulu*. Madison: University of Wisconsin Press, 2015.
O'Brien, Geoffrey. "Magnificent Obsessions." Liner notes for the Criterion Collection DVD release of the Stahl and Sirk versions of *Magnificent Obsession*.
Paalman, F. J. J. W. *Cinematic Rotterdam, The Times and Tides of a Modern City*. UvA-DARE, University of Amsterdam (thesis supervised by Thomas Elsaesser), 2010.
Peary, Gerald. *Samuel Fuller: Interviews*. Jackson: University Press of Mississippi, 2012.
Perez, Hiram. "Alma Latina: The American Hemisphere's Racial Melodramas." *Scholar and Feminist Online*, vol. 7, no. 2, Spring 2009.
Petley, Julian. "Sirk in Germany." *Sight & Sound*, Winter 1987/88, pp. 58–61.
Porter, Eleanor H. *Oh, Money! Money!* In *The Works of Eleanor H. Porter*, e-book, 2010.
Powers, James, Rochelle Reed, and Donald Chase. "Fritz Lang." *Dialogue on Film*, American Film Institute, April 1974.
Rasner, Heinz-Gerd, and Reinard Wulf. "An Encounter with Douglas Sirk." *Filmkritik*, no. 203, November 1973 (translation by Virginia Soukup).
Ray, Robert B. *How a Film Theory Got Lost and Other Mysteries in Cultural Studies*. Indiana University Press, 2001.
Reimer, Charles. *Cultural History Through a National Socialist Lens: Essays on the Cinema of the Third Reich*. Rochester, NY: Camden House, 2000, pp. 65–77.
Remarque, Erich Maria. *A Time to Love and a Time to Die*. New York: Harcourt, Brace and World, 1954 (translation from the German by Denver Lindley).
Rentschler, Eric. *The Ministry of Illusion: Nazi Cinema and Its Afterlife*. Cambridge: Harvard University Press, 1996.
Rentschler, Eric. "Sirk Revisited: The Limits and Possibilities of Artistic Agency." *New German Critique*, no. 95, Spring–Summer, 2005, pp. 149–61.
Rosenberg, Bernard, and Harry Silverstein. *The Real Tinsel*. London: Macmillan, 1970.
Ryan, Tom. "The Adaptation and the Remake: From John M. Stahl's *When Tomorrow Comes* to Douglas Sirk's *Interlude*." *Senses of Cinema*, March 2014.
Ryan, Tom. "The Bleakness of the Unhappy Ending: Sirk's Uncomfortable Comedies." *Senses of Cinema*, February 2015.
Ryan, Tom. "Douglas Sirk." *Senses of Cinema*, February 2004.
Ryan, Tom. "Obsessions, Imitations and Subversions, Part One: on *Magnificent Obsession*." *Senses of Cinema*, December 2014.
Ryan, Tom. "Obsessions, Imitations and Subversions, Part Two: on *Imitation of Life*." *Senses of Cinema*, December 2015.
Ryan, Tom. "On *A Time to Love and a Time to Die*." *Australian Journal of Screen Theory*, no. 4, pp. 49–57.
Ryan, Tom. "Sirk, Hollywood and Genre." *Senses of Cinema*, March 2013.

Sarris, Andrew. *The American Cinema*. New York: E. P. Dutton, 1969, pp. 109–110.
Sarris, Andrew. "Sarris on Sirk." *Bright Lights*, no. 6, Winter 1977/78, p. 5.
Saxton, Christine. "The Collective Voice as Cultural Voice." *Cinema Journal*, vol. 26, no. 1 (Fall 1986), pp. 19–30.
Schaub, Martin. "Watch Out, Douglas Sirk! I Own You: The Memorable Rediscovery of the Hollywood Director, Douglas Sirk." *Tages-Anzeiger Magazin (Zurich)*, no. 12, March 23, 1974, pp. 28–35 (translation by Virginia Soukup).
Schrader, Paul. "Notes on Film Noir." *Film Comment*, Spring 1972, pp. 8–13 (also in Alain Silver and James Ursini, eds., *Film Noir Reader* [New York: Limelight Editions, 1996], pp. 53–63).
Schulte-Sasse, Linda. "Douglas Sirk's *Schlussakkord* and the Question of Aesthetic Resistance." *Germanic Review*, Winter 1998, pp. 2–31.
Selig, Michael. "Contradiction and Reading: Social Class and Sex Class in *Imitation of Life*." *Wide Angle*, vol. 10, no. 4 (1988), pp. 13–23.
Shearer, Stephen. *Patricia Neal: An Unquiet Life*. Lexington: University Press of Kentucky, 2006.
Silberman, Marc. *German Cinema: Texts in Context*. Detroit: Wayne State University Press, 1995.
Smith, Robert E. "Love Affairs That Always Fade." *Bright Lights*, no. 6, Winter 1977/78, pp. 11–15.
Staggs, Sam. *Born to be Hurt: The Untold Story of Imitation of Life*. New York: St. Martin's Press, 2009.
Stern, Michael. *Douglas Sirk*. Boston: Twayne, 1979.
Stern, Michael. "Douglas Sirk: Interview." *Bright Lights*, no. 6, Winter 1977/78, pp. 29–34.
Strick, Wesley. *Out There in the Dark*. New York: Thomas Dunne Books, 2006.
Truffaut, Francois. *Hitchcock*. New York: Simon and Schuster, 1967.
Trumpener, Katie. "The Rene Clair Moment and the Overlap Films of the Early 1930s: Detlef Sierck's *April! April!*" *Film Criticism*, vol. 23, no. 2/3, Winter/Spring 1999, pp. 33–45.
University of Connecticut Film Society. *Douglas Sirk: The Complete American Period*. Program booklet with edited essays, 1974. http://mikegrost.com/sirk.htm.
Vaughn, Robert. *Only Victims: A Study of Show Business Blacklisting*. New York: Proscenium, 1972.
Vidocq, Eugene Francois. *The Memoirs of Detective Vidocq: Convict, Spy and Principal Agent of the French Police*. Enhanced Media, 2015.
Walker, Michael. "*All I Desire*." *Movie*, no. 34/35 (Winter 1990), pp. 31–47.
Walker, Michael. "Film Noir: Introduction." In Ian Cameron, ed. *The Movie Book of Film Noir*. London: Studio Vista, 1992, pp. 8–38.
Weinstein, Valerie. "'White Jews' and Dark Continents: Capitalist Critique and Its Racial Undercurrents in Detlef Sierck's *April! April!* (1935)." In Barbara Hales, Mihaela Petrescu, and Valerie Weinstein, eds. *Continuity and Crisis in German Cinema, 1928–1936*. Rochester, New York: Camden House, 2016, pp. 132–48.
Will, David, and Peter Wollen, eds. *Samuel Fuller*. Edinburgh Film Festival, 1969.
Willemen, Paul. "Distanciation and Douglas Sirk." *Screen*, vol. 12, no. 2 (1971), pp. 63–67.

Willemen, Paul. "Towards an Analysis of the Sirkian System." *Screen*, vol. 12, no. 2 (1971), pp. 128–34.
Wood, Robin. "Film Studies at Warwick." *University Vision*, no. 12, December 1974, pp. 27–36.
Zuckerman, George. "On Sirk." *Bright Lights*, no. 6, Winter 1977/78, p. 27.

INDEX

Page numbers in *italics* indicate an illustration.

Aaker, Lee, 140
Adams, Gerald Drayson, 144, 146
Adventures of Huckleberry Finn, The (novel, 1884), 216
Affair to Remember, An (1957), 213
Alberich, Enrique, 255
Aldrich, Robert, 150
Alexander (2004), 124
Alexander, Kurt, 53
Alexander the Great (Alexander III of Macedonia), 124
Alger, Horatio, 217
All About Eve (1950), 60
All About My Mother (1999), 256
Allen, Chet, *137*
Aller, Luis, 255
All That Heaven Allows (novel, 1952), 8, 173–74, 283n
Allyson, June, 206, 215, 287n
Almodóvar, Pedro, 255–56
Altes Theatre, Leipzig, 24
Alvarez Kelly (1966), 212
Amari, Raja, 253
Ameche, Don, 87, 102
American Tragedy, An (novel, 1947), 180
Anders, Allison, 161, 254
Andriot, Lucien, 96
Anneler ve kizlari (1972), 286n
Anthropoid (2016), 273n
Antonioni, Michelangelo, 124
Apache (1950), 150
Arden, Eve, 158
Arlen, Harold, 100

Arnold, Elliott, 281n
Arthur, Robert, 231
As Before, Better Than Before/Come prima, meglio di prima (play, 1919), 190
Ascheid, Antje, 19
As You Like It (play, 1603), 137–38
Attack (1956), 289n
Attentat/The Assassination (1965), 273n
At the Circus (1939), 158–59, 281n
Attila (1954), 125, 126–28, 278n
Attila the Hun, 124, 125, 278–79n
Aunt Jemima, 217, 218, 221, 286n
Awful Truth, The (1937), 101

Baberske, Robert, 39
Babington, Bruce, 19, 52, 109, 252, 277n
Baby Doll (1956), 159
Bacall, Lauren, 46, *185*, *240*, 241
Back Street (1961), 224, 284n
Bad and the Beautiful, The (1952), 100
Baedeker travel guide, 50
Bailey, Pearl, 223
Ball, Lucille, 75, 275n
Balz, Bruno, 272n
Barbarian and the Geisha, The (1958), 145
Barton, Ruth, 276n
Basserman, Albert, 270n
Battle Hymn (autobiography), 144
Battle of Apache Pass, The (1952), 146–47
Baudelaire, Charles, 78
Beethoven, Ludwig van, 35, 37, 117
Before Sunset (2004), 213
Begin Again (2013), 279n

Bennett, Charles, 80
Bennett, Joan, 160, 179
Bentazky, Ralph, 271n
Bentley, Eric, 4, 34
Berkeley, Martin, 135
Berlant, Lauren, 222, 252
Berliner Staatstheater, 19
Bernhardt, Curtis, 174–75
Bigelow, Kathryn, 254
Big Heat, The (1953), 231
Billington, Kevin, 213
Birgel, Willy, 47
Bitter Rice (1949), 275n
Bitter Victory (1957), 289n
"black is beautiful," 223, 226
Black Magic (1949), 73, 79–81, 275n
Blees, Robert, 166, 201
Blood Brother (novel, 1947), 281n
Blue Angel, The (1930), 271n
Blue Veil, The (1952), 201
Blyth, Ann, 121–22, 136
Boefje (children's book, 1903), 54
Bogdanovich, Peter, 275n
Bombardier (1943), 280n
Bonaventure (play, 1949), 120–24
Book of Mormon, The (play, 2011), 269n
Bosse, Peter, 38
Bourgeois Gentilhomme, Le/The Would-Be Gentleman (play), 20, 23
Bourget, Jean-Loup, 6, 200, 204, 238, 242, 252
Bowie, David, 288n
Boyer, Charles, 79, 85, 116, 128, 210, 215, 285n
Brando, Marlon, 289n
Brazzi, Rossano, 206, 213, 215, 256, 286n, 287n
Brecher, Irving, 158
Brecht, Bertolt, 9, 45, 62, 173, 273n
Breen, Joseph, 75, 220, 224
Brel, Jacques, 243, 288n
Brink, Carol Ryrie, 166
Brinken, Lydia, 14, 243, 272n
Brion, Patrick, 6
Brodney, Oscar, 124, 139, 144, 279n
Broken Arrow (1950), 146–48, 281n
Bronte, Emily, 282n

Brosnan, Pierce, 70
Brown, Geoff, 50
Brune, Lothar, 271n
Brunette, Peter, 208
Brunner, Mathias, 254
Brusse, Marie Joseph, 54
Bunuel, Luis, 255
Burke, Billie, 209
Burnett, W. R., 144, 151
Burnham, Terry, 225
Burton, David, 100–102
Buscombe, Ed, 281n
Buzzell, Edward, 158–59
Byington, Spring, 132

Cagliostro, Alessandro, 80
Cahn, Sammy, 183
Caignet, Felix B., 286n
Cain, James M., 65, 206, 207–8, 209, 211, 212–14
Calderón de la Barca, Pedro, 3
Callahan, Dan, 176
Call Me by Your Name (2017), 254
Camper, Fred, 7, 12, 252
Cannes Film Festival, 53
Cape Fear (1991), 254
Capra, Frank, 98, 109, 252
Captain Lightfoot (novel, 1954), 144, 151
Carney, John, 279n
Carradine, John, 63, 64
Cather, Willa, 234
Caught (1949), 84
Chain Lightning (1950), 144
Chandler, Jeff, 125, 146
Chapman Report, The (1962), 135
Chekhov, Anton, 14–15, 66, 67, 69, 70, 274n
Chevalier, Maurice, 76
Church, David, 255
Cimino, Michael, 281n
Clair, Rene, 23
Clouzot, Henri-Georges, 288n
Coates, Paul, 11, 49
Coburn, Charles, 78, 132
Cocke, Inez, 212
Coen, Franklin, 212
Cohen, Albert J., 103

Colbert, Claudette, 223, 286n
Collins, Bill, 12
Come Back, Little Sheba (1953), 223
Comolli, Jean-Louis, 6, 266n
Companeez, Jacques, 75, 77
Company She Keeps, The (1950), 90
Concert, The/Das Konzert (1948), 271n
Conflict (1945), 84
Connery, Sean, 70
Constable, John, 14
Constant Nymph, The (1943), 285n
Cooper, Gary, 71
Correll, Ernst Hugo, 19
Corsican Brothers, The (1941), 79
Count of Monte Cristo, The (1934), 79
Court-Martial of Billy Mitchell, The (1955), 278n
Courtship of Eddie's Father, The (1963), 105, 280n
Cousins, Mark, 173
Crawford, Joan, 86, 275n
Cromwell, John, 90
Crothers, Scatman, *137*, 279n
Crowther, Bosley, 160, 171
Cukor, George, 84
Cummings, Robert, 87, 276n
Curtis, Tony, *110*, *111*

Dailey, Dan, 135, *137*
Dallas (TV series, 1978–91, 2012–14), 187, 256
Dalsum, Albert van, *56*
Daney, Serge, 6, 271
Daniels, William, 99
Dante, 3
Dark Corner, The (1946), 177
Dark Purpose (1964), 285n
Darnell, Linda, 67, *68*, 96
Daumier, Honore, 14
Daves, Delmer, 146–48
Dea, Marie, 76
Dean, James, 177, 279n
Deception (1946), 285n
De Concini, Ennio, 124
Defiant Ones, The (1958), 216
Defore, Don, *111*
Delacroix, Eugene, 14

De Laurentiis, Dino, 124
De Laurentiis, Martha, 124
del Toro, Guillermo, 252
Denning, Richard, 277n
de Poligny, Serge, 271n
De Santis, Giuseppe, 275n
De Sica, Vittorio, 80
Desperate Hours, The (1955), 282
Deutsch, Helen, 87, 91
Devil's Doorway (1950), 150
DeWolf, Karen, 100
Dial M for Murder (1954), 84, 276n
Diamond, I. A. L., 283n
Dicker, Karin, *225*
Dieterle, William, 190–91
Dietrich, Marlene, 71
Dietrich, Ralph, 92
Dime a Dance, A (story, 1938), 275n
Donna Reed Show, The (TV series, 1958–66), 191
Double Indemnity (1944), 83, 214
Double Indemnity (novel, 1943), 214
Douglas, Lloyd C., 7, 193, 195–200, 205, 279n, 284n
Douglas, Melvyn, 283n
Dreiser, Theodore, 180
Dr. Hudson's Secret Journal (TV series, 1951, 1955), 224, 284n
Dumas, Alexandre, 60, 79
Dunne, Irene, 195
Dunning, Decla, 276n
Dynasty (TV series, 1981–89, 2017), 187, 256

Ebert, Roger, 255–56
Edinburgh Film Festival, 7, 254
Ees, Annie van, 53, 54, *56*
Eggerth, Martha, *42*, 268n, 271n
8 Women (2002), 255
Einstein, Albert, 13
Eisler, Hanns, 275n
"Elegy Written in a Country Churchyard" (poem, 1751), 137
Ellis, Sean, 273n
Ellis-Fermor, Una, 32
Elsaesser, Thomas, 7, 10, 60, 159–60, 252, 273n

Elton, Ben, 279n
Emerson, Ralph Waldo, 89
Endfield, Cy, 276n
Ertugrul, Muhsin, 25
Evans, Victoria L., 13, 36, 161, 200, 252
Evans, Vincent B., 145
Ewell, Tom, 177
Experiment Perilous (1944), 84

Fabares, Shelley, 191
Fain, Sammy, 287n
fairy tales (and legends), 23, 37–39, 41, 51–52, 71, 72, 73, 101, 112, 130, 139, 141, 192, 200, 204–5, 206, 208, 214, *215*, 218, 220, 247, 285n, 287n
Fallen Angel (1945), 67
Far from Heaven (2002), 173, 253, 266n
Farkas, Arkos, 53
Farrell, Colin, 124
Fassbinder, Rainer Werner, 6, 7, 15, 169, 173, 206, 251, 252, 253, 254, 255
Father of the Bride (1950), 108, 177
Father's Little Dividend (1951), 108, 177
Faulkner, William, 53, 231–32, 234–37, 239–40
Faust, 3, 287n
FBI (Federal Bureau of Investigation), 110, 279n
Fear Eats the Soul/Angst essen Seele auf (1972), 173, 252
Female Trouble (1974), 256
Ferber, Edna, 187
Fiction Factory (TV series, 2002–), 254
Fields, Herbert, 7, 100
Filmarbeit mit Douglas Sirk (1987), 266n
First Legion, The (play, 1934), 116–19
Fischer, Lucy, 10, 252, 255
Fischer, Robert, 254
Fitzgerald, F. Scott, 53
Flame of the Timberline (story, 1953), 139
Flaus, John, 216, 283n
Fleming, Victor, 188–89
Flight from Glory (1937), 288n
Flowers of Evil/Les Fleurs du mal (book of poetry, 1857), 78
Flynn, Errol, 283n
Force of Arms (1951), 244

Foreign Correspondent (1940), 240n
Fort Apache (1948), 146
Fort Worth (1951), 270n
Four Aces, 183
Francisci, Pietro, 124
Frank, Nino, 275n
Freiberg, Freda, 219, 287n
French, Brandon, 172, 282n, 283n
Fromm, Freddy, 59
Fuchs, Daniel, 212
Fuller, Samuel, 87–88, 91, 276n

Gantillon, Simon, 75
Gardner, Ava, 274n
Gas, Food, Lodging (1992), 254
Gaslight (1940, Thorold Dickinson), 275n
Gaslight (1944, George Cukor), 84
Gavin, John, *246*, *248*
George, George W., 92, 106
George, Heinrich, *30*, 31, 270n
Geronimo: An American Legend (1993), 281n
Giant (1956), 145, 187
Gilbert, Lewis, 273n
Gill, Frank, Jr., 103
Gillmann, Karl Peter, 31
Girl from the Marsh Croft, The (novel, 1908), 25–29
Girl from the Marsh Croft, The/The Woman He Chose (1917), 25, 27–29
Godard, Jean-Luc, 6, 244, 255, 288n
Goebbels, Joseph, 14, 17–19, 40, 53, 75, 234
Goffman, Erving, 271n
Golitzen, Alexander, 15
Gomberg, Sy, 224
Grace of My Heart (1996), 254
Grant, Cary, 72, 85, 101, 236
Grant, Earl, 287n
Gray, Thomas, 137
Grayson, Charles, 144
Great Companions, The (novel, 1951), 8, 135–37
Greatest Show on Earth, The (1952), 125
Great Impostor, The (1961), 231
Greer, Jane, 90
Grido, Il (1957), 124
Griffin, Eleanor, 224

Gross, Larry, 281n
Grost, Michael E., 102
Grosz, George, 23, 269n
Guadagnino, Luca, 254–55
Gunn, James, 166

Hak, Sabine, 252
Halliday, Jon, 5, 6, 7, 9, 11, 18, 35, 58, 79, 95, 99, 109, 119, 120, 135, 144, 145, 167, 171, 180–81, 199, 200–201, 206, 213, 223, 229, 230, 231, 233, 252, 266n, 267n, 271n, 274n, 276n, 277n, 283n, 288n
Hamilton, Patrick, 84
Hamlet (play, 1609), 199
Handel, George Frideric, 37–38
Hangman's Village (novel, 1943), 64
Hangmen Also Die! (1943), 61–62, 65, 274n
Harbich, Milo, 39
Hardwicke, Sir Cedric, 78
Harlow, Jean, 189
Harriet Craig (1950), 166
Harvey, James, 7, 59
Harwood, Ronald, 273n
Haskell, Molly, 10, 170, 172
Hastings, Charlotte, 120–24
Hawks, Howard, 234–36, 298n
Hayden, Sterling, 114, *140*
Haynes, Todd, 173, 253, 254, 255, 266n
Heaven Can Wait (1943), 102
Hecht, Ben, 278n
Heinecke, Kurt, 40
Hemingway, Ernest, 58
Henderson, Joe, 279n
Henreid, Paul, 285n
Herbert, Frederick, 135, 280n
Hess, Colonel Dean, 144, 145, 153, 281n
Heung, Marina, 287n
Heuser, Kurt, 35, 43
Heydrich, Reinhard, 61, 62, 64
High Heels (1991), 255
Hill, Walter, 281n
Hillier, Jim, 61
Hirschbien, Peretz, 64
His Girl Friday (1940), 101
Hitchcock, Alfred, 60, 71, 80, 84, 275n, 278n

Hitler, Adolf, 11, 14, 17, 32–33, 36, 51, 58, 243, 244, 270n, 271n
Hitler Youth program, 233
Hoffman, Charles, 191
Hoffman, Joseph, 106, 109, 131
Holliday, Judy, 209
Holman, Libby, 188
Hood, Thomas, 137
Hopper, Jerry, 189, 191–92
Horak, Jan-Christopher, 45, 55, 64, 272n, 273n, 274n
Horton, Edward Everett, 23, *68*
Howard, Leslie, 285n
Hudson, Rock, *4*, 15, 47, 48, *134*, 145–46, *148*, 149–50, *151*, 153, *154*, 168, *185*, 188, 191, 195, *201*, 202–3, 215, *240*, 251, 277n
Hugenberg, Alfred, 17
Hughes, Howard, 92
Hunter, Ross, 15, 48, 139, 141, 166–67, 169, 172, 182, 193, 201, 223
Hunter, Tim, 7, 254
Hurlbut, William, 182
Hurst, Fannie, 7, 216–24, 226, 230, 286n
Hutchinson, Ivan, 12

I Am a Camera (1955), 159
I Am Love (2009), 255
Ibsen, Henrik, 20, 29–34, 270n
Ignatius of Loyola, 278n
Iles, Francis, 84
Imaticao da Vida (1960), 286n
Imitation of Life (1934, John M. Stahl), 182, 193, 216, 220–23, 224, 229–30, 281n, 284n
Imitation of Life (novel, 1933), 216–26, 230, 286n
Impekoven, Toni, 40
In a Lonely Place (1950), 120
Incredible Shrinking Man, The (1957), 231
In Love and War (1958), 289n
Interlude (1968, Kevin Billington), 213
Intermezzo (1939), 285n
Island in the Sun (1957), 158
It's a Wonderful Life (1946), 98
Itzkovitz, Daniel, 219, 286n

Jackson, Mahalia, 223
James, Henry, 213
Jane Eyre (1944), 84
Jane Eyre (novel, 1847), 209
Jannings, Orin, 244
Jarrott, Charles, 285
Jary, Hilde ("Mrs. Sirk"), 14–15, 53, 58–59, 144, 150, 201, 233, 251, 268n, 272n
Jeanne Eagels (1957), 212
Jeavons, Clyde, 288–89
Jennings, Humphrey, 61
Jimenez, Cedric, 273n
Johnny Belinda (1948), 201
Johnny Dark (1954), 212
Joker Is Wild, The (1957), 120
Jordan, Miriam, 100
Joseph, Albrecht, 64
Joseph, Rudolph S., 64, 116
Jourdan, Louis, 285n
Jud Suss (1940), 270n
Juha (1999), 256

Kaiser, Georg, 24
Kant, Emmanuel, 66
Karloff, Boris, 77
Kaurismaki, Aki, 256
Kelly, Grace, 72
Kern, James V., 283n
Kettelhut, Erich, 39
Klaren, Georg C., 31
Klinger, Barbara, 10, 189, 252
Klorer, John, 190
Knight, Patricia, *83*, 88
Knoteck, Hansi, *28*, 268n
Koch, Gertrud, 11, 49
Koehler, Ted, 100
Koepnick, Lutz, 45
Kohner, Susan, 225
Korvin, Charles, 190
Krahn, Maria, *28*
Kraike, Michael, 120, 278n
Kramer, Stanley, 216
Kreimeier, Klaus, 18, 40

Lady Chatterley's Lover (novel, 1928), 170
Lady Eve, The (1941), 213

Lady Possessed (1952), 285n
Lagerlof, Selma, 25–29
Lamaar, Hedy, 67, 95, 276n
Lamour, Dorothy, 277n
Landers, Lew, 287n
Landis, Jessie Royce, 72
Lang, Fritz, 39, 60, 61–62, 273n, 274n
lang, k.d., 54
Langley, Lee, 213
Laurie, Piper, *110, 111, 134*
Lavery, Emmet, 116–19, 278n
Lawrence, D. H., 12, 170
Lawton, Charles, Jr., 83, 90, 99
Lean, David, 213
Leander, Zarah, 19–20, 45–46, *47*, 48, 50, *52*, 272n
Leave Her to Heaven (1945), 96
Leave It to Beaver (TV series, 1959–63), 282–83n
Lee, Edna, 8, 173–74
Lee, Harry, 169, 173–74
Lee, Leonard, 190
Legend of Lylah Clare, The (1968), 100
Lehman, Peter, 9
Leigh, Rowland, 69
Leonard, Hugh, 213
Let's Fall in Love (1933), 7, 100–102
Letter from an Unknown Woman (1948), 165, 204–5, 285n
Levy, Melvyn, 64
Lewis, Sam, 279n
Lidice, 61–65, 113, 273n, 274n
Lili (1953), 91
Limmer, Wolfgang, 3, 7, 266n
Liszt, Franz, 165
Litschke, H. W., 20
Littauer, Kenneth, 206
Little Black Angels/Angelitos Negros (1948), 286n
Little Black Angels/Angelitos Negros (TV series, 1970), 286n
Little Palace Concert, The (operetta, 1935), 40, 271n
Little Women (1949), 120
Long Gray Line, The (1955), 231
Lopez, Robert, 269n
Lorenz, Lovis Hans, 43

Losey, Joseph, 276n
Lost Horizon (1973), 15
Love Affair (1939), 210, 213, 285n
Love Affair (1994), 213
"Love and Life" (poem), 283n
Loveless, The (1981), 254
Love Me or Leave Me (1955), 212
Lover Come Back (1961), 231
Loving (2016), 216
Lowe, Edmund, 100
Lubitsch, Ernst, 40, 204
Ludwig, Emil, 64
Luhrmann, Baz, 124
Lyndon, Barrie, 125
Lytton, Bart, 64

Macbeth (1948), 81
MacDonald, Ian, 146
Macdonald, Ross, 276n
MacMurray, Fred, 9, 160, 163, 175, *177*, *179*
Madden, David, 206
Maddin, Guy, 255
Magic Flute, The (opera, 1791), 73
Major Dundee (1965), 120
Malloy, Doris, 64
Malone, Dorothy, 186, *240*, 256
Maltese Falcon, The (1941), 83
Maltz, Albert (Michael Blankfort), 281n
Man, The (1972), 135
Man Called Peter, A (1955), 224
Mangano, Silvana, 275n
Man in the Iron Mask, The (1939), 79
Mankiewicz, Joseph L., 60
Mann, Anthony, 150
Manning, Bruce, 190
Man with the Iron Heart, The (2017), 273n
Marin, Edward L., 270n
Markey, Gene, 8, 135, 137
Marlowe, Christopher, 124
Marlowe, Jo Ann, 96
Marquez, Gabriel Garcia, 16
Martin, Adrian, 37, 240, 241, 252, 269n, 283n
Marx, Groucho, 158–59
Mason, James, 285n
Mayer, Louis B., 65

Mayring, Philipp Lothar, 25, 269n
McBride, Joseph, 234
McCarey, Leo, 210
McCarthy, Todd, 288n
McGuire Sisters, 285n
McKelway, St. Clair, 85
Mecholsky, Kristopher, 70, 71, 81, 206, 252, 275
Meek's Cutoff (2010), 281n
Meisel, Kurt, 42
Mele, Anniello, 80
Melody of the Heart (1929), 271n
Memoirs of a Physician/Balsamo, the Magician (novel, 1893), 61
Memoirs of Casanova, The (novel, 1822), 70
Menzel, Gerhard, 48, 49–50, 272n
Merry Widow, The (1934), 40
Mescall, John J., 197
Metty, Russell, 15, 125, 203–4, 228, 285n
Meyer, Leo, 53
Midnight (1939), 102
Midnight in Paris (2011), 213
Mildred Pierce (novel, 1941), 208
Milius, John, 281n
Milland, Ray, 276n
Millay, Edna St. Vincent, 63, 274n
Miller, Alan, 111
Miller, F. E., 279n
Minnelli, Vincente, 105, 108, 160
Mi Vida Loca (1993), 254
Moliere, 3, 20, 23, 24
Monroe, Marilyn, 288n
Monsieur Verdoux (1947), 84
Montgomery, Monty, 254
Moon Is Blue, The (1953), 159
Moore, Juanita, 223, 225–27
Moore, Roger, 70
Morgan, Ralph, *64*, 198
Morocco (1930), 71
Morris, Gary, 96
Morris, Richard, 139, 279n
Morrow, Jeff, 150, *151*
"Mort, La"/"My Death" (song, 1959), 238, 288n
Motion Picture Production Code/Hays Code/PCA (Production Code Administration), 75, 158–59, 170,

208–9, 220, 222, 223, 224, 277n, 281n, 284n
Mozart, Wolfgang Amadeus, 73
Mr. Deeds Goes to Town (1936), 98
Mr. Smith Goes to Washington (1939), 98
Muller, I. A. L., 24
Mulvey, Laura, 7, 10, 189, 252
"Murder of Lidice, The" (poem, 1942), 63, 274n
My Antonia (novel, 1918), 234, 238, 241
My Reputation (1943), 174–75, 253

NAACP (National Association for the Advancement of Colored People), 223
Nadar, Thomas, 45
Nagel, Conrad, 171, 282n
Nason, Richard W., 278n
National Velvet (1944), 91
Nebenzal, Seymour, 64, 65
Nelson, Evi, 269n
Nesselson, Lisa, 255
Neubach, Ernst, 75
Never Say Goodbye (1946, James V. Kern), 283n
Never Say Goodbye (1956, Jerry Hopper), 103, 189–92, 284n
Nichols, Jeff, 216
Nick, Edmund, 40
Nielsen, Asta, 13
Noames, Jean-Louis, 6, 88, 271n
Now, Voyager (1942), 222
Nutcracker, The (ballet, 1892), 38, 39

Oberon, Merle, 190
Oh, Money! Money! (novel, 1918), 131–33
Olsen, Chris, *238*
Olsen, Moroni, *126*
Once (2007), 279n
Once Upon a Honeymoon (1942), 270n
One Hour with You (1932), 40
Only Angels Have Wings (1939), 235–36, 288n
Only Yesterday (1933), 182
Operation: Daybreak (1975), 273n
Ophuls, Max, 53, 160, 165, 204–5
Out of the Past (1947), 83, 90
Out There in the Dark (novel, 2006), 234

Oxford English Dictionary, 84, 256
Ozon, Francois, 255

Palace Scandal/Das Kleine Hofkonzert (1948), 271n
Palance, Jack, 86, 125, *127*
Pallette, Eugene, 23
Palm Beach Story, The (1942), 98, 277n
Panofsky, Erwin, 13
Parker, Eleanor, 283n
Parker, Trey, 269n
Parrott, Ursula, 7, 182, 283n
Partie de campagne, Une (1936), 272n
Partridge, General Earl, 145, 153
Paths of Glory (1957), 289n
Peary, Gerald, 208
Penthesilea, 20
Perrault, Charles, 84
Perreau, Gigi, 104, 106, 132
Phantom Lady (1944), 177, 275n
Pichel, Irving, 79
Pickford, Mary, 86
Pieges/Snares/Personal Column (1939), 60, 75–76, 77, 79, 275n
Pillars of Society/Pillars of the Community (play, 1877), 29–34, 270n
Pinky (1949), 223
Pirandello, Luigi, 190
Player, The (1992), 100
Pollyanna (novel, 1913), 131
Polyester (1981), 256
Pommer, Erich, 40, 271n
Pons, Antulio Jiminez, 286n
Ponti, Carlo, 124, 126
Pope Leo I, 278n
Pork-Chop Hill (1959), 289n
Porter, Eleanor H., 131–33
Postman Always Rings Twice, The (1946), 67, 83, 97
Postman Always Rings Twice, The (novel, 1934), 65, 214
Powell, William, 189
Preminger, Otto, 278n
Pretty Little Liars (TV series, 2010–), 256
Prize, The (1963), 135
Pulp Fiction (1994), 256
Pulver, Lilo, *246, 248*

Pylon (novel, 1935), 231, 234–35, 237, 240, 288n

Queen of Sheba, The (1952), 124
Quillévéré, Katell, 255
Quinn, Anthony, 125

Rabourdin, Dominique, 6
Rainbow's End (novel, 1975), 214
Rains, Claude, 190
Rappaport, Mark, 189, 251
Rasner, Heinz-Gerd, 6, 163
Ratoff, Gregory, 79–81, 100, 102
Ray, Nicholas, 160
Ray, Robert B., 11
Reason, Rex, 125, 148
Rebel Without a Cause (1955), 177
Reckless (1935), 188
regle du jeu, La (1939), 66–67
Reichardt, Kelly, 281n
Remarque, Erich Maria, 6, 232, 243, 245, 247–49, 289n
Renoir, Jean, 60, 66–67, 76, 272n
Rentschler, Eric, 11, 18, 49, 52–53
Reynolds, Zachary, 188
Riefenstahl, Leni, 271n
Ritter, Rudo, 20, 24
River's Edge (1986), 254
Robe, The (1953), 166
Rock Hudson's Home Movies (1992), 251
Rodriguez, Joselito, 286n
Romeo and Juliet (play, 1597), 138
Root, Wells, 201
Root of His Evil, The (novel, 1952), 206, 207–9, 212–13
Rosen, Milton, 135
Rosten, Leo, 77, 85

Salter, Hans J., 128
Sanders, George, 15, 47, 59–60, 67, *68*, 70–71, *72*, *74*, 75, 79, 95, 135, 190, 248
Sarafian, Richard C., 124
Sarris, Andrew, 6, 183, 254, 266n
Satin Rouge (2002), 253
Saul, Oscar, 120
Saxton, Christine, 184

Schayer, Richard, 80
Schiller, Friedrich, 35
Schmidt, Eckhardt, 19
Schoenfeld, Bernard C., 176–77
Schrader, Paul, 82
Schulte-Sasse, Linda, 11, 13, 37, 51, 52, 252, 270n
Schwarz, Hanns, 271n
Scorsese, Martin, 124, 254
Scott, Allan, 224
Scott, Lizabeth, 90
Scott, Randolph, 270n
Scott, Ridley, 124
Secret Beyond the Door . . . (1947), 84, 85
Selznick, David O., 189, 190
Sequens, Jiri, 273n
Serenade (novel, 1937), 206, 211, 214
Seven Year Itch, The (1955), 177, 288n
Sex Kittens Go To College (1960), 231
Shakespeare, William, 13, 130, 137–38, 163
Shape of Water, The (2017), 252
Shean, Al, *64*
Shearer, Stephen, 277n
Sheridan, Ann, *140*
Sherman, George, 146–47
Shoeshine (1943), 80
Shooting Party, The (novel, 1883), 14–15, 65–67, 69, 274n
Shurlock, Geoffrey, 224
Siedel, Erhardt, *21*, 23
Sierck, Claus Detlef, 14, 232–34
Silberman, Marc, 17, 45
Silent Village, The (1942), 61, 63
Silverheels, Jay, 146
Silver Lake, A Winter's Tale, The/Der Silbersee Ein Wintermarchen, 24
Since You Went Away (1944), 270n
Sing Street (2016), 279n
Siodmak, Robert, 60, 75–77, 275n
Sirgo, Otto, 286n
Sirk, Douglas: arriving in the US, 14–15, 58–59; born Hans Detlef Sierck, 13; at Columbia, 58, 87, 91, 99, 115; leaving Europe, 14, 53, 58; into retirement, 14, 268n, 289n; theater career, 6, 13–14, 17, 23, 28, 30–31,

59, 269n, 270n; with Triangle Productions, 86; at UFA, 11–12, 14, 17–18, 19–20, 24, 32–33, 35–36, 40, 45, 48–50, 52–53, 58, 59, 65, 231–32, 244, 268n, 271n, 272n; at Universal-International, 6, 15, 48, 59, 92, 99, 120, 124–25, 135, 144, 145, 171, 190, 192, 193–94, 224–25, 231, 244, 256, 282, 288; at Warner Bros., 58, 244

Works: *Accord Final* (1938), 272n; *All I Desire* (1953), 10, 34, 36, 67, 83, 90, 91, 117, 141, 159, 162, 163–68, 169, 171, 172, 175–78, 180, 181, 184, 187, 190, 191, 201, 236, 270n, 285n; *All That Heaven Allows* (1955), 5, 8, 10, 21, 36, 48, 107, 132, 159, 161–62, 168–75, 177, 180, 184, 187, 191–92, 203, 212, 236, 252–53, 255, 266n, 282n, 283n; *April! April!* (1935), 14, 20–24, 25, 28, 41, 269n; *Battle Hymn* (1957), 5, 14, 57, 114, 144–57, 205, 206, 212, 244, 281n; *Boefje* (1939), 4, 20, 53–57, 113, 269–70n, 273n; *Cagliostro* (unmade), 79–81; *Captain Lightfoot* (1955), 124, 139, 144–45, 150–53, 156, 240, 281n; *La Chanson du souvenir* (1936), 271n; *Christian Brothers at Mont La Salle, The* (1941), 59; *Final Chord/Schlussakord* (1936), 10, 34–39, 40, 42, 43, 57, 271n, 272n; *The First Legion* (1950), 5, 57, 58, 64, 114, 115–21, 122, 123, 127, 128, 278n; *The Girl from the Marsh Croft/Mädchen vom Moorhof* (1935), 4, 25–29, 34, 63, 89, 114–15, 122, 236; *La Habanera* (1937), 10, 18–20, 48–53, 271n, 272n; *Has Anybody Seen My Gal* (1951), 4, 21, 56, 94, 99, 106, 129–35, 136, 138, 139, 140, 145, 277n, 279n; *Hitler's Madman* (1943), 14, 59, 60, 61–65, 66, 69, 95, 113, 116, 244, 250, 273n, 274n; *Imitation of Life* (1959), 4, 5, 10, 36, 96, 159, 182, 193, 216–30, 287n; *Interlude* (1957), 36, 193, 206–15, 256, 285n, 286n; *The Lady Pays Off* (1951), 99, 103–8, 236, 280n; *Lured/Personal Column* (1947), 10, 59, 60, 75–79, 80, 82, 95, 116, 275n; *Magnificent Obsession* (1954), 5, 47, 48, 114, 125, 128, 140, 155–56, 157, 166, 168, 172, 175, 185, 193, 195–205, 240, 255, 279, 284n, 285n; *Meet Me at the Fair* (1952), 56, 103, 130, 135–38, 140, 277n, 279–80n; *Mystery Submarine* (1950), 82, 83, 84, 92–95, 106; *No Room for the Groom* (1952), 90, 94, 99, 106, 109–12, 129, 131, 132, 140; *The Palace Concert/Das Hofkonzert* (1936), 18, 40–43, 268n, 271n; *Pillars of Society/Stützen der Gesellschaft* (1935), 20, 29–34, 51; *A Scandal in Paris* (1946), 59, 60, 62, 70–75, 80, 81, 95, 96, 114, 115, 270n, 274n, 275n; *Shockproof* (1949), 82, 83, 84, 87–91, 276n; *Sign of the Pagan* (1954), 114, 124–28, 139, 278–79n; *Sleep My Love* (1947), 10, 80, 82, 83–87, 97, 121, 276n; *Slightly French* (1949), 7, 99, 100–102, 277n; *Summer Storm* (1944), 4, 7, 14–15, 47, 59, 60, 64, 65–69, 82, 96, 113, 116, 236, 248, 254, 274n; *Take Me to Town* (1952), 8, 56, 114–15, 124, 129, 130, 139–42, 165, 277n, 279–80n; *The Tarnished Angels* (1957), 4, 10, 36–37, 144, 185, 206, 231–32, 234–42, 272n, 288n; *Taza, Son of Cochise* (1953), 125, 144, 146–50, 151, 185, 235, 280n, 281n, 285n; *There's Always Tomorrow* (1955), 7, 9, 10, 83, 107–8, 117, 159, 160, 161, 162–63, 167, 175–83, 184, 187, 203, 236, 283n; *Thunder on the Hill* (1951), 114, 120–24, 127, 278n; *A Time To Love and A Time To Die* (1958), 6, 10, 37, 42, 115, 223, 231–34, 241, 243–50, 288–89n; *To New Shores/Zu neuen Ufern* (1937), 10, 18–20, 43–48, 51, 58, 236, 244, 271n, 272n; *Week-End with Father* (1951), 92, 94, 99, 106–9, 110, 131,

277n; *Wilton's Zoo* (unmade), 14, 273n; *Written on the Wind* (1956), 10, 37, 47, 52, 68, 96, 102, 144, 145, 159, 160, 162, 183–89, 231, 235, 238, *240*, 241, 248, 254, 255, 256, 272n, 277n, 284n
Sjostrom, Victor, 25–29
Skinner, Frank, 128, 183, 200, 212, 285n
Slavin, George F., 92, 106
Slingerland-Nusink, Tineke, 273n
Sloman, Edward, 7, 176, 182–83
Small, Edward, 79
Solt, Andrew, 120
Song of Love (1947), 285n
"Song of the Open Road" (poem, 1856), 137
Son of Monte Cristo, The (1940), 79
Sorry, Wrong Number (1948), 84
Sothern, Ann, 100
Soul Has No Colour, The/El alma no tiene color (1997), 286n
Sperling, Milton, 278n
Spier, William, 275n
Stack, Robert, 47, 102, 145, 149, 163, *185*, *240*, 241, 248
Staggs, Sam, 224, 256
Stahl, John M., 96, 182, 193–94, 195, 197–205, 206, 208–11, 213, 216, 220–23, 224, 225, 226, 227, 229, 230, 284n, 285n
Stanwyck, Barbara, 160, 163, 165, *166*, 167, 175, 176, *177*, *178*
Star Is Born, A (1937, 1954, 1976, 2018), 100
Stationmaster Death/Bahnmeister Tod (play, 1919), 13
Stella Dallas (1925, 1937, 1990), 222
Stern, Michael, 10, 99, 110, 112, 125, 138, 141, 162, 181, 202, 230, 238, 252, 266n, 280n, 282n
Sternberg, Joseph von, 6, 71, 255, 271n
Stevenson, Robert, 92, 276n
Stine, Clifford, 83, 94, 99
St. Joseph, Ellis, 69, 72
Stoltz, Robert, 271n
Stone, Matt, 269n

Stone, Oliver, 124
Stopover (novel, 1951), 163, 166
Strange Woman, The (1946), 60, 67, 80, 95–97
Stratton, David, 289n
Streetcar Named Desire, A (1951), 120
Strick, Wesley, 234, 254
Stroheim, Erich von, 77
Stromberg, Hunt, 79, 95
Sturges, Preston, 98, 277n
Sudden Fear (1952), 84, 86
Summer Stock (1950), 224
Summertime (1955), 213
Susann, Jacqueline, 91
Suzanne (2013), 255

Tamburlaine (play, 1590), 124
Tamiroff, Akim, 73, 79, 80
Tarantino, Quentin, 256
Tartuffe ou l'imposteur (play, 1664), 269n
Tásnadi, Mária v., *38*
Taylor, Dwight, 211, 212
Taylor, Robert, 85, 182, 195, 201, 202
Teilhet, Darwin L., 109
Tex (1982), 254
There's Always Tomorrow/Too Late for Love (1934), 7, 176, 182–83
Thin Man series (1934–47), 70
This Love of Ours (1945), 190–91, 284n
Thoeren, Robert, 69
Thoreau, Henry David, 170, 282n
Thoroughly Modern Millie (1967, and play, 2002), 139
Threepenny Opera, The (play, 1928), 9
Three Summers (2017), 279n
Thunderbolt and Lightfoot (1974), 281n
Toast of New Orleans, The (1950), 224
To Catch a Thief (1955), 71–72
Tone, Franchot, 189
Touch of Evil (1958), 231
Tourneur, Jacques, 90
Tracy, Spencer, 177
Triumph of the Will (1935), 271n
True Believer (1989), 254
Truffaut, Francois, 275n
Trumbo, Dalton, 278n
Trumpener, Katie, 23

Twelfth Night (play, 1602), 17
Two Mrs. Carrolls, The (1947), 84

UFA (Universum Film-Aktien Gesellschaft), 11, 14, 17–20, 24, 28, 33, 40, 45, 48, 49, 59, 65, 231, 244, 268n, 271n, 272n
Ulmer, Edgar G., 64, 67, 95–97, 276n
Undercurrent (1946), 84, 85
University of Connecticut Film Society, 8–9

Valentine, Joseph, 83
Valley of the Dolls (1967), 91
Vanishing Point (1971), 124
Vecsey, Ferenc, 40
Veitshochheim Castle, 40
Venice Film Festival, 39
Verhoeven, Paul, 40, 271n
Vertigo (1958), 278n
Vertov, Dziga, 28
Vicki Cristina Barcelona (2008), 213
Vidor, King, 124

Wages of Fear, The (1957), 287n
Walden (book, 1854), 170, 173, 282n
Walker, Dusty, 280n
Walker, Michael, 141, 167–68, 181, 252
Walker, Scott, 288n
Wallace, Irving, 135
Wallner-Baste, Franz, 40
Walsh, Raoul, 270n
War and Peace (1956), 124
War Game, The (1965), 61
War of the Worlds, The (1953), 125
Waters, Ethel, 223
Waters, John, 255, 256
Watkins, Peter, 61
Waxman, Franz, 197
Webster, Paul Francis, 275n, 287n
Weihmayr, Franz, 271n
Weill, Kurt, 24, 45
Weinstein, Valerie, 24
Weitz, Chris and Paul, 225
Welles, Orson, 79–81
Wexley, John, 62, 273n
When Strangers Marry (1944), 84

Whirlpool (1949), 120
White, Patrick, 16
White Horse Inn (operetta, 1931), 271n
"white Jew, the," 24
Whitman, Walt, 137
Wigton, Anne, 288n
Wilde, Cornel, 83, 88, 90
Wilder, Robert, 183
Willemen, Paul, 7, 252
Williams, Ben Ames, 96
Williams, John, 72
Williams, Tennessee, 187
Wilmot, John, Second Earl of Rochester, 283n
Wilson, Michael, 278n
Wilson, Rex, 270n
Winterstein, Willie, 28
Wolfe, Thomas, 53
Woman on Pier 13, The/I Married a Communist (1949), 92, 276n
Woman's Face, A (1941), 270n
Wood, John, 20
Woolrich, Cornell, 76, 275n
Written on the Wind (novel, 1945), 183, 187–88, 189, 284n
Wulf, Reinard, 6, 163
Wuthering Heights (novel, 1847), 282n
Wyler, William, 252, 282n
Wyman, Jane, 45, 48, 132, 163, 168, 171, 172, 195, 201, 202–3, 205, 282n

Yearling, The (1946), 201
Young, Brigham, 137
Young, Joe, 279n
Young, Robert, 283n
Young, Victor, 183
Young Lions, The (1958), 289n

Zuckerman, George, 15, 185, 189, 232, 235, 240, 280n
Zuckmayer, Karl, 53
Zugsmith, Albert, 15, 188, 231

CPSIA information can be obtained
at www.ICGtesting.com
Printed in the USA
BVHW030532030519
547141BV00003B/3/P